e fought near *LAKE GEORGE* on the 8th of September 1755, between 2000 English with 250
HNSON and 2500 French and Indians under the Command of General *DIESKAU*
ating the French General with a number of his Men, killing 700 and putting the rest to flight.

THE ENDPAPERS

The Battle of Lake George, where Sir William won his baronetcy, drawn by Samuel Blodgett, who had been with Johnson's army. Blodgett, who believed you could not get too much into a picture, shows the main battle at the right and, on the left, the Bloody Morning Scout which resulted in the death of the sachem Hendrick. Across the top is "a plan of Hudson's River . . . with such marks as will be of great service to navigation." We see Forts Edward and William Henry which Johnson built, although not until after the battle, and in the left-hand corner a prudent dedication by the New England engraver to Governor William Shirley of Massachusetts who disliked Johnson as a New Yorker and hated him as a military rival. (*Courtesy, New York Public Library*)

Books by James Thomas Flexner

AMERICAN PAINTING
I. First Flowers of Our Wilderness
II. The Light of Distant Skies
III. That Wilder Image

AMERICA'S OLD MASTERS

THE POCKET HISTORY OF AMERICAN PAINTING
(also published as *A Short History of American Painting*)

JOHN SINGLETON COPLEY

GILBERT STUART

THE WORLD OF WINSLOW HOMER
(with the editors of Time-Life Books)

NINETEENTH CENTURY AMERICAN PAINTING

THE FACE OF LIBERTY

DOCTORS ON HORSEBACK:
Pioneers of American Medicine

STEAMBOATS COME TRUE
(also published as *Inventors in Action*)

THE TRAITOR AND THE SPY
(also published as *The Benedict Arnold Case*)

LORD OF THE MOHAWKS:
A Biography of Sir William Johnson
(previously published as *Mohawk Baronet*)

WILLIAM HENRY WELCH AND THE HEROIC AGE
OF AMERICAN MEDICINE
(with Simon Flexner)

GEORGE WASHINGTON
I. The Forge of Experience (1732–1775)
II. In the American Revolution (1775–1783)
III. And the New Nation (1783–1793)
IV. Anguish and Farewell (1793–1799)

WASHINGTON: THE INDISPENSABLE MAN

THE YOUNG HAMILTON

Lord of the Mohawks

To Richard Fielder
With admiration,
James Thomas Flexner

William Johnson
This earliest likeness reveals that the fierce frontiersman and
forest warrior, whose imagination enabled him to think like an
Indian, had a sensitive, poetic face. (*Public Archives Canada*)

Lord of the Mohawks

A Biography of Sir William Johnson

JAMES THOMAS FLEXNER

Newly Illustrated and with a New Foreword

LITTLE, BROWN AND COMPANY · BOSTON · TORONTO

To Beatrice and Nellie

Lord of the Mohawks was originally published in 1959 by
Harper & Brothers under the title *Mohawk Baronet.*

LIBRARY OF CONGRESS CATALOGING IN PUBLICATION DATA
Flexner, James Thomas, 1908–
Lord of the Mohawks.

   First ed. published in 1959 under title: Mohawk
baronet.
   Bibliography: p.
   Includes index.
   1. Johnson, Sir William, bart., 1715–1774.
2. United States—History—French and Indians War,
1755–1763.   3. Indians of North America—Government
relations—To–1789.   4. Indians of North America—
Wars—1750–1815.   5. Soldiers—Great Britain—Biog-
raphy.   6. Colonial administrators—Great Britain—
Biography.   7. Colonial administrators—United
States—Biography.   I. Title.
E195.J63F57   1979   973.2′6′0924 [B]   79-14843
ISBN 0-316-28609-5

MV
*Published simultaneously in Canada
by Little, Brown & Company (Canada) Limited*
PRINTED IN THE UNITED STATES OF AMERICA

Contents

Contents

List of Illustrations

ix

The part title drawings (*pages 5, 43, 221, 285*) reveal how Louis XIV was encouraged to envision the Canadian Indians he regarded as his subjects. The name of the artist is under dispute, attributions including Bécard de Granville (or Grandville), an attorney at Quebec, and Louis Nicolas, a defrocked Jesuit missionary. Once in the library at Versailles, the drawings are here reproduced from *Les Rapetés des Indies, Album Manuscript de la Fin de XVII Siècle,* Paris (1930). (*Courtesy, New York Public Library*)

Foreword to the Revised Edition

It was the autumn of 1757, during the French and Indian War. The American colonial defenders of Fort William Henry possessed only one hope. The woods around their clearing boiled with hostile Indians. Drawn up in ranks, French regulars fired in unison. Cannonballs were smashing down ramparts of sod and wood. In all directions, the wilderness hemmed in the battlefield, except to the north. To the north, placid water stretched beyond eyesight between swelling hills. However, Lake George flowed not to British America but to Canadian France. More enemies appeared on its smooth surface paddling down to join the siege. Fort William Henry would soon fall, unless—

The one hope concentrated on a narrow gap in the woods at the end of the long clearing in front of the fort. Beyond, although invisible to the straining eyes of the defenders, a narrow road burrowed under primeval branches for fourteen miles to Fort Edward. At Fort Edward there was a British regular army detachment of some 3,500 men. Surely their commander, Major General Daniel Webb, was leading them to the rescue. Surely the defenders of Fort William Henry would soon see the gap in the woods brim with red coats!

But Major General Webb was sitting nervously in the log room that served him as headquarters. How could he forget that the road to Fort William Henry was a tunnel through enveloping foliage which presented endless opportunities for such an Indian ambush as had recently, in the wilderness behind Virginia, decimated the regular regiments of another British regular major general, Edward Braddock? Beside Webb's own fort, there was a waterway that pointed blissfully in the opposite direction from Lake George: the Hudson River flowed into well-settled New York, away, far away from any immediate danger. How imprudent it would be to march off from so providential a line of retreat!

Suddenly there sounded in Webb's ears a chorus of war whoops. Had Fort William Henry fallen and were the enemy upon him? Fortunately, no. Webb was informed that reinforcements, frontiersmen and Indians, had arrived from the Mohawk Valley. Webb was smiling with relief when his narrow room suddenly filled with gaudy Iroquois warriors and frontiersmen equally painted and feathered. In the lead, limping a little from the French bullet still in his thigh, was a huge white man in Indian garb who Webb realized, although it seemed impossible, was a British baronet. Sir William Johnson "proposed to General Webb to march at once to the French lines."

Webb knew that Johnson, an untrained and only occasional soldier, was being hailed in England by a phrase in itself insulting to the regular army: "the heaven-taught general." The frontiersman had been made baronet because, two years before, with a ragtag army of woodsmen, apprentices, and Indians, he had captured what had always been known as "Lac St. Sacrement" and renamed it after the British king: "Lake George." At the very spot where the present French commander in chief, the Marquis de Montcalm, was besieging Fort William Henry, Johnson and his rabble had defeated Montcalm's veteran predecessor, famous on European battlefields, Baron Dieskau. Johnson had then built the fort under siege and Fort Edward, where he was confronting Webb. But the English general could no more think of this giant, whose face was hidden by war paint, as "Sir William" than he could take seriously strategic suggestions from such a barbarian.

A Mohawk witness to the interview was that winter to chase a deer so far northward that he met a brave from Sault St. Louis. They smoked a pipe together, and the pro-French tribesman carried the story to Montcalm's aide-de-camp, Louis Antoine Bougainville, who preserved it for posterity in a letter to a young lady in France.

Thus we know that Major General Webb watched the nose-pendants bob against the soot-blackened faces of Johnson's followers, thought what indignities a regular officer assigned to America must endure, and patiently explained "that he did not wish to expose himself to complete defeat in woods already drenched in English blood."

At this, the Indians mumbled to each other, their nose-pendants flashing. Johnson—his warriors could protect Webb's British regulars from ambush—exclaimed that the shores of Lake George "would be as fatal to Montcalm as they have been to Dieskau. . . . French bones will again cover the battlefield." He raised his tomahawk and his dagger and swore by these weapons to conquer or die. At which the Indians held up their own weapons and, in a storm of gutturals, swore.

There is a limit to a British gentleman's condescension, and Webb had reached it. He turned, but before he could get out the door something struck his foot. The wilderness baronet had unfastened and thrown one of his leggings. Now each Indian was doing the same. As the major general looked down with amazement at the mounting pile of leather, Sir William said, "You will not go?"

"No," said Webb.

Johnson stooped and his Indians stooped; each disengaged his other legging and threw it at Webb's feet. Johnson took a step forward, and there was menace in his voice, "You will not go?"

"No!" shouted Webb.

The Indians and their titled leader came no closer. They merely undressed and threw their clothes, piece by piece, at the colonel. After each volley, Johnson reiterated, "You will not go?"

When the chiefs and the baronet were stripped to their breechcloths, as one man they raised their tomahawks. Webb opened his mouth to cry out, but the weapons fell to the ground in a coordinated gesture of disgust. Johnson departed at a gallop with his troop.

"Where," asked the French narrator, Bougainville, "is Homer to paint these scenes greater than anything Greek?"

William Johnson had as a young man immigrated to the edge of the wilderness from a farm near Dublin. The former Irishman prospered on the banks of New York's Mohawk River. He came to combine, more than any other American who ever lived, Indian and white power. As Sir William, he represented his colony and then the British Crown itself, becoming official ambassador to the tribes. As Warraghiyagey, an adopted Mohawk and the advisor of many Indian nations, he kept burning in his personal back yard the Council

Fire that was the capital of the wilderness, a territory many times larger than all the white settlements. To his forest mansion, there journeyed from the east royal governors and colonial statesmen; from the west, sachems who ruled in savannahs no white man had ever seen. All were received hospitably. Johnson could entertain more than a thousand guests in a style both rough and grand. Through the fur trade and through the colonizing of western land he had made himself one of the richest men in America.

Content in forests, Warraghiyagey was uneasy in cities: he was a true frontiersman, certainly the most influential America has ever known. Although he never visited London and avoided the colonial capitals, the letters he dispatched from primeval forest could make or destroy officials in gilded rooms. Warraghiyagey spoke to his white brothers with the force of his personal Indian alliances; the menace if need be of many thousands of raised tomahawks. He was one of the only two Americans who were elevated, by the British Crown, to the rank of baronet.

Had, as is quite possible, the British lost the French and Indian War, American history would have flowed in an altogether different channel: the Colonials, menaced on their own shores by a Catholic and truly foreign power, could not have revolted against Great Britain. The continent would probably have developed into another Europe, divided between separate nations speaking various languages. Johnson, because of his influence with the Indians and his own military prowess, made a determining contribution to the victory that drove the French from Canada and opened the road to the establishment of the United States.

Johnson's prestige in the English-speaking world reflected his achievements. Twice he broke a British commander in chief; often he created imperial policies that His Majesty's government had no choice but to follow. In 1768, he overruled the Crown and personally added to the Thirteen Colonies the area that now comprises all of Kentucky, a corner of Alabama, much of West Virginia and Tennessee.

In character, Sir William was gargantuan: physically overwhelming, of tremendous appetites. His prowess in drinking is testified to by his death from cirrhosis of the liver; rumor found reason to assert that he had fathered seven hundred children, on women Indian and white. He was addicted to the outdoors, hunting, fighting, and fishing, but also to the arts of peace. In the wilderness he planned in advance, for the settlers who were to clear his acres, efficiently organized agricultural communities. A tyrant in his own bluff way, he could not, within his own domain, be gainsaid. Violent upon occasion, he was also benevolent, surprisingly tender to anyone, white or Indian, who was wounded or sick or bereaved, or for any other reason in need of aid. Those who were dependent on him felt toward him, for the most part, a passionate loyalty. Untutored, he was highly intelligent, able to defeat not only regulars in battle but politicians in the schemes of power.

Johnson's gifts of leadership were crowned with a mental dichotomy which in its extent and depth may well have been unique: he was able to be at home equally in cultures that were, within the development of human institutions, thousands of years apart. Sir William was a well-adjusted European man; Warraghiyagey thought and acted as an Indian. These two personalities lived together without strain in one keen mind and passionate heart.

A man so rare and so picturesque and also so determining in the history of America should certainly occupy one of the most brightly lighted niches in American historical memory. How can it be that Johnson's name and achievements are well known only to experts?

Both narrow-minded and conservative, national historical memory repudiates figures who do not fit accepted national preconceptions, unless, of course, the deviants were punished by failure. Sir William prospered, although he did not conform. His sexual activities have horrified. (Flamboyance in that direction is permitted to literary but not historical figures.) Among the deepest of American shibboleths is that belief that the frontier was by its very nature a spawning ground of egalitarianism. How shocking to realize that the most effective of all American frontiersmen was not an egalitarian, not even a Tory in the conventional sense, but a feudal chief! Sir William was closer to Achilles than Daniel Boone, to King Arthur than Benjamin Franklin.

But the most serious impediment is that a truthful account of Warraghiyagey's career explodes those myths about the American Indian which were fabricated to justify conquest and virtual extermination, and are a cherished part of American legend. The Indians who walk these pages are not a stupid, incompetent, treacherous, sadistic race who needed to be purified by Christianity, justified by welcoming the stealers of their land, and, during the eighteenth century, given respectability by servile assistance to the British-American forces in their battles with the French from Canada.

The Indian nations can be no more accurately defined as "French-Indians" or "English-Indians" than the settlers can be considered "Huron-Whites" or "Iroquois-Whites." Sachems and chiefs, like colonial governors and Assemblies, were concerned with the welfare of their own nationals, and when the Indian leaders changed alliances as their national interests seemed to change, it was no more "treachery" than the similar shifts—say those of Prussia and France after the Treaty of Westphalia—which European statesmen were at that historical moment making.

If the Indian policies usually attributed to childish waywardness are examined with an effort to discover their logic, logic can usually be found. The tribes were in a situation like that of the Balkan States before the recent Russian conquest. All small and mutually hostile, they were caught between great powers. They tried similar maneuvering to assure their safety, and failed no more dismally.

It is common for historians to write that the Indians' military power should not be underestimated, and then, because of dedication to white thinking, white testimony, and the usual archives, blithely to underestimate. (Thus Pontiac has been considered the greatest Indian warrior of the mid-eighteenth century for the very reason that made him one of the most incompetent: he tried to fight in the white manner.) Complete acceptance of the fact that in forest warfare one Indian following "savage" strategy was worth ten conventionally drilled white regulars upsets accepted explanations of the French and Indian War and Pontiac's Conspiracy. Debates around council fires loom as important as debates in legislatures; and Sir William Johnson, the man who brought Indian power to the English side, rises to his actual historical stature.

For any man who enjoys writing picturesquely, the chance to depict Indians as gorgeous and terrible bugaboos is an alluring one— but it was snatched away from me by my protagonist. Treating the Indians not as haunts or exotics but as fellow men, Johnson emphasized not their cultural differences from European-Americans, but their common humanity.

Respect for Indians brings to the fore impressive personalities. We find walking these pages Tiyanoga, the Mohawk sachem known in English as Hendrick, a statesman of rare perception, subtlety, and gifts, worthy of a place in histories of diplomacy. And the woman who was undoubtedly the most powerful member of her sex during the Revolutionary period comes into focus. She far overtops the currently accepted heroine Abigail Adams, who has become a cult figure because she occasionally and ineffectually expostulated to her important husband about women's rights. Degonwadonti, known as Molly Brant, the Mohawk wife and then widow of Warraghiyagey, was a major military commander: she controlled the Indian armies that, as allies of the British, fought the revolting whites, decimating the Mohawk and Wyoming Valleys. "One word from her," wrote the colonel officially in charge of His Majesty's Indian forces, "goes further with them than a thousand words from any white man without exception."*

In addition to unearthing heroes, the Indian-view reveals previously unrecognized villains, most conspicuously Sir Jeffery Amherst. Through his injustice and savagery to the tribes, Amherst incited Pontiac's Conspiracy, even as he subsequently was to play, as advisor concerning America to the British government, an important role in defining the policies that detonated the Revolution and then lost the war that followed.

Lord of the Mohawks does not deal with the American Indians in the generalizing terms of anthropologists seeking to define a culture. We are here concerned with historical happenings at definite times in specific places. We follow individual Indian leaders on documented warpaths, and sit cross-legged at council fires where policies that determined events were actually made. Yet our story has tremendous implications because every event is lit by the sunset glow that presaged the destruction of the greatest northeastern Indian confederation, the Iroquois, the Five or Six Nations. It becomes painfully manifest that, despite their brains and power and grandeur, every Indian nation which appears on this book is doomed. But that is not all: the historical process working itself out under our eyes will travel westward until not a single Indian nation anywhere will control in freedom its hunting ground.

* Except when otherwise stated, the spelling and punctuation of quotations has been modernized.

When it seemed as if his white enemies would succeed in stripping Warraghiyagey of his power to help the Indians in the white world, the great sachem Hendrick keened, "He has large ears and heareth a great deal and what he hears he tells us; he also has large eyes, and sees a great way, and conceals nothing from us. . . . We had him in wartime, when he was like a tree that grew for our use, which now seems to be falling down, though it has many roots. His knowledge of our affairs made us think him one of us, and we are greatly afraid."

PART ONE

An Irish Immigrant

1

Dark Entry

William Johnson was born into one of the world's winters, a society so prostrate that no greenness showed anywhere. Yet strong seeds lay underground.

The place: Ireland, certainly County Meath, probably the Manor of Killeen near Warrenstown. The date: unrecorded, perhaps 1715, as tradition says, but maybe a year or two earlier. His parents' marriage: unequal, as so often happens when important families crumble.

Years later, when preparing an inscription for the impressive monument with which he would replace his parents' ragged gravestones, William could only boast that his father, Christopher Johnson, had come from a line "honorable in its alliances." The most honorable had been with William's mother, whose ancestors were "possessed of an estate . . . from the first arrival of the English in Ireland." Anne Warren had stooped from the stone manor house at Warrenstown to marry a tenant of the nearby Earl of Fingal. They had three daughters and then, when the father was about thirty-six, a male child.

William grew up about twenty miles from Dublin. A nearby priest traced his ecclesiastical lineage back 1,300 years directly to St. Patrick. Tara, a swelling of land that had up to the sixth century been the seat of Irish kings, was only two miles from Johnson's boyhood home. There among broken mounds of earth, Thomas Moore was to swoon his days away listening for "the harp that once through Tara's halls

7

the soul of music shed." William was to make that harp resound down strange forest aisles, but the vanished palaces were for the boy an insubstantial dream compared to the reality of a field beside the River Boyne where his childhood delvings could exhume human bones. Here his grandfather Warren had ridden as an officer of King James' own regiment, and fled to be attainted for treason. Here, at the Battle of the Boyne, old Ireland had finally collapsed under the English conqueror's heel.

No one who was anyone lived in Ireland any more. Southwest and northeast of the family farm, William's boyhood rambles brought him quickly to the ditches under high hedges that closed off the demesnes of Baron Dunsany and the Earl of Fingal. He might wiggle through and explore as much as he pleased without coming on a baron or an earl. With their families, they were all in London, dancing court on George II, sending back to their overseers calls for more cash. The overseers responded by evicting more farmers and replacing them with more sheep. More sturdy beggars took to the roads and Christopher Johnson's millstones turned less often.

He rented from the Earl of Fingal 199 acres and a grist mill in the Manor of Killeen. Since Catholics—who were forbidden by law to buy land—could not rent for more than thirty-one years, the Johnsons were forced, as they did in 1728, periodically to renew their lease. This was a stop to ambition. An Irish landlord would do nothing for his tenant, and if the tenant did anything for himself, the improvements would revert to the landlord, who would use them, when the term was out, as an excuse for charging more. Dwellings, even of farmers who paid "great rents," were commonly built to fall down at the end of the thirty-one years; they were, as Dean Swift wrote, less convenient than "an English hogsty."

The Johnsons were plagued always by self-comparisons with their Warren connections, who, despite heavy fines for treason, had preserved some of their ancestral estate. Christopher wrote himself down in deeds as "gentleman," but could not be completely sure of his right. While the Warren children were hurried to England to hatch importantly under the wings of important relations, the Johnsons—there came to be three sons and four daughters—wandered about their ailing farm and ramshackle mill in the situation later described by one of William's brothers: "No money, interest, nor friends. Consequently can't expect to rise."

It was not common in William's generation for Irishmen with any pretense to position to mourn the lost cause: rather the contrary. Dean Swift upbraided his compatriots for automatically preferring anything English to everything Irish. Since oppressive laws blocked for Papists every road to advancement, only priests, martyrs, and peasants could stay in the British Empire and adhere to their ancestral faith. The ambitious fled to Catholic nations or into the Church of England. Choosing the latter course, William admitted to no conflict between being an Irishman and being an Englishman. He was proud of both allegiances, and was to be, if anything, overwarm in his love for the Crown. As for the Anglican church, he became one of its most powerful American supporters without ever implying that its doctrines were closer to divine truth than Indian worship of Manitou.

Although old conceptions might be jettisoned, her defeats had brought on Ireland an inescapable scourge: the absentee landlord. Once, in feudal times, the citadels and defense of the people, the empty castles of Dunsany and Fingal now cast baleful shadows on the countryside. Better, so it would seem, to have even vicious tyrants to appeal to than no one at all, just great rooms where dust sifted and in back offices functionaries carried out orders sent from afar by unreachable men who did not know (or care) whether they were being kind or cruel. Seeing peasants on rent-gouged land starving in "birds' nests of dirt wrought together with a few sticks and straws," seeing sheep-displaced families fighting in the gutter for a few blades of grain dropped from a cart, Johnson dreamed of landlords who lived at home and took care of their people.

People were Ireland's asset, though ignored like unmarketable grain withering in a field. Knowing no social organization but the feudalism that no longer functioned, too weak to defend themselves except with their fists, unable by their own efforts to keep economically upright, the Irish peasants clung to any human power they could find. The Johnsons' mill might be rickety, their farm sterile, their house cracked, but they had food and warmth and a few coins for liquor: their kitchen teemed.

William learned to read, write with an illiterate energy, and figure a little—but his real education was people. They were his triumphs, his failures, his strength, his element, as a swimmer's element is water. On them he tried out his powers: his imagination that could enter another man's mind and operate there as if it were his own; his affection, his anger, his generosity, and his violence.

He grew into a big man for those days, almost six feet tall, dark of hair and skin, given to silences and passionate speech, his eyes, which changed with the light from gray to dark hazel, made strange by a slight lack of alignment between the pupils. He was "of a most comely aspect and in every way well formed for the most manly exercises." Men loved him and women loved him. He loved liquor and masculine jokes; fast horses, hunting and fights; he loved soft-breathing women and their tenderness. Although without anything but the most rudimentary schooling, he could quickly teach himself what he needed to know. His mind was ingenious, strong, and practical. He was a leader of people—with nowhere to lead them.

That he was bitter at the lack of opportunities presented him is revealed by his inability, once he escaped, to send letters home. In reproaching him for neglect, a brother pointed out that Christopher Johnson had been "so good and indulgent a father. . . . He seems really to be doting on you above all his children, for in all his discourses about you, they usual[ly] end in tears." It hardly helps a father to be indulgent if he presides over years of frustration from which an ambitious son can discern no escape.

Yet escape was opening, still invisible. Thousands of miles from County Meath there flowed a river, of which Johnson had probably never heard, for what was to become one of the world's great commercial waterways now rarely bore craft heavier than an Indian canoe. Primeval forest threw branches far out over the water. However, at the point where this river, the Mohawk, was joined by Schoharie Creek, the mingling waters reflected cleared fields and two wooden forts. One was Teantontalogo, the Lower Mohawk town, or "castle," as stockaded Indian villages were called; the other was His Majesty's crumbling outpost of Fort Hunter.

In 1733, when Johnson was about eighteen, the commandant of Fort Hunter, Captain Walter Butler, carried along the wilderness road from Albany a large piece of parchment on which his lawyer had made many marks with a pen. Soon Butler gave a party for the inhabitants of the Indian fortification: rum flowed, knives and blankets changed hands, and at last tipsy sachems, holding the pen clumsily in their fingers, drew on the bottom of the parchment turtles, bears, and wolves, symbols of the three clans of which the Mohawk nation was made. Butler wrote down next to each symbol the name, as it could best be transcribed in English letters, of the signer and added the legal phrase "his mark." The captain had secured an Indian deed for 86,000 acres on the south bank of the Mohawk.

The Corporation of Albany possessed a previous Indian deed for the same land, but Butler had as a partner in his speculation William Cosby, the Royal Governor of New York. Cosby expressed doubt that the Albany deed actually existed, was handed it for inspection, handed it on to an Indian named Arie, who, at his request, threw it into the fire. The parchment gave off a smell of burning flesh which Cosby sniffed with pleasure: his friends would have the land, and he would take for himself the 14,000 acres closest to the meeting of the rivers.

William Johnson was involved because of another event thus described in the New York *Gazette:*

> This day, young Mars in wedlock band was tied,
> And got the chaste Susannah for his bride.

"Young Mars" was William's uncle, Peter Warren. Removed from Ireland when a child by his own uncle, Admiral Matthew Lord Aylmer, Peter had entered the navy at the age of twelve; he was the captain of a major warship when, at the age of twenty-eight, he married into one of New York's richest merchant families. "The chaste Susannah" was sister to Cosby's chief justice, James De Lancey. It was an easy matter for Warren, after Cosby had coughed his life out, to secure for a mere £110 the governor's share of Butler's purchase.

Johnson's life had moved in its restricted round for twenty-two years or more when he received from his uncle "most kind and affectionate letters" asking him to recruit peasants who would work in return for their passage to the Mohawk. William was himself to cross the ocean and, as Warren's agent, set up a plantation.

In the mud huts of County Meath, William expounded the possibilities of the New World with overwhelming eloquence. He had never seen an Indian or a forest. He could not visualize the American wilderness beyond the fact that it was huge in every dimension—and that was all he needed to know. A farm not of 199 but of 14,000 acres; trees that scraped new heavens for thousands of miles; a place where a man's destiny awaited his own making.

2

Greenhorn's Progress

Late in 1737 or early in 1738, Johnson joined his uncle in Boston. Peter Warren was short and sturdy, with blue eyes, red hair, and a freckled skin; Peter Warren was voluble, indiscreet, and childishly vain. To see the little captain preen, no one would suspect that he would prove on the high seas the most effective British corsair of his generation. Johnson's appearance was equally illusory. Lumpy in his ill-fitting Irish clothes, he became more taciturn the faster his uncle talked. He seemed dark and slow, hardly competent for the business entrusted to him.

Although only twelve years older than his nephew, Warren was full of fatherly admonishments. Paternalism, indeed, so dominated that the roles of the two aggressive men in their joint enterprise were never clarified. Johnson concluded that his uncle's motive was the charitable one of getting him started in the world, while Warren felt he was employing a poor relation who would be grateful for any recompense thrown his way.

Johnson's duties, the uncle explained, were to cultivate a farm with servants and slaves Warren would supply, to lease Mohawk land to settlers, and to establish a store primarily for the tenants. William got the impression that the farm was to belong to him in return for his labor.

The cocky sea captain had not deigned to consult his fur-trading De Lancey relations about conditions in the backwoods. He had bought for his store, at a cost of more than a thousand pounds, stock suitable for a County Meath crossroads. To this William added what he himself had been able to scrape up for the enterprise: less than ten pounds' worth of Irish linen. The frontier marriage between prosperity and pelts was known to neither Hibernian; they thought of the Indians not as hunters to be employed, but as irascible neighbors to be bought off with an occasional gift.

Johnson's first stop on his way to his destiny was Albany. Thrust by the navigable Hudson deep into the wilderness, that little city seemed to have been imported entire from urban Holland. Bijou houses, tiled in bright colors, turned their stepped gables to the street. Dutch gutturals resounded; and in the midst of the shaggy forest everything was neat: orchards were tended as carefully as drawing rooms. If an Indian came by, he seemed a mirage, but soon there was another.

Since Mrs. Warren had relatives in Albany, Johnson was invited to smoke a pipe on the porches built out over the street. The birds that had been encouraged to nest under the eaves as fly-catchers made the principle sound, for William's hosts sat in silence, clearly hating him, he did not know why. When they did speak, it was to attack his project as a "visionary establishment." The Mohawk, they told him, was not ripe for settlement. Strangely enough, they did not seem to wish it to be. And the richest of them all, the patroon Jeremias Van Rensselaer, cheated him on the sale of some horses.

From Albany, Johnson rode westward over a sandy track through scrub pine to Schenectady, a smaller Dutch town half huddled behind walls for fear of Indian attack. Below it, he saw for the first time the river he was to make his own: 300 yards wide and turbulent now with the excitements of spring. This was the foot of navigation, for Cohoes Falls blocked the actual joining of the Hudson and the Mohawk, and Johnson noted men unloading from a canoe little nondescript packages of furs.

His enthusiasm soared when, a few miles out of town, he came on farms that belonged in Paradise. The river wound between fields so continuous and even that, as his mount paced along, he was overtaken by a plough. Behind three horses hitched abreast, it was turning up at a trot rich black loam.

But as Johnson advanced toward his uncle's territory, low wooded hills pulled in toward the river, particularly on the south side, where he rode and where the tract lay. Now there were long miles during which he could see only packed foliage. The occasional farms were windowless cabins, half-naked children, plough-scratchings around tree stumps.

Twenty-one miles from Schenectady Johnson reached what his uncle had grandly dubbed Warrensburg. Rising rapidly for about 600 feet were what Johnson still considered after seventeen wilderness years "the thickest timbered woods I ever saw." He plunged up the hillside to feel, to experience the land. Locking over his head, a perpendicular maze of spring verdure strained away the sun; branches brushed at his eyes, underbrush and fallen trees tangled his feet, his face was assaulted by the stinging insects that rose from every impenetrable thicket.

From the rivers alone could he see any distance, learn that the land lifted in all directions to low hills. He could drift past Warrensburg's green ramparts, and, where watercourses burrowed beneath foliage, peer inland along quick water to shaded silver falls. For three and a half miles, Warrensburg bordered the Mohawk, and then, when found again on the Schoharie side, twisted and turned for five miles more. In all, twenty-two square miles, a hidden package of undiscovered wonders.

Warrensburg did not include the point of land at the actual meeting of the rivers. Here was a clearing, where William was amazed to see people milling as thick as on Dublin's central square. Fort Hunter, a chunky, crenelated, blockhoused rectangle of horizontal logs, pointed its cannon from higher ground at the sprawling, unsteady, random stockade around the Lower Mohawk Castle, where there were no cannon. Yet the balance of power was not so much in favor of the English fortification as one might suppose. When moved to visit Fort Hunter the Indians did not wait for the scientifically designed portal to open. "Except they are quite drunk," a missionary complained, "they'll run over the wall like so many cats."

At the time of Johnson's arrival, the tensions in the Valley were relaxed, and on warm days the inhabitants of the two fortifications fraternized. Half-naked soldiers lolled and spat and swore, their whims served by the squaws who were their Indian wives. The

Rev. Henry Barclay stalked around, trying to uphold the dignity of the Church of England, scolding the soldiers for corrupting the Mohawks. Indian women, with papooses strapped to their backs, labored in adjoining cornfields, while the braves cleaned guns or sat motionless. The little boys, who alone used bows and arrows, twanged their strings at the wild pigeons that from the bordering forest filled every silence with sibilation.

Inside the fort were quarters for twenty soldiers, a manse for the missionary, and a tiny church with, over the doorway, the royal arms. The communion plate was inscribed, "the gift of Her Majesty, Anne, by the grace of God of Britain, France, Ireland, and her plantations in North America, Queen, to her Indian chapel of the Mohawks." Scattered like jackstraws inside Teantontalogo, the Indian castle, were "long houses" typical of the Iroquois Federation to which the Mohawks belonged: low, windowless clan tenements, about thirty feet wide and sometimes a hundred in length. Down every central hallway burned a succession of fires, flanked with the quarters, resembling box stalls, of individual families. When the whole village met at the Council House, there were about 360 braves, squaws, and papooses.

The Mohawks noticed Johnson only to beg food and drink, but he could not resist staring at the braves who wrapped dirty blankets around them like mantles or, on hot days, wore only a patch between their sinewy legs. Another newcomer wrote, "they paint and grease themselves much with bear's fat clarified, cut their hair off from one side of their heads, and some of that on the other they tie up in knots upon the crown with feathers. Tufts of fur upon their ears, and some of them wear a bead fastened to their noses with a thread hanging down to their lips; beads and wampum about their hocks and wrists."

"The ladies," the dandified army officer, John André, was to write his fashionable sister, appeared on ordinary occasions in "a blanket tolerable impregnated with bear's grease and vermilion, which they wear capuchin fashion. Their finery is a man's shirt copiously besprinkled with vermilion; fine bead necklaces, earrings, etc.; a little sort of winding blue kilt or petticoat coming down to their knees; and blue cloth leggins—a sort of trousers—with fine shoes worked with porcupine quills, black, red, yellow,

Guerrier Iroquois

JOHNSON'S NEW NEIGHBORS

The drawings of Iroquois, here and on the following three
pages, are by Grasset de Saint Sauveur (*Courtesy of the New-
York Historical Society, New York City*)

Iroquois allant a la Decouverte

J. Grasset St Sauveur inv. direx.   J. Laroque Sculp.

Grand Chef de Guerriers Iroquois

J. Grasset S. Sauveur inv. direx.   J. Laroque Sculp.

Sauvagesse Iroquoise

etc., with fringes of red hair (not carroty locks) but scarlet horse-hair or something of that kind."

Only the most worthless Indians of either sex admitted to a knowledge of English, and they had learned it from the lowest order of traders. By pure flowing streams, Johnson heard Mohawks mouth the most disgusting obscenities.

Years later, Johnson wrote that "a man of sense and observation" could learn nothing useful about Indians except through "a long residence amongst them, and a desire of information in these matters superseding all other considerations." In 1738, he was more concerned with setting up his farm and store.

Johnson was meeting the problems of the wilderness on a large scale. He had recruited twelve families in County Meath and brought along, as an intimate companion, his cousin Michael Tyrrell. There were already seven or eight tenants on Warrensburg, mostly Germans, and he rented land to others in 200-acre lots on the long term of two or three lives. Warren sent up some slaves and Johnson hired an overseer. Although the Irish contingent suffered from a perennial wilderness hazard—lack of limes for a good punch—the immediate problem was to get in a crop that would ripen before winter.

The Albany surveyors procrastinated, until the risk of clearing a neighbor's land seemed to all the lesser risk. Then everyone girdled tree trunks with deep gashes. To the pungency of shed sap, a bit of forest sickened slowly, and finally, after a night of wind, perpendicular skeletons cast only thin shadows on soil for the first time open to the summer sun. As the ground dried and became enslavable by man, mists flitted away like the ghosts of savage millennia.

Warrensburg was pocked with bits of dead forest when Johnson received a letter from his uncle advising him to change the forest into "square fields, leaving hedge-rows at each side, which will keep the land warm, be very beautiful, and subject you to no more expense than doing it in a slovenly, irregular manner." Johnson replied by asking with suppressed testiness that the store be supplied with "goods proper for the country."

As soon as the winter wheat ripened, Johnson's wilderness neighbors had floated on laden rafts or scows to his store. They were mostly Germans, marked by privation and hard labor: the girls "broke before twenty-five years of age"; the women as rough appearing as men, often with beards they had to cut with scissors; the men seemingly haughty but actually suspicious—frowning and unfriendly.

These refugees from the Palatinate had weathered injustice and agony to achieve the crop they were now bringing to market. In Germany, they had been so harried by armies and tax collectors that in their final destitution they had been unable to protect themselves from packs of wolves. They had fled in such numbers to England that they were attacked there by mobs fearing this influx of cheap labor. Queen Anne relieved the pressure by sending two or three thousand to New York.

They sailed with high hopes, but in 1710 found themselves virtual serfs on the Hudson River patroonship of Robert Livingston. The most determined bought land from the Mohawk Indians and, defying edicts from the Royal Governor, established seven villages up the Schoharie from Warrensburg. For a year and a half they lived on roots and berries as they cleared away the forest, but as soon as they had managed to achieve crops that could banish hunger, they were notified that their Indian title was worthless; all the results of their anguished labors belonged to land speculators who had been sitting comfortably in Albany. At this point, the Germans ran amuck. Efforts to make them pay rent for their own land were met with gunfire; enraged housewives blinded a sheriff; but it was a hopeless battle against forces too powerful. Their leaders imprisoned, the Germans were evicted from the Schoharie Valley, where second growth soon rose in most of their fields.

Again there was a division between the stouter and weaker of heart. Many secured freeholds in more democratic Pennsylvania, but a stubborn minority refused to leave the Valley, forcing a break at last in the determination of the Albany landlords to allow no freeholders on their frontier. Granted land on the Mohawk beyond Warrensburg in the Indian country, they established the villages of Stone Arabia and German Flatts. This was fifteen years before Johnson's arrival. Since then the Germans had been reinforced by new immigration and had produced tremendous families; they were spreading up and down the Valley.

At Johnson's store, the Germans did not yearn over the fine

linen he had brought from Ireland with his own hand; they glow-
ered at it as a symbol of the luxurious world which had, before
they found a wilderness haven, visited on them every conceivable
horror. Standing on bare feet pounded to the consistency of
leather, they were amused by the piles of stockings. A boy picked
up in bewilderment a bottle of ink. Having in gestures and exple-
tives expressed their opinion of Johnson's merchandise, the German farmers stepped into their produce-loaded scows and drifted
for Schenectady.

Other potential customers came lightly laden: Indians, and white
men to Johnson's unpracticed eye distinguishable from Indians
only by a lack of nose rings and scalp locks. With the pride of men
establishing great credit, they unpacked piles of beaver. Finding
no goods suited to forests, they repacked and also disappeared
toward Schenectady.

Tyrrell laughed at William's discomfiture and wrote Warren
begging for a commission in the navy that would enable him to
live like a gentleman. But Johnson felt no urge to escape. He was
building on the farm he regarded as his personal share of the enterprise "a house, barn, stables, barracks [for servants and slaves]
etc.," which he later valued at £160.

Calls at Schnectady and Albany stores where, under suspicious
eyes, he made little purchases and looked around him, educated
him in the merchandise which, although called "Indian truck,"
appealed to frontiersmen as well as Indians. He learned to order
black, crimson, and "common red" strowds (a coarse woolen
shoddy); gartering of many colors; blankets "made to the sample
every way," as Indians were very particular; ruffled and plain
shirts without buttons; deep red, blue, green, and yellow ribbons;
calico in "lively colors"; women's and children's scarlet, green, and
blue worsted hose with and without clocks; fowling pieces with
four-foot barrels, each to have some distinguishing mark; shorter
guns for boys; "middling pistols with ramrods"; bars of lead and
bullet molds; goose, duck, and pigeon shot; gunpowder; cutlasses
"of the cymeter kind"; hatchets; beaver and fox traps; iron spears
for striking fish and beaver; flint and steel for striking fire; knives,
scissors, needles, and shoemakers' awls; hair cockades; combs; brass
wire; "toys" of silver "which the Indians wear, of different kinds";

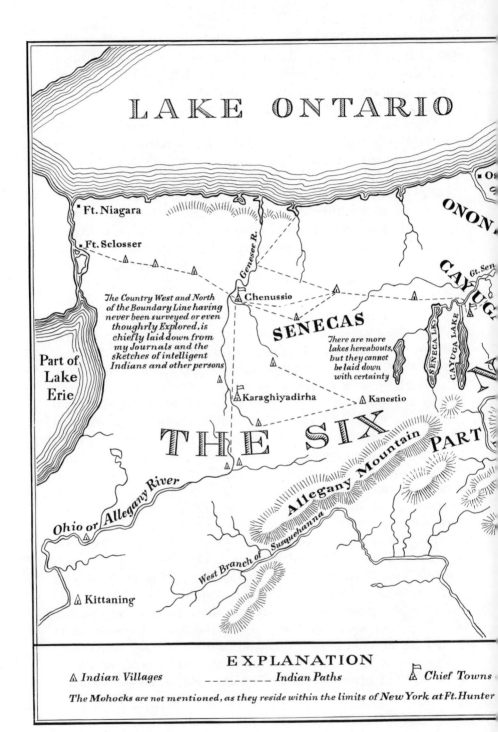

LAKE ONTARIO

ONON

CAYUG

Gt. Sen

■ Ft. Niagara

■ Ft. Sclosser

Genesee R.

Chenussio

The Country West and North
of the Boundary Line having
never been surveyed or even
thoughrly Explored, is
chiefly laid down from
my Journals and the
sketches of intelligent
Indians and other persons

SENECAS

There are more
lakes hereabouts,
but they cannot
be laid down
with certainty

SENECA LK.

CAYUGA LAKE

Part of
Lake
Erie

Karaghiyadirha

Kanestio

THE SIX

PART

Allegany Mountain

Ohio or Allegany River

Susquehanna

West Branch of Susquehanna

Kittaning

EXPLANATION

△ Indian Villages   - - - - - - - - Indian Paths   ⚑ Chief Towns

The Mohocks are not mentioned, as they reside within the limits of New York at Ft. Hunter

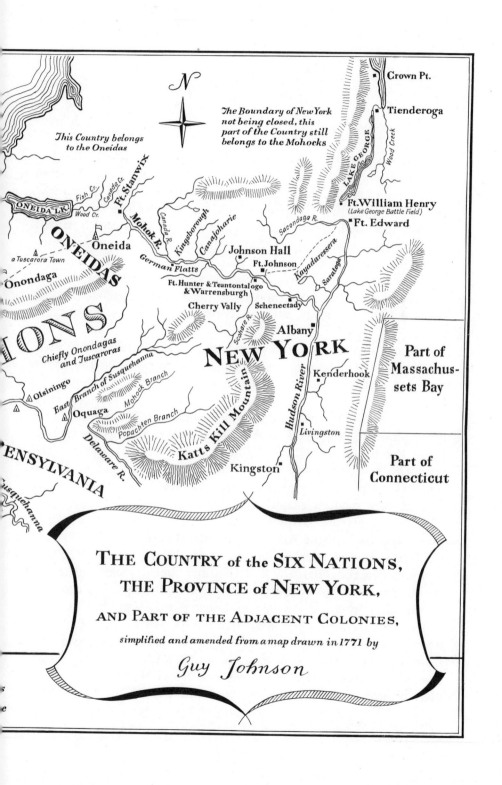

This Country belongs
to the Oneidas

*The Boundary of New York
not being closed, this
part of the Country still
belongs to the Mohocks*

Crown Pt.

Tienderoga

N

ONEIDA LK.

Fish Cr.

Canada Cr.

Ft. Stanwix

Wood Cr.

Mohok R.

ONEIDAS

Oneida

a Tuscarora Town

Canada R.

Kingsborough

Canajoharie

Sacondaga R.

LAKE GEORGE

Wood Creek

Ft. William Henry
(Lake George Battle Field)

Ft. Edward

Onondaga

German Flatts

Johnson Hall

Ft. Johnson

Kayadaressera

Saratoga

IONS

Ft. Hunter & Teantontalogo
& Warrensburgh

Cherry Vally

Schenectady

Chiefly Onondagas
and Tuscaroras

East Branch of Susquehanna

Mohock Branch

Schoharie R.

Albany

NEW YORK

Part of
Massachus-
sets Bay

Olsiningo

Oquaga

Popachten Branch

Delaware R.

Katts Kill Mountain

Hudson River

Kenderhook

Livingston

Part of
Connecticut

ENSYLVANIA

Susquehanna

Kingston

THE COUNTRY of the SIX NATIONS,
THE PROVINCE of NEW YORK,
AND PART OF THE ADJACENT COLONIES,
simplified and amended from a map drawn in 1771 by

Guy Johnson

mirrors, kettles; "red leather trunks in nèsts"; tobacco, snuff boxes, and pipes; black and white wampum; and, of course, rum.

When, in desperation, Johnson ordered on Warren's credit Indian truck worth £160, his uncle protested from Boston: he was far from persuaded that anyone would buy such outlandish merchandise.

Johnson shivered, as winter came on, in the shadow of the hill the sea captain had bought sight unseen, while the other bank of the Mohawk lay golden in the sun. The forest had to be driven like a stubborn beast from Warren's high acres, while the north shore was bordered with level "flatts" that were kept clear and fertilized by the spring-flooding river. Last night's snow had not been disturbed on the road that limped past Johnson's store and ended at Fort Hunter. Across the thinly-iced river he could see farmers sliding on the main road in sleighs laden with merchandise; he could see Indians under strange Western headdresses go by at a trot.

If Warren had not been a greenhorn, he would have bought on the north bank. Locating there "the properest place on the whole river for a storehouse and shop in winter," Johnson bought the tract—a quarter of a mile long and a mile deep—on June 30, 1739, for £180, not in his uncle's but in his own name. He seems to have been genuinely surprised at Warren's disapproval. And Warren could not bring himself to abandon his patriarchal grandeur by stating in so many words that his nephew had no right to act except as his agent; he puffed instead that the raw dependent had undoubtedly made a stupid investment.

William's defense is quoted exactly as written and shows the prose style he brought with him to the Mohawk: "I find yu. are displeased att my purchaseing the land, Which in Everry Bodys Opinion is a good Bargain and Can any time I please Sell it for the Money And More So that I hope, D^r. Uncle y^l. not continue y^r. Opinion when y^u see it and know My Design (w^h. is this) to have a Carefull Honest Man there Who will Manage the farm, w^h. will at least Clear I am sure £30 ℔ Annum, Moreover the Chief thing is a fine Creek to build a Saw Mill on, haveing Loggs Enough att hand, half of w^h. Creek belongs to Me, so that I intend after a little time, please God, to build a Mill there, w^h. May

Clear £40 ℔ Annum and that w^thout Much trouble, so that the Income of that may Enable me the better to go on in the World tho I must Acknowledge D^r. Uncle that w^t. great favours y^u. Were please to do me, was a Sufficient Beginning And am wth. all the Gratitude Imaginable Contended wth. it and for the future shall be no way Expensive, nor troublesome to y^u. . . . As to my Moveing over where I made the purchase, to live there I never had the least Notion in the World of it."

Johnson was already eying the fur trade in the belief that he could reform it to his advantage. The some eighty traders who frequented Oswego, the English outpost on Lake Ontario, were, he wrote, "a parcel of mere bites." Envisioning no clothes but rags, no food but slops, they carried only enough cargo to "maintain them in idleness for nine months in the year." Johnson decided to see what he could do with £200 of goods at Oquaga, a new Indian town created on the east bank of the Susquehanna by refugees from white encroachment. He had "a fellow here who I would take with me that understands their tongue and way of dealing."

Since the records preserved from the years of William's obscurity are sparse, no account remains of his trip to Oquaga. Yet we can reconstruct it from accounts by other travelers.

When there was no snow and little mud, when rivers were fordable and the streams kept their banks, the wilderness was for a few months open to horses. Thus, Johnson certainly led pack animals from a saddle as he veered into the Catskills up a steep path where rattlesnakes rested in the grooves worn by generations of Indian feet. The way was "obscured by fallen trees, old logs, mirey places, pointed rocks, and entangling roots which were not to be avoided." Even horses famous for being "very sure footed" needed an attention almost impossible for Johnson to give when his own head was menaced by the ragged ceiling of branches that pressed down whenever he rode on heights or through valleys, for the vegetation curved with the land. Leaves blocked all view except of the unchanging glades and shadowed the forest into a perpetual glooming which even hardened travelers found sad.

Eventually dimness sank to black; Johnson stretched out on a blanket and slept in a world devoid of stars. And when he awoke in a pale diffusion of twilight that signified dawn overhead, there was no jubilation of birds; songsters avoided the deep forest. But during the night he had listened to the howling of wolves, wild voices crying of freedom and space without end.

The horses were saddled and the arduous advance resumed. Sometimes the sameness was broken by a glow far ahead on the trail; in a moment, dark stems were silhouetted against radiance; and then the horses trotted out into a clearing, a bright gem set in the dark forest. Tall grasses rippled their kaleidoscope of hues, bordering trees took on height and color, and, if the clearing were on a hillside, the land revealed its basic shape: mountains swelled and tightened into declivities, valleys were outlined by shadow. Ancient apple trees were miraculously alive with singing birds. A clay pipe bowl that crushed beneath the foot, a turfy square of broken rampart, told of an Indian village lost to history beyond recall.

Eventually, the Indians in Johnson's party reined in, took looking glasses from their belts, and, mouthing like fine ladies in boudoirs, streaked their faces with vermilion, lampblack, and white lead. They shouted; there was an answering shout, and the party galloped up to the Indian hamlet of Towanoendalough. Seventeen years later, it consisted of "three wigwams and about thirty souls." Beyond was the Susquehanna. Here, Johnson probably left his assistants to come on with the horses, and took to the water.

Oquaga proved to differ from Teantontalogo by being so deep in Iroquois territory that it needed no stockade for defense. Straggling without any order along the banks, the loghouses each possessed "a paltry garden," where the squaws cultivated corn, beans, watermelons, etc. There were cows, hogs, fowl, horses, but no sheep. "Their fences are miserable," a later traveler reported, "and the land back of the village very indifferent."

Since Indians knew well the privations of the long trail through the dark forest, even the bearers of vital messages were not questioned until they had rested and been fed. Johnson would have been taken to the end room of a long house, which had been quickly and sketchily swept out for his reception, and given food, a kettle of boiled corn or, if a hunt had been successful, venison. After what must have seemed an age to the impatient Irishman, sachems filed in gravely. But even then he could not state his business. There was a long period of silence, while the Indians sat cross-legged and a pipe was handed round.

The tempo at Oquaga remained slow. For days, no one in the village had any furs to sell. And when shouts from the forest presaged a successful hunting party, they brought only a retail lot of pelts. There would be a brisk session of trading; a drunken orgy on the rum Johnson had exchanged, and then another long wait for another few packages of pelts. In all probability, Johnson soon rode home. He had learned his lesson. Trading in Indian villages was for "mere bites"; prosperity lay in encouraging small traders to come to his store.

When Johnson reached his clearing, he was greeted with kisses. Facts about Catherine Weisenberg are few, but since her womb swelled with the future of the Mohawk Valley, she is well remembered by legend. Gossip states that this "uncommonly fair and wholesome looking maid" was a German indentured servant, coming, strangely, from Madagascar and bought on a New York wharf by two brothers named Phillips who lived next door to Warrensburg. One brother was soon complaining, "Johnson, that damned Irishman, came the other day and offered me five pounds for her, threatening to horsewhip me and steal her if I would not sell her. I thought five pounds better than a flogging and took it, and he's got the gal." Against this story is the statement of her descendants that her family was among the original settlers of the Valley.

Whether or not she had been an indentured servant whose time was bought and sold, Johnson's girl had probably been a lone newcomer to the Valley. Not land or church records or any mention in Johnson's papers indicate a Weisenberg family among his neighbors. (Rumors concerning a married sister named Servis will be discussed in due course.) Although Catherine's mother certainly lived in Johnson's household at a later date, there is nothing to show that she had not been imported after the daughter had become established there.

A further clash between traditions—Catherine came to Johnson as his bride, proclaimed their descendants; as his mistress, gossip whispered—is incontrovertibly resolved by a battered, paper-bound "Register Book," which, in his later years, Johnson would have paid well to destroy. This record, kept by the Rev. Barclay at the

Indian Chapel in Fort Hunter, notes a baptism: "June 8th, 1740: Ann, daughter of Catherine Wysenberg." Again on February 7, 1742: "John, son of Catherine Wysen Bergh." And again, on October 14, 1744: "Mary, daughter of Catherine Wysenberk."

Although he must have known that "Catty"—as Tyrrell called her—brought her wriggling bundles from Johnson's nearby house, in all three notations Barclay suppressed the father's name. The future rector of New York's Trinity Church realized that young gentlemen carving their fortunes out of the wilderness could not expect the porcelain-tinted ladies they would eventually marry to share their initial hardships, nor should they be embarrassed by records of their youthful high spirits.

To understand the relationship of William and Catty, twentieth-century readers will have to forget their equalitarianism, their women's rights. The patrician's nephew and the servant girl were joined two centuries ago, not according to the then revolutionary middle-class morality of the Puritans, but in the conservative, time-tested feudal and aristocratic manner. "Landlords of consequence have assured me," wrote a traveler in Johnson's native Ireland, "that many of the cotters would think themselves honored by having their wives and daughters sent for to the beds of their masters." Johnson was to say of his German neighbors, "If one gets a Dutch girl with child, 'tis not minded."

Modern writers have postulated for Johnson fits of conscience at the ravishment of the girl whom tradition paints as so young and innocent and fair. Certainly, he came to mourn that the fruits of that lower-class body were irretrievably illegitimate, yet, when the babies were conceived, the possibility of marriage could not have occurred to either parent. William would have slammed in his own face all the doors of ambition; Catty would have been as miserable in the role of a gentleman's wife as she would have been screamingly out of place. But the lovers, when they went upstairs together publicly, were behaving suitably for their respective stations. As a "housekeeper," Catty played a recognized role. Thus, one of William's friends wrote him, "I begin to have fine taste and flatter myself I shall have an opportunity of getting a French mademoiselle for a housekeeper in the summer."

So many matters that motivated her lover were outside Catty's philosophy that she could not expect to understand him. She could only bend to him as a flower bends to the sun, opening her petals to gleam, closing them to darkness. She had a handsome man and a passionate one, who was kind to her as he was to all people. She could entertain her friends well, even if only in the kitchen; she lived, according to her own standards, luxuriously. Although it was understood that she would move on when her William brought home a bride of his own station, she had her children, who could count on his favor, and he would provide for her generously, in spinsterhood or marriage. As a friend wrote, it was in his character always to do more than he promised, and it was increasingly clear that Johnson would be able to do much.

He spent more and more time away from Warrensburg on his land across the river, where he was building a stone house unnecessarily substantial for the overseer for whom he assured his uncle it was intended. Catty could not have been surprised when, as her first pregnancy approached its termination, he showed her the nursery and the bedroom they would share; told her to pack all his possessions.

On February 9, 1740, at the age of twenty-five or -six, Johnson headed a letter not "Warrensburg" but "Mount Johnson." He had declared an independence he was never to relinquish, not to any Colonial Assembly, to any Royal Governor, not even to the Crown itself. But he still had to find the philosopher's stone of his true greatness.

3

A Political Forest

Gradually Johnson cleared a high mental plateau from which he could see the wide topography of his situation. He saw the Mohawk River flowing, not only in its physical channel, but westward until a visionary extension of its waters rippled over the huge central valley of the continent, broke against mountains so distant they were known only to hearsay and dream. Eastward, the Mohawk seemed to move in a shining current through the dark Atlantic, until at last it lapped the thrones of England and France and washed them into conflict. For the river that moved through Johnson's dooryard was a key to a new empire over which the two old empires yearned. Rarely had destiny placed a man in so important a spot at so important a time.

The long Appalachian mountain range, which, as it roughly paralleled the Atlantic Ocean, marked the limits of British settlement, broke only twice to allow water communication with the North Central plain. The St. Lawrence River gave the Canadian French easy access to the Great Lakes and the whole center of the continent; Johnson's river, on a less lavish scale, did the same for the English. Sloops sailed up the Hudson from the ocean to the Mohawk; smaller boats moved past Mount Johnson to a marsh which was one of the most strategic spots in North America, for water flowed from it in two directions: some to New York harbor,

some to the Great Lakes. Vessels which had been carried the short
distance overland from the Mohawk were propelled by the current
to Wood Creek and thence on the Onondaga River to Oswego on
Lake Ontario. This was roughly the route of the Erie Canal that
was to make New York the greatest city in America.

During more than a century, the French had used their waterway to explore millions of acres, to erect trading posts and Jesuit
chapels. However, the Dutch and the English had ventured only
occasionally on theirs. Exertion was for them unnecessary, since
they had touched off in the wilderness one of those nationalistic
explosions that bloody and change history.

Probably during the sixteenth century, five related Indian nations had fled into what is now northern New York from some
Algonquin conqueror, and had stockaded themselves in a long,
diffuse line on hills. These refugees were in no unusual situation—
American prehistory was a slow churning of tribes, the vanquished
receding from the victor—but the Iroquois had, after their defeat,
made an amazing move. In a hunting culture, where every nation
is automatically at war with every other, they had formed a federal
government.

Whether the Iroquois League was established, as legend tells
us, at a single constitutional convention attended by supernatural
beings, or was the result of evolution, it was given permanence by
being a carefully worked out expansion of the customs of the individual tribes. Thus the Iroquois territory was thought of as a
long house, with each nation occupying a room around its own fire.
One door opened on the Hudson: the Mohawks were the keepers
of this door. Next, as the trails weaved westward, came the Oneidas,
the Onondagas, the Cayugas, and, at the other door on the Genesee,
the Senecas. Although the main council fire burned in the central
chamber of the Onondagas, the Mohawks, who were reputed to
have initiated the federation, remained the leaders of what was
now called the Five Nations.

(By Johnson's time, the League was sometimes also called the
Six Nations, for in 1710 the Tuscaroras, who had fled from white
penetration in North Carolina, were taken in. They were, however, allowed no representatives of their own at Onondaga, being

spoken for by the Oneidas, on whose territory they were quartered and whose "children" they were considered.) *

The fifty sachems on whom executive, legislative, and judicial responsibility rested operated on three levels: As members of the Onondaga Council, they governed the League; they presided over their own nations in local affairs; and they were dignitaries in their personal clans, which helped cement the alliance since the clans extended beyond the boundaries of the individual nations. Every such means toward coherence was necessary, for the League, although it functioned more effectively than today's United Nations, was like it a union of states that had not abandoned their individual sovereignties. No Iroquois nation could be coerced by the others; all decisions of the Onondaga Council had to be unanimous.

When in 1609 the first Dutch ship sailed up the Hudson to the Long House's eastern door, the League had suffered no major trials; it was still passive on its defensive hilltops. But the warriors came down to exchange gifts.

It was a meeting of spring and autumn in the evolution of man, and if the result was to be tragedy for the younger culture, that was at first not evident. The two economies fitted neatly together. Unlike the Englishmen who were flocking into territories to the north and south, the Dutch were happy in their native land: They sent to New Netherland, not a flood of homesteaders, but a trickle of traders. The Dutch burghers coveted, not the Iroquois hunting grounds, but the products of Indian hunting. They imported cheaply from Holland goods that the Indians were enchanted to receive in exchange for furs which brought in Europe tremendous prices. Everyone was pleased, and, to keep the lucrative trade under strict control, the Dutch West India Company, which governed New Netherland, gave Albany a monopoly, and opposed any settlement in the Mohawk Valley that would clog that vital highroad of supply.

Before the white man came, the Iroquois were evolving toward an agricultural economy, their women supplementing the achievements of the hunters by cultivating ever larger fields of corn. Their society was a solid unit—but like that of all other Indians who

* Since the Tuscaroras were not full members, I shall, in my own text, refer to the League as the Five Nations, but quotations will contain whatever designations were used by the original writers.

were exposed to European goods, it was soon pulled into a shape that could not stand by itself. The collection of furs as a cash crop placed a new emphasis on the ancient tribal preoccupations with the chase and the warpath, but discouraged agriculture—the corn fields shrank—and handicrafts. The Indians lost most of their traditional skills in shaping wood and bark and clay, in shooting arrows: they became dependent on manufactured kettles and beads and paint and knives and—most grievous for their future power— guns and ammunition. These things they could not learn to make themselves, for their men were now more than ever convinced that all occupations were womanly except hunting animals—and man.

War soon became a necessity for the Iroquois, since in their eagerness for European manufactures they decimated the game in the Long House. To secure furs elsewhere, they enacted, between 1640 and 1685, a saga of conquest. Although they never boasted more than 2,500 warriors, they overran tribes occupying a huge territory that extended north to Hudson's Bay, south to the Carolinas, west as far as the Mississippi, and east to the white frontiers. In their pride, the Iroquois insisted that in the human race they alone were "men," and so great became their reputation for invincibility that, if a single Mohawk were discovered near a New England tribe, the cry, "A Mohawk! A Mohawk!" would echo from hill to hill, "upon which they all fled like sheep before wolves, without attempting the least resistance."

The Iroquois objective was to gain control of the fur trade of the entire continent. Alien hunters they either drove away to make room for their own marksmen and trappers, or else forced to sell them raw pelts, which they carried to Albany to be exchanged for European goods, some of which they used to buy more skins. Rival nations of middlemen, particularly the Hurons, France's business agents on the Great Lakes route, the Iroquois decimated and dispersed. Such activities, of course, outraged the French, since every Iroquois success meant that fewer furs were routed to Canada, more down the Mohawk Valley to New York. The French tried to stop Iroquois imperialism by counter-warfare, missionary penetration, and treaty, but, during their period of great expansion, the Five Nations resisted conquest and responded to blandishments only when their armies were occupied elsewhere.

Albany prospered, so much so that when New Netherland fell to the British in 1664, the English governors, far from wishing to disrupt the Dutch-Iroquois alliance, were eager to dip their own hands into the proceeds. The Albany monopoly was continued; settlement on the Mohawk supply line still discouraged. The future site of Mount Johnson remained deep in wilderness.

But while New York rejoiced, the Iroquois began to wonder. Although, like the Romans, they adopted into their nations many individuals they had captured, such transfusions did not keep their population, as war followed war, from a slow decrease which meant, despite their mounting military glory, a drop in absolute power. And, as the death wail mingled perpetually in their castles with rejoicings over enemy scalps, military fervor began to slacken, and the sachems increasingly reckoned cost against gain.

Despite all their victories, furs still moved to Canada: The Ottawas had taken over the Hurons' burnt camp sites and were paddling laden canoes up the St. Lawrence. And every year, the French were becoming more powerful and more able to defend their own. (In 1687, an army led by Denonville laid waste Seneca towns.) Furthermore, the Albany merchants, whose trade had gained so much from Iroquois aggressions, were making good use of the fact that those aggressions blocked the Indians from selling in Canada. As the only market the Iroquois could reach, Albany paid the low prices for furs made possible by monopoly.

Having pondered these things, the sachems substituted in the 1680's for their forty-year-old policy of wholesale warfare a new reliance on diplomacy. They signed and adhered to a peace treaty with France. The result was electric and delightful. Competition between buyers lifted the value of furs, and the French and English, both anxious to propitiate the military power that dominated their common frontier, showered on the Five Nations gifts and favors. Tasting the fruits that come to those who control the balance of power, the sachems congratulated themselves on having solved their problems. Actually, they had opened their forests to forces that were to make them dependent on an Irishman not yet born—William Johnson.

No longer able to count on their Iroquois allies, the English built Fort Hunter to dominate the Lower Mohawk Castle, and placed a missionary there to pull against the Jesuits. When, in their eagerness for a competitive market, the Senecas allowed the French to establish a fortified trading post at Niagara, the English voided the Albany monopoly, built Fort Oswego, moving their fur frontier to the Great Lakes. The Mohawk Valley was now a supply route for the army. Glad to have it protected by bulwarks of flesh, the English authorities, disregarding the screams of the Albanians, (as the inhabitants of Albany were called) allowed German refugees from the Palatinate to secure freeholds there.

The ancient organization of New York's fur trade had crumbled, but the former Dutch monopolists of Albany were far from defeated. Their activities had brought prosperity to the transshipping merchants of New York City, with whom they had intermarried to form an oligarchy that included almost all the old, influential families in the colony. Under the system of limited sufferage, these families controlled the colonial government, and now they worked together to establish a new frontier policy that was almost completely successful until Johnson arose as an opposing champion.

Since their Iroquois allies would no longer fight to keep the Canadians away from the fur harvest, the Albany merchants went into partnership with the Canadians. New York could import products Indians coveted more cheaply from industrialized England than Canada could from agricultural France. Sending these goods on to French possessions was a violation of English law, but smuggling was an eighteenth-century institution, and it was very profitable to slip Indian truck up Lake Champlain to Montreal across customs barriers obliterated by foliage. French voyageurs carried British manufactures (and also Massachusetts rum, which the Indians liked less well than French brandy but welcomed as less expensive) into the wilderness. In payment, Albany received a valuable share of Canada's furs.

This trade was in many ways to the disadvantage of Albany's former allies, the Iroquois. Every fur that came into New York via Canada dodged around the Long House, depriving the Five Nations of their traditional commission as middlemen. The English guns that voyageurs sold in the forest armed Indian nations whom the Iroquois had made during the years, when they had fought Albany's fur battles, into confirmed enemies. And, most grievous of all, the Canadian trade enabled the Albanians to be completely indifferent to the welfare of their own Indian neighbors. The low prices they had paid for furs dropped even lower, until the most assiduous Iroquois could hardly buy with a year's labor a year's supply of white man's goods. The Indians complained endlessly to Johnson against their former friends in Albany. "They have cheated us," the Mohawks would say. "They treat us as slaves."

Now that the Mohawk Valley had been opened to settlement, the Albanians foresaw that the Indians would in the end be driven away, and they were determined that the white expansion should be on their own terms and to their own profit. Over a period of years, they had befuddled their Mohawk "friends" with liquor and induced them to sign deeds which the Indians, after they had sobered up, did not remember signing. Thus, the Albanians secured legal control of almost all the best land on the river. Having no excess population of their own to export, they tended to let their purchases lie, for the time being, unexploited, but it was necessary to tie down their claims with surveys. This was done surreptitiously. Coming on the indentations made by surveyors' tripods in their soil, the Indians were filled with suspicion and rage.

We have seen that Governor Cosby had been forced to burn an Albany deed in order to wrench Warrensburg away, and that this had opened the Mohawk to Johnson. Naturally, the Irishman had not been enthusiastically received when he arrived in Albany full of grandiose plans.

Those outsiders, mostly German, who had previously forced their way into the Valley had not been prosperous or influential enough to give the Albany Dutch much trouble. They were either small fur traders, who went to Oswego and competed with the Iroquois as middlemen, or small farmers producing wheat as a cash crop. Through financial and political manipulation, the Dutch faction had forced these settlers to deal with them, thus keeping control of the wholesale aspects of both trades. What was their anger when Johnson opened a store between them and the fur-bearing forests, in the middle of the wheat-bearing lands!

Captain Warren was, of course, basically to blame for the interloper. Used to bellowing from a quarter-deck and kept by his profession always on the move, the naval officer had sent his nephew into the Valley without detailed conversation with his wife's relations: he had not realized that he was balking their interests. Actually, his brother-in-law, James De Lancey, was the most powerful political leader of the Dutch faction. Had the Mohawk Valley speculation remained under Warren's control, the two men would have probably worked out a compromise which would have incorporated Warren's interests into the Dutch system. But Johnson had destroyed this possibility when he had declared his independence by moving to his own property across the river.

He had not intended the break to be as sharp as it proved to be. Knowing that his uncle's true ambition for Warrensburg was to establish a populated manor, he sought no tenants for himself—he tilled his own farm with servants and slaves—and continued to sign leases for Warren, securing twenty-three families in all. This was an impressive number for the time and place, but Warren was not placated. William had set up a store at Mount Johnson that obliterated the one at Warrensburg; his nephew had been insubordinate.

Johnson visited New York in 1740, 1741, and again in 1742, and on each occasion Warren gave him an acknowledgment of indebtedness to sign. Unwilling to admit any nonpatriarchal motives, the uncle explained grandly that he wanted the bonds from his relation "chiefly with a view to make him frugal and diligent in his business"; he might never demand payment. And Johnson, "so easy I was about it," kept no record of his promises to pay the large sum of £1,820—nor did he save any money toward the debt. Johnson put most of his earnings into goods for his perpetually expanding store, and what was left he invested in farmland and mill sites.

Warren had no need for payment. The conflict with Spain known as the War of Jenkins's Ear made vulnerable the treasure ships of the Indies, and, as a brilliant British raider—he dumped on his nephew more captured slaves than the Mohawk Valley could afford—the stocky sea captain was lifted by prize money to great wealth. Considering Warren "my only father in this part of the world," William felt he had received only his "reasonable expectation of sharing some part of his fortune." His uncle's naval triumphs, he wrote, cast "everlasting credit" on the family; he would do his part, "when in my power," by adding in his own right to the family influence and glory. Warren wished to be paid in cash. However, when Johnson's first note came due in 1744 and was not met, he did not sue. He secretly set up a dynastic booby-trap for William in his will.

Both uncle and nephew had been trained to despise trade. Although Warren would not himself engage in the bourgeois occupation of keeping accounts, he urged William to do so, and even sent him ledgers. William threw the ledgers to the field mice.

In the Johnson store, money rarely changed hands. As his stock diminished, his bins of furs and flour filled higher, and, when they almost spilled over, he shipped to agents in New York City, who sold his goods locally or to England or the Indies. Despite perpetual complaints of amateurish labeling and packaging, the produce was excellent and sold well.

After his achievements made Johnson an object of curiosity to all Europe, the *Gentleman's Magazine* noted with wonder that he sat down with the local Germans, "smokes tobacco, drinks flip, and talks of improvements, bears, and beaver skins." This made the burghers of Albany, who could hardly be induced by the most pressing business reasons to shake hands with a German backwoodsman, puff convulsively at their pipes. How could Captain Warren's nephew eat on with relish while a peasant's wife gave suck to her baby at his table? How could he join wholeheartedly in a German dance and, when it was over, strip to the waist like the other men and lie before the fire in a pile that included the women in their petticoats? How could he prefer such rough occasions to a polite evening on a Dutch patrician's stoop?

As a matter of fact, Johnson bore against the Albany Dutch a grudge that went back to his childhood: They were using their mercantile monopoly to play the role that had been played in County Meath by the hated absentee landlords. Unconcerned with the welfare of the peasants, they sought from them only one thing: profits. "The devil is a Dutchman," an inhabitant of the Valley would say. Another, considering this an understatement, would add, "A trading Dutchman would cheat the devil himself." Although Johnson's neighbors had more to eat, in other ways they were as poor and ignorant as the gillies who had crowded his father's kitchen by the mill of Killeen.

In Ireland, a peasant found protection before the law only

through the intervention of some powerful relation or patron. The same was true of the Mohawk Valley Germans, who could not read or write English and were completely unrepresented in the centers of power where statutes were being continually passed to their disadvantage. Without conscious plan, Johnson stepped into the role of their protector. (A supplicant too shy to come into the parlor at Mount Johnson could slip into the kitchen where his fellow-German, Catty, would listen to his tale, and, if necessary, lead him to her lover.)

Johnson adopted what he called a policy of "fair dealing with the German settlers, etc." Contracting in advance for the crops, he took no advantage of penury, and the mills he had built ground with strict rectitude. He would set up able neighbors in the fur trade and back them in paying high enough prices for pelts to out-bid at Oswego or in the forest the representatives of the profiteering Albany wholesalers.

Expansive generosity came naturally to him. He would sternly instruct his overseer to be strict in collecting debts, but respond in person to every story of misfortune. Since he rarely left his estate except for a deer chase or a wolf encounter, the wife of a sick farmer had no trouble finding him to borrow slaves who would at no charge bring in the harvest.

In return for kindness, Johnson expected loyalty. If traders to whom he had extended credit wished to sell their furs in Albany, they found it wise to drift by Mount Johnson in the dark. Calling down the law on a neighbor who had absconded owing him £4.3.8, Johnson wrote typically, "I don't value the debt so much as the evil intent of the fellow to impose upon me."

The amazement and also the uneasiness of the Albanians grew when Johnson added to those he cherished and protected the wild aborigines of the forest. As a friend wrote, "Something in his natural temper responded to Indian ways. The man holding up a spear he had just thrown on which a fish is now impaled; the man who runs, with his toes turned safely inward, through a forest where a greenhorn could not walk; the man sitting silent, gun on knee, in a towering black glade watching by candle flame for the movement of antlers toward a tree whose bark has already been streaked by the tongues of deer; the man who can read a bent twig like an historical volume—this man is William Johnson, and he has learned all these skills from the Mohawks. How can an admirer of ability fail to revere their control of their forest environment; how can a lover of liberty fail to adore their denial of all exterior restraint?"

However, Johnson's "singular disposition" included a quality much rarer than the appreciation and practice of Indian skills—throughout American history thousands of white men joyfully exchanged breeches for breechcloth. His unique gift was his ability to feel simultaneous loyalty to both Indian and white institutions, to move with no sense of strain according to conceptions thousands of years apart in human evolution. For this feat, he had been to some extent prepared when overwhelming worldly pressure had forced him as a boy to abandon the Catholic religion of his forefathers. Since he felt no need for philosophic reassurance, he had not fled to any other religious belief or even an aggressive skepticism; whole areas of his mind remained unencumbered with those seemingly revealed preconceptions, based on early training, that make most people unreceptive to exotic thought. Add to this that, although transcendantly able, he was the least introspective of men, that he never tried to codify his ideas and was thus unaware of theoretical inconsistencies, and that his instinctive human sympathies were warm.

Johnson believed that trading Indians should be allowed to get as drunk as they pleased—he had opposed the Rev. Barclay's desire to establish prohibition at Teantontalogo—but the braves who dealt with him or his representatives awoke from their stupors to a novel experience: the pains in their heads had not been added to by financial pains. They could hardly believe their eyes' to see that, although the rum had been paid for, they still had pelts that would buy ammunition, clothes for their families, and even jew's-harps to while away the tedium of the long trail home. The jew's-harps soon strummed away in distant glades, and to the flickering of council fires the strange tale was told. In 1752, some Moravian missionaries were almost trampled to death in a stampede of Onondagas to offer their furs and ginseng roots at a tent set up by Johnson's representatives.

More important for Johnson's future than the mounting affection of his German neighbors was the secret surveyance of his actions by the Mohawk's political wizard Tiyanoga, known to the Dutch as King Hendrick. This great sachem commonly denied any knowledge of English, but one day he addressed Johnson in that tongue. Being adept in dramatic gesture, he may well have dressed himself, for this act of confidence, in the much belaced blue court costume which Queen Anne had given him with her own royal hand. His cocked hat under his arm, he could have stepped from the gilt frame of one of Sir Peter Lely's portraits, had it not been for his dark color, his high, hooked nose, and the tomahawk scar that seemed to continue his mouth the whole width of his left cheek. "He appeared," declared a man who had seen him, "as if born to command, and possessed a majesty unrivaled."

Hendrick was one of the "Four Indian Kings" who had in 1710 gone on a famous embassy to London. He could tell Johnson, who had never seen so great a city, about the streets as long as rivers, the white faces that stared, the gem-starred ladies who had curt-seyed to him as royalty in gilded halls. But that was all a fading dream. New problems plagued the Mohawks. Gravely sipping Johnson's rum, watching every change of the white man's expres-sion, Hendrick let drop a question about white policy toward his nation which he did not understand. For the Mohawks distrusted New York's official Indian commissioners with whom they were supposed to consult but who belonged to the Dutch faction they resented and believed had betrayed them. Like Johnson's white neighbors, the Indians needed a champion adept in threading the political mazes of the English world.

For his part, Johnson was learning the Mohawk tongue, a task so difficult that even the Albanians officially entrusted with Indian affairs rarely attempted it. A missionary complained that "their verbs are varied, but in a manner so different from the Greek and Latin" that he could discover no rule and assumed "every verb has a peculiar mode." Furthermore, the Iroquois "compound their words without end," that for wine being "oneharadesehoengtseragh-erie," meaning "a liquor made of the juice of grapes." Johnson concluded that their language, although limited in vocabulary, "is extremely emphatical, and that their style abounds with noble images, strong metaphors, and equal in allegory to many of the eastern [European] nations."

As he became increasingly able to communicate with the Indians he became increasingly fascinated with them, and they responded with growing friendship until, at a date never exactly ascertained, he was adopted as a Mohawk. We can reconstruct the ceremony from the account of another man similarly honored.

After the neophyte had stripped off his clothes and put on a breechcloth, braves drew on his face and body designs in various colors, put a large belt of wampum around his neck, silver bands on his wrists and right arm. Then an old chief shouted "Coo-wigh!" several times in quick succession, which brought all the inhabitants of the castle at a run. They gathered around the chief, who made "a long speech very loud." Then three young squaws led the future Indian into the river, plunged him under and washed him, rubbing, as our informant wrote, "severely, yet I cannot say they hurt me much.

"These young women then led me to the Council House, where some of the tribe were ready with new clothes for me. They gave me a new ruffled shirt, which I put on, also a pair of leggins done off with ribbons and beads, likewise a pair of moccasins, and garters dressed with beads, porcupine quills, and red hair; also a tinsel-laced cappo. They again painted my head and face with various colors. . . . They seated me on a bear skin, and gave me a pipe, tomahawk, and polecat pouch, which had been skinned pocket fashion, and contained tobacco and killegnico, or dry sumach leaves, which they mix with their tobacco—also spunk, flint and steel. When I was thus seated, the Indians came in dressed and painted in their grandest manner. As they came in, they took their seats and for a considerable time there was a profound silence: everyone was smoking. At length, a sachem announced 'My son, you are now flesh of our flesh and bone of our bone.'"

The Mohawks renamed Johnson "Warraghiyagey," which he translated as "a man who undertakes great things."

The Albanians, so Johnson was warned, "look upon you with a more sour eye and a darker face than a bull can do." What had happened was even worse than their most pessimistic fears when the energetic young Irishman had started large-scale operations in the Indian country. "Loved, caressed, and almost adored in the Mohawk Valley," he had made his store a barrier past which almost no pelts penetrated; he was growing rich on merchandise

Hendrick, the great Mohawk sachem who was Johnson's dearest Indian friend, as depicted by I. Faber in 1710 during his visit to Queen Anne (*Courtesy of the New-York Historical Society, New York City*)

The SOUTH VIEW of OSWEGO on LAKE ONTARIO

General Shirley in 1755 strengthen'd & inlarged this Fort
and erected two others; one Westward 170 Square with
a Rampart of Earth & Stone. Another on the Opposite side of the Onondaga River 470 Yards distant from the Old
Fort. This which is call'd the East Fort, is built of Logs and
the Wall is surrounded by a Ditch. The Projec-
tion of the Rocks renders the Channel at the Entrance into the Onondaga River very Narrow, and
our Vessels are generally warp'd from the Lake
into the Bason.

Explanation.
1. The River Onondaga.
2. The Lake Ontario.

which, since the first pale face had glimmered in the wilderness, had seemed the Albanians' right.

They put through the New York Assembly a licensing and inspection law which designated leading Dutchmen overseers of the fur trade. Since Johnson was entirely unwilling to submit to such control, he was summoned, on July 23, 1743, for breaking the law. He considered this "the height of ill-treatment" and threatened reprisals. In the end, the Albanians did not dare do more than fine the Mohawk Valley's champion, lest the inhabitants of the frontier, white and Indian, rise angrily to his defense.

Although still unknown except locally and among his business correspondents and competitors, Johnson had in his five American years risen far by applying to the frontier an anachronistic social philosophy which he had imbibed in oppressed Ireland and which chimed with the ancient institutions of the Indians. He did not in the bourgeois manner see his neighbors as independent workers and purchasers from whom a profit could be earned by buying cheap and selling dear. Nor did he in the aristocratic manner regard them as inferiors, as a different breed of creation to be manipulated from high above. He saw the German immigrants and the Iroquois aborigines as adopted clan brothers whose prosperity was intertwined with his own.

This identification, which he gradually expanded to larger and more distant groups, was the key to Johnson's character and the basis of his career. Matters he did not bring into personal focus he tended to ignore. For the rest, he was convinced that what was good for him was good for his followers, a not unusual conclusion to which he drew a rare corollary: He believed that what was good for them would in the end prove to his own advantage.

Like a dictatorial, devoted father operating within his own household, he determined issues according to intelligent expediency tempered with partiality for his own. Considering himself one with his supporters, he could never convict himself of cruelty toward them, but, on the other hand, conscious cruelty toward his own would be a form of masochism (Johnson was a hedonist). His brutalities were to be failures of imagination, willful sometimes, more often temperamental.

The achievements of such a man, although winged by the force of his intellect, are given scope by the impressionability of his heart. Since the role played in most men's consciences by principle is played in his by love, he can operate sympathetically no further than he can love, and his mental conflicts will not be between right and wrong but between rival loyalties. His career will have consistency only as far as his emotions are consistent: It will reflect his character as the wax duplicates a seal. He will find it difficult to obey the orders of his superiors; nor will he be able to co-operate with equals unless they agree with him in everything—a most unlikely chance. He will have to stand by himself at the head of his cohorts, a difficult position in the eighteenth century when the age of personal champions had passed to make room for the courtier, the institutional general, the politician, and businessman. And William Johnson had not yet faced any real test.

He was soon to go through an ordeal of blood, for in 1744 England and France sprang to war over the Austrian Succession, each throwing into the cockpit its American colonies.

PART TWO

French and Indian Wars

4

The Old French War Begins

King George's War, the American offshoot of the War of the Austrian Succession, began on the northern seacoast where the French and New Englanders had long disagreed over fisheries. From their Nova Scotia fortress of Louisburg, the French captured an English island in May, 1744, before the Colonies had been notified from their homeland that they were at war.

This brought into action one of the most able statesmen in our colonial history, Governor William Shirley of Massachusetts. An English-born lawyer, he was to inspire colonial efforts in two wars against the French, but fight the truly decisive engagement of his career with William Johnson. However, the backwoodsman had not swum into Shirley's ken—except perhaps as an insubordinate nephew of Captain Warren—when the governor promoted retaliation against Louisburg. The French base fell in June, 1745, to an English fleet under Warren and New England militia commanded by the merchant-general William Pepperell. Warren won an admiralship and above £20,000 in prize money. Pepperell was made America's first baronet.

Johnson was to be the second American baronet. Already hungry for military glory, he saw in the fighting with Canada a chance to serve not only his king but also the Mohawk Valley, which would be restored to its former importance by a bloody disruption of the Albanian-French fur trade. However, the New York merchants who

45

profited from that trade were not blind to their interests. More Dutch than English in background, they saw no reason to damage their prosperity because King George had a disagreement with Louis XV—or because Massachusetts wanted fishing rights off the Grand Banks. Whatever happened elsewhere, they were determined to keep their own frontier open and at peace.

New York's royal governor, Sir George Clinton, was supposed to further the war, but the New York Assembly found endless reasons to delay raising an army, and, in any case, the Five Nations had followed their now-traditional policy of declaring neutrality. Those Albany Dutchmen the Commissioners for Indian Affairs assured Clinton that nothing would make the Iroquois change their minds. And without the Iroquois, there was no hope of attacking the enemy, for the League dominated the foliaged, craggy desert that separated New York from Canada. No English army could expect to survive there without Indian protection, and to invade this territory without permission from the Iroquois proprietors might well drive the most redoubtable of all American forces to the French side, bringing inevitable destruction to the frontier and perhaps putting the entire Colony at the mercy of the French.

What was an easygoing man like Clinton to do? He was by definition a fighter—as Vice Admiral he held one of the highest ranks in the British navy—but he disliked bother. A younger son of the Earl of Lincoln, he had allowed his relationship with the great Whig family of Pelham to waft him gently upward in life. Even his compliant relations had balked at securing him the governorship of New York, but they had been forced to open up to him this chance for "honest graft" to save the family the embarrassment of having Sir George thrown into debtors' prison.

When in 1743 Clinton had entered Manhattan's provincial society, he had been delighted to encounter there "a youth of prompt parts" who had studied law in England and was a political leader in America. James De Lancey's "uncommon vivacity with the semblance of affability and ease, his adroitness at jest with a show of condescension to his inferiors," so impressed the good-humored admiral that he allowed De Lancey to handle all governmental affairs, while he himself concentrated on madeira and port, late retirings and late risings. As Warren's brother-in-law, the new Grand Vizier was, of course, kin to Johnson, but he was politically allied to Johnson's enemies, the Albany faction, whose peace policies he supported.

At first, he handled Clinton with extreme tact. When the governor's relaxations became soured by qualms of conscience about not fighting the enemy, De Lancey had the Assembly vote him money to hold an Indian conference at Albany. In October, 1745, while the Dutch commissioners smiled sarcastically, Clinton threw at the feet of the Iroquois a string of black wampum embroidered with a hatchet, and demanded that that they "knock the French on the head." The sachems kept their warriors from going into a war dance. Delegates from warlike New England blamed this passivity on "the intrigues of the people of Albany," but Clinton indignantly denied all accusations against his friends.

Sometimes Clinton fretted for fear that his own frontier might not be safe—France's traditional Indian allies had not, like England's Iroquois, declared neutrality—but De Lancey told him not to worry: Even if the Five Nations would not fight, they certainly loved their old Dutch allies too much to let any enemy brave ruffle a single hair on any New Yorker's head. Such complacency made Albany feel perfectly safe, but Warraghiyagey, who was familiar with Mohawk dissatisfaction, was far from sure that his Indian neighbors would refuse to let French raiders through.

Northward from Johnson's clearing, a green ocean stretched continuous until it lapped the enemy settlements; through it scalping and burning parties could move as silently as barracuda through the sea. When the wind thrashed leafy billows from the Mohawk to the St. Lawrence, Johnson would awake at Catty's side to listen for sounds that might betray a bloody secret. During eight months, he could turn to sleep again, and then, in January, 1745, he heard from the direction of Teantontalogo the "dead cry" which Indians gave in moments of mortal danger, "Quee! Quee! Quee!"

There was a great scurrying at Mount Johnson. Neighbors rushed in, arms were distributed, sentinels posted, and then William advanced gingerly at the head of a posse across the frozen river to the Indian castle. He found it deserted except for the Rev. Barclay, who was close to tears. The minister's flock had told him that he was "the chief contriver of the destruction intended against them." The dead cry had been inspired not by the French nor France's Indian allies.

For months, rumors had been reaching the Mohawks that "Albany people agreed to kill us and drive us away from our land, which they covet." The braves were warned to watch out for the first snow and, sure enough, the instant the road was white, sleighs loaded with ammunition slid into Fort Hunter.

That January evening, a runner dashed through their gate. "The white people of Albany," he shouted, "are acoming with drums and trumpets, with several hundreds to kill the Mohawks!" Abandoning their stockade that Fort Hunter dominated for nature's fortress, the forest, the Indians sent messengers to the other Iroquois nations "to alarm them" and hurriedly organized an ambush for advancing Albanians. But the braves peered in vain down the glimmering white track, and when a brilliant winter dawn touched sky and snow, scouts reported that they could find no enemy.

As the Indians filed back into Teantontalogo, the alarm moved east to freeze blood from Virginia to Maine. Anti-Albany hysteria among the Mohawks, who were traditionally the most pro-English of the Iroquois, was terrifying news. If the Mohawks asked the French for protection, the whole League, with its system of alliances that covered thousands of square miles, would join the enemy with results that the most massacre-haunted imagination could only dimly conceive.

Very much on the spot, the Albanians insisted that some villainous agitator must have temporarily deluded Albany's dear Mohawk friends. Johnson was among those accused, but the evidence must have been very flimsy, since his enemies pushed no charges. They decided to blame the French operatives known collectively as Jean Coeur. But Pennsylvania's grizzled Indian agent, Conrad Weiser, suspected that the rumors had been floated by the Mohawk's own star politician: Hendrick had frightened his own people to dramatize, for all English eyes to see, the Mohawk's resentment of the Albany commissioners. Weiser was outraged at such duplicity, but Johnson, if he had similar suspicions, certainly chuckled. As the years passed, he was to concoct with Hendrick many a similar charade, and this one had publicized brilliantly what Johnson agreed was a very dangerous situation.

The French were calling Mohawk sachems to Montreal to receive showers of presents and sending messages which, so Johnson wrote, "may be of vast disservice." Then, in November, 1745, enemy raiders advanced unmolested through Mohawk territory to Saratoga, only thirty miles north of Albany. At about dawn, a friend wrote Johnson, "400 French and 220 Indians appeared, and did beset all the houses there, burnt and destroyed all that came before them, left only one sawmill standing, which stood a little out of their way it seems; and took along with them such booty as they thought fit; killed and took captives 100 or 101 persons, black and white." Albany was so terrified that the inhabitants were sending down the Hudson "an abundance of goods" and "a good many women."

A thin, discontinuous line of settlement entangled in forest, the Mohawk Valley was much less defensible; most inhabitants fled their clearings as death traps. Warned that the French had put a price on his head because he was a nephew of Admiral Warren (they were soon to double the price for his own sake), Johnson was invited to spend the winter in Albany: "I beg that you will not be too stout." Did the sentence "there is room enough for your servants if you will bring them down" make the invitation include Catty and her children?

Although Johnson may have sent these irregular dependants to a safer spot, he himself was "too stout." Admitting himself "in great danger," he secured from Warren a brass cannon and some swivels; he fortified Mount Johnson as best he could. His presence was the bolt that held what was left of the Valley together. When the Mohawks themselves prepared to flee into the woods at reports of an invading cloud of Frenchmen and French Indians, Warraghiyagey "beat them out of the notion by showing them I had never moved any of my effects away, though of as much value as perhaps the whole river."

During the winter of 1745-6, the Valley suffered from nothing but rumors; the crucial battle was a dining-room Donnybrook. Bored by managing the governor with "a smile or a joke or a promise or a bottle," and convinced that his brother-in-law Warren, as the hero of Louisburg, would soon supplant Clinton anyway, De Lancey, when drinking after dinner with his superior, insisted on "some favorite point with great imperiousness." But for once the wine, instead of dissolving Clinton's backbone, had strengthened it; he stated "with some tartness his resolution to maintain the dignity of his station. The altercations," a contemporary continued, "ran so high that Mr. De Lancey left the table with an oath of revenge, and they became thenceforth irreconcilable foes."

More effectively than he had intended, Clinton had released himself from bondage to the New York oligarchy. Needing, like a frock coat, a pair of shoulders to keep him upright, he substituted for the mercurial De Lancey a slow, grave, polysyllabic Scotch-Irishman. Cadwallader Colden had published on a dozen learned subjects and was trying to extend, according to the obsolete techniques of scholasticism, Newton's scientific theories. Although the springs of human action were outside this ponderous savant's understanding, he had for Clinton various appeals. He was self-assured, a veteran of New York politics unallied with the great families with whom Clinton had quarreled, and a devoted servant of the Crown eager to fight the French. Furthermore, he had personal knowledge of Indians. Like Johnson an adopted Mohawk, he had written the only book in English on the Five Nations.

Clinton's change of allegiance only increased the determination of De Lancey and the Assembly to walk their own path. After the first shock of Saratoga's fall had passed, the Albanians had concluded that their trade was so valuable to the enemy that, whatever else happened, they would be spared. As for the Mohawk Valley, since its furs profited only Johnson, it was expendable. The Assembly refused to send any militia there on the grounds that all the inhabitants had fled. Fort Oswego on Lake Ontario was left dangling on a long line of unprotected communications; and the Dutch merchants, who traditionally supplied it, refused to continue "unless a very considerable allowance was made for escorts." At this point, a voice spoke up from the theoretically deserted Valley. William Johnson would be happy to supply Oswego on the old basis.

With malicious glee, the Dutch monopolists supported a bill to give him the contract. The intruder would bankrupt himself. If necessary, the Assembly could help things along by holding up the payment of his appropriation. They would be rid of him at last.

Johnson had agreed to keep supply boats moving through miles of blank wilderness. There were innumerable carries around rapids and between watercourses; squalls on Oneida Lake could swamp laden bateaux; but Wood Creek headed the boatmen's cursing list. Wood Creek was a long, watery hole under foliage that connected a morass beside the Mohawk River with Oneida Lake. After bottoms had stuck in sand and mud, groaned on snags and banged on submerged rocks, a sudden pelting of rain would invoke a flood that pulled the shore out from beneath great trees and laid them athwart the channel. To angry men trying to get purchase with axes they swung from bobbing bottoms, it sometimes seemed as if the forest were growing sideways. And always eyes had not only to scan the four directions of the earth but also to look upward to green tangles where the heavens should be but whence braves might drop like tomahawk-toothed catamounts.

On April 14, 1746, Johnson sent his thanks to Clinton for "the kind favor" of the appointment. He intended to send off the first shipment "the latter end of this present week, which is very expeditious considering the little notice I have had."

Johnson ranked only as a justice of the peace—Clinton had so appointed him in April, 1745—but the main stream of history was shifting in his direction. Early in June, 1746, positive orders arrived from England that New York was to join other colonies in an attack through the Iroquois country; the Assembly was forced to approve a militia levy. The orders further provided that the Five Nations be enlisted as allies; the Assembly voted funds for a full-dress conference with the sachems, although they continued privately to back the statement of their Indian Commissioners that the Iroquois "are very unwilling to enter the war," and that it was "much better for us" that the Indians "should not intermeddle."

Johnson was as pleased as an athletic captain who learns that his team will be matched against the champions. He loved a contest not only for advantages to be gained but for its own exciting sake, and insisted that his followers, however much it might seem to their disadvantage, play sanguinary parts. Yet he never hated the enemy, admiring always French skills in forest warfare and Indian management, which he considered far superior to any that the English or Colonials possessed. His respect for the enemy gave to his hopes that he could now fight them an additional zest.

At Teantontalogo, he set roasting "a large bull of five years old" and added "bread and liquor equivalent." He told the Mohawks that English armies were about to overwhelm Canada, and that "I hoped they would be as ready as well, which would be the only way of recommending themselves to the favor of the government, and all brothers here, and a great deal more too tedious to mention. Their answer to me was that they would all as one man join heart and hand to fight with us against the French, our common enemy." They promised to "receive the interpreter all painted, feathered, and dressed." The interpreter was to bring an official invitation to Clinton's war parley at Albany.

When "His Excellency, the Honorable George Clinton, Captain General and Governor in Chief of the Province of New York and Territories thereon depending in America, Vice Admiral of the same and Vice Admiral of the Red Squadron of His Majesty's Fleet," entered in July, 1746, the Albany Fort which he had hoped to find clamorous with warlike Colonials, vivid with shouting Indians, empty rooms echoed hollowly to his tread. Most of the members of his own Provincial Council* had stayed in New York City; and the citizens of Albany went about their business ignoring him. The interpreter had been unable to bring any important Indians, even Warraghiyagey's Mohawks having been stopped by a decision of that central governing body of the Five Nations, the Onondaga Council, that neutrality was still official policy.

In a great rage, Clinton summoned the official Commissioners for Indian Affairs, who replied to his upbraiding that they lacked enough interest with the savages to make them fight. When Clinton asked if anyone possessed the requisite influence, they replied "that they knew of none." But Clinton and his advisor Colden summoned William Johnson.

Only the young Irishman gave any hope that His Majesty's orders for an overland attack against Canada could be obeyed; and he admitted that his influence was limited to the Mohawks. The official interpreter was sent to the more westerly Iroquois nations.

* The Council, its members appointed by the Crown for life, was the upper body of the New York legislature, the lower being the Assembly, elected by property holders. Althought the Council was usually sympathetic to royal prerogative and the governor, Clinton, when he broke with De Lancey, lost the support of both houses.

Warraghiyagey hurried to Teantontalogo to stage a ceremony that can be reconstructed from various sources.

It was dusk in the Mohawk Castle. The odor of roast bull and rum filled the air. In one of the lodges, Warraghiyagey was surrounded with the braves who were his particular friends. They had eaten ceremoniously of dog meat and were now arraying themselves for a war dance. Johnson put on moccasins, a kilt of deer skins embroidered with porcupine quills, and a feather-tufted skull cap bound with a silver band and crowned with a great eagle feather revolving from a little tube. He painted designs on his naked torso and then, grimacing into a hand mirror, on his face. To his arms, his wrists, and his knees he attached rattles of dried deers' hooves that, with those of his companions, enlivened the firelit chamber with a crackling rustle.

Outside there was also activity. The red-painted hatchet Johnson had driven into the war post had been pulled out by the sachems and ceremoniously buried. The old men were trying to keep the tribe away from the feast and out of the Council House, where the dance was to be enacted. But when from Warraghiyagey's lodge there came again and again the wild yell, delivered from a wide-open mouth, that had for centuries meant slaughter in the forest, the Council House filled in a moment.

The summer air was soft on his seminakedness as Johnson led his band in single file past silent long houses to the room full of argument where burned an unofficial council fire. Entering, he gave a war whoop that was echoed down the screaming line. Then the drums spoke; at every beat, he came down hard on his heel in rhythm with his companions; the packed earth trembled. So violent were his gestures that in a moment his bare flesh dripped with sweat. His fellows squatted down, but he could not: as the warrior who had initiated the dance, he had to sing the first personal war song. He strode back and forth, past excited young faces, past old faces tight in frowns; he looked up to where children clung from rafters, saw squaws leaning over the solid wall of male shoulders; he felt the heat and the tension and the anxiety, and he chanted about the power of King George, about the great army that was going to help the Iroquois drive into the ocean their ancestral enemies. At last he stopped, and reaped an adequate harvest of approving shouts.

Now the general dance resumed: Warraghiyagey certainly was careful to avoid grace, for he knew that the more grotesque his gestures, the more manly they would seem. Others sang their solos, but he found the moments of personal inaction inadequate even to get his breath. The war dance was a rhythmical contest of endurance. The fate of empires might depend on how high he leapt, on his ability to prance on after the other warriors collapsed.

Suddenly one of the sachems who had tried to keep the dance from taking place stopped the drums with a shout. Throwing off his blanket, he chanted of his own prowess, celebrated wherever the eagle flew—and then he joined in the dance. The other sachems followed, and now the blood lust rocked unimpeded through the chamber where the women and children swayed to the beat of the drums.

Round and round Johnson went, yelling as he drove an imaginary hatchet into an imaginary skull, and gradually his mind was washed clean of every European thing. No longer was he an ambassador on a ticklish mission from another world: he was one with his fellow dancers, one flesh, one heart, one brain. And when he too sank to the ground in exhaustion, his war-painted body was hardly distinguishable from the bodies that lay around it. But when he awoke the next morning, his mind awoke with him, and he returned to his scheming for English ends.

His difficulties had to a large extent been nurtured by the Albanian trade system which sent British goods to Canada in exchange for furs. When the English alliance had flourished, Iroquois' activity as middlemen had joined all the Five Nations to New York with economic bonds. But the changed trade pattern encouraged the western Iroquois nations, particularly the Senecas, to trade directly with the French, either by traveling northwest to Niagara or in their own villages, where *couriers de bois* (but never an English merchant) often lived with them the long winters through.

As a result, the huge Seneca nation, which boasted almost as many warriors as all the rest of the Iroquois put together, was strongly drawn toward a French alliance. The Cayugas, next to the east, and the Onondagas in the middle of the Long House, had also been infiltrated. Thus, there was much pro-Canadian sentiment in the Onondaga Council.

However, the territories of the Oneidas and their wards the Tuscaroras almost abutted against English settlements at several places, and the Mohawks were living side by side with Englishmen. Their castles vulnerable to Colonial attack, these eastern or "lower" nations could only join in a French alliance if they abandoned the graves of their fathers.

The ghosts of dead Iroquois that flitted through the woods, always just out of sight, like vanishing deer; the ancestral voices that spoke from dream or waking vision, urged the living to fight their own old enemies, the French. The Mohawks, who were traditionally the chief of the Five Nations, the Oneidas and the Tuscaroras had no particular love for the English, but joined in wishing the League not actually to make war on but rather to frighten New York into an Indian policy more favorable to the Iroquois. Among the central and upper nations brash young warriors unattuned to ancestral voices, the greedy (France was always lavish with presents), and the Catholic (Jesuits had made many converts) called for an ax to swing in concert with the French. In this confusion, neutrality seemed to the Onondaga Council the only policy that would not tear the League apart, and also they subscribed to the conviction, which Colden had to admit privately was "politic," that if they allowed either the English or French to achieve a victory that would make them "absolute masters," the Indians would become "slaves." However, Warraghiyagey hoped that by using his personal friendships to drag the Mohawks into the war on the English side he could draw the other nations after.

Although his war dance had been a great success, Teatontalogo, which it had filled with martial fervor, was only one of two major Mohawk castles. At the Upper Castle of Canajoharie, some thirty miles further up the river, Hendrick and his fellow sachems insisted that it was to the common interest to "remain neuter," and that, in any case, the Mohawks were bound to inaction by the Onondaga Council. Warraghiyagey was, indeed, trying to undermine the federal structure of the Iroquois League.

The structure depended altogether on unanimous consent, not

only at the Onondaga Council, where any negative vote was a veto, but in the minds and hearts of individual braves. Prisons were to the liberty-loving Indians an inconceivable barbarity; fines had no meaning in an economy based on communal ownership; the only feasible punishment was death, but much recourse to this would, as Johnson pointed out, "defeat their grand political objective, which is to increase their numbers by all possible means." To keep order, the Five Nations relied on taboo, the force of public opinion.

No force can be stronger as long as a society remains in almost unanimous agreement—but, by Johnson's time, contact with the whites had snapped many sinews of Indian tradition and bent others into a tangle that made impossible true unanimity on anything except the most basic cultural canons. Foreign policy was not one of these, and, indeed, Iroquois neutrality was in itself a trimming to the European wind. According to tradition, all neighbors not in alliance were enemies, and fighting was the only road to glory.

Johnson observed that the Indians, "particularly those living close to our settlements," submitted to less "order and government" than they once had done. A sachem's power had become largely personal, and depended on "his merit, and the number of warriors under his influence, which are seldom more than his own relations.*

Thus Warraghiyagey did not despair of overriding Hendrick. He hoped by giving blankets, ammunition, and rum, by promising scalps and glory, to whip to an incontrollable height that yearning for martial honor that inhabited every Indian breast.

* Although anthropologists would have us believe that sachems were sedentary statesmen and that war parties were led by a separate group of "chiefs," this seems to have no more been the case than that the class officers in an athletically minded college are normally a different group from the athletes. Since Indian society elevated war, to be great one had to be a great fighter. A corollary of this was that the introduction of firearms undermined Indian statesmanship.

In the days of bows and arrows, warriors wore bark armor and fought in close array; a hero could command the warriors of a whole nation. But the Indians recognized at once what it took European generals several centuries to recognize: that gunpowder had made close-order fighting obsolete. They dispersed behind obstacles. Since they had no elaborate means of communication, one officer could lead only a handful of troops. With the shrinkage of command, the political authority of the sachems also shrank.

Warraghiyagey had begun with a family of French agents a tug of war across the Long House that was to continue for thirteen years until they met at last on the field of battle. The progenitor was Louis Thomas de Joncaire, Sieur de Chabert, who had been captured by the Senecas in 1692 or 1693, spared, adopted into the nation, and made, by mutual agreement, France's ambassador to the Senecas and through them to the Iroquois League. He educated some of his children in the Indian villages, and when he died in 1739, two skillful sons, Philippe Thomas de Joncaire and Daniel Joncaire, Sieur de Chabert et Clausonne, inherited his position and his prestige. So continuous was this line of French influence over the Iroquois, which predated by more than a half century Johnson's nascent influence, that English officials failed to realize that there were three Joncaires. All were rolled into one long-lived, almost supernaturally powerful Gallic schemer known as "Jean Coeur."

The Joncaires labored to frustrate Clinton's emissary who carried to the middle and upper nations renewed invitations to the war parley at Albany. They made sure that the most lavish outpourings of rum would fail to stir up the tiniest pro-British war dance. However, some of the sachems finally agreed that they would "come to Albany and hear what the Governor of New York had to say to them."

On "the ambassadors' trail" which connected the far-flung castles of the League, Senecas started eastward from the Genesee, picking up at each council fire their fellow sachems. When they reached the Mohawk country they found, so Colden wrote, "that Mr. Johnson had already engaged many of the young men there to join the army against Canada." The massed legislators stated angrily that the Mohawks ought to have remembered, before breaking orders, that they were "the smallest in number of any of the Six Nations."

The Mohawks answered, "It is true we are less considerable as to number than any of the other nations,* but our hearts are truly English and all of us are *men,* so that, if our force be put to the trial, perhaps it will be found greater than you imagine." Hands

* The Mohawks had originally rivaled the Senecas as the most populous of the Iroquois. However, they had, during the period of collaboration, enjoyed the closest contact with the Dutch, been the soonest and best armed by them, borne the brunt of the fighting, earned the greatest glory, and most grievously sacrificed their manpower.

reached for knives, muskets were raised, and the age-old League was in danger of bloody collapse when the sachems remembered their skill in compromise. For once the cleavage was so great that even a pretense of unanimity could not be achieved, but fortunately the Mohawk had two banks, and roads stretched to Albany along both sides of the river.

On August 8, 1746 settlers hurried from their cabins to stare at the most unusual sight they had ever seen. Down the southern road knots of western sachems were advancing, in the shirts and blankets they wore every day. But on the northern, Mohawk braves moved in single file, stripped to breechcloths, their bodies painted hideously for war. They gave a jubilant scalp halloo as a pale figure, similarly stripped and painted, stepped from a white man's house to the head of the column.

Soon it was the turn of the Albany burghers to stare, and their surprise was mingled with consternation. The wild young Irishman who led the savage parade was demonstrating what he had achieved what all the policy makers of New York, all the Albanians with their traditional skill at Indian negotiation, had believed was impossible. He had mobilized for war a Mohawk army. With such assistance, the military force that the Crown had ordered to invade Canada but which the great New York families had counted on the Indians to block might march after all, with incalculable effect on the frontier.

Eyes front, face grave, Warraghiyagey led his band down the crooked Dutch streets to the fort where His Majesty's governor leaned entrancedly over the ramparts. Under the shadow of the walls, Johnson fired his musket into the ground. As each Mohawk reached the same spot, he too fired, making a long, rambling salute. Clinton's cannon roared over city and forest a deep, martial reply.

Stripped, feathered, tinted with bear's grease, William Johnson had emerged from what a contemporary called "the obscurity of a solitary residence in the wilderness" into the bright light of history.

5

Colonel of the Six Nations

Receiving the sachems in the fort hall, Governor Clinton "treated them with a glass of wine." The earl's son could not help smiling to see Admiral Warren's nephew squatting cross-legged in paint before him, but he was mightily impressed. So were the representatives of embattled New England who were eager to get on with the war.

This eagerness was not shared by provinces too far south to have any common boundary with Canada—the very title that the Colonials gave the conflict, "King George's War," implied it was not theirs—and thus Pennsylvania's Indian agent, Conrad Weiser, long the most influential white man in the forests, watched Warraghiyagey with disapproval. Seeing the feathered Irishman drinking with the braves, Weiser considered him a playboy. Hearing how Johnson had dared flaunt the Onondaga Council, Weiser suspected that he would be quietly assassinated by the sachems—and a good thing too!

The official congress opened on August 19, 1746. In the presence of the leading Indian negotiator of the Dutch party, Philip Livingston, Johnson was no more than a spectator, moved by the "extraordinary regularity and decorum" of the Indian forms.

Political discussion occupied the central role in the aboriginal social scheme which sex occupies in the modern American: Debate involved as much etiquette; congresses were fraught with similar

59

beauty, excitement, and possibilities for shame. White men might dress the Indians in the cheapest European shoddy and make free with their women, but from congresses everything European was banned. His Majesty's own representatives had to gesticulate, intone ritualistic replies, throw wampum, and keep their tempers just as if they were Indians.

Congresses were characterized by calmness and prolixity. Since the objective was not to worst your opponent but to achieve the unanimity without which no Iroquois decision was binding, the Indians never contradicted or interrupted. Such rough words as are sometimes spoken in the United States Senate would dissolve an Indian congress, being regarded as a declaration of war.

Oratory was the Iroquois art, comprising all others. Its eloquence was their literature; its metaphors painted the skies and the forest; its cadences were their music. Like all great art, it served a deep practical need. In a society without writing, the tablets of history were listeners' brains; to be indelible, the message had to be eloquent and engraved over and over. What seemed to Europeans an endless repetition of traditional phrases was basic to Indian statecraft.

As official documents and aides to memory, the Indians used strings of elongated beads made from sea shells. "Their belts," Johnson wrote, "are mostly black [actually dark purple] wampum, painted red when they denote war. They describe castles upon them as square figures of white wampum, and in alliance, human figures holding a chain of friendship, each figure representing a nation. An ax is also sometimes described, which is always an emblem of war."

A belt, varying in size according to the importance of the subject, only marked with hieroglyphics for occasions of great moment, was "thrown" by a speaker on initiating each point of discussion; it was publicly displayed while the subject was being considered; and then, as a record of the decision was reached, stored away to be brought out again if the matter were referred to at a subsequent conference.*

---

* Although New England frontiersmen, in their lust for currency, used wampum as money, the thousands of records examined for this volume fail to reveal that the Indians ever did so. As the Iroquois leader, Joseph Brant, was to write, "Money is of no value to us, and to most of us unknown."

The first day of every congress was given over to a formal oration by the nation which had called the meeting: in this case, the English. The speaker had to begin by condoling with the Indians for all their nationals who had died since the last congress, "wiping off," as the Iroquois put it, "the sorrowful tears from our eyes, by which the stoppage of our throats are opened and the bloody bed washed clean."

The next step was for every English orator (the French, of course, told a different story) to rehearse in traditional metaphors the history of the Iroquois-New York alliance. A few years later, Johnson was himself to do this as follows: "Our first friendship commenced at the arrival of the first great canoe or vessel at Albany, at which you were much surprised, but finding what it contained pleased you so much, being things for your purpose as our people convinced you of by showing you the use of them, that you all resolved to take the greatest care of that vessel, that nothing should hurt her. Whereupon it was agreed to tie her fast with a great rope to one of the largest nut trees on the bank of the river. But on further consideration in a fuller meeting it was thought safest, fearing the wind should blow down that tree, to make a long rope and tie her fast at Onondaga, which was accordingly done, and the rope put under your feet that if anything hurt or touched said vessel, by the shaking of the rope you might know it; and then agreed to rise all as one, and see what the matter was, and whoever hurt the vessel was to suffer."

The Governor of New York was so pleased that he substituted for the rope a "Covenant Chain" to bind them "forever in Brothership together, and that your warriors and ours should be as one heart, one head, one blood, etc; and that what happened to the one happened to the other. . . . Our forefathers, finding it was good . . . ordered that if ever that silver chain should turn the least rusty, offer to slip or break, that it should immediately be brightened up again, and not let it slip or break on any account, for then you and we were both dead. Brethren, these are the words of our wise forefathers, which some among you know very well to be so."

Clinton had stayed away from the 1746 conference, claiming a fever. Speaking for the governor, Colden congratulated the Five Nations on having reached that happy time when, by co-operating with the English, they could re-establish their "fame and renown over all the Indian nations" and "revenge all the injuries their country had received from the French." Already some thousands of soldiers had arrived from England (which was a straight lie) and the Colonies had raised a cloud of warriors (which was a great exaggeration). How the Iroquois' ancestors would rejoice at this chance to revenge them on the deceitful French!

The oration was delivered in strophes, broken with the throwing of belts. At every stop, a sachem called out "Yo-hay?" (Do you hear?) and the audience answered with a shout which meant, "We hear and remember." When the interpreter had finished, a sachem from each nation cried out an individual "Yo-hay!" To Colden's amazement, there were not six but eight shouts. One of the extra nations the English Indian experts never could identify (how the French would have laughed!); the other Colden finally discovered was an Iroquois ally, the Missisaugas, a nation "of five castles containing 800 men . . . living near a place called De Troit" (by which he meant Detroit).

After the Iroquois had conferred among themselves for four days, their spokesman sang, "We are now heartily entered into the war with you." They promised to join the English army which they had been told was about to march, and to bring with them as many of their allies as they could mobilize. This said, the Indians helped themselves to the presents that had been laid out to reward such a favorable reply.

On the official record, the congress had been a great triumph for Clinton, Johnson and the war party, but a Mohawk sachem told Weiser that the English "never spoke from their heart to them, and therefore they could do no otherways but speak with their mouth." The New York Assembly was sceptical when Clinton crowed to them, and the governor himself was far from sure he had achieved anything practical.

He was kept from putting the matter to an immediate test by French naval action that blocked the arrival of the English regulars considered necessary to give any militia action backbone. The full-scale invasion the Iroquois had agreed to join was indefinitely postponed. But, since the eating was good in Albany, they sent for their families: Clinton soon had 700 as hungry guests, many of whom came down with smallpox. One of the two Missisauga delegates died. After the other had built over the grave a canopy of birch mats, he also sickened. He called Clinton to his deathbed and, as the vice admiral tried not to breathe in lest he suck up infection, begged that the first French scalp be sent to his mother. Fatalities mounted. The poor governor could not enjoy his port because of wailing squaws. There was only one thing to do: dump the whole problem on William Johnson.

He created Johnson "Colonel of the forces to be raised out of the Six Nations," and ordered that, from his own settlements or Schenectady he "send out as many parties of the said Indians as you possibly can against the French and their Indians," under the leadership of any "Christians" he could himself recruit. He was also to act as his own commissary, although he could not be sure of being repaid any disbursements except the scalp bounties the Assembly had enacted: for the hair of adult males, £10; for their bodies as prisoners, £20; for male children, dead or alive, £10. Female scalps and prisoners were on the house. (In enacting her own scalp bounties, Massachusetts avoided this discrimination against the ladies.)

New York's official Indian relations were now in Johnson's hands, but the sidetracked Albany commissioners saw a bright side. They were sure the Indians would disgrace Johnson by refusing to fight. And, in the meanwhile, he was in just the predicament you would wish on your best enemy.

After the Albany Conference finally broke up, carts full of groaning Indians changed Mount Johnson into a hospital where new cases of smallpox broke out daily. Brave after brave, sitting upright as if ready to spring to his feet in pursuit of celestial deer, was buried, with his equipment beside him, by relations who had discarded their breechcloths as mourning. The survivors who crowded around Warraghiyagey's food kettles "appeared very uneasy" at the halting of the expedition they had been asked to join. Naval blockades meant nothing to them; they attributed the English delay to cowardice. They were not, Johnson warned Clinton, "a people of so little thought" that they would singlehanded fight England's battles.

Furthermore, there existed a major impediment to Mohawk war

fever. Long ago, the Jesuits had been active in the Valley, and, when they were finally expelled, they had carried to Canada with them enough "praying Indians" to divide the Mohawk stock almost in half. The emigrants, whose hunting grounds now bordered the French settlements directly to the north, were a pro-French nation, the Caughnawagas, outside the League and with a hairstyle of their own: they pulled out all their hair except a tuft on the top. Yet the émigrés remained, as individuals, members of the Iroquois clans. Fighting their clan brothers was to the Mohawks repugnant, but no raiding parties could reach the Canadian settlements without passing through Caughnawaga-controlled forests.

The French sent the Mohawks messages stating that the Caughnawagas would not let them through and urging continued neutrality as the only alternative to fratracidal bloodshed. The Caughnawagas added, "Be not angry at our destroying Saratoga last fall. Colonel Schuyler dared us to do it by saying he wished to see a French army there. We gratified his wish." Johnson was far from pleased when Hendrick, so recently lukewarm in the British cause, responded by setting out for Canada to discuss the future of the war with the Caughnawagas and the French governor.

Warraghiyagey had, of course, no intention of waiting the result. Playing on their "natural inclinations" for "warlike enterprises," he recruited individual warriors as mercenaries and sent them araiding with "Christian" officers selected from his friends in the Valley. On October 21, he could write Clinton that "several parties are out against the French."

To stay at home himself, as Clinton had ordered, became an increasingly nervous task when red leaves fell away from gray forests in a slow drifting unbroken by the triumphant shouts of returning warriors. Leaders of the Dutch faction who had previously avoided him sought him out to sneer. Were the Indians he had sent out, they asked, using the equipment with which he said he had supplied them to shoot quail, or had he in fact distributed no equipment but pocketed the money he said it had cost? Certainly, it was strange that all Johnson's claimed activity had not harvested a single prisoner or scalp!

His dark face flushing with anger, Johnson made what replies he could, but he could not help fearing that his Indian mercenaries were disobeying their Christian officers and merely using his ammunition to keep their stomachs full of bear. He cursed the confusions of forest loyalties. Why did the Caughnawagas exist to get in everyone's way; why did Hendrick have to bustle around on missions? He could only hope that the French Mohawks would kill some of his Mohawks by mistake, which would, he believed, set the Iroquois "and the French and their Indians by the ears."

Mocking smiles broadened in Albany and then, in the third week of November, vanished. Down the neat streets there came a parade. Ten rangers in buckskin preceded twelve Indians, stripped to their breechcloths and waving, at the ends of sticks, hoops decorated with red ribbons on which were stretched little circles of hair, the mortal remains of four Canadians: a man, a child about seven years old, and two women whose disembodied tresses rippled like banners. Eight white prisoners, "painted and clad in Indian dress," shuffled after: a captain of French militia, two more men, two women, and three pretty girls about twenty-two, fifteen, and thirteen years old. These were Catrine, Angélique, and Catiche Vitry. Angélique could hardly take her eyes off the leader of the procession, the tall, silent, fierce "Colonel of the Six Nations," William Johnson.

The parade disappeared into a sloop and sailed down the Hudson. Clinton, who had been as mocked in New York City as Johnson had been in Albany, was put into a happy twitter by the arrival of this dramatic proof that Mohawks were actually fighting on the English side. He forbade Warraghiyagey to lead his demonstration off the vessel until a company of militia could be deployed as a guard of honor. Keeping step to "the very mournful" scalp cry of the Indian captain, the barbarous pageant moved through New York's streets to the fort where, as cannon boomed, the vice admiral received the scalps and thanked the Indians. The administration press was jubilant, while Peter Zenger's New York *Journal* gave the event the briefest possible mention.

Warraghiyagey and his triumphant braves presented Clinton with a petition aimed at Philip Livingston, the very summit of the forces inimical to the inhabitants of the Mohawk Valley, white and Indian. It was Livingston's father who had tried to hold many of Johnson's German neighbors as virtual serfs on his estate. And

Philip himself, although New York's Secretary of Indian Affairs and thus officially charged with the protection of the tribes, was trying to perpetrate the most audacious of all land frauds.

During 1730, three Canajoharies had been induced at a drunken orgy to sign a deed which conveyed to Livingston and his dependents their Upper Mohawk Castle, the very houses in which the tribe lived. The "sellers" remembered nothing of what had happened. The "purchasers" waited three years. Then a bold party, certain that, if the Indians caught them, "they should all be murdered," surveyed the tract by moonlight while the true owners slept. They drew a line "which took in all the Indian planting land and castles." Johnson having not yet reached the valley, there was no one to warn the Canajoharies when a patent was granted in New York City that could be used to force them all into exile. But now Warraghiyagey gave Clinton a protest which he had drawn up for Indian signature.

In forwarding it to London, the governor wrote, "I think it necessary for retaining the affections of the Indians that Philip Livingston be removed from the office of Secretary of Indian Affairs." Then he urged Johnson "for His Majesty's favor," as an "eminent" leader in the common cause who "has run great hazards of losing his life."

While Johnson was in New York with his triumph, Hendrick returned to the Mohawk Valley, eager to communicate his adventures. He had "spent fine days in Montreal," so Johnson's chief deputy, John F. Lydius, recorded, "where he was extremely well entertained and renewed the covenant [of peace] with the Governor, who clothed him and his company from top to toe, and gave them some guns, knives, hatchets, and ammunition." Governor Vaudreuil capped his generosity with a note urging French commanders everywhere to supply the Mohawk delegation with anything they wanted.

Hendrick went on to Caughnawaga, where he found the Mohawks' cousins disgruntled because the French were not taking their military consequence seriously enough to keep them well fed. To the sachem's suggestion that he might lift a Canadian scalp or two, they answered, "It was high time that Canada ought to be alarmed."

Using Vaudreuil's paper to borrow a French canoe, Hendrick

floated with his party down Lake Champlain, but disembarked when an opportunity arose to ambush two French Canadians. The Mohawks killed and scalped one, captured the other. Then they met head-on in the forest three more Canadians and four pro-French St. Francis Indians who were returning empty-handed from a raid on the colonial frontier. The Mohawks' prisoner clamored to be rescued, but the St. Francis Indians admired him and the scalp as one group of anglers might admire the catch of the other. The Canadian rangers did not dare interfere but huddled in fright with the prisoner as the Indians smoked a comfortable pipe together. Then each group repossessed its white men. Hendrick proceeded to the Mohawk Valley, where he pushed his prisoner and tossed the scalp through the door of Johnson's deputy: "There is your dogs which I fetched for you!"

According to Indian ideas, the tricks Hendrick had played on Vaudreuil proved him not a dastard but a strategist. War chiefs did not, like white generals, rate their fellow nationals so lightly that they were willing to balance expected casualties against the importance of an objective. Not one brave was expendable. Military skill consisted of gaining scalps without losing any, and thus the maneuvering necessary to set up surprise attacks was basic to Indian strategy. Negotiators who believed blindly what Indians told them the Indians regarded as fools who deserved what happened to them.

Although Hendrick described his adventures with an innocent air, he knew that there was much in his frank account that would annoy the English. He had acted out and was now reporting a parable intended to make clear that the Mohawks had no intention of serving New York as a cat's-paw. Like the other tribes, they would serve no interest but their own. Under existing circumstances, it was to the interest of Indians on both sides of the border to allow war parties free passage through their respective territories, so that young braves could, without hurting one another or lowering the total Indian manpower, enjoy collecting white scalps and profit from the bounties so generously offered by both Canada and the Colonies for human hair. If Clinton wanted more exclusive services, he would have to make them very much to the Indians' advantage.

The sachem undoubtedly chuckled, after he had completed his

own dramatic recitation, to hear of Johnson's city-stopping parades. And when he learned that Warraghiyagey had followed up with a protest to the governor against Livingston, the key Indian oppressor, and that the protest had been forwarded to Hendrick's big brother, George II, he did some hard thinking. This was the kind of thing he was working to achieve. And Johnson, as soon as he returned to the Valley, sweetened the situation by giving "to Hendrick and party, in private presents," the large sum of £60.

Warraghiyagey's next business was a reception, enlivened with "rum, etc.," for the division of scalps and prisoners. He sent one scalp, accompanied by a belt of wampum, to the mother of the Missisauga delegate who had died after the Albany conference, an act of piety that paid off in bloodshed on the western French frontiers. Since Indian custom often gave captured warriors an opportunity to win back renown by demonstrating the fortitude with which they withstood mortal torture, the three adult male prisoners were in great danger; Johnson persuaded their captors to give one to the Governor of Massachusets, two to Clinton. The women and children were safe—the population-hungry Iroquois would adopt them into their clans as complete equals—yet Johnson gave £14 for Catiche and Angélique Vitry. Catiche went to live with Lydius and Angélique became the property of William Johnson.

When Johnson had been in New York City, Clinton had commissioned him—secretly, lest the Assembly "insist on sending persons in whom I could not confide"—to go to Onondaga and press the central government of the League for a formal declaration of war against the French. Johnson stayed home, probably because Hendrick assured him he would only lose face in making such a request before the English mounted the great army which Clinton had promised would co-operate with the Iroquois.

Although the British regulars that had been supposed to give backbone to a colonial invasion of Canada never arrived, Governor Shirley would not sit quiet. During the winter of 1746-7, he maneuvered the New York Assembly into a position where, in order to indicate loyalty to the Crown, they had to authorize a militia levy for the following summer. The troops were to join with those of Massachusetts and New Hampshire in an attack against Crown Point, the base on Lake Champlain whence the French staged their raids on the colonial frontiers.

When asked to prepare the Indians for this venture, Johnson wrote, "I make not the least doubt of bringing as many in the field as will be sufficient for the enterprise. I only wish our forces were all so ready and willing." He broadcast in the forest reports of an impending English army, but carefully "fixed no certain time, fearing a disappointment."

He continued to place his reliance on his own activities with mercenaries. During the thaws of 1747, he wrote Clinton jubilantly, "I am of opinion we shall make the French smart this spring by taking, scalping, and burning them in their settlements."

Hendrick and his fellow Mohawks had attached to Warraghiyagey their hopes of getting justice and favor from the English; they wanted his ability to serve them to be great in New York and London. Since experience taught them that a chief's prestige depended on his ability to mount successful war parties, Mohawk braves flocked to Mount Johnson, bringing with them as many of their clansmen from other nations as they could persuade to enjoy the fighting and share the spoils. Hendrick offered his services as a commander.

When a party was ready to march, Johnson gave a feast. He himself led the strenuous war dance, and the next morning he was on hand for the ceremony of departure. Still in the gaudy and clanking regalia of ceremony, the braves marched a short distance into the forest, followed by women carrying the breechcloths, blankets, and utilitarian moccasins of the trail. By a great tree they halted. The war chief peeled off a wide area of bark, and then the warriors painted on the wood—using "the utmost of their skill," as Johnson noted, "to represent the thing intended"—one male figure for each member of the party. A traditional animal indicated their objective. Having left much empty space on which to record scalps and prisoners, the braves stripped off their finery and were reclothed by their women. Then, silently and in single file, they vanished into the forest.

Twenty-three Indians led by Lieutenant Walter Butler, Jr.,*

---

*Walter Butler, Jr., was the son and namesake of the biblious Irish officer who, as commandant of Fort Hunter, had originally bought from the Indians the tract that included Warrensburg. Johnson found the younger Butlers—Walter, Jr., and his brothers John and Thomas—very useful assistants in administering the Valley and Indian affairs. Later, John and his son, Walter N. Butler, gained an unenviable eminence in American history as Tory raiders.

hid unobserved for two days on a hill overlooking Crown Point. They saw two loaded canoes set out toward the New York frontier, and by the shouting "concluded they were going to scalp." On the third day, thirteen of the Iroquois descended the hill, followed a fresh trail, and eventually crept under an embankment to within a few feet of twenty-three French soldiers and three Indians who were resting on fallen trees.

"Our Indians," Johnson later described the action, "fired upon them and killed three, whereupon the enemy flew to their arms and returned the fire briskly, but without any execution. Our Indians having loaded again gave them a second volley, killed one more and wounded three, upon which the enemy retreated, but one of their officers brought them back to their ground again, and then they fought smartly, and the chief of our Indians was wounded through the breast and one arm, and another slightly on the knee, upon which it was said our Indians, enraged, fought more like devils than men.

"One of our Indians run up, on observing one of the French Indians presenting his piece, within ten yards of him and discharged his piece loaded with swan shot into his breast, upon which he fell down dead. The other two French Indians on this run for it; this discouraged the French so much that they all likewise fled towards the fort, except two officers and a sergeant, who continued fighting bravely till they all three fell. . . . One of the French officers, the Indians say, was a young man dressed in blue with a broad gold lace, who fought with undoubted courage till he was grievously wounded, and then he called out for quarter in the Indian language; but perceiving that his wounds were mortal, they dispatched him. . . .

"Part of our Indians, in the meantime, pursued those that fled, till they came within musket shot of the fort." They counted seven wounded men being carried in, and "then returned to the place of action; but observing a party from the garrison coming after them, they had only time to take six scalps. The enemy pursued them closely two days, till they came to a lake from whence a river issues that runs towards the Mohawk Castle. . . . This is esteemed the gallantest action performed by the Indians since the commencement of the present war."

Johnson was undoubtedly particularly pleased to learn that, in the heat of battle, a French Indian had been killed. He believed—as did that historian of the Five Nations, Colden—that the tribes were so bound by custom that such a casualty would inspire automatic revenge that would in turn force counter-revenge until, as the sachems watched without power to intervene, their policy—raids against *both* white frontiers but peace among Indians—would be overwhelmed. Hendrick may well have looked grave when he heard of the Indian casualty, but he hid more skills in his blanket than Warraghiyagey yet imagined. No more than before did the Indians fight each other.

However, the six black symbols of death with which the triumphant raiders completed their record of the trip on an oak tree near Mount Johnson, and the £60 Warraghiyagey paid in cash for the scalps they sold him induced such an eagerness to bruise the Canadian frontier that "not three men fit to bear arms" were left in the Mohawk castles. As other war parties returned, warriors from the Upper Nations, who had sneaked to Johnson's recruiting office behind their sachems' backs, strutted openly home to boast of martial prowess, to display new guns and clothes and kettles. The 7,200 jew's-harps and 4,320 hawk bells Warraghiyagey distributed assaulted French ears with an English cacophany in France's re motest wilderness crannies.

That the enemy were worried was revealed by a surprising delegation which, in mid-April, filed out of the forest: sachems of the pro-French Senecas, and with them delegates of the Tionontati, a nation outside the League and allied to the Hurons, who were the mainstay of French power near Detroit. After the braves, some of whom had never before seen English territory, had rested and refreshed themselves, Warraghiyagey, with the ceremonial assistance of Mohawk sachems, lit in front of his house, for the first recorded time, the official council fire that was to become the center of Indian negotiation for the whole continent.

Although friends of those French agents, the Joncaires, the delegates offered to call together against the French not only the Iroquois but "all the distant nations," if only Warraghiyagey would delay the invasion of Canada long enough to enable them to persuade their cousins, the Caughnawagas, to change sides. Johnson smiled at the trap the Joncaires had laid, for it eased him of his greatest embarrassment. The New England militia were being kept at home by rumors of a French naval attack on Boston and, although some New York troops were gathering at Albany, the Assembly had ruled that the invasion in force which the Indians had been promised was "impractical" and were allowing it to die.

"Such a large body of men," Johnson told the Indians, "and such a number of ships takes a long time to prepare and moves but slowly on. You may, if you exert yourselves . . . perhaps have time" to win over "your brethren there . . . e'er our army is in their country, which I should be glad to see and heartily thank you for." Expressing their gladness that Johnson would not "delight" in spilling French Iroquois blood, the delegation drank rum, accepted presents, and went home.

Soon his deputy Lydius was writing from Albany, where the militia waited unpaid and unsupplied for a march that was never ordered, of "a general tumult, rather a rebellion among the new levies . . . and the lord knows what will be the end of it. I pray God I will never live to see the like! . . . Their officers have no more command as a slave hath over his master. This city is in a general consternation for fear of being plundered by them. They say they have so often been deceived and wronged! . . . 150 of them went away in one body. . . . I do dread the consequences if it comes to the ears of the Indians."

This letter was followed by a message from Onondaga which seemed to indicate that, while war fever was smoldering out in the English settlements, it was ablaze in the forests: A French emissary who had asked the Onondaga Council by what authority the braves had enlisted with Johnson had been told "that it was done by the whole body, meaning the Five Nations."

Johnson's conclusion that "all the nations are entered heartily into our cause" only made his Mohawk friends look very grave. Did Warraghiyagey not realize, they asked, that every increase in Iroquois war fever would only make more terrible the reckoning when the western sachems discovered that the colonial army was disintegrating in Albany and figured that they had been betrayed? Johnson wrote Clinton that, should the Iroquois and their allies enter the war before the colonial expedition was ready to receive them, it would create a more "weighty and troublesome" affair than he could handle.

He was in desperate need, he continued to Clinton, of weapons and supplies. "Every Indian fitted out for the first time," Lydius noted, "must have a gun if they have none," or forty shillings in cash if they had. "Also one blanket, one shirt, one pair of stockings, a lap or Indian breeches, a skin for shoes, a hatchet, two knives, three boxes of paint, two pounds of powder, four of lead, six flints, two [illegible] cutlasses. Between four or five, a kettle. All these things they are to have every time they go out, excepting the gun. A quantity of rum, besides the maintenance of their wives and families."

Appealing to Clinton over and over again for funds, Johnson explained that this maintenance was "vastly expensive." He had kept the Mohawks "from hunting this long time to be ready at call . . . they cannot have anything but what is given them." The old men, the squaws and children seemed to have stomachs like whales', but to let them go hungry would end Warraghiyagey's influence.

The greatest beneficiaries of his largesse were two rum sellers: Joseph Clement, who had set up bar "within twenty yards of my house," and George Klock, "another grand villain," who was to be his gadfly for the rest of Johnson's life. The bartenders took in exchange for rum what the Indians had been given, sending them back surly with hangovers and "as poor as rats." If New York were to have any war parties, all had to be supplied again. To protests, Klock answered that Johnson "might hang myself!" Johnson begged Clinton to make an example of the miscreants.

Unable to imagine what would happen if his rising influence brought the western tribes flooding in, Johnson further urged Clinton to send to Oswego with £500 of goods an agent who would intercept the Oneidas, Cayugas, and Senecas and send them out on raids from there. He himself would have more than he could handle when the raiders he had already dispatched returned. There were 119 Indians in the two largest forces, "besides seven other parties who are all out this long time and soon expected. We shall soon have an abundance of prisoners and scalps; wherefore will require a great deal of money, which they expect will be ready here at their return. . . . Wherefore I hope it may be seriously considered in time."

Clinton wrote Colden, "I have just received some letters from Colonel Johnson, but my head aches so much I am not able to read them."

As Johnson had hoped and dreaded, the woods reverberated five times in a few weeks with the death cry. Raiders came in with twenty-seven prisoners and six scalps, worth £305 in prizes. "All plague me daily for their money."

"I have my houses, etc., now all full of the Five Nations," Johnson would write one day. "My houses," he wrote the next, "are full of French." Although he could plan to burn and scalp French families in their own settlements, when they were brought as prisoners to his settlement, he was so kind to them that for the rest of his life French beggars besieged his door.

One captive accompanied the colonel on his rounds. Sparkling in such fine clothes as during her previous fifteen years she had never seen, Angélique was imperious to the servants, condescending to her fellow Canadians. The antics of the flashing brunette lightened the grim seriousness of her protector's war-torn days, and certainly he found comfort at night in her budding charms. He needed all the relaxation he could get, for it seemed as if England and New York had left him to fight the war alone.

Although Clinton, when he finally got around to reading Johnson's letters, took them so seriously that he forwarded some to his superiors in England, he was unable to help his subordinate. The New York leaders saw, in the Crown's desperate need for money with which to fight, an opportunity to further colonial self-rule; the bills they passed contained provisions which reduced the governor's power. Clinton either had to accept them in their entirety or, by vetoing them, put a stop to what little chance there was of New York's co-operation in the war. He was forced to notify Johnson that he could give no more money for scalp bounties: the Indians would have to go for their pay to the Assembly's Commissioners in Albany. Johnson replied that the Indians would rather never fetch another scalp—and he continued to pay the bounties out of his own purse.

He was enabled to do this because the border raids he was inciting had closed the forests through which Albany had exchanged with Canada goods for furs. Whatever pelts reached the Colony of New York now came along the all-Iroquois Mohawk Valley route. Johnson gathered them in, thus gaining a monopoly of what was perhaps the most lucrative trade in British America.

To find any merchant in Albany outside the hostile Dutch faction who could receive his merchandise and forward it down the Hudson, Johnson had been forced to employ as his business agent John L. Lydius, a renegade Dutchman whose skill with the Indians Johnson had acknowledged by making him also his military aide. While ancestral Albany countinghouses gaped empty, Lydius could hardly wedge himself into his shop between the bales. If an hereditary trader could not resist peeking in at this profusion, he would catch Lydius' good eye ashine with triumph, while the empty socket seemed, behind its tomahawk scar, clenched in derision. Lydius would dart out of his shop and dare the burgher to fight. This invitation refused, he would offer his muscle to be felt, confiding that it was so big and firm because he ate nothing but hard-boiled eggs.

Only two years before, Lydius had tried to destroy Johnson by spreading rumors that he had incited the Mohawks' notorious anti-Dutch riot: he considered himself Warraghiyagey's rival for Indian influence. His wife was a Caughnawaga, and he had lived with those "praying Indians" until their Jesuit mentors had come on him painting with his own hand on Indian torsos mysterious designs which they suspected were hidden Protestant propaganda. Despite his brave charge that he was being persecuted as a devout Catholic by Jesuits who were secret Protestants, he was banished from Canada. Settling at Saratoga on land claimed by both New York and Massachusetts, Albany-born Lydius got a cheap New England deed. Although, as a younger man, he had been forced to flee the Massachusetts police, that colony employed him as its unofficial ambassador to the Iroquois. New York officials objected that he was probably a Catholic, but he replied that he was being persecuted as a good Protestant by men who had secretly financed Bonnie Prince Charlie's Catholic rebellion.

In 1745, Johnson had indignantly refused to support Lydius' candidacy for the Assembly, but now that he needed him he felt he could handle him as he handled all types of men. And Lydius wrote his Massachusetts employers that he found it politic, for the moment, "to do what I have done under a color of Colonel Johnson." However, he insisted in his reports that he himself was largely responsible for the Indian raids against Canada that were so grateful to New England's war policy, and he begged perpetually for supplies with which to outfit the Indian warriors. When Massachusetts finally sent some supplies, he forwarded them for distribution to Johnson.

Johnson's eyes must have gleamed as he read the inventory of arms and equipment—so much that he needed!—but he returned the boxes unopened to his assistant. "It would be demeaning myself too much," he wrote, "to act as deputy agent to Colonel Stoddard [the Massachusetts Indian agent] or anybody else [i.e. Lydius], but, if it had been desired in a proper manner, I might for the good of the common cause have complied with it. . . . My kind compliments to Mrs. Lydius, etc."

Involved, in addition to Johnson's personal prestige, was an intercolonial issue. Since the Iroquois were the dominant Indian force on the frontiers from Virginia to Maine, many colonies felt the need to be represented and influential in the Long House, but the Long House was in the specific jurisdiction of New York, and that colony wanted no outside interference. The issue was dramatized by Weiser's tendency to come dashing to Onondaga and the Mohawk Valley at every crisis—Pennsylvania was outraged when Clinton sternly sent Weiser home lest he interfere with Colonel Johnson—and particularly by Lydius himself who, as he argued with the Indians for Massachusetts' military policies, pushed that colony's pretensions to land around Saratoga that New York also claimed.

Were Massachusetts allowed to distribute goods to the Iroquois without prior consultation with Johnson, the New England colony would have scored a point in the long game of one-upsmanship on frontier claims. Thus Governor Clinton protested to Governor Shirley. Shirley apologized and added, for he was mightily impressed with New York's Indian colonel, that he had never imagined that "these Indians had been engaged in acts of hostility against the French by any person's influence except his, under Your

Excellency's directions." Johnson seems in the end to have got the goods on his own terms; and Lydius testified to his power by continuing to serve him with smiles: resentments would have to wait for a more propitious time.

Although too busy to notice his subordinate's anger, Johnson was increasingly worried by the Indians' protests at the delay in the appearance of the effective colonial army which they had been promised. "At the latter end," he wrote Clinton, "should things miscarry, it will be the entire ruin of me, for I cannot pretend to live anywhere near them, as Your Excellency may be sensible of, they being a bloodthirsty, revengeful set of people to any they had a regard for, should they be misled or deceived by them; which (as I said before) if affairs take another turn will be the case with me, which makes me very uneasy at present."

Could Weiser have read this letter, he would have smiled with prophetic satisfaction, since he had long been sure that Johnson would get himself assassinated. All, indeed, that Warraghiyagey's Mohawk bodyguards would have to do was relax their vigilance. Since the French had put a price on his head, he was a clay pigeon for Canadian Indians. They had not yet got close enough to hit him with the inaccurate firearms of the time, but if the Mohawks no longer patrolled, they could crawl through roadside underbrush practically to his horse's feet.

Through the porous wilderness, rumors passed from mouth to mouth until they reached someone who could put words on paper. Thus, Lydius rushed to Johnson the warning that "John, the River Indian" had seen "300 birch canoes" set out at some unnamed French fortification "to come this way!" The canoes turned up at Saratoga, where New York had just rebuilt her fort. The commandant sent a friendly Indian galloping off with the password "Ogeewana is my name" and advice that Johnson run. Then he picked up his own militiamen and ran.

Warraghiyagey stayed on the Mohawk, but sent increasingly anguished messages to Clinton. If the governor could do nothing else, at least he should honor that ancient custom of holding an annual conference with the Iroquois, at which presents were given and the covenant chain rebrightened! But Clinton had no desire to get in at close quarters with disgruntled Indians. Although he sent

Hendrick affectionate messages, he stayed out of reach until forced to Albany by the need to quiet the unruly militia.

After a conference with the sachem, Johnson rode to town and, with a straight face, told Clinton that Hendrick could not be restrained from calling on the governor. The Indian had "proposed to be very loud and speak very plainly," but, thank God, he had been able to persuade the savage that such behavior to a royal official and a vice admiral too "would not be suitable."

Clinton was to complain to Colden that Hendrick and about thirty Indians cornered him "in my little parlor just over the kitchen, and a monstrous hot day." The sachem, "notwithstanding his promise" (we can visualize Johnson's pious expression of surprise), "was exceedingly angry indeed, and very impertinent, that I was hardly able to bear him. He called upon the Mohawks, and told them I had drawn them into the war, and that he was come down to see the army. Instead of seeing it, he found they were betrayed; that the French no sooner proposed anything but they set about it; and then hit me in the teeth of [the flight from] Saratoga. . . . As for his part, he would leave his castle and take all his people with him—and so we parted in a sort of a pet."

That evening, Hendrick sent word that he wanted to see Clinton in private. The governor replied, "I would have nothing to say to him, but at last I thought it was well to hear what he had to say, but the scene was greatly changed, for he was all goodness, and we parted the best of friends that ever was, and did everything but hug and kiss, and he was quite sober, as, to do them justice, they every one was. I was forced to fill the dog's pockets. They leave me, God be praised, this afternoon."

Hendrick's good humor had been secured by the governor's promise that he would put Warraghiyagey completely in charge of New York's Indian affairs, by-passing the Assembly's Indian Commissioners (who promptly resigned their now-empty office) and paying such charges as scalp bounties from the royal purse. This Clinton could do, but when, in response to Hendrick's taunts, he ordered the Albany militia to reinforce Johnson's personal army in the Mohawk Valley, the militia refused to march.

Johnson's "disappointment" was, he wrote, made doubly "miserable" by the contrast with increasing Indian preparedness. "I will engage to bring 1,000 warriors into the field in six weeks' time, provided I have clothes, arms and ammunition for them, or forfeit £1,000." It was more to the point whether he could stop the warriors from coming. The Five Nations, he was told, had sent war belts to their allies, and he was "far short of a proper supply for the numbers that may be expected." To Clinton, he cried out that should Indians who ruled a huge area of wilderness arrive and find him empty-handed, it might "effect the whole continent."

Then an "Indian express" came from Oswego to report "a great number of Senecas and some of the foreign Indians with them, called the Flatheads, coming down to me." They were carrying a huge war belt which, from its description, resembled the one that Colden had given the sachems a year and a half before to solemnize his promise of an English army. If that belt were really approaching down the ambassadors' trail, the sachems were planning a formal demand that their white ally keep this solemn promise.

Where was Warraghiyagey to find an army?

6

A Raveling War

North America was still innocent of man when an advancing grumble of ice blocked with rubble the exits from a slim valley. Water mounted into a long lake starred with 220 wooded islands. In their primordial migrations, the tribes of pre-history found the water a smooth highway north and south through mountains. Eventually, Iroquois war parties made the loons shout and dive, and added to their domain this liquid pass. Then, in 1646, a new type of invader, the Catholic Saint Isaac Jorges, stared reverently at the downward reflections of lifting forests and called their mirror Lac St. Sacrement. For more than a century this name graced maps of the New World until in 1755 the lake found a new conqueror who named it permanently, after an English King, Lake George. Already in 1747 this conqueror was seeing in the lake a hope of rescue from a desperate situation.

As William Johnson had awaited the war parties that might cut his throat, seven Indian scouts came in to report a new French base at Lac St. Sacrement. "They lay two days in the sight of the enemy," he wrote, "whom they compute five and six hundred men encamped upon an island, from which they daily send large parties among us, who seldom fail of doing us mischief."

Johnson resolved to attempt, with these French raiders as his objective, what the British governments on both sides of the ocean had failed to achieve. He would himself create a white army to co-

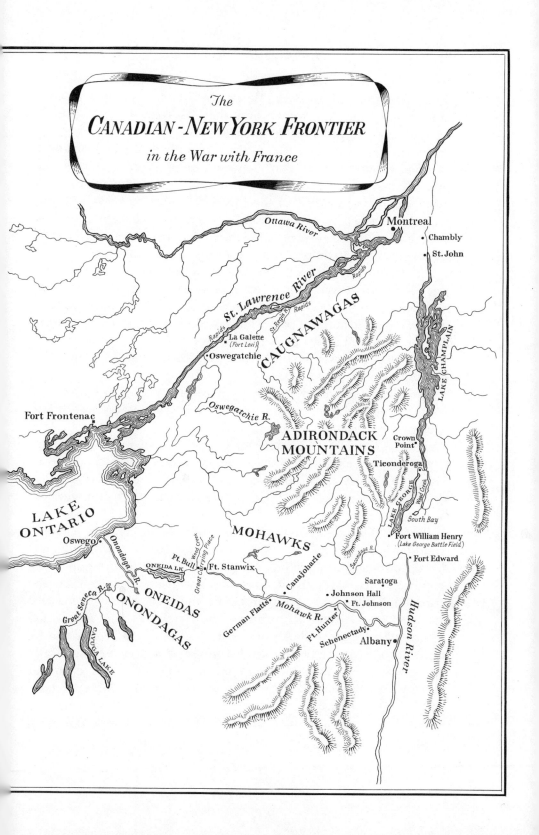

The
CANADIAN-NEW YORK FRONTIER
in the War with France

Ottawa River

Montreal
• Chambly
• St. John

St. Lawrence River

Rapids

St. Regis R.

Rapids

CAUGNAWAGAS

LAKE CHAMPLAIN

Rapids

La Galette
(Fort Levi)
• Oswegatchie

Oswegatchie R.

Fort Frontenac

ADIRONDACK
MOUNTAINS

Crown
Point•

Ticonderoga•

LAKE GEORGE

West Creek

South Bay

LAKE
ONTARIO

Oswego •

Onondaga R.

MOHAWKS

Fort William Henry
(Lake George Battle Field)

• Fort Edward

West Creek

Ft. Bull •

Great Carrying Place

ONEIDA LK.

• Ft. Stanwix

Canajoharie •

Saratoga

Sacondaga R.

Great Seneca R.

ONEIDAS

German Flatts •

Mohawk R.

Johnson Hall •

• Ft. Johnson

ONONDAGAS

Ft. Hunter •

Hudson River

CAYUGA LAKE

Schenectady •

Albany •

operate with the Iroquois in an attack through the no-man's wilderness above New York. When the western warriors reached Mount Johnson, they would find that less-tardy braves were already off on the promised English warpath.

His efforts to frighten Albany into co-operation merely made a "council of war" resolve that "it would be hazarding the preservation of this city in the present situation to detach any body of men." So Johnson called to the Mohawk Valley that was in much greater danger: 331 of his neighbors left isolated cabins to join their leader. Warraghiyagey also recruited 318 braves representing all the Iroquois nations and a scattering of western tribes.

On August 28, Johnson led this army into the forest on what was his own first war path. After several days of rapid advance, he clambered out on branches to peer across Lake St. Sacrement at France's island camping place. He saw no smoke, no troops patroling the shore. The fires proved cold; the raiders had vanished. But Warraghiyagey was sure that from the denser thickets French Indians were watching.

"To show the enemy the strength of our Indian alliances," he wrote, "I desired each nation to affix their symbol to a tree." The Mohawks delineated "a steel such as is used to strike fire out of a flint"; the Oneidas "a stone which they painted red"; the Onondagas "a great mountain"; the Cayugas "a pipe"; and the Senecas, being "the most numerous and most distant of the Six Nations," drew various symbols for various towns which Warraghiyagey was at a loss to interpret.

Having done what he could to frighten the French, Colonel Johnson led his army to Albany to frighten the Dutch. Unadorned by dead hair and quaking captured flesh, the procession Warraghiyagey led through the city was less awful visually than the triumph he had staged a year before, but the Albany merchants found it more deeply disturbing. The roughs, Indian and white, whose mass footsteps choked their streets, were, in effect, a private army at the command of the wild frontier colonel who energetically led the energetic line. At that moment, Johnson could have put Albany to tribute, and many who saw him pass would not have put it beyond him.

Leaving Lydius and some trusted Mohawks to disband the army,

Warraghiyagey took chiefs representing all the Iroquois nations down the Hudson with him to storm the colonial government. He found reason to wish that he had been less aggressively self-reliant in his relations with the paternalistic Warren.

Sir Peter Warren, K.C.B., now Vice Admiral of the White and a member of parliament, was the hero of the American war theater; he had become the British government's advisor on American affairs. Dreading his enmity, Clinton and Colden had tried to please him by praising his nephew William: they were puzzled by how little this had achieved in counteracting the influence of De Lancey who, indeed, had secured through Warren an appointment as Lieutenant Governor. Sure this was the first step toward having De Lancey succeed him, Clinton had refused to deliver the commission, a gesture that had helped his temper more than his prestige.

Johnson was hardly in New York before the De Lancey-dominated Assembly passed a "remonstrance" which stated that Indian affairs had tangled into an expensive disaster since the authority of the Albanian Commissioners had been superseded. The Assembly insisted that accounts of Iroquois hostilities against the French, of scalps and prisoners, were "mere amusements" to justify Johnson and Clinton in billing the governments for presents and supplies that never reached Indian hands. Although they could secure no witnesses more convincing than the rum-seller Clement, whom Clinton had finally at Johnson's request put out of business, the Assembly either refused to appropriate money to reimburse Johnson for supplying Oswego and for his other services to the colony, or used legal maneuvers to prevent payment. Having run out of royal funds, Clinton paid him what was owed by the Crown in drafts that the treasury might honor if Warren exerted his influence. Johnson secured in cash little more than Clinton's personal loan of £1,400. Only his control of the fur trade kept him from going bankrupt.

Collecting debts was merely one of Johnson's objectives in New York. With Clinton's and Colden's blessing, he led his Iroquois delegation through the hostile labyrinths of colonial politics in an appeal for a major military campaign in the spring. Nothing less, he argued, could save the English Indian interest, since the Joncaires were radiating down the snowy trails the all-too-plausible rumor that the English wished the Iroquois to commit suicide by fighting alone, so that their lands would be opened to settlement.

Fortunately, the lobbying sachems had returned to their castles before word arrived that, to "defend the liberties of Europe," the British government had abandoned all plans to attack Canada. It seemed inconceivable that the colonies would continue the unpopular war on their own, but Johnson, trembling at the reaction in the forests, lobbied on.

Since Hendrick's truce had successfully kept Indians from fighting Indians, reports at Mount Johnson that Caughnawagas were hovering near inspired, during the colonel's absence at New York, no more than a routine scout of three "Christians" and three Indians. When they encountered a large party of Caughnawagas, they began a prudent retreat, but taunts came to them over the frozen thickets. "Pursue them!" cried the Caughnawagas. "We are men! We will have them all!"

At this, the Mohawk leader dodged behind a tree trunk and lifted his rifle. "I am Gingego, a Mohawk, a man, who will never fly from you or all mankind!" Gingego was quickly shot down, as was one of his companions.

The third brave told the dread news at Teantontalogo, but there was not a large enough force there to sortie from the palisade. And, in Warraghiyagy's absence, the Indians could not induce a single white man to go with them.

When he returned, he sent some fifty Mohawk Valley farmers out with the same number of Indians. They found the headless bodies of Gingego and the other Mohawk mangled most frightfully, sticking in the snow with their heels up. Nearby, over a bed of ashes, were the heads, not only scalped and flayed, but with the noses, ears, and lips cut off, and what was left half roasted. Gathering together the remains, the wailing Indians carried them, not to their own castle, but in anger to Mount Johnson.

"I assure Your Excellency that I have a hard time of it, [they] telling me it was all my fault by bringing them so far into the war, and now can have no help from us, when they are murdered in our cause." As the Indians screamed with sorrow, shouted threats, Johnson noted impassively that "there would never be a better time to engage them and all their allies most steadfastly in the British interest." He would, of course, need a small army of "brisk" white men to fight alongside of them. "Otherwise, there will be no possibility of continuing in these parts for any of the inhabitants, for this cruel and unprecedented beginning portends a bloody spring and summer." This was March, 1748.

Clinton did his best by appointing Johnson colonel of the Albany regiment. However, on being asked by the new colonel for a list of the officers, the second in command resigned with the statement that he had no list.

The Gingego incident had been, according to Indian law, extremely provocative, for the Mohawk casualties had been scalped, which proclaimed the killing an act of state, and mutilated, which added an insult. The Onondaga Council would have been amply justified, had they wished, in declaring war on the Caughnawagas, but they did not wish. And the Caughnawaga sachems were, when they heard what had happened, as horrified as the Mohawks. Even the French in Montreal were upset, for they wanted no Iroquois hordes on their frontiers. Only Colonel Johnson wished to blow the incident into war, and he was not backed by his own government with the troops that would encourage the Five Nations actually to fight.

Indicated to history only by its results, an ancient rite was solemnized somewhere beyond the boundaries of the written word. To a band of wailing Iroquois, Caughnawagas came wailing. The chief of the murderers' clan ceremonially conveyed a present to the chief of Gingego's: "By this I remove the hatchet from the wound and make it fall out of the hands of him who is prepared to revenge the injury." Another present: "By this, I dry up the blood of that wound"—and so on through sixty or more gifts, each canceling some part of the offense or quieting some symptom of sorrow.

The way was opened for a new French maneuver. Three of Warraghiyagey's Mohawks had during the raids of the previous summer been captured by the enemy, and now ashen Iroquois appeared at Mount Johnson to repeat a report that the prisoners were not only locked in cells but held motionless by chains. To Indians "uninured to any restraint," this was a horror past imagining.

After the shock had gone deep, the French announced that they would free the sufferers if Iroquois sachems would come to get them. When Hendrick threatened to lead the deputation, War-raghiyagey wrote that should he do so, "all other endeavors are vain." He was sure that the French governor would inflame the already dangerous fear that the English were trying to trick the Five Nations out of existence.

Johnson felt the situation so menacing that he determined to go himself to "all the nations and stop them" from sending deputations to Canada. Since Hendrick did not tell his former confidant that peace was being re-established with the Caughnawagas, but rather encouraged his fears, Warraghiyagey believed that "the open rupture between the Indians" would make his trip "very dangerous." However, he intended to march westward, by-passing Onondaga, to the Seneca country on the Genesee, and then loop back to attend a formal meeting at the central Council Fire. He estimated that he would have to "march through thick woods for above a hundred miles"; the distance, actually, was closer to 200.

He set out on April 11, 1748, with fifty of his German and Irish adherents, a Mohawk bodyguard, and six Mohawk sachems, including Hendrick.

In every castle along the way, Johnson conferred with the local sachems. Since the Onondaga Council was not a forum of debate—the open sessions served the oral Indian culture as a means of publication—he would be limited there to stating his views and his propositions; he was trying to influence in advance the secret sessions at which the sachems would reach the conclusions that would eventually be publicly announced as unanimous. He found it far from easy, as the Indians were "quite out of humor at the many disappointments they have met with since the beginning of the war."

Often the talk lasted late into the night, but he could look forward to comfort in the end. On his arrival at every castle, "some of the prettiest girls" would wash and dress themselves in their best apparel," and then present themselves in his long house cubicle for his choice. The young squaws were charmingly modest, "put out of countenance" if a man happened by as they were playing ball; but taboo imposed on them no sexual restraint. After a few drinks, they would throw off their clothes and chase terrified

Anglican missionaries up trees. (They found French Jesuits more conciliatory.) The squaws were usually unslaked, because their own men found it difficult to serve them. Warraghiyagey explained that the braves "did not sport or marry until thirty years of age, for they imagined it enfeebled them, and, when going to war, are not very fond of their wives on the same account." Braves on the warpath (unlike white soldiers) were impelled *not* to rape captives.

The rumor was to circulate in London that Johnson fathered seven hundred Indian children. Although Clinton considered this statistic an exaggeration, Warraghiyagey certainly took much pleasure in the warm-tinted forest beauties whose black hair, which they so carefully tended, half hid athletic charms. And if the natural increase followed, everyone was pleased. Warraghiyagey had helped the tribe toward its great political objective, the growth of population, and the question of illegitimacy never arose. Among the matrilineal Iroquois, paternity had no dynastic significance: a child belonged only to its mother's clan and its nearest male relations were its maternal uncles. Thus Hendrick, although his father was a Mohegan, secured through his mother one of the great Mohawk sachemships. Thus, despite a paler skin, Johnson's forest children had, according to Iroquois science, precisely the same bloodline as their all-Iroquois half brothers.

On April 24, Johnson entered "a very beautiful and fertile" valley cut by a narrow river "full of trees fallen across or drove on heaps by the torrents." The Iroquois capital, Onondaga, was spaced along the river like a modern garden suburb. An eighteenth century traveler considered it "a strange mixture of cabins interspersed with great patches of high grass, bushes and shrubs, some of peas, corn, and squashes."

At the outskirts, so Johnson wrote, "I was received by all the sachems and warriors who stood in order with rested arms and fired a volley, after which my party returned the compliment. Then I was conducted by some of the principal sachems to my quarters, which was a large Indian house cleaned out, with new mats laid on the cabins to lie in. . . . In about an hour after I arrived, they called all the sachems of every nation together, and then sent for me to the meeting, which was a very full one."

The Onondaga speaker welcomed Johnson "to our fire or meet-

ing place" and then burst into complaints. By keeping them on
call for an invasion of Canada, Warraghiyagey had prevented them
"from hunting now almost two years (except a trifle about home)
and that all for nothing, as we can see no sign of your doing anything with your army as we expected." Add to this that the war
had made goods very expensive at Oswego, "so that we are to be
pitied. . . . What shall we do now to live, being in a miserable,
poor condition?"

Johnson took the traveler's privilege of saying he was too tired
to answer until the next day. However, "I will this night provide
a feast for your sachems, and another for the warriors and dancers
who I hope will be merry, which is my greatest pleasure to make
and see them do."

The next morning, Johnson blamed all frustrations on the
Senecas who had asked him to postpone any major expedition
against Canada until they had tried to win the Caughnawagas to
the British cause. "While our hands were tied here by you, . . . we
have got the Frenchman's axe sticking fast in our heads day after
day, and the Five Nations also." Although the Iroquois had not
"hurt the Caughnawagas as yet," those miscreants, inspired by
French treachery, had murdered Gingego in his own fields. "I now
desire you, if there remains the least spark of the noble spirit in
you which your brave ancestors were noted to have through the
world, that you may follow your brother's desire, and use the axe
against them, which you have so long in your hands." He threw "a
very large belt."

Warraghiyagey was certain that this appeal would be in vain.
Nothing, indeed, could have embarrassed him more than having
the fifty senators break into a war dance in anticipation of major
English military action. He had wished only to create an emotional climate that would make the sachems agree not to go to
Canada for their prisoners. But the Iroquois, as he noted, were "a
cool people"; and, his emotional appeals having failed, he was
forced to take a rash step. Without Clinton's knowledge, he promised that Clinton would arrange for the prisoners' release. "I desire
you now, by this belt of wampum, not to try any more, but leave
it entirely to your brother."

At the next session, the Onondaga speaker, walking with a slow even pace up and down the long hall of the Council House, chanted his reply: "We, the Five Nations now assembled here, can't help telling you that we think it very hard and cruel to be hindered from fetching our own flesh and blood from thence, who lie rotting and dying in irons, when we are offered them only to go for them." Yet they would not go to Canada "before you make a trial for the redemption of our people. And, as you say you have so many French prisoners, we think you may easily do it if you have a love for us."

As Johnson rode home from "the most troublesome and fatiguing journey I ever undertook," he realized that the promise he had been forced to give added to his situation a new, tremendous danger. If Clinton failed to secure the prisoners, it would be "the means of souring their tempers more than anything ever happened yet." Indeed, by simply refusing Clinton's request, the Governor of Canada could now enrage the Iroquois against the English and endanger Warraghiyagey's scalp more successfully than all his blood money had done.

The French, indeed, showed no eagerness to get their enemies off the hook. As the negotiation limped to an unsatisfactory start, Johnson communicated his concern so effectively to Clinton that the sighing governor agreed to hold that autumn the long-postponed full-dress conference with the Iroquois. But after the invitations had all been dispatched, while the hordes of disgruntled Indians were actually converging on Albany, Clinton received, as he wrote Johnson, "news that will startle you." England and France had signed an armistice; the King had abandoned the Indian allies he had lured into the war, just as the French had warned he would do. Terrified of the Iroquois reaction, Clinton considered postponing the conference, but he did not dare do that, either.

Johnson was thankful that his request to hold the Congress at his own personal council fire had been ignored. He was happy to make no speeches, let Clinton and Shirley, who was also present, bear the brunt. According to the official report the governors circulated, the Iroquois were mild as milk: they made no complaints and expressed undying loyalty to England. However, Shirley thought it necessary to warn them that, if they wavered in this loyalty, they would be "rooted out"—not by the English, of course, but by the French, in whose power England would leave the ungrateful savages.

As usual, the tribes were dumped on Johnson when the conference was over. He was, he wrote, "prodigiously tormented with the Indians," but on August 10 he was able to add, "I have just now got rid of all the Indians from my house except the Seneca, called the Grota Younga, who stays to be cured of the ulcer he has in his leg. . . . Thank God, the greatest hurry is now over for the time!"

As the Indians receded into the forest, they carried with them the unresolved question of Warraghiyagey's destiny. Over many a council fire, the future of the white Mohawk was passionately discussed. The unilateral peace with France was a final indication that England had not kept faith with her Iroquois allies, and Warraghiyagey, as England's representative, had, on the face of the record, let his Indian brothers down.

Yet the sachems had not permitted themselves to be tricked very far. In all probability, the Onondaga Council had never been convinced that the great English army Clinton had promised them would ever march, nor had they really wished it to. Although they would have considered it expedient to join a triumphant English campaign, any damage to Canada that upset the balance of power was less to Iroquois advantage than a continuation of conditions that permitted the League to play the Europeans against each other. Hindsight makes the historian wonder whether the sachems' perpetual calls for the promised English army, the scares they continually threw into Warraghiyagey were not ruses intended to strengthen their bargaining position by keeping England and her representative in the wrong.

As things had turned out, Warraghiyagey had kept every promise that was within his personal power to keep, and the fighting he had initiated had been to the League's advantage and taste. Although the Gingego incident had been unfortunate, although the prisoners in Canada presented a continuing problem, the warriors had enjoyed much warfare and earned good pay without suffering many casualties. The sachems could congratulate themselves on having warded off the only kind of war which the Indians, who scorned white soldiers, feared: a war among themselves. And the peace between the European powers had not caught them by surprise. Since even the martial Warraghiyagey had made no real effort that summer of 1748 to send braves ascalping, it had been clear that the hostilities were petering out.

After the peace, the Senecas, as the most pro-French members of the League, certainly argued that the British had proved themselves perfidious and cowardly. This Hendrick could not deny, but the fact remained that the Mohawks, because they lived so close to the English settlements, had to get on with the miscreants willy-nilly. That presented serious problems.

If the Indians tried to protect themselves from white land pirates and crooked white traders with the only means in their control—the ax and the musket—the "murdering" of white men, however justified by Indian law, would be terribly avenged. Theoretically, the nation could appeal to the white man's law, but the courts were far from the forests, and, in any case, the testimony of an Indian had no legal validity. The only way the Mohawks could stave off death, ruin, and even slavery—Warraghiyagey was at that moment urging on Clinton the release of some kidnaped Indian children—was through white protectors.

In their desperate need, the Indians leaned on such protectors as offered—even the disreputable Lydius—for the ideal protector needed to combine attributes and abilities seemingly irreconcilable. Although living on the frontier, he should exert influence on the centers of government, abroad as well as in America. He should be rich, so he could meet instantly the needs of sick and starving Indians—tomorrow means nothing to people balanced on the edge of subsistence—but he should not get his riches by cheating Indians. To earn the respect of the tribes, he should be a physical man, brave, expert enough in their lore not to be a fool in the forest, yet he needed to know how to make his way through the very different labyrinths that led to white power. During the eighteenth century, men who, like Pennsylvania's Indian agent Weiser, were not gentlemen, could exert only servants' power. Above all, the protector had to extend his patronage consistently with Indian pride, which meant no condescension, but the ability to feel the way an Indian does, to understand tribal customs by instinct as well as will. But he must not in his sympathy with Indian ways lose contact with the European world it was his mission to handle. Nor could he be expected to undertake every battle on the Indians' behalf since, if he betrayed basic English interests, he would lose his power to serve the tribes. Yet he must wish to serve them.

The ideal protector would belong equally to the two cultures which were so contradictory in institutions and philosophy. Although Warraghiyagey was far closer to the ideal than anyone else, Hendrick was much too shrewd to believe that his loyalties were in fact altogether equal. But then, how could a patriotic Indian expect that a white man would not feel his deepest allegiance to his own race and the nation where he was born?

Since the whites as a group were more concerned with money than glory, the return of peace would bring speculators crowding over Indian lands from which the soldiers had shuddered. Crucial problems were certain to arise, and toward their solution Hendrick would give Warraghiyagey a further chance. There would always be time to brush William Johnson aside should his services to the Indians be less than could be expected—or should, miraculously, a better white alternative appear.

7

Sunset at Noon

As the American phase of the War of the Austrian Succession, King George's War was brought to an official end by the Peace of Aix-la-Chapelle (October, 1748). King George betrayed the colonial war party by returning to France, in exchange for territory of no interest to Americans, the major fruit of American arms, Louisburg.

Naturally, the New York Assembly, which had always opposed the war, showed no interest in recompensing Johnson, who had stubbornly insisted on fighting: They took double precautions to see that he did not receive the more than £5,000 he claimed the colony owed him for supplying Oswego, and other services. As for the Crown debt of £2,836 for scalp bounties, Indian supplies, etc., no member of the British government was interested in paying it. The Iroquois were far from pleased with the way they had been treated as allies, and Johnson's non-Indian Mohawk Valley supporters expressed annoyance at having been lured into a conflict which had closed with a peace that they considered very dishonorable.

William Johnson had begun King George's War hidden in underbrush; he ended it dangling high from fraying ropes. In such a perilous situation, a man can hang motionless, hoping for unforeseeable succor, or can risk all in violent efforts to extricate himself. Johnson had no genius for staying still, and there beckoned to him a course of action that could be as effective as it was dangerous.

In various treaties, the Iroquois had agreed that they were

"children" of the British king, but they had meant no alienation of sovereignty, only that they accepted English protection for lands exclusively their own. They were, indeed, at that very moment furious because Clinton, in a letter which the French were assiduously circulating through the forests, had referred to them as subjects of the British Crown.

However, at the Treaty of Utrecht (1713), which ended the War of the Spanish Succession and to which the Iroquois were not a party, the French had accepted English sovereignty over the Five Nations. On this recognition, which the Canadian governor was now trying to negate, hung those shadowy legal claims with which statesmen like to justify aggression. Since the French had traveled the wild continent while the English had stayed in their settlements, they claimed all the northern frontier and the Ohio Valley through discovery. But the English argued that the Iroquois had owned the land before the French came and were British subjects.

When Clinton had demanded the return of the imprisoned Mohawks under an agreement that England and France would exchange each other's nationals, the Canadian governor had replied that, as an independent federation, the Iroquois would have to make their own peace. Should they do this, the French would have a sound basis for arguing that the Five Nations did not acknowledge British sovereignty and that thus their lands belonged by right of discovery to Louis XV. That the Indians had in themselves any sovereignty was an idea so repugnant to European diplomacy that it was not considered worth mentioning.

If Warraghiyagey could, despite the return of peace, still keep the Iroquois sachems from fetching their prisoners until they were somehow disentangled by Clinton, he would make a major contribution to the British empire, and demonstrate an influence over the Indians that might make both the colonists and the Crown consider him indispensable. The white diplomatic considerations could not, of course, be stated to the sachems, who would rather take Warraghiyagey's scalp than allow any Englishman to claim in their presence sovereignty over the Long House. Yet, since neither France nor England would under any circumstances acknowledge ultimate Iroquois sovereignty, the outcome of the Anglo-French argument would have no basic effect on the control by the Five Nations of their hunting grounds. Their safety would depend, as before, on their own ability to defend themselves through diplomacy and arms. And Warraghiyagey could argue to Hendrick that if the Mohawks continued to rely for the rescue of their captives on Clinton's good offices, their father, King George, would be so pleased that they would place his government under an obligation which they would in future negotiations find valuable. The Mohawks did, indeed, need to propitiate the British power that was their traditional ally and so contiguous to their hunting grounds, and Hendrick had resolved to give Warraghiyagey, for the time being, his head. The sachem acquiesced, and, since the prisoners were all Mohawks, the Onondaga Council did not intervene.*

The Governor of Canada countered by insisting on an immediate exchange of all white prisoners. Although Clinton saw the trap, he found it politically impossible to keep Yorkers in duress until Iroquois were liberated. Thus Mohawk scouts watched boatloads of English captives float home down Lake Champlain while their own compatriots still lay in irons. To underline the contrast, the Canadians routed the returning French nationals to Oswego through Five Nations territory, past Mount Johnson, Teantontalogo, and Canajoharie.

The arrival at Mount Johnson of the cheerful band elicited screams and tears. Angélique was a Canadian prisoner, but she did not wish to rejoin the ragtag and bobtail with whom she had been captured. This flourishing plantation was now her home, she insisted; did not William realize the value of her love? William realized that if he did not grasp this opportunity, he might have the ignorant, imperious little beauty with him forever. To Clinton he wrote, "I sent my French girl along with the rest." A gift of money somewhat stayed her tears, but hardly was she gone before he received a lachrymose letter saying that she had been robbed of the purse by the *garde magasin* at Fort Frontenac. Her father

* Indians claimed by the French to be "the principal chiefs" of the Senecas, Cayugas, Onondagas, and Oneidas signed, it is true, a French-prepared document stating that the Iroquois were not British subjects, but this paper did not keep the Canadians from continuing to use the Mohawk prisoners as hostages to force more official Iroquois action. It was a well-known fact that some Indians could be bribed to sign anything.

next entered the lists, writing in illiterate French to thank "Monsieu Jeanson" for "kindness" to "your little Angélique" who "cannot forget you for a single moment." The other sisters joined in passionate regards and the hopes of the whole family that Johnson would do something for them. His reply is lost, but it was in his character to respond liberally.

However, to request generosity rather than grant it was for him extremely difficult. He undoubtedly resented being forced by his situation to swallow his pride and ask of his uncle three favors: to assist him toward some royal recognition of his services, an office or an honor; to secure from the Ministry what was owed him by the Crown; and to persuade De Lancey to have him paid what New York owed.

Warren answered that, far from seeking "preferment at home," his nephew should "decline all public business and attend only his own private affairs." If the admiral offered to help with the Crown debt, nothing came of it for the time. As for De Lancey, Warren urged William to appeal to that official himself.

Obediently, Johnson went to New York City, but he could not bear to behave like a petitioner. Deciding to happen, as if by chance, on De Lancey in "the coffee house he used morning and night," Johnson cramped his long legs under a table and waited. Day after day, for eight days he waited, trying to keep his eyes from staring anxiously at the door lest someone guess his ignominious mission, increasingly sure that the dandified laughter around him was directed at him. Finally it occurred to him that he might wait till the crack of doom: De Lancey was purposely avoiding him.

There was nothing for it but to seek De Lancey out and admit his errand. The politician laid away his suavity for the occasion; he was blunt, scorned the wilderness overlord, implied that to receive "notice" he would have to "submit entirely. . . . Which surprises me," William wrote his uncle, "as I never disobliged him or any of the family."

Why should he submit, Johnson asked Warren, "I having set out in whatever I have done for the public on my own personal interest, independent of the governor and him [De Lancey] too?" By fair dealing, he had secured control of "the German settlers, etc. up the Mohawk's River, who are grown considerable and will in time possibly be the majority in the County of Albany." Furthermore, he had "a superior interest" with the Indians for whom "the tame people of America, notwithstanding their vaunts, are not a match." The colonials might be more numerous, but "the wolf never values how many the sheep are." Why should he knuckle under to any politician in a laced stock?

For that matter, he could wear a laced stock as well as anybody. "I am busy," he continued, "to build me a good, strong dwelling house in the Mohawks' by my mills, all of stone. I have purchased one of the best houses in Albany last winter, and another in Schenectady, also a very good low clear farm adjoining to the one I live on. I thank God my estate begins to increase, so that again[st] the time I may have the happiness of seeing you and dear Aunt here, I hope to be able to receive and entertain you tolerably well."

The new Mount Johnson, which he started to build late in 1748 and occupied early in 1750, was separated by a mile of farm, pasture, and hillside from the old, with its flanking store. Sixty feet long by thirty-two wide, it had two main floors, a daylit cellar that contained the kitchen, and an attic under so high a gambrel roof that boards could be put across the rafters to make two tiers of servants' sleeping quarters. From London, Johnson ordered a beam "with my name and the year upon it," lead for the roof, a knocker, paint, locks, latches, bolts, hinges, and even nails. But the paneling, mantles, and banisters were carved in America from cherry and black walnut in semiclassical designs that were both gracious and austere. With its broad central hallway and harmoniously proportioned rooms it was, as Aaron Burr noted, characterized by "commodiousness and elegance." Two centuries later, the spirits still lift when one walks across the threshold.

After Johnson had moved in, he had recourse again to London, ordering "globe in the hall for light"; books on natural philosophy and English history; "a good French horn with notes, a good common hunting horn, a good loud trumpet." On the walls he hung engravings including Titian's "Loves of the Gods" and portraits of race horses, but none of the portraits of the temporal great which graced most eighteenth-century homes. Warraghiyagey followed no star but his own.

Behind the house were "two swells of mountain." From the

eastern one, a brook tumbled to a dam that divided its flow: one half meandered through gently sloping lawn into the river, while the rest hurried along a raised aqueduct to the mill that groaned within fifty paces of the mansion. From the windows, Johnson could also see houses for the miller and cooper, tenements for servants and slaves; barns and stables; a bakehouse with a cupola for pigeons; and, encircling an imposing council house, sheds, tents, and cabins for the Indians. In the day, creaking of carts and the purposeful ululations of voices rose to his window; at night, he closed his eyes to the wailing of Indian flutes. Peace was to him a beating of tides of people, over whom he presided as the moon presides over the sea.

He gathered around him a group of merry Irishmen. His overseer, Thomas Flood, who came from County Meath, was efficient until too drunk to stand. Despite warnings from home, Johnson had taken in Matthew Farrell, a scapegrace brother-in-law. Charles Lewis Riley, a one-time pedagogue, served as jester and universal genius: he made pleasure carriages, swore in Latin, and, as he boasted, played "now the bagpipes, now the German flute, then the hautboy, then the violin." These companions, a horrified visitor noted, "drink punch at victuals at twelve o'clock in the day, even in winter." Travelers were taken in as a matter of course and, after staying as long as they pleased, thanked Johnson, as a Quaker did, for "the favors I so bountifully received with so much easiness at thy house."

Warraghiyagey played with that toy of eighteenth-century gentlemen, science. The screams in his candle-lit parlor were issuing from a pretty squaw whose tresses had mysteriously risen in the air as she held her hands against a whirly contraption. Much plagued by witchcraft, the braves glanced at Warraghiyagey nervously, but, like his white companions, he was rocking with laughter. Soon he was comforting the ingénue on his lap and, as the rum ladle circulated, the glass dome on his electrical machine was broken—he had to send to England for another.

Johnson's three children sometimes came to visit. "I hope you have got rid of your family," a friend wrote testily in August, 1748, "and that you have been fully sated with the joys of their music." It was more convenient to let them be educated in New

York City, and to be told, as he was in September, 1749, "the children is all well and desires their duties may be accepted by you." The letter fails to mention Catherine Weisenberg, whose whereabouts remain a mystery, but records for the first time the existence of her mother, known familiarly as "the Old Woman." The children's grandmother is in New York with them, and has just returned from escorting to Mount Johnson a cargo precious to rum-drinkers: "300 ᶜᵗ. limes."

Underfoot in 1750 was "little Will," a half-Mohawk William Johnson (Tagcheunto) whose presence suggests that his mother also lived in his father's house. Since the boy was sometimes known as "William of Canajoharie," she probably came from the Upper Castle. Authentic documents give no further hints on the woman who seems to have been Warraghiyagey's first formal Indian wife.*

Warraghiyagey usually made no gesture toward acknowledging the offspring he sired in Indian castles, but one lad who grew up in a Mohawk long house he did acknowledge. Born during 1747 or 1748 (he was thirty-five in December, 1783), he was called in his father's will "young Brant, alias Keghneghtaga," and commonly known as Brant Johnson. From the similarity of names, we may conclude that the boy was some relation of the Molly Brant who was to be Johnson's greatest love but who was, when Brant Johnson was born, herself only a child.

Warraghiyagey introduced his white friends to Indian charmers —"My compliments," a militia officer wrote him, "to little Miss Michael at the Mohawks [Teantontalogo] and Mme. Curl'd locks at Canajoharie"—but insisted that "the young Indian ladies" were just as "polite a set" as "the Albany ladies here;" he demanded that they be treated with equally courtly manners. In fact, he was beginning to conclude that red beauties were more agreeable companions than white. When his cousin who had fled the Valley for a polite life in the army made a conventional marriage, Warraghiyagey referred to "poor Tyrrell" and added dubiously, "I heartily wish it may be for the best."

* The story that she was Caroline, Hendrick's niece, and that she also had by Johnson two daughters, can be authenticated in no particular, and, since it was first published in a most questionable source during 1901, cannot even be dignified as local legend.

In 1750, Johnson sat for a fashionable portraitist—to their mutual frustration. John Wollaston, who was conquering New York society, had been the pupil of a noted English drapery painter, but his skill in making provincials look elegantly dressed and stiffly aristocratic left him when faced with the frontiersman. He caught primarily his sitter's massiveness, and the uneasiness Johnson always felt in cities. The broad brow under black hair which Wollaston limned, the large hazel eyes, the long nose ending in a bump, the wide cheeks and nervously chiseled mouth combine to express a shy melancholy, a dumb appeal for kindness, like a spaniel's. When Warraghiyagey got the portrait home, he found it increasingly annoying, particularly the tasteful drapery and the "narrow, hanging shoulders. . . . Mine," he growled, "are very broad and square." He would have had the picture painted over had the Mohawk Valley possessed an artist.

As Warraghiyagey continued laboring to keep the Five Nations from ransoming the Mohawk prisoners with a separate peace, he found himself supporting the Crown's cause almost completely on his own and at his own expense. Not only in New York but in every province battles between the local legislatures and the English governors centered on the control of the purse. Since dissatisfaction in the wilderness, although a deep tide, moved slowly and was invisible in the capitals, money for Indian affairs was the first to be denied. Clinton complained that his Assembly "will rather give up the Indians to the French . . . than yield any of their claims or expectations of power."

Untroubled by local legislatures, the Governor of Canada suffered from no such impediments. Johnson reported that when some Onondagas were upbraided for listening to Canadian blandishments, they replied that "the French were a very stirring people, and never still, but constantly inviting the Indians to come see them, where they are no sooner came but were clothed from head to foot, besides powder and lead in plenty, all for nothing." From his own purse, Johnson was trying to match the largesse of the King of France—he expended £595.12.8 in about two years—but the British interest continually lost ground.

To Clinton and through him to the British cabinet Johnson now spelled out the plan that summarized his convictions and also his

William Johnson in his late thirties
The fashionable portrait painter, John Wollaston, did not
please the frontiersman by endowing him with an elegantly
tapered figure (*Courtesy, Albany Institute of History and Art*)

high personal hope. Indian affairs, he argued, were "of much more importance to His Majesty's government than the whole act of ruling" the white colonists. The colonists were being refractory to royal control and could not be relied upon to fight British battles. But the Indians could be made into loyal allies and were, as a military force, stronger. They were also economically more valuable. Did not the fur trade offer to the Crown a surer revenue than all the multifarious and besmuggled activities of the settlers?

Permitting "the narrow minds of an American Assembly" to interfere in matters as important as Indian relations was madness. He himself had suffered great economic loss because he was forced to rely for "my just dues" on New York's colonial government. If he were to remain dependent on such authority, he would have to resign. However, he would be happy to continue to manage England's forest alliances if he were given an appointment that, by basing his office directly on the Crown, would make him independent of Colonial opposition.

While Warraghiyagey was calling for power from abroad, his own Indian world was invaded by a brilliant Jesuit, the Abbé Picquet. To win the Onondagas and Cayugas to the French cause as the Mohawks of Caughnawaga had been won, the priest established a new mission, at Oswegatchie on the upper St. Lawrence. Some pro-English Mohawks burned the buildings, but Picquet rebuilt them in a stronger form, and his ability to give "large presents," or so Johnson complained, enabled him to collect with amazing rapidity a populous settlement. The Oswegatchies were now added to the Caughnawagas as Iroquois in alliance with the French. This further drain on the manpower of the original League was highly distasteful to the sachems, who could only blame the contrast between French activity and England's supineness, which Warraghiyagey's singlehanded activities had failed to overcome. In the Seneca country, the brothers Joncaire were arguing that more emigrants would leave unless the League abandoned its official opposition to an alliance with the French.

The Joncaires were also inciting the Five Nations to renew their ancestral war with the Catawbas of South Carolina, as this would keep the long English frontier in turmoil. Commissioned by both Virginia and Pennsylvania to stop the conflict, Weiser hurried to the Mohawk, but found that Johnson had already arranged for a truce until a Catawba delegation could come north to make a formal peace with the Iroquois.

These issues were continuations of conflicts that had for a century bred fighting but had never set the continent aflame. A new issue was in less than five years to make the Colonies and Canada clash in a war so passionate that it could only end with the conquest of one by the other.

The cause was a three-pronged migration—Indian, English, and French—into the Ohio Valley, long an Iroquois hunting preserve with few permanent residents. As game had become increasingly scarce in the Long House, and also to avoid the dislocations of King George's War, more and more Iroquois had stayed the year round on the Ohio. Their settlements were swelled by Missisaugas and Tionontati who, under Johnson's urging, had raided the French, and were no longer safe on the banks of Lakes Erie and Huron. Miamis, fleeing hostile tribes from the north, gathered on what are now called the Miami and Maumee Rivers; while Delawares and Shawnees, who were displaced by Pennsylvania farmers, flooded across the Alleghenies. The tribesmen in the Ohio Valley, Johnson wrote in 1750, had become "double the number of the Six Nations," a fact which, the Governor of Pennsylvania commented, "will give a remarkable turn to Indian affairs."

This concentration of Indian hunters induced some 300 traders from Virginia and Pennsylvania annually to lead pack animals across the mountains, and then walk Indian trails from village to village. Their reports of fertile land without rocks or hampering hills came as a surprise to the English authorities and inspired their cupidity. During 1749, the Ohio Company, organized by powerful Virginian families including the Washingtons, secured from George II a grant of 500,000 acres, acres which Louis XV considered his own.

"Those that fortify first in Indian country," Johnson wrote, gained a control that could only be upset by actual war; he joined the royal governors in urging immediate action. But the colonial legislatures denied necessary appropriations as France prepared to wall the Colonies away from the west by fortifying the river line—Allegheny to Ohio to Mississippi—that linked their bastions of Louisiana and Canada.

In July, 1749, Indian news was relayed to Fort Johnson, and from there to New York and London: a French army had "gone to the Ohio." Warraghiyagey's reaction was to send through the woods war belts warning his allies to keep their warriors home lest the French surprise them.

However, Céleron de Blainville's expedition, which between June and October traveled 2,000 miles in thirty-three birch-bark canoes, sought not bloodshed but political advantage. During the following February, Hendrick gave Warraghiyagey a roundup of the reports that had filtered through the forest. The Ohio Indians, although they had refused Céleron's demand that they drive away all English traders, had been shaken to see a French army of 214 men where no English army had ever been.

In May, 1750, a runner, followed by lamenting squaws from both Mohawk castles, handed Warraghiyagey a belt of wampum dangling fifteen bloody sticks. This had been fashioned by Mississaugas who had sneaked from a French-inspired war dance to warn their neighbors, the Senecas, that fifteen Ottawa castles had "joined the French to spill their [the Iroquois'] blood."

The squaws flocked around Warraghiyagey, begging him to mend the stockades protecting their castles, "which I immediately got done, and promised them . . . my house for a refuge in case of need." He could not refuse "anything in my power" to friends "who have been so ready to assist us when they were called upon, and by that means have brought this trouble on themselves."

Johnson appealed to Clinton for some militia companies—reinforcements would "be of more service than a present of £5,000"—but the militia law had expired, and the governor was too deep in his squabbles with the Assembly to ask that it be renewed.

Although no soldiers were available to reinforce pro-English Indians menaced by France, between invasion scares there was no lack of English subjects on Mohawk territory. Surveyors sighted brass tubes along vistas the tribesmen swore they had never sold, and ominous rumors swelled that the Livingstons were again pushing their fraudulent claim to the Canajoharie Castle. The appeals for redress, for protection Johnson forwarded to New York City fell on deaf ears.

At this moment, when French influence was at such a flood that Warraghiyagey feared he could no longer keep the Iroquois from signing a separate peace with France and fetching their prisoners, the Canadian governor—it appeared inexplicable—abandoned his three-and-a-half-year agitation for a separate peace. He freed the three Mohawks that had been imprisoned all that time. As pleased as he was surprised, Johnson invited to a party in honor of the returned captives every brave, squaw, and papoose in both Mohawk castles.

Banners and gustatory odors filled the air. Warraghiyagey waited smiling at the edge of his clearing. Ranged behind him a little unsteadily—they had been scrupulous as rum-tasters—were his Irish companions with Mount Johnson's loudest musical instruments in their hands. A glimpse of moving shapes elicited a fanfare on trumpets and hunting horns, but when the massed Mohawks came into clear view, they exhibited no smiles. Several hundred copper faces were contorted in a single "great passion."

Leading the column, Hendrick refused to shake hands. Nichus, the chief of the captives, turned his back. The rest tightened into a halt, cold, menacing, and silent. "I asked them," Johnson remembered, "what they meant by such behavior?"

Hendrick answered that "they had sufficient reason"; Johnson and Clinton were "all French."

To Warraghiyagey's indignant denial, Hendrick replied, "They were all assured of it"; and Nichus added that the truth of the charge was known to everyone in Canada. The French governor had shown Nichus the "very large belt of wampum" Clinton had sent to urge Canadian cooperation in the English plot, "which was to fall upon the Indians on both sides and destroy them." The Iroquois were not at that moment under attack only because the French governor "would by no means agree to any such thing, having too great a regard for all Indians whatsoever."

As Hendrick led the accusations, Warraghiyagey studied the sachem's face for a sign that he was acting and did not really believe. If such a sign appeared, Johnson failed to tell Clinton: "The Indians imagine it to be actual fact . . . which, I assure your Excellency, gave me three hard days' work to get the better of, but at last convinced them it was French policy."

Johnson had for some time been threatening to resign his post as New York's sole Commissioner for Indian Affairs unless some way was found to relieve him of carrying personally all the expenses of that office. Now Hendrick had, with typical dramatic indirection, served notice that the Mohawks, having consummated Warraghiyagey's greatest political wish by not signing a separate peace with Canada, would no longer support him unless he could bring about a real improvement in the Indian policy of his English superiors. In writing Clinton of Hendrick's anger, Johnson reiterated his own determination to resign.

Since Clinton felt himself too rushed by more immediate problems to give the least attention to Indian affairs, he was comforted to have Colonel Johnson on the frontier handling matters. His subordinate's primary pains, he assumed, were financial; he brushed aside the resignation and urged Johnson to come to New York City personally to push for the payment of his bills. Did the frontiersman feel again, at this suggestion, the constraint in his knees he had felt as he had waited day after day in De Lancey's coffee house while that city politician avoided him?

In any case, a new turn of events was so alarming that Hendrick was being forced to collaborate with him once more. Red Head, the chief sachem of the Onondagas, had long been subject to French influence, and now secret word came that he was in Canada arranging to sell land within a stone's throw of the Iroquois capital to the French for a trading house. Such trading houses blossomed imperceptibly into forts, and thus, if the scheme went through, the Onondagas would be tied by proximity to the French even as the Mohawks were by proximity to the English. How then could the League survive in unity another French-English war?

Hendrick and Warraghiyagey summoned as many sachems as they could to Mount Johnson and dilated on the danger. The Indian conferees then hurried to Onondaga. After shock waves of conflict had beat against the traditional Iroquois unanimity, word was sent back to Warraghiyagey that a way out had been discovered. Accordingly, he drew up in his own name a deed to the whole area in which the French wished to place their trading house—the territory around Onondaga Lake for two miles in every direction—and sent it to the Council Fire with a gift of £350. The deed was signed by all the Onondaga sachems, including Red Head.

The tract with its salt springs was to become very valuable, since it included most of the modern city of Syracuse, but Warraghiyagey had bought it as a political expedient, with a promise to keep it unimproved. He offered the deed to the Crown and asked to be reimbursed its cost.

Inconspicuously and unheralded even by a thunderclap Sacanghtradeya, a Cayuga sachem, came to Mount Johnson on December 4, 1750. He handed Warraghiyagey a square lead plate, and asked him to translate the "piece of writing which the Senecas, our brothers, got by some artifice" from one of the Joncaires. (Actually, an Indian had dug the plate up from a river bank where it had been buried.)

Johnson translated, "In the year 1749, during the reign of Louis XV, we, Céleron, commander of a detachment sent by M. the Marquis de la Galissonière, commander in chief of New France, for the restoration of tranquility in some villages of these districts, have buried this plate at the confluence of the Ohio and Tchadakoin, this 29 July, near the river Ohio, otherwise Beautiful River, as a monument of the renewal of possession which we have taken of the said river Ohio and of all those that therein fall, and of all the lands on both sides as far as the sources of the said rivers, as enjoyed or ought to be enjoyed by the preceding Kings of France and as they therein have maintained themselves by arms and by treaties, especially by those of Riswick, of Utrecht, and of Aix-la-Chapelle."

Warraghiyagey did not fail to argue that this claim to Indian land showed "the vile designs of the French"; the Ohio tribes should be notified. He himself hurried the plate off to Clinton who rushed it to London so that the King might know those "vile designs." The gauntlet that was to touch off the eighteenth century's most destructive war had been thrown at Warraghiyagey's Council Fire.

In repose, Hendrick's face was sad and gentle, a poet's face struck with a tomahawk scar. The nervous mouth could not always speak in anger, simulated or real; the amazingly virile back— Hendrick was now an old man—could not always stiffen with pride. Looking in his eyes, Warraghiyagey saw the sorrow of a Mohawk adept at prophecy.

Two weeks after he had interpreted the lead plate Johnson sent Clinton "perhaps the last piece of Indian news I shall ever have occasion to trouble Your Excellency with"; the French were planning to build trading house and garrisons at all passes between Oswego and the Ohio. Then he took what Colden complained was "a very odd step, such as nothing of the kind had ever been done before."

Across the midwinter wilderness Indian runners moved from castle to castle, west through the Long House to the Seneca country, south into the embattled Ohio Valley. In windowless cabins shut tight against the bitter weather, through the smoke of innumerable council fires, they delivered this message: Warraghiyagey had extinguished his own Council Fire: he would no longer represent the Colony of New York to the Indians, nor the Indians to the Colony of New York. Every politically conscious Indian knew that this was a protest against England's refusal to keep faith with her forest allies.

Sachems who had been cursing Warraghiyagey felt suddenly bereft, and Hendrick keened, "He has large ears and heareth a great deal and what he hears he tells to us; he also has large eyes, and sees a great way, and conceals nothing from us. . . . We had him in wartime, when he was like a tree that grew for our use, which now seems to be falling down, though it has many roots. His knowledge of our affairs made us think him one of us, and we are greatly afraid."*

* The Indians highly valued bravery and also the fortitude that enabled a captured warrior to be the hero of his own execution by exhibiting, in the presence of the entire enemy tribe, calm defiance as he was being tortured to death. But as these pages again and again reveal, the tribes freely acknowledged fear. The seriousness of their plight had made them realists in matters political and (when they could hold on to themselves) military. They knew that if they failed to procure from the whites guns and ammunition, clothing and (when their hunting was impeded) food, they were, as the Senecas put it, "dead." Furthermore, because of their paucity of manpower, they could not prudentially sacrifice one brave in payment for ten or even more white casualties. Hence the fact that, when menaced by a strong force which they could not ambush, the braves would gather up their sick, their old men, women and children, and, without resisting, abandon their orchards and villages to the invader's torch.

8

Rider Without a Saddle

Mount Johnson seemed to have moved deeper into the wilderness.
Fewer dispatches came there, more belts of wampum were thrown.

The Iroquois were so familiar with the white man's injustice that
Warraghiyagey's failure to overcome it seemed to them less significant than his willingness, when it was clear that he had failed, to
resign his white office. At long last, they had found a white champion they could certainly trust!

Indian politicians went into tantrums when, on their way to Warraghiyagey's Council Fire, they discovered that their squaws had
forgotten to pack their ceremonial eagle feathers. In Johnson's
sheds, maidens wrapped around their waists the doeskin skirts of
formality and, as lithe thighs flashed where the soft leather divided,
trembled with eager fear at the hope of catching Warraghiyagey's
eye. Briefing him by the hour on the personalities and prejudices
of the western sachems, Hendrick confided in him as if he were
truly a Mohawk.

Although Johnson was touched by the love of his adopted compatriots, he could not help mourning his vanished office in the nation to which he had been born. He argued with Clinton over personal financial dealings—"It seems as if you suspected me, which I
should be glad to know!"—and read unintended insults into the
letters of his friends. Denouncing the "cursed clan" of Albany
Dutchmen, he wrote that it was only with "silent heartscaldings"
that he could bear "the yoke of oppression, envy, and malice here."

Colden charged that Johnson's resignation helped the enemy—
it had occasioned "extraordinary speculations among the Indians"
—but Clinton concerned himself with trying to get the Indian-
tamer back into service. He sent him a monkey and a parrot, and,
by pulling wires in London, had him appointed to the Provincial
Council.

Although membership in this upper house of the New York
legislature was a lifetime post much coveted by city politicians,
Johnson would not leave the frontier to take the oath of office.
Nor would he resume his Indian commissionership as Clinton's
appointee. An effective appointment, he was still convinced, would
have to come from the Crown—but to raise his subordinate to this
independent role, Clinton did not agitate.

In July, 1751, representatives of New York, Massachusetts,
Pennsylvania, Connecticut, and South Carolina met with the Five
Nations at Albany. Hendrick opened for the Indians: "We desire
His Excellency will be pleased to reinstate Colonel Johnson, or
else we expect to be ruined."

Clinton replied, "He absolutely refuses to continue in the management of your affairs," and had, although invited, stayed away
from the congress.

If Colonel Johnson would not come at New York's request,
Hendrick suggested, Warraghiyagey might come at the Iroquois'.
Clinton growled about unnecessary delay; Hendrick assured him
that the Indian messenger would "go sooner than a horse"; and,
sure enough, Warraghiyagey was there in a jiffy. Now, he took his
oath as a member of the Provincial Council, but only to complain
of his unpaid debts.

Into the full assembly of Iroquois, a Catawba peace embassy was
introduced by the South Carolina commissioner. Two singers came
first, carrying ensigns of feathers and shaking calabashes; after
them came their king, loud with solemn song. When the little
procession had circled, the singers pointed their plumes at the
senior sachems and halted. The king prepared and lighted a calumet. He smoked himself and handed it to each sachem, who smoked
and handed it back. "The Catawba singers then ceased and fastened their feathers, calumets, and calabashes to the tent pole." The
king now delivered a long paean to peace with the Iroquois.

Having listened contemptuously, the Iroquois speaker tossed a tiny bit of wampum. "This belt," he said, "serves to make you more powerful and give you small horns." When the Catawbas had unilaterally returned their Iroquois prisoners, "the peace shall be completed, and your horns lengthened." In awaiting such further submission, the Five Nations would condescend to accept a year's truce.

This armistice, for which Warraghiyagey had prepared, was the principle achievement of the congress. On the main British objective, the result was failure. Urged to protest French penetration of the Ohio Valley, the Iroquois stated that, before taking any action, they would confer with the French. How could they be expected to trust the English, they asked, until Warraghiyagey was again put in charge of their affairs?

If the Iroquois had hoped thus to worry their champion's enemies, their strategy boomeranged. Thoroughly outdone, Clinton and Colden damned Johnson and the former Albanian Commissioners of Indian Affairs in the same paragraphs and for the same reason: because they all scrambled for furs. Trade rivalries between individuals, the officials insisted, were blocking all efforts to establish an intelligent Indian policy. Urging at long last that the Indian commissionership should be removed from local pressures as a royal appointment, Johnson's former superiors asserted that he should be ineligible because of his business interests. Clinton recommended Colden.

In the meanwhile, the governor appointed no one to handle the tribes, lest he be forced to accept minions of the Assembly. Johnson's suggestion that Clinton make Lydius New York's Indian commissioner—did he assume he could control his former subordinate?—was amazingly unperceptive, and was fortunately ignored.

In November, 1751, Warraghiyagey finally overruled his repugnance to cities and white politics. He journeyed to New York, took his seat in the Council, and tried, by promoting a conflict with the De Lancey-controlled Assembly, to get £500 appropriated for Indian presents and repairs to Fort Oswego. The vigorous gyrations of the frontiersman elicited in the city only smiles, for he had entered the political war just at the moment sophisticated politicians had declared it over.

That the Clinton-De Lancey feud was crippling the New York

Lapowinsa, by John Hesselius
One of the sachems who were cheated in the infamous "Walking Purchase," when the whites did not walk but ran; his face is a melancholy prophecy (*Courtesy, Historical Society of Pennsylvania*)

government had suddenly become manifest on both sides of the ocean: an investigation was begun in England, and in America a cry arose for action and efficiency. The astute duelists promptly hid their swords and vied in unctuous gestures of love. Clinton shelved Colden in favor of a more moderate advisor, and De Lancey smiled benignly on the governor's little grafts. Late in 1752, the two-year vacancy in Indian authority was filled by commissioners most of whom, Clinton admitted, were Johnson's "inveterate opposers."

Back in the Valley, the Iroquois sachems assured Warraghiyagey that they would support him "with all their might"; they would ignore the newly appointed commissioners. He promised that he would "live and die among them."

That winter, processions of Indians arrived daily at Mount Johnson to commiserate with Warraghiyagey on the death of his uncle, Sir Peter Warren. With all the prolixity of Indian oratory, each group gave the same traditional lachrymose orations; they dilated on their host's "melancholy condition"; they desired him "to wipe away your tears, and to open your mouth and ears that you may again see, hear, and speak to us, your brothers." Staging a continuous wake that cost £132, Warraghiyagey delivered the correct grief-stricken replies, although Warren's death had sprung the booby-trap his vengeful uncle had laid for him. Stating in his will that Johnson owed him £11,000, Warren had forgiven a third of this amount in a beneficient gesture, and nastily made the other two-thirds his legacy to Johnson's brothers and sisters.

Johnson felt it his duty to help his family—he was just setting his sister Katherine up in his Albany house—but he was damned if he would be prodded by Warren's dead hand! To the anger of his father and siblings, he asserted that he owed his uncle no money. His uncle, he insisted, owed him money because he had never received the farm which was to be his pay for setting up Warrensburg.

Arbiters were appointed in New York City, and each side presented a statement of costs: Warren, it was claimed, had supplied Johnson with goods valued at £4,807; Johnson had spent £753 on Warrensburg and £4,587 on the disputed farm. The arbiters accepted both accounts and ruled that Warren's estate owed Johnson the difference—a sum which he made no serious effort to collect.

As Warren's executor, James De Lancey's brother Oliver, who was hardly a Johnsonite, did not protest. However, Lady Warren asked angrily from England, "I should be glad to know what he has done with the produce of all the labor he charges for?" The lack of information on this point is so obvious a flaw that we can only assume the accounts were more an excuse than a basis for settlement. The arbiters, indeed, stated that they had taken into consideration a nephew's right to largesse from a rich relation; and Johnson, when threatened by Lady Warren with a lawsuit, gave dark hints. "Purely through a tender regard for my uncle's memory and character," he had omitted to list expenses "which, if Lady Warren cannot recollect, I will not mention," beyond pointing out that litigation would exhume matters it would be better to suppress. The suit never materialized. If Johnson's Irish family remained unhappy about being thus cut out of their rich uncle's will, their rich brother would make it up to them at his own time and in his own way.

Actually, Johnson could not have secured the more than £7,000 in cash which Warren's will demanded without sabotaging a new activity. He was turning his major energy to the purchase and colonization of land.

He bought from the Mohawks, for "£300 and goods," 130,000 acres on the Charlotte River, a tributary of the Susquehanna flowing from the mountains south of Schoharie Creek. Hendrick was among the nine Indians who signed the deed, as was "Brant, alias Aroghyiadecker." Was Brant accompanied by his children? Did Warraghiyagey notice how sturdy was the nine-year-old Joseph, who was to be to him as a son? Did he exchange glances with the fifteen-year-old Molly, who was to be his destiny?*

After land had been purchased from the Indians, a patent had to be granted by the governor and his council. At the same time as Johnson sought such approval for the Charlotte River tract, he made another request, in which he had much less interest, since it

* The report circulated by some historians that Joseph was actually Johnson's son has no discernible foundation other than a confusion between Joseph Brant and William's undoubted offspring, Brant Johnson.

presented no foreseeable possibilities of settlement. The government having failed to take over Onondaga Lake and pay back his purchase money, he asked that it be granted to him as well.

This brought a smile to a pair of deceptively guileless blue eyes and a very firm mouth over a receding chin. As perpetual Under-Secretary of New York, Goldsbrow Banyar was manipulating the routine services of government to give himself a nice fortune and inconspicuous power. Banyar foresaw a new war with France: the best way for a fat little functionary to stay strong in wartime was to attach himself to a hero. The huge Indian colonel looked like such a hero, and certainly needed guidance through the china shop of colonial politics. Pointing out that it was illegal to grant more than 1,000 acres to a single individual, Banyar urged Johnson "to follow the custom" by suppressing his own name in all land petitions in favor of "the names of friends," one for each 1,000 acres, who could be relied on to convey the land to him after it had been patented.

Johnson replied proudly that his contributions to the frontier were so great that he should be excused by the government from engaging in the subterfuges of lesser men. The government gleefully granted him the Onondaga purchase, which he considered almost valueless, as payment of all the debts the colony owed him; the Charlotte River purchase, which he passionately desired, was refused. There might, the council ruled, be a conflict there with the jurisdiction of Pennsylvania.

Johnson's next petition was more sophisticated. Having bought 20,000 Mohawk Valley acres from the Indians, he drew up his request for a patent in the names of the interpreter, Arent Stevens, and twenty other neighbors. Clinton was secretly assigned a sixth share in the land which, after he had shepherded the grant through his council, he sold back to Johnson for £213. The ostensible patentees were given presents and a fine party during which they signed over all their rights.

Adding to this "Stevens Purchase" through more surreptitious patents and also through purchase from prior patentees, Johnson amassed what he called Kingsborough, where he was to build his capital of Johnstown. North of the Mohawk River, behind the village of Stone Arabia and other Palatine settlements, the tract stretched west from Mount Johnson some ten miles deep for some fifteen miles. Since these interior woods were difficult to reach, hard to clear, and extremely open to Indian attack, Johnson would have preferred the banks of the Charlotte River, but he swore to place 500 families on what he had. When he could get only a few extremely tough Germans, he accused the Albanians of thwarting him with "villainous and idle rumors." However, whispering campaigns were unnecessary.

On April 20, 1753, Warraghiyagey was awakened about midnight by Mohawks who, "whooping and hollowing in a frightful manner," reported that a major French force was mobilizing at Fort Frontenac, where the St. Lawrence flowed from Lake Ontario. A few days later an express came from the Senecas asking succinctly, "Are we dead?" Johnson thereupon gave England the first warning of the French army that was to cut and fortify a path to the headwaters of the Ohio River system, where they would build Fort Le Bœuf, and crouch for a leap into the heart of the continent. Frightened Indians normally in the English interest were soon begging to carry the baggage of such enterprising warriors.

Hendrick selected among the many laced coats Johnson had given him those most suitable for his embassy and led a Mohawk delegation to New York City; Johnson followed in his capacity as a member of the Governor's Council. Before that body, Hendrick stated with great violence that, had the British not broken their promises to persevere in the last war, the Mohawks would have "torn the Frenchman's heart out"; and now the British were leaving their allies "naked and defenseless, and don't care what becomes of our nation." Furthermore, Indian land was being stolen through fraudulent deeds and crooked surveys. Unless all old deeds were resurveyed under Indian supervision, and no new ones granted except in the presence of Indian representatives, the Mohawks "would take a little rod and whip" away the squatters on their land.

To Clinton, this seemed "insolent." He replied that the Indians, if they had legitimate grievances, could get redress from the recently reappointed commissioners in Albany.

Those commissioners, Hendrick bellowed, "are no people but devils. . . . As soon as we come home, we shall send up a belt of wampum to our brothers, the Five Nations, to acquaint them the covenant chain is broken between you and us. So, brother, you are not to expect to hear of me any more, and, brother, we desire to hear no more of you!" He stalked out of the meeting, followed by seventeen angry braves, and returned to the forest.

The councilors stared at each other in a terror that soon communicated itself to the Assembly. If the Mohawks went pro-French, nothing could keep the League in line, and, with unanimous Indian support, the French might well overrun the colony. Hearing in their imagination war whoops echo down New York City streets, Johnson's foes in the Assembly begged him to go to Onondaga on a peace mission. They even voted him for expenses £450.

Sourly studying the situation from the Pennsylvania woods, Weiser insisted that Hendrick's threats and furious departure had been a put-up job to advance Warraghiyagey's interests.* And, indeed, it was a miraculously placated Hendrick who, when the pair arrived together at Onondaga, acted as the orator who delivered Warraghiyagey's speech:

"Brethren of the Six Nations, it grieves me sorely to find that the road hither [from New York] has been so grown up with weeds for want of being used, and our fire almost expiring at Onondaga. . . . I am now sent by your brother, the governor, to clear the road and make the fire with such wood as will never burn out." Hendrick threw a belt; the audience responded, "Yo-hay!"

"Brethren of the Six Nations, I have now renewed the fire, swept clean all your rooms with a new white wing, and leave it hanging near the fireplace, that you may make use of it for cleaning all dust, dirt, etc. which may have been brought in by strangers [the French], no friend to you or us." (A string of wampum.)

"Brethren of the Six Nations, I am sorry to find on my arrival among you that the fine shady tree [of English protection] which was planted by our forefathers for your ease and shelter, should

* This suspicion is given credibility by a sequence of events that might seem to disprove it. It was known that a faction of the Mohawks had accused Johnson of claiming that his Stevens Purchase contained more land than the Indians had intended to sell; Hendrick repeated the charge before the council. Johnson thereupon produced documents which Hendrick (who was daily in his company) received with surprise. Having examined them, the sachem announced in the most public manner that, unlike other white men, Warraghiyagey treated Indians with perfect rectitude.

Lord of the Mohawks

be now leaning, being almost blown down by northerly winds. I shall endeavor to set it upright, so that it may flourish as formerly." (A belt)

"Brethren of the Six Nations, your fire now burns clearly, at the old place, the tree of shelter and protection is set up and flourishes: I must now insist upon your quenching that fire made with brambles at Swegatchie [Father Picquet's mission]. . . . 'Tis formidable news we hear that the French and some Indians are making a descent on the Ohio. Is it with your consent or leave that they proceed in this extraordinary manner?"

This was delivered by Hendrick with all the eloquence of a great orator, yet Warraghiyagey had been unable to promise military help or redress of grievances. Nor was it encouraging to see, sitting among the Indians, some Frenchmen who claimed to be on a trading mission and whom the Iroquois had invited to attend.

After conferring for two days among themselves, the sachems gave Warraghiyagey back rhetoric for rhetoric, and then replied to his leading question: "It is not with our consent that the French have committed any hostilities at Ohio. We don't know what you Christians—English and French together—intend. We are so hemmed in by both that we have hardly a hunting place left. In a little while, if we find a bear in a tree, there will immediately appear an owner of the land to challenge the property, and hinder us from killing it, which is our livelihood. We are so perplexed between both that we hardly know what to say or think." (A belt)

How could the Iroquois be expected to renew the English alliance when the English could find nothing with which to answer French armed might but words? From Virginia, a militia colonel traveled to Fort Le Bœuf to ask politely that the French withdraw from His Majesty's territory. That the emissary's name was George Washington impressed no one: he was a stripling on his first mission. With scorn, the Indians watched Washington go home, having accomplished nothing.

Like a man in a nightmare shouting fire to a stone-deaf multitude, Johnson cried out for action before all the Indians in the Ohio Valley went French, pulling the Iroquois after them. To most colonials, the land behind the mountains seemed further away than Europe, and of less concern to the busy seacoast society. The Penn-

sylvania Assembly expressed doubt that the British had any claim
to the Ohio Valley, and all the colonies saw in the King's desire to
hold this land an opportunity to bargain for local liberties. The
Governor of Virginia had the greatest difficulty getting, on terms
he could accept, money to build a fort at the key Forks of the Ohio,
where Pittsburgh now stands. The project advanced so half-
heartedly that in April, 1754, the French took it over by sounding
a few drum rolls, and substituted their own Fort Duquesne.

New York having got quickly over its panic, Johnson's enemies
renewed their opposition, and they soon rose to complete control
of the province. Clinton was recalled to England; his successor, Sir
Danvers Osborn, took one long look at his new capital and committed suicide; as Lieutenant Governor, James De Lancey stepped to
the helm. In reports to London, he blamed New York's continuing
Indian troubles on Johnson's interference with the Albany officials.

Yet in the forests Warraghiyagey remained among Englishmen
supreme; he gave Pennsylvania an object lesson in how hard he was
to get around. Worried lest Weiser die, leaving their province no
champion against the New York frontiersman, the Pennsylvanians
sent Daniel Claus to the Mohawk Valley to learn Indian speech
and ways.

Born twenty-three years before at Württemburg, Claus had entrusted his little inheritance to a respectable-seeming minister's son,
who enticed him to Philadelphia and stranded him there. He met
Weiser and was soon, to the amazement of the frontier, emerging
from Indian cabins as grave, washed, and neat as an ambitious
city apprentice. Having efficiently examined the situation on the
Mohawk, Claus annoyed his Pennsylvania sponsors with eulogies
of the Yorker he was intended to oppose: "All the Six Nations
carry their belts and news to his house . . . nor will they see or hear
of the fourteen Commissioners of Indian Affairs. . . . He suffers, to
my surprise, a vast deal of trouble and charges, when the others
sit quietly at home and mind not to send any message at all to
them. . . . I dare say, if Colonel Johnson should neglect or take no
notice of them, they would be already in the French interest."
Claus added that he himself had gone to live with Johnson who
"introduces me to all affairs necessary."

When Pennsylvania objected to this kidnaping, as it seemed, of

their fledgling champion, Johnson banished Pennsylvania's paragon—but not very far. He kept control of the youngster by placing
him with his own dear friend, Hendrick. And Claus was too honest
not to continue sending back praises of Johnson. Pennsylvania
huffed and puffed, but was soon forced to beg the New Yorker's
help in handling the current link in a long chain of events.

Determined to use an old, vaguely worded deed to get title to
the valleys of the Delaware and the Lehigh, which were occupied
by the Delaware Indians, the Proprietors of Pennsylvania, the
Penn family, had in 1737 interpreted the phrase "as far as a man
can go in a day and a half," by which the Indians had meant a
comfortable forest stroll of some thirty miles, into the 150-mile
gallop of a trained runner along a prepared trail. When the Delawares screamed with rage, Pennsylvania had recourse to the Iroquois, who had long previously conquered the disunited Delaware
tribes, and still considered them their "women," unauthorized to
fight or to own land. As overlords of the disputed territory, the
Iroquois confirmed Pennsylvania's claim and moved their vassals
to the Wyoming Valley. The League and Pennsylvania both
pledged that the Wyoming should be reserved to the Delawares
and the Delawares' "grandsons," the Shawnees, who had joined
them from the South.

Where industrial Wilkes-Barre now reeks, the Wyoming Valley
was then a broad green plain, watered by the Susquehanna, which
extended roughly north and south for thirty-five miles between
black heights of oak and pine. The Delawares could have been
happy there, but no sooner had they moved in, with their legions
of tailless dogs and their occasional cow, than they heard the
twanging of New England voices.

In the imperial mare's-nest of conflicting royal charters were
documents permitting Connecticut to leapfrog over New York and
extend her jurisdiction to the Pacific: the Wyoming was included.
For Connecticut speculators, Lydius had secured from some
drunken Iroquois a deed to the delightful pass. Pennsylvania was
outraged at this invasion of what she considered her territory, and
terrified lest the appearance of Connecticut settlers drive the Delawares and Shawnees into the arms of the French.

The Connecticut speculators wanted the Onondaga Council to

approve Lydius' shaky deed and offered to pay Warraghiyagey well for his help. Although he had been warned against Johnson, Richard Peters, the Secretary of Pennsylvania, was forced, that summer of 1754, to send him a counterappeal. What was Peters' delight when the New Yorker replied that "the pretended saints of New England, the crafty inhabitants of the New Jerusalem," were more characterized by "the subtlety of the serpent than the meekness of the dove!" The Connecticut deed was fraudulent, and Warraghiyagey would keep the Five Nations from being "imposed upon by any strategem whatsoever." Thus Johnson chose sides in a battle that was greatly to effect his subsequent career.

The Indians were celebrated for how far their voices could carry but paper and boats could carry their messages even further. After it had been almost forgotten in New York, Hendrick's threat that the enraged Mohawks would lead their League out of the English alliance echoed at Whitehall. The horrified Board of Trade ordered all the colonies involved in English-Iroquois relations to meet as a group with the Five Nations, and work out a continental Indian policy that would make the League faithful to the Crown. Thus was born the famous Albany Congress of 1754.

It was at this Hendrick-inspired meeting of commissioners from seven colonies, which Johnson attended as a member of the New York Council, that Benjamin Franklin proposed his famous plan for federation of all British America under a single legislature and a President General appointed by the Crown. "It would be a strange thing," argued Franklin, "if Six Nations of ignorant savages should be capable of forming a scheme for such a union, and be able to execute it in such a manner as that it has subsisted ages and appears indissoluble; and yet that a like union should be impracticable for ten or a dozen English Colonies." Although Johnson voted with the other commissioners for Franklin's plan, the "ignorant savages" kept their lead. Neither the Colonial Assemblies nor the Crown would accept such encroachment on their respective prerogatives. The most important immediate effect of the Albany Congress was to give wings to Warraghiyagey's career.

Hendrick dominated the Indian sessions. He was unimpressed with a marvelous belt of wampum into which had been woven the King of England embracing equally the Thirteen Colonies and the Six Nations, "with a space left to draw in other Indians." During a speech which the *Gentleman's Magazine* stated contained "strains of eloquence which might have done honor to Tully or Demosthenes," the sachem twitted the English for their lack of preparedness: the French were "men fortifying everywhere," while the Colonies were "all like women, bare and open without fortifications." He accused the Albanians of selling arms to the French in return for beaver; he complained of land frauds; he insisted that neither the French nor English had any business in the Ohio Valley; he demanded the reinstatement as Indian agent of William Johnson.

"Since Colonel Johnson has been in the city," the Iroquois warned, "there has been a French Indian at his house who took measure of the wall around it." English preparedness was doubly important because Warraghiyagey was "in very great danger. . . . If he fails us, we die."

As Acting Governor of New York, De Lancey was alone in the position to right most of the wrongs about which the Iroquois complained. He said he could do nothing until all the grievances had been carefully investigated: he would report back the following year. In the meanwhile, the Iroquois should continue to deal with the Albanian commissioners, their old and dear friends. Hendrick's brother, Abraham, insulted those commissioners to their faces, and it was clear that, although the sachems stayed for the distribution of presents, they departed far from placated.

Prevented by protocol from interfering, New York's sister colonies had watched unhappily. If the Iroquois joined the enemy, so the delegates as a body warned the Crown, "there is the utmost danger that the whole continent will be subjected to the French." And the record indicated for officials on both sides of the water to see that only William Johnson had the influence with the Iroquois needed to save British America from this "utmost danger."

Although the Albany Congress was a desperate effort to win over the Indians, even while it was in session, land hunger would not down. Lydius set up one saloon, Weiser another. At Lydius' bar, the sachems tipsily confirmed the Connecticut deed to the Wyoming Valley. At Weiser's bar, Pennsylvania created another cause of contention. To invalidate French claims (and forestall rival

English colonies) Weiser bought from drunken Indians, for £400 down and the promise of another £400 when the land was finally settled, a vast empire on the Ohio: all the territory northwest of the Susquehanna "as far as your province extends, let it reach beyond the River Ohio and Lake Erie and wherever it will."

Probably because of the rising land conflict with the French, Warraghiyagey, who had blocked previous Pennsylvania attempts to buy on the Ohio, did not object in 1754. But he was annoyed when he learned that Hendrick had, in a drunken moment, signed Lydius' paper. He sent the sachem to Philadelphia at the head of a delegation to "retract what they had so shamefully done." Hendrick agreed with the Pennsylvanians that Warraghiyagey should mediate the matter the following spring at Onondaga. Had this been achieved, it might have prevented a war between the Delawares and Pennsylvania, a war between Pennsylvania and Connecticut, and one of the Revolution's most bloody episodes, the Wyoming Massacre. But the conflict with France was moving too rapidly to allow a solution in the Wyoming Valley.

Although no war had been declared, Colonel Washington had been placed in command of a small Virginian army. Too impatient to wait for his force to finish gathering, he led a tiny band of militiamen across the mountains. In the Ohio Valley, he annihilated a French scouting expedition, firing, at the age of twenty-two, the shots that opened on this continent the French and Indian War, and were to set Europe on fire. He expected retaliation from Fort Duquesne, where France's troops far outnumbered his own. However, he did not retire. Instead, he built in three feverish days the indefensible works he called Fort Necessity. He was promptly forced into surrender, leaving not a single English flag afloat in the Ohio Valley.

"The unlucky defeat," Johnson wrote, would "animate" the pro-French Indians and "stagger the resolution" of the pro-English. He wished that Washington had "acted with the prudence and circumspection requisite in a officer of his rank," and had "avoided an engagement until all our troops were assembled. . . . I doubt his being too ambitious of acquiring all the honor, or as much as he could, before the rest joined him."

It cannot be denied that the youthful Washington had made a

disastrous mistake because he lacked the ability Johnson possessed superlatively: the ability to understand Indians. He had driven away his own warriors by—so they complained—treating them "as his slaves"; and in his anxiety to show Virginian courage, he had failed to realize that the allegiance of thousands of braves depended on his not damaging the prestige of British arms. "There was never the like seen," wrote Claus, "how quick the nations turned after Col. Washington's defeat." Warraghiyagey's influence was more than ever needed.

From De Lancey and Governor Shirley of Massachusetts came offers. De Lancey offered to pay at long last what the colony owed Johnson, if he would support the colony's Indian commissioners. Shirley wrote, "I am persuaded His Majesty hath not a subject who knows so well how to gain the hearts of the Indians and an absolute influence over them as yourself . . . and, if you will be pleased to let me know in what particular manner you think you can be most instrumental in that service, I will represent and recommend it." To De Lancey, Johnson sent a curt no, but he lay awake many nights worrying about what to say to Shirley.

During more than fifteen years in the Mohawk Valley he had been engaged in the fur trade, and pelts had lifted him from a poor relation to one of the richest men in America. Were he to walk out to his store, he would find there almost every fur that had, for the last several months, legitimately entered New York. The inevitable war would soon stop again the illegal trade with Canada, giving him, once more, a monopoly of the most valuable commodity New York produced. He had a means of wealth that could be relied on to shower him with gold, probably for every day of his life. To throw it away would, he knew, seem to any merchant actionable madness.

Yet in his heart of hearts, this new lord in an ancient forest agreed with those who argued that the independent royal Indian commission he desired should not be given to any individual engaged in trade. He was no John Jacob Astor who enjoyed grubbing in countinghouses. He enjoyed diplomacy and war; he enjoyed clearing fields and building settlements. In his heart of hearts, he was a medieval man who considered buying and selling an ignoble activity unworthy of men worthy of power. He believed—quite wrongly, for the Lords of Trade had already recommended his appointment to the Crown—that his trading activities stood between him and his ambitions for office, between him and his ability to serve both his king and the Five Nations who had, through adversity, been his faithful friends.

"I laid it to account in the best light that I should be a considerable loser," but he found he was "contented to be so, as far as I can prudently bear." On December 17, 1754, he wrote Shirley that, "should his Majesty deem me worthy of that important trust," he would abandon the fur trade and devote the rest of his life to the public service.

9

A New French War

Although officially at peace, England finally resolved to stop French "encroachments" in North America. Major General Edward Braddock sailed, in January, 1755, to Virginia with regular regiments and orders to liberate the Ohio. As commander under Braddock of forces raised locally, the Crown appointed Governor Shirley; he was to recapture Louisburg and plan whatever other expeditions seemed advisable. Shirley decided to block off the hive from which French bees stung the frontier, by building just south of Crown Point an English fort that "may command the French fort there and curb the city of Montreal itself." As general of the expedition to do this, he selected William Johnson. The frontiersman, he explained, understood wilderness fighting, knew the terrain, and could enlist Indians.

But Johnson, who had undoubtedly dreamed during his shackled youth of that escape to the army that had released many of his relations, realized how little he resembled a professional soldier. (He had never even seen a battle!) His sudden appointment as top commander of a major army filled him with dismay. "You must be convinced," he wrote Shirley, "that the little experience I have of military affairs cannot entitle me to this distinction. . . . I should have exerted my utmost interest among them [the Indians] if Your Excellency had fixed on some other person, which would still be very agreeable to me."

In the same letter, the wilderness officer made a suggestion that could have saved the regular, Braddock, from annihilation. Instead of traversing deadly mountains and deadlier thickets in a march on Fort Duquesne, the main British force should float comfortably to Niagara, "leaving a few men towards the Ohio to keep the French on expectation of a visit there." If the French lost control of the Niagara River, their communications would be cut not only with the further Great Lakes and the posts on them dependent, but also with the Ohio Valley: they would be forced to abandon not only Duquesne but all their northwestern posts. Parkman was to attribute this brilliant strategy to his hero Shirley, but Shirley himself wrote Johnson, "I shall not be unmindful, when I see the general [Braddock], of what you mention about Niagara."

In April, Johnson journeyed to Alexandria, Virginia, his first trip to the American South. In a flat land under a moist sky, he met Braddock, and was electrified to learn that the Crown had ordered his appointment to the office he had so long coveted. As Colonel of the Six Nations and their Allies, he was to manage English relations with the northern Indians, accountable only to Braddock as commander in chief and supported with funds from the royal treasury. He asked to be relieved from the Crown Point command, lest it "interfere with my administration of Indian affairs," but Braddock insisted that he accept both responsibilities.

One of Johnson's first official acts as Indian colonel was to write George Croghan, a Pennsylvania frontiersman whom he may have passed on the streets of Dublin when they both were young, but whom he had never met. Croghan was now, after some fourteen American years, the most influential trader over the mountains and into the Ohio Valley. When Johnson had kidnaped Claus, Pennsylvania had considered making Croghan Weiser's successor as its Indian representative, but the authorities could not really put up with the athletic and almost illiterate Irishman, a "vile rascal" who pitied gentlemen for their effeteness.* He was accused of dis-

---

* From England, where he was serving as Johnson's representative in 1764, Croghan reported back in spelling and punctuation that deserves to be preserved: "There has been Nothing Don Sence I Came to London by the Grate one* butt squbeling & fighting See who will keep in power the publick Intrest is Neglected to Serve privet Intrest & I blive itt is hard to Say wʰ. party is yᵉ. honistist was I to Spake My mind I wold Say they were all R-g-e-s [rogues] aLicke I am nott Sorry I Came Hear as it will Larn Me to be Contented on a Litle farm in amerrica if I Can gett one when I go back Butt I ashure yʳ. honour I am Sick of London & harttily Tierᵈ. of yᵉ. pride and pomp of the Slaves in power hear which are to be pitied tho they Dont Deserve itt."

honesty and even of treasonous correspondence with the French. These charges Johnson must have heard, but he knew that no one could rival Croghan's influence with the Shawnees and Delawares and Mingoes.

As his previous trust of Lydius had revealed, Johnson felt he could use as instruments men others considered disreputable, and in this case his faith was eminently justified. Croghan accepted with alacrity the commission to recruit Delawares for Braddock's army; he became in 1756 the first deputy superintendent in Johnson's department, and served him with good will, energy, and even genius for more than fifteen years. While Johnson presided particularly over the Long House, Croghan dealt with the Indians of Pennsylvania and the Ohio, extending his personal contacts eventually to the Great Lakes and the Illinois. He became second only to Johnson as the most powerful white Indian on the continent.

During their conferences with Braddock, Johnson and Shirley had urged the commander in chief to change the objective of his own army from Fort Duquesne to Niagara. Braddock replied that he was committed. However, his "secret orders" from England had suggested an attempt on Niagara if it could be made without interfering with his expedition against Fort Duquesne; he ordered Shirley to lead on that attempt the two royal Massachusetts regiments. Thus was created a confusion of commands that was like tying two tomcats together by the tail.

For colonial troops, Shirley was Johnson's superior; for Indian troops, Johnson was Shirley's. Each was to mount an independent expedition at the same time in the same little city, Albany. Then Johnson was to march northward toward Crown Point along the borders of Shirley's New England, while Shirley was to advance up the Mohawk and through Johnson's Iroquois country to his embarkation point of Oswego. Since Shirley's force was supported by the Crown, while Johnson had to rely on colonial appropriations, Shirley had more money than Johnson, but, the militia having been assigned before Shirley's expedition was planned, Johnson had most of the manpower.

The frontiersman was not sophisticated enough to notice the confusion, and the governor was too sophisticated to be worried. Snapping his blue-black eyes, sniffing through his bony nose, and

William Shirley, by Thomas Hudson
The brilliant politician, Governor of Massachusetts, Commander of the British army in America, who was unseated by William Johnson (*Courtesy, Frick Art Reference Library; owner, Mrs. Norman J. Marsh*)

Daniel and Ann Johnson Claus,
Sir William's daughter and
son-in-law, artist unknown
(*Public Archives Canada*)

gesticulating with a tenseness that belied the self-satisfaction of his little smile, Shirley was irritable, intellectually brilliant, and adept in the world of cities; he looked on the massive Johnson as a blunt instrument created to be wielded by a quick hand.

De Lancey also saw in Johnson a hammer to be manipulated. New York's acting governor had, it is true, opposed the appointment of his long-time opponent to the Crown Point command, but his opposition had been based more on habit than any existing disagreement. Since Johnson's abandonment of the fur trade had ended his economic rivalry with the Dutch faction, and the growing French threat had made even the Albany merchants agree that the fighting with Canada they had for so long blamed on him was now necessary, there was no real reason why De Lancey should not use him as a weapon against a new menace.

That the Governor of Massachusetts should, as deputy commander in chief, exert continental authority outraged the chief executive of New York for his colony had serious land disputes with Massachusetts. Furthermore, Shirley had insulted De Lancey personally. To De Lancey's request for some military graft to which he felt his office entitled him, Shirley had replied "with a tartness not to be forgot."

When Shirley tried to pry loose for his own undermanned expedition some of Johnson's troops, De Lancey responded with a rousing attempt to send all available men and supplies to Johnson. To discredit Shirley by sabotaging the Niagara expedition became a major object of New York's ruling politicians. They were joined by Thomas Pownall, an adventurer well connected in England who was combing America for political office and saw himself as Shirley's successor in Massachusetts. With the cabal's blessing, Peter Wraxall, a civil servant experienced in intrigue, went up the Hudson as Secretary of the Indian Department. Wraxall's presence at Johnson's right hand brought the first twinge of worry to Shirley's supporters. Although they concluded that the frontier soldier lacked the "sense and penetration" to be an effective political opponent, they feared Wraxall's "art and genius."*

* Both Pownall and Wraxall had been present at the Albany Congress of 1754 and had at that time sent messages to London urging that Johnson be appointed to manage the Indians.

Warraghiyagey needed a political advisor. His troops were to comprise 600 men from New Hampshire, 1,000 from Connecticut, 400 from Rhode Island, 800 from New York, and 1,200 from Massachusetts. Each group was in effect a separate army, with its own officers, its own commissary, its own budget to be voted by its own legislature. (In order to have legal command, Johnson had to be elected major or lieutenant general in the militia of every participating colony.) As the various governments wrangled over which should pay for what that had to be bought commonly, Johnson angrily foresaw not a shooting but an "argumentative war." And how he cursed when he discovered that the mountain boys of New Hampshire were too afraid of the water to sail down the coast, but, by marching overland, were risking ambush by the French.

Having puzzled his already spinning head with a book on fortifications, Johnson bullied Braddock into sending him a trained artilleryman. Like a girl awaiting her lover, Johnson awaited this paragon, who was highly billed as having taken part in the defense of Bergen Op Zoom. Captain William Eyre, indeed, proved highly useful; he took over, not only the artillery and the engineers, but the duties of quartermaster and adjutant. Obliged to help recruits put up their tents, being blithely told that, if a shell were too small for the gun, you could fill in the space with clay, Eyre wrote Johnson, "Hitherto, I have been successful, and it makes me grave when I consider to be embarked in so extraordinary an undertaking."

Warraghiyagey's first act on returning from Braddock's Virginia headquarters had been to summon the Mohawks to Mount Johnson and declaim, "I transport the shade of that fire which was in Albany, and rekindle the fire of council and friendship in this place."

The Mohawks replied, "We are charmed to see you again and greet you with this string of wampum." However, to Johnson's request that they reinforce Braddock's army, they replied, as Johnson reported, that they would first send a delegation "to pay their duty to your Excellency," which meant they would look Braddock over and report back what they had seen. Warning that the success of wilderness marches depended on Indian protection, Johnson urged the European general to receive the Mohawks with every courtesy. However, he should not try to enlist the Mohawk delegation; they should be sent back with presents. The Onondaga Council was about to meet, and the other Iroquois nations would be displeased if the Mohawks engaged in hostilities "without the general concurrence."

Johnson's policies and possibilities had changed since the outbreak of King George's War. Then he had possessed only some influence among the Mohawks; in order to recruit them, he had fostered local revolution against the Onondaga Council. But now that he had power in that council, he did not want to tear the fabric of Iroquois government—particularly as French infiltration of the upper nations might enable them to turn anarchy to their own advantage—but rather to mesh that fabric with the English interest.

Warraghiyagey had invited the sachems to Mount Johnson for a great congress that might determine whether North America would be an English or a French continent. Perhaps he could enlist the Iroquois in the war; perhaps he would have to settle for neutrality. But one thing was certain: His own hand would be desperately weakened, as would Hendrick's ability to help him, if the arriving sachems found that the Mohawks had betrayed League unity by agreeing independently to fight.

All was still in abeyance when Shirley demanded that Indians be assigned to convoy advance units of his army to Oswego, and to serve him personally as a bodyguard. Johnson answered that no special protection was needed in the Iroquois country; he would postpone recruiting the warriors until the Niagara expedition was ready to embark from Oswego for enemy soil.

To Shirley, this reply seemed a revelation of insubordination and villainy. Believing, as most Europeans did, that the Indians could be shunted around like white soldiers, the deputy commander in chief could only conclude that his order had been disobeyed because General Johnson had joined the cabal against him. If his Niagara campaign was not to be naked of Indians he would have to recruit them himself! And so there dawned the opportunity for revenge against Johnson which that one-eyed man of many wiles, Lydius, had long awaited.

In mid-June, the crucial Iroquois conference convened at Warraghiyagey's council fire. Since the sachems had brought with them entire villages to witness the deliberations and enjoy the food," Johnson's clearing boiled with 1,104 Indians. "Numbers of them," he wrote, "came ahorseback, and they must not at this critical time be controlled. They have spoiled my meadow and destroy every green thing about my estate." Fearing the result on this unfriendly throng, he promulgated orders against the sale of rum— but from the surrounding settlements, rum flowed in unabated.

Warraghiyagey found all the nations except the Mohawks "extremely averse" to fighting the French, partly from fear "owing to our long passivity and their activity," partly "from a real attachment in many of their leading men to the French interest. . . . I am fully persuaded that had this meeting not taken place, there would very speedily have been a defection of the major part of the upper nations."

Between the copious formal sessions, Warraghiyagey appealed to each important Indian as seemed best in that individual case: with arguments, with promises, with presents, with assurances of affection. The private conferences lasted "from early in the morning to twelve o'clock at night and sometimes later. . . . The fatigue I have undergone has been too much for me. It still continues, and I am scarce able to support it."

Enter Lydius. He showed Johnson a commission from Shirley as colonel of Indian forces in the Niagara expedition. Johnson assured him that when such forces were needed, they would be supplied, but Lydius had not been instructed to wait on Johnson's pleasure. He took aside members of the turtle clan, into which he had been adopted, and enlisted them for Shirley.

As Warraghiyagey reopened his private talks the following morning, he was inundated with protests against such recruiting before official policy had been determined. Johnson stormed downstairs to find Lydius and order him "not to speak to any Indian." Lydius then presented a letter from Shirley empowering him to act independently of Johnson.* The man who had just, after years of urging, been entrusted with the exclusive control of Indian affairs replied that when he saw Governor Shirley, "he would talk smartly to him."

---

* Shirley was to deny that his letter had thus encouraged the violation of royal orders, but he continued to invade Johnson's prerogative by recruiting Indians.

Later that day, Lydius pushed into a public meeting, whereupon an Oneida sachem, who recognized him as the instigator of Connecticut's Wyoming Valley deed, arose and addressed Johnson, "Brother, you promised us that you would keep this fireplace clean from all filth, and that no snake should come into this Council Room. That man sitting there is a devil and has stole our lands. He takes Indians slyly by the blanket, one at a time, and when they are drunk, puts some money in their bosoms, and persuades them to sign deeds for our lands." Johnson answered that Lydius "came without any invitation from me."

However, Lydius kept whispering to Indians until, as he munched his eternal hard-boiled eggs at Johnson's supper table, a great row convinced him he was "unwelcome." He exited grandly, leaving Warraghiyagey more than ever determined that Shirley should have no braves until he actually needed them on sailing from Oswego toward New France.

Braddock's need was immediate. Johnson was cautiously paving the way for supplying him with warriors when the emissaries the Indians had sent to the British general returned. They reported that "the great man in Virginia did not seem to love Indians and made but little account of them."

To Braddock, Johnson dispatched a lecture on Indian relations: "Without generosity, patience, and a winning civility of behavior, nothing can be done with them when compliances on their side are wanted." He could not know that this was a belated warning to a ghost. Reaped by Indian gunfire, Braddock and his great army lay prone in the blood-soaked wilderness.

On the banks of the Mohawk, Warraghiyagey threatened Indians: he would "demit the management of your affairs entirely and leave the country." He also made promises which he later asked the Board of Trade to honor: that the Indian land grievances be settled without interference from "some very powerful and wealthy people in this province"; that wooden forts be built and garrisoned "at the chief residing place of each nation who can be prevailed on to admit it"; that "gunsmiths or armourers" reside at the forts to mend the Indians' weapons; and that trade with the Indians be limited to "residents and interpreters" at the forts who would be kept from unfair dealing by being directly accountable to Johnson: "no other person or persons to presume to interfere in the said business."

Finally, Warraghiyagey cried, "My war kettle is on the fire, my canoe is ready to put into the water, my gun is loaded, my sword by my side, and my axe sharpened! I desire and expect you will now take up the hatchet and join with us!" However, he was satisfied with a vague promise that the Iroquois would at some unspecified time "join and assist you in your undertakings." This he took as an authorization to recruit at once individual Indian warriors.

In the way of recruiting stood that old stumbling block, the Caughnawagas. No more than in King George's War would the Iroquois let their own blood. Warraghiyagey promised that he would make every effort to win the French Mohawks over and, despite Shirley's shrill screams that the Canadian Indians were spying on his army, ordered that any Caughnawagas who came atrading to Albany should "receive no disturbance or injury whatsoever." This further persuaded Shirley that Johnson had sold out to De Lancey and the Albany Dutch.

When Shirley received a copy of the official record of the Indian congress which Wraxall, as secretary, had prepared, he was lifted into a nervous fury by a footnote. There at the bottom of a page it was stated, for the government in London to see, that he, the deputy commander in chief, had disobeyed royal orders by dispatching a disreputable character to interfere in the Indian department that the Crown had declared Johnson's sole responsibility.

To Shirley's shrill protest, Johnson replied that the footnote had been included without his "direction and privity"; he had now ordered it scratched out. Shirley countered that Johnson should have expunged the footnote on first seeing it. Unless he would promise to supply as many Indians as Shirley wanted instantaneously on demand, Shirley would consider Johnson guilty of insubordination to a superior officer and would be justified in recruiting Indians for himself.

Wraxall drafted for Johnson's signature a reply which lacked, as he put it, "blameable mildness," but Johnson preferred to inform Shirley in a brief note that he would let the Indians "know your request, but whether I shall be successful, and what number I may be able to obtain are points which I cannot answer you on with any certainty."

Late in July, Johnson received "the incoherent, unexpected, unintelligible, not to be credited damned bad news" that Braddock's army had been annihilated. "Very far from well . . . in the present hurry of my spirits," he wrote Acting Governor De Lancey that when the Indians found out "the greatest part of them" would undoubtedly seek self-preservation and "join our enemies against us." It would be "madness" to continue the Crown Point campaign without Indians; let it be stopped and what forces could be spared from defense of the Colonies be concentrated under Shirley against Niagara. He himself would leap into the forest, "go through all the nations or try to get some of their most leading men to meet me at Onondaga, lay matters before them, use all the arguments and influence I am master of to prevent the dissolution of our Indian connections."

Johnson had just penned his fear that the English faced "the last and worst of all evils, namely to perish infamously," when "some of the most leading men of three Upper Nations" filed into his clearing. He put on a passive face and greeted the arrivals, whose faces were equally uncommunicative. After the warriors had eaten and rested, questioning elicited that they had not heard of England's disaster. Beginning in a minor key, he finally communicated the defeat "pretty nearly in its true light."

To De Lancey he reported, "They assured me they would stand by their engagements, and I am now fitting them out with arms. . . . The Crown Point expedition will be pushed on with alacrity. . . . If the Indians stand by us and God bless our endeavors, I hope we shall raise laurels that will overshadow our cyprus."

10

Death of a Sachem

As in the bloodstained forest of Braddock's defeat, Indians had stripped and scalped dead bodies, stripped living prisoners for death by torture, Frenchmen had searched for papers. They found Johnson's orders to attack Crown Point.

The high command had intended to advance on Oswego, but they now resolved to cut Johnson off in the wilderness as Braddock had been cut off, and then to sweep on to Albany, leaving Shirley's army at Oswego to wither at the end of severed communications. Up Lake Champlain to Crown Point sailed the main French army: 700 regulars, 1,600 Canadians, and 700 Indians. The French commander in chief, Marshal Ludwig August, Baron Dieskau, a German professional in the French service, a protégé of the famous Marshal Saxe and the veteran of many a European battlefield, was now—although Warraghiyagey did not know it—opposed to the frontier general who had never even heard the sounds of battle.

When the time approached for his army to march, Johnson had to leave his Council Fire to attend to a thousand details of mobilization at Albany. Into his Valley poured Shirley, Lydius, and a host of Indian agents. They treated the official interpreter, Arent Stevens, with "such insolent rudeness" that the old man felt obliged "to strip and challenge to fight any of them"; they pushed the old man aside. They laid hands on warriors Warraghiyagey had recruited for Crown Point and almost pulled them to pieces in importunities that they go instead to Niagara.

Although Anglo-Iroquois affairs were already in a precarious state due to Braddock's defeat, Shirley, so Johnson wrote their superiors in England, labored to tear down the prestige of the Crown's Indian representative. Shirley told the Mohawks that he had made Warraghiyagey a great man and could as easily break him, adding "that he had given me £5,000 sterling for them, that pay and appointments were ordered them, which I concealed from their knowledge."

As he had done in King George's War, Johnson was enlisting warriors for their equipment, maintenance for their families, and promised rewards after a successful campaign. Now Shirley offered salaries, an expensive precedent that was to plague the English service throughout the French and Indian War.

Johnson was trapped in Albany with his gathering army, but Hendrick traveled the Valley as his champion. The sachem insisted that, as immediate fighting impended at Crown Point, any warrior who waited for the Niagara expedition to get under way would be a coward. The Shirleyites managed to recruit thirty Mohawks, but Hendrick got four back.

The squabble over ownership of the Wyoming Valley that was, in the person of Lydius, adding fuel to Indian controversy, had been deeply embedded in the white army by the Connecticut Assembly, which had forced the appointment as Johnson's second in command of the leading Wyoming speculator, Phineas Lyman, and had included in their act commissioning him major general arguments for the Connecticut claim Johnson so strongly opposed. Lyman was soon closeted with Shirley.

An issue came easily to hand. The New England levies that were to make up two-thirds of Johnson's army had heard in their native elm shade rumors that the general under whom they were supposed to serve luxuriated in a harem of beauties so seductive they could have inspired the more exciting curses in the Old Testament. Ministers had wrestled with the problem in prayer, and the recruits had been frightened: would not such immoral leadership call down on the army God's wrath? And when the New Englanders reached Albany, their forebodings had been redoubled:

camp followers openly served the New York regiment and could be induced to bestow sweet, secret damnation on New England's trembling sons. Lyman wrote Johnson that, if the women were not instantly banished, the Northern saints "will either mob or privately destroy them."

As he prepared to visit the bedroom of his latest delight, Johnson let Wraxall draft his reply: "Immoralities of all kinds I will use my utmost power to suppress and chastize. . . ." He scrawled down his signature, but was undoubtedly glad he was not present to have his heart wrung by a scene thus described in a soldier's diary: "Saw Nelly and Polly in a great taking, for the women were ordered away."

As the New England levies eyed General Johnson uneasily, he surveyed them with misgivings. "The officers and men," he wrote, "with very few exceptions, are not only strangers to military life, but show an averseness to discipline and regularity, which gives me no small trouble and uneasiness." Yet the general and his soldiers were made for each other. A Massachusetts surgeon soon decided that he had never been so misinformed about anyone: "I must say he is a complete gentleman, and willing to oblige and please all men, familiar and free of access to the lowest sentinel, a gentleman of uncommon smart sense and even temper; never yet saw him ruffle or use any bad language." And Johnson concluded that his troops were "brave though not regular."

Reports circulating in the army that "the Indians painted up the general" were shuddery, yet it was reassuring to have a leader so at home with the barracuda of the forests. To reduce the shudders, Johnson staged war games during which, the Boston *Gazette* reported, Indians, "naked and painted," scrimmaged with the farm boys.

The same account states that an English officer, in Albany with Shirley's force, asked one of Johnson's subordinates why he did not drill his troops. "To load quick and hit the mark," the American replied, "that is our whole exercise."

"What! Do you take aim at the enemy?"

"Yes. Good aim or not fire."

"So, if an officer appears, twenty should aim at him?"

The American nodded.

"Absolute murder!" cried the horrified English officer.

As Warraghiyagey was training his troops, he sent back to Mount Johnson a housekeeping memorandum of which a fragment has survived. Fires and candles were to be lighted in all bedchambers at suppertime, water and towels with "slippers and a chamber utensil brought." A special maid was to see that clean linen for the table and the family was always in readiness; and the house was to be washed twice a week, beginning at daylight with the parlors and proceeding to the bedchambers after the family had arisen.

Since Johnson himself gave such orders, that family may not have included his former housekeeper, Catherine Weisenberg, so long missing from all records. But her three children were now conspicuous figures in their father's life. They had completed their hegira from nameless bundles to heirs-in-residence on one of New York's richest estates.

Although fourteen-year-old John possessed his father's gray eyes, the rest of his physique seems to have come from his mother. He was blond and slight, with a round face more pretty than imposing, and a delicate mouth pulled back petulantly over a receding chin. His huge father bent over him with love and admiration, and saw in the boy a successor to his own prowess. John was allowed to get drunk with the loud-singing Irishman, and urged to test his puberty on the Indian and white pretties. General Johnson enlisted him in the Crown Point army as a volunteer.

For his daughters—fifteen-year-old Ann (Nancy) and Mary, now eleven—Johnson had other ideas. The forest maidens, so a little girl growing up in Albany was told, lived at the wild frontier outpost in a room apart, under the care of a widow who shunned life "from which she seemed to wish her pupils to remain forever estranged. . . . Never was anything so uniform as their dress, their occupations, and the general tenor of their lives. In the morning, they rose early, read their Prayer Book, I believe, but certainly their Bible, fed their birds, tended their flowers, and breakfasted; then were employed some hours with unwearied perseverance at fine needlework for the ornamental parts of dress, which were the fashion of the day, without knowing to what use they were to be put, as they never wore them, and had not . . . ever seen a lady, excepting each other and their governess. They then read, as long as they chose, the voluminous romances of the last century, of which their friend had a vast collection, or Rollin's *Ancient History*, the only books they had ever seen. After dinner, they regularly in summer took a long walk; or an excursion in the sledge in winter, with their friend; and then returned and resumed their wonted occupations, with the sole variation of a stroll in the garden in summer or a game at chess or shuttlecock in winter.

"Their dress was to the full as simple and uniform as everything else. They wore wrappers of the finest chintz and green silk petticoats, and this the whole year round without variation. Their hair, which was long and beautiful, was tied behind with a simple ribbon; and a large calash shaded each from the sun; and in winter they had long scarlet mantles that covered them from head to foot."

When at home, Warraghiyagey escaped from his military camp into this dovecote once every day to savor a half-hour of innocence and gentleness. The door was locked against all other males but their brother. This suited Mary—she was happy with her birds and books—but in Nancy young womanhood flowered no less surely because it was unwanted and unacknowledged.

Daniel Claus had left the Pennsylvania service and was now a member of the Johnson household, to which he brought a methodicalness that was sometimes as much needed as his air of shopkeeper respectability seemed always out of place. Regretting drunken brawls between Indians and Irishmen (whose war cries were almost indistinguishable), the butt of practical jokes which he deplored, he invoked, in moments of fear, strangeness or suppressed anger, the vision of Nancy scudding under her long cape down these roaring halls—silent, remote and pure. When the ladies took their prim walks, he managed sometimes to be in the garden, and, if his eyes met Nancy's, it seemed to him that she was looking with equal wonder on his face.

Finally, the moment came when the governess left her charge for the moment unguarded. A few hurried syllables, and each knew for certain. No action followed. For Nancy, the avowal was enough. And Claus realized that this was no time to try to interest Johnson in a retainer's love for his daughter.

By early August, Johnson had sent some 2,000 militiamen about fifty miles up the Hudson from Albany to the Great Carrying Place (now Fort Edward) where the river turned southeast. From there, a road was to be cut either northwest to Lake St. Sacrement or north to Wood Creek:* both flowed to Lake Champlain and Crown Point.

Down below at Albany, Johnson was laboring to get the remainder of his force in motion. The New Hampshire troops were invisible in some unreported forest; artillery stores were lacking and the boats to carry the guns leaked. "No one," the general wrote, "is more sensible of the importance of dispatch, and the most sanguine does not burn with more impatience. I cannot be everywhere. I give strict orders. I entreat. I animate."

Unable to wait any longer, Johnson joined the army on August 14, bringing "our artillery and many other wagons loaded with provisions, which made great rejoicing." He also brought some fifty Indians who frightened James Gilbert of Morton, Massachusetts, out of what little ability he had to spell: "My pen is not abel To Describe The odiesnes of Their Dress. They had Juels in Their noses. Their faces painted with all Colouers. They appeared very odious To us also." Among these Indians was a seventeen-year-old warrior with a great future—Joseph Brant.

Militiamen, glancing uneasily at the fierce, tattooed faces of four Mohawks passing through their encampment, did not recognize ambassadors returned from an embassy on which the life of the army might depend. Warraghiyagey had sent them to urge neutrality on the Caughnawagas; in his tent, they gave their discouraging report.

"Brethren," the Caughnawaga speaker had told them, "the French priests, by throwing water upon our heads, subjected us to the will of the Governor of Canada, but, as you are a free people, be careful of your safety and do not engage yourself in the quarrels between the English and the French. . . . Where the French go, we must go also." Then the Caughnawagas had said that not only every pro-French Indian warrior, but 8,000 white soldiers—6,000

* Men who deserve the eternal curses of historians gave the same name to two of New York's vital waterways, the "Wood Creek" that connected the Mohawk Valley with Lake Oneida, and the "Wood Creek" that flowed into Lake Champlain, along which Burgoyne was to advance during the Revolution toward his famous surrender.

of them regulars just arrived from France—were on their way to crush Warraghiyagey's army.

After allowing for "the natural boasting and vapors of the French," Johnson deduced that his white army was outnumbered. (Actually, when the New Hampshire troops finally wandered in, he had 3,100 to 3,200 white effectives, about 900 more than the enemy.) Since the Caughnawagas' refusal to withdraw discouraged the Iroquois, he expected to remain greatly outnumbered in Indians. He had with him "not quite sixty," and these were "very cold to their brother" and "most provokingly insolent, which at present I must bear with silence. . . .

"Imagine," Johnson continued, "that you see my tent from morning to night crowded with Indians, with officers, etc., all impatient to be heard, each thinking his own affairs more important than the others. I am obliged to hear them all . . . which, I assure you, renders it miserable." A regular army general would have handled this situation by shouting an order, but Johnson fled with his tent to an island. When the water was instantly black with militiamen's boats and the bobbing heads of aquatic Indians, he mourned. " 'Tis in no one's power to relieve me."

Since the Caughnawagas had told the Mohawks that the French intended to ambush the Wood Creek route, the militiamen cutting a road in that direction were called back and pointed toward Lake St. Sacrement. A fort which Johnson tactfully named after Lyman was started at the Carrying Place before the major part of the army began its advance toward the Lake on August 26.

Behind platoons of axmen who were still clearing the sap-fragrant road, the troops moved slowly, taking three days to cover the fourteen miles. Johnson had plenty of leisure to dispense hospitality. A general, he believed, should keep a fine table: "the troops will naturally expect to see it, the officers to feel it." Colonel Seth Pomeroy felt it. He noted on the 27th, "Eat pieces of ham, broken bread, and cheese, drank some fresh lemon punch and the best of wine with General Johnson." The next day, "Dined with General Johnson by a small brook under a tree. Eat a good dinner of cold boiled and roast venison, drank some fresh lemon punch and wine. We came to the lake about four of the clock."

Under its hills, around its islands, the water gleamed and darkened, unmindful of man and all his murders—yet this was a murderers' path, leading from as well as to New France. At the southern end, General Johnson's army floundered in "a thick wood: not a foot of land cleared." Despite frenzied chopping, plough-hands and apprentices had to spend the nights prone in a tangle through which they could not see or hope to run. They had been told that enemy Indians with scalping knives could land a short distance down the lake and stroll up to them as along a boulevard. When on September 1 dawn came at last, there was a stirring in the copses, "a great uneasiness tending to mutiny in our army. In Captain Jones' company," so Colonel Pomeroy noted, "thirty or upwards marched off with their packs on their backs and guns clubbed. Others threatened to go. . . . At night, the army seemed more composed."

"This lake," Johnson wrote, "which the French call Lake St. Sacrement, we have called Lake George . . . not only to honor His Majesty, but to ascertain his undoubted dominion here."

Johnson intended to sail down Lake George to Ticonderoga, an easily fortified narrows at the inlet to Lake Champlain. The French were there, but, so Indian scouts told him, not in force. He would drive them out, and build a fort while he awaited the rest of his army. Then he would assault Crown Point, fifteen miles northward. To keep open his line of communications, he ordered Eyre to plan a fort at Lake George—but the immediate necessity was to find a suitable encampment for his army while it awaited the 600 bateaux that would have to be moved overland from Fort Lyman on the Hudson before the advance could begin.

The place Johnson selected had its rear on the lake, its right flank on a marsh, and its left on a hill where the fort was to be and where Eyre had already mounted his cannon. The encampment would only be attacked from the southwest over level ground which Johnson ordered cleared of trees.

Everything was still in preparation when he received a most welcome reinforcement. Hendrick, who had effectively carried his middle-aged body on the war path in King George's War, was now so old and fat that he could only travel on horseback, yet War-raghiyagey needed him as never before, and he came at the head of about 200 braves. "The Indians," wrote Pomeroy, "fired off their guns at the entrance to our camp, and with our cannon we fired two rounds."

Some of Hendrick's braves wished to go scalping, but the sachem restrained them until he had sent another message, "which is to be the last," to the Caughnawagas. It did not have to travel very far. Quick, silent, and undeviating as bird shadows, Hendrick's emissaries advanced to a nearby glade from which the day before three signal shots had sounded. Had a sentry stumbled on the conference between so-called French and theoretically English Indians, he would have suspected treason, but the belts which the Iroquois handed the Caughnawagas had been supplied by Warraghiyagey. The results of the low-voiced oratory the future would show.

Although the French had anticipated Johnson by moving their main force to Ticonderoga, Dieskau was operating not on information but from guesswork; his lines of intelligence had crumbled. Theoretically, he commanded 600 Indian eyes, but Warraghiyagey had misted those eyes over.

The Caughnawagas made up half of Dieskau's Indian force. Their priests had threatened them with hell-fire, yet many had eaten well at Mount Johnson. Warraghiyagey was known to them as the Indians' friend, and in his camp were their Iroquois brothers. Dieskau doubted the loyalty of the Caughnawagas, and believed that their influence "spoiled" the "good" warriors.

"Never was I able to obtain from them a faithful scout," the French marshal complained. "At one time, they refused to make any. At another time, seeming to obey me, they set forth, but, when a few leagues from the camp, they sent back the Frenchmen I had associated with them, and used to return within a few days without bringing me any intelligence." Dieskau suspected "mischievous intrigues."

Among his Indians were Abnakis, displaced New England tribesmen who had every reason for hating the colonists. Finally, he managed to send out some of these without the knowledge of the Caughnawagas. They brought back an English prisoner who reported correctly that Fort Lyman was lightly garrisoned and not complete. But the captive added the false intelligence that Johnson's main army had retired to Albany.

Dieskau resolved to sail up Wood Creek and then march overland to Fort Lyman with 200 regulars, 600 Canadians, and all his 600 Indians. Since no artillery could be carried along the narrow trails, had Dieskau realized that Johnson's large army was within fourteen miles of Fort Lyman, he probably would not have taken the risk—yet the marshal's faulty intelligence seemed likely to pay off with victory. Johnson was convinced that, if they advanced, the French would bring cannon in the only way that was practical, in boats up Lake George; he was concentrating there his preparations for defense. The 500 men who were building Fort Lyman were camped outside the uncompleted works. Dieskau seemed bound to overrun this little force, cutting Johnson's supply line and leaving the larger English army half trapped, incapable of withstanding a second, a more formal French attack.

On September 6, 1755, a sachem appeared in the English headquarters to murmur that he had just awakened from an ominous dream: no straggler should go out to the left of the camp. The evening of the seventh, some braves came in from a northward scout. Having interviewed them, Hendrick reported that they had picked up the tracks of two men which soon converged with the tracks of three more. Then they heard six guns fired. The next morning, "we heard so many guns fired we could not count them." Exploration revealed three deeply-packed trails "made by a great body of men yesterday." They seemed to be marching toward Fort Lyman.

A wagoner called Jacob Adams volunteered to carry a warning to that encampment: Johnson lent him his own horse and saddle; he disappeared into the gloaming. It was dark when he encountered part of the French army. He pressed hard with his spurs, relying on the speed of his mount to carry him through. Some deserters who were hiding in the woods heard shots and a voice cry, "Heavens: have mercy!" They fled back to Lake George to report the capture or death of Adams—but Johnson had already sent other messengers.

Before the English even realized that there was an enemy in their forest, Dieskau had penetrated to within a few miles of Fort Lyman. He was planning to attack at nightfall, but the Caughnawagas, as he wrote, "refused point blank to march." When the marshal insisted that he would go on without them, they seemed to change their minds "and immediately set forth to lead the van, as if to make a parade of their zeal." As the light faded, the veteran European commander, the Canadians, the regiments of La Reine and Languedoc followed the Indians, ducking under limbs, thrashing through underbrush, encircling fallen branches. Finally, it was pitch black. The Caughnawagas were terribly sorry; they could not imagine how it had happened. They had lost their way.

As he cursed in German, Dieskau was handed Adams' scalp and the dispatch found on the courier's body, which revealed that Johnson's army was not in Albany but nearby. A prisoner, who was soon brought in, added that the army, although large, was encamped without conventional defenses in a clearing, and—this was incorrect—that Johnson was like Dieskau devoid of cannon. "I immediately," the marshal wrote, "gave the Indians the choice of proceeding the next day to attack either the fort or this army." The Indians wanted to go where there was no artillery: they voted for Johnson's encampment at Lake George. "Very happy for us," was that general's comment. At Fort Lyman, the "victory probably would have been a very cheap one, and made way for another here."

A council of Johnson's officers decided to send 500 men to Wood Creek to find and destroy Dieskau's boats, and another 500 to relieve Fort Lyman, but Hendrick objected to this division of forces. He promised to lead the march with his warriors if the general would send all the thousand militiamen down the road toward Fort Lyman. This maneuver, which was undertaken as September 8 dawned, has gone down in history as "the Bloody Morning Scout."

Conspicuous on horseback, Hendrick began the procession; behind him, 200 Indians advanced in a single file, a thin line in the center of the road. Next came Colonel Ephraim Williams (whose will, made operative later that day, was to found Williams College) leading the thousand militiamen. Marching five or six abreast, they filled to its edges the newly-cut gash in the forest. On both sides, huge, prone tree trunks, piled-up branches on which the dying leaves still hung, increased the possibilities of ambush, but Hendrick moved steadily ahead on his horse, hardly looking to left or right, and his braves trotted after him. When the militia halted to close their ranks more tightly, the Indians went on alone.

Dieskau was approaching down the same road. Notified by scouts of the English sally, he ordered his "Indians to throw themselves into the woods, to allow the enemy to pass, so as to attack them in the rear, whilst the Canadians took them on the flank, and I should wait for them in front with the regular troops."

The trap was set, and Hendrick rode into it followed by his warriors. But he had not gone very far when a warning shot was fired and a voice called out from a thicket to ask, in the Iroquois tongue, who went there?

Hendrick reined in with slow dignity, and then replied, "We are the Six Confederate Indian Nations, the heads and superiors of all Indian nations on the Continent of America."

Caughnawaga faces and torsos popped up from the leafy tangles, on both sides of the road, while, in the narrow clearing, the Iroquois gathered in a tight crowd behind their leader. Finally, a venerable spokesman gave voice: "We are the Seven Confederate Indian Nations of Canada, and we come in conjunction with our Father, the King of France's troops, to fight his enemies, the English, without the least intention to quarrel or trespass against any Indian nation. We therefore desire you will keep out of the way, lest we transgress, and involve ourselves in a war among ourselves."

Hendrick replied that the Six Nations had come to assist their brethren, the English, against the French who were encroaching on Indian lands in the Ohio. The Caughnawagas should join this worthy cause, or keep out of harm's way.

So the oratory rolled until a young Mohawk who was standing behind Hendrick committed one of the most tragic acts in the history of his nation: he fired at the Caughnawaga spokesman. Instantly, on both sides of the road the heads of the French Indians vanished. For a moment, crickets could be heard in midsummer silence, and then gunfire poured on the Iroquois, a packed target in the open road. Flight was attempted, but some forty Indians fell.

At the first musket crack, Hendrick had slipped from his horse; he fled with the other survivors. But, being old and heavy, "grayheaded as silver," he could not keep up. All alone, thrashing in the forest, conscious that he could not move fast enough to escape if he were seen or heard, he veered to the west, away from both armies, into wilds he assumed were empty of man.

It was a slow progress, but, as he fell over contemptible obstacles, rose bruised and scratched, certainly in his mind he ran as swiftly as of old, holding high the tomahawk of memory. He had seen London and the Queen and all the packed white faces; at a thousand council fires his voice had been the most eloquent; he had defeated his enemies with wiles and with war. How many scalps he had won with the sure hands and quick feet that now trembled and tripped and would not do his bidding!

His reveries were shattered by high voices: the old chief had strayed into an encampment where Caughnawaga women and children were awaiting the outcome of the battle. Boys too young for the warpath brandished miniature axes; others flexed toy bows and arrows. The great statesman was brought to earth, as the squaws applauded, by a whooping haggle of infants.

Johnson, after the bustle of battle had subsided, realized that his longtime mentor, coadjutator, and intimate was missing. Anxious days passed without news. Then the body was found lying where it had fallen. Warraghiyagey wept to see missing from his friend's hoary head only a tiny bit of skin, the size of a small coin, proof, disgraceful according to Indian tradition, that the warrior and diplomat who had shaken the world had been inexpertly scalped by squaws and children.

Hendrick, as Sir William Johnson knew him,
etched from an original drawing by T. Jeffreys during 1756
(*Courtesy of the New-York Historical Society, New York City*)

Fort Johnson, previously known as Mount Johnson,
drawn before 1759 by Sir William Johnson's nephew and son-in-law, Guy Johnso
(*Courtesy, New York Public Library*)

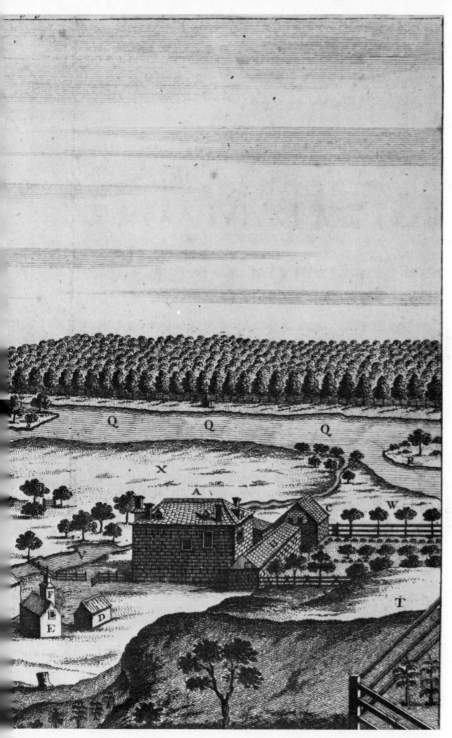

house, or Fort Johnson. B The wall and ramparts. C The block-house in the corner,
front, and barracks that flank the gate; the same on the other side. D Cooper's house.
bake-house. F A pigeon-house. G The mill. H An aqueduct from the mill-dams to
... I The Indian council-house. K Indian encampments. L A sheep-house; but now
a block-house built there. M A very large barn and stables. N Mount Johnson, very
...d steep. O The house where Sir William Johnson lived before. P The barn for ditto.
Mohawk river. R Part of an island opposite to the fort, 100 acres. S Thirteen smaller
...elonging to Sir William Johnson. T Another block-house, to defend the back of the
V A fine creek that runs by the fort into the river. W A garden. X Fine pastures.
Y Corn-fields. Z The road to Schenectady.

(*Courtesy, New York Public Library*)

Lord Loudoun, at whom Warrigahey and his army of Indians angrily threw their clothes when he cravenly refused to lead the British regulars he commanded to the rescue of Fort William Henry
(*Courtesy, New York Public Library*)

11

The Battle of Lake George

After the Iroquois who led the Bloody Morning Scout had dropped under Caughnawaga fire or vanished, the French Indians and the Canadians appeared in the woods around the colonial militia "a small distance" down the road. From his encampment, Johnson heard "heavy firing . . . which we judged was about three or four miles from us. We beat to arms, and got our men all in readiness."

The main army occupied a large, stump-filled clearing, their rear protected by the waters of Lake George. Since the alarm of the previous night, they had built across the front, more than a musket shot back from the tall forest, a breastwork of overturned wagons and felled trees. Now, while the stoutest of heart pulled in more branches, the rest ranged themselves nervously behind the barricade.

"The fire," Johnson wrote, "approached nearer, upon which I judged our people were retreating, and detached Lieutenant Cole with about 300 men to cover their retreat." The reinforcements advanced nervously through the woods, heard footsteps, raised their guns, saw in the gloaming their fellow Colonials running with Indians at their heels; the reinforcements lowered their guns and joined the flight. The forest road disgorged the fugitives into the clearing for a final anguished sprint. They clambered over the improvised ramparts "with all the marks of horror and fear in their countenances." This, Wraxall remembered, "infected the troops in our camp. . . . Our general harangued them and did all in his power to animate our people." He knew that if Dieskau attacked during such confusion, the army would be helpless.

Dieskau, too, realized his opportunity. The Colonials, he wrote in a hasty dispatch, were running "like a flock of sheep." Expecting, as he explained, to spend the night in Johnson's bed, he led his regulars at double-quick down the road.

Soon he came on his Indian allies milling around, while the Canadian militiamen stood on their arms and watched anxiously. The Abnakis had captured three Iroquois and were determined to roast them; the Caughnawagas, lachrymose over what had already happened, were determined to release their cousins. When the French commander in chief shouldered into the center of the argument, shouted that matters of roasting could wait, and ordered an immediate advance, the tribesmen turned unanimously on him. They stated that it was not Indian custom, after you had fought one battle, to fight another: they would rather go home with their scalps and spoils. The Canadians added that they preferred not to fight without Indians. Dieskau replied, so Claus was to be told, "The liquor is drawn: it must be drank." He ordered his regulars to advance—but the delay had given Johnson time to calm his troops.

Over their shield of boughs and wagon bottoms, the Colonials saw the road burrow like a pipe into the woods. From it flowed a stream of white-uniformed bodies that rippled on identically swinging black legs. The bodies wheeled until they stretched in three perfectly spaced straight lines across the far end of the clearing. Each line was fronted with "glittering" bayonets which "daunted" the Colonials. The front rank raised their muskets, aimed for a suspenseful moment, and then, as one musket, fired. The guns were lowered in unison; their possessors melted backward through the other two lines which were stepping forward; the new front rank lifted their guns, paused, and emitted in unison a blast of smoke and bullets.

Johnson was now so hoarse "with calling the troops and running along the lines" that he could not speak. But wherever he was, there were certain to be lemons for punch. He called for a lemon, sucked it and was able to shout again. Even more steadying to his troops were the voices of Eyre's cannon. Although the balls only cut branches above and behind the Frenchmen, the bellow and the power to reach that far were reassuring. The Colonials looked around and saw that, although impressive to eye and ear, the enemy's platoon firing "did not great execution, being," as Johnson wrote, "at too great a distance, and our men defended by the breastwork."

But Johnson exposed himself. As he slumped over, Wraxall "thought I saw the shot enter. I judged it to be near the small of his back, and feared 'twas mortal." Actually, Johnson had been shot in the hip. He pressed a hand to the wound, staggered to his feet, and tried to keep going, but Wraxall "found he grew stiff, and led him off to get him dressed." After receiving first aid, Johnson returned, at least for a time, to the breastwork. He was to boast that he had been "very active."

The French regulars advanced. As effectively as the stump-filled terrain would admit, they held their even lines, "until the warm and constant fire of our artillery and troops put them in disorder." From his command post in the rear, Dieskau saw most of his Indians squatted down in the woods as spectators, his Canadians "scattering right and left, firing Indian fashion." He hurried across the field to remonstrate. His marshal's uniform was now clearly visible to colonial sharpshooters; he was hit in the leg. While an aide was trying to stanch the wound, the same leg received two more shots. The aide called a pair of Canadians to carry the general away. They tried, but one fell dead on top of Dieskau—as the marshal wrote, "to my great embarrassment." The other Canadian fled. Ordering that his aide assume the command, Dieskau crawled to the woods and, with his back against a tree, achieved a sitting posture.

The French army was suffering for their lack of cannon, since the jerry-built breastwork withstood all the fire power they had. But the regular officers could not believe that anything so unconventional could be so effective, or that raw Colonials could really repulse their trained man-killers. They rallied their troops again and again; more and more white-clad bodies reddened in the clearing.

Some Canadians and a few overexcited Indians were maneuvering behind what cover they could find on the flanks. The rest became sated with the horrifying spectacle of musket-carrying men sacrificing themselves because sword-carrying men told them to. The forest men drifted off to scalp the casualties of the Bloody Morning Scout. In the meanwhile, the French regulars, having failed at the center, tried the left flank, and then, in desperation, shifted over to the right, "still keeping up their fire in other parts of the line, but not very strong." At the end of four and a half hours, the assault collapsed, "when," Johnson continued, "our men and the Indians jumped over the breastwork, pursued the enemy, slaughtered numbers, and took several prisoners."

In the panic, the French forgot their wounded commander who had gradually slumped to the ground. He opened his eyes to see a Colonial aiming at him from behind a tree. Dieskau motioned with his hands not to fire, but the man did so, the bullets passing through both his hips. Then the assailant jumped on him and cried, in good French, "Surrender!"

"You rascal," Dieskau remembers he replied. "Why did you fire at me? You see a man lying on the ground, bathed in his blood, and you fire, eh?"

"How did I know but you had a pistol? I prefer to kill the devil than that the devil kill me."

"You are a Frenchman, then?"

"Yes. It is more than ten years since I left Canada."

"Whereupon," Dieskau's account continues, "divers others fell on me and stripped me. I told them to carry me to their general, which they did."

Johnson was on his bed, a doctor probing his hip, when "an elderly gentleman" was helped in. The marshal, although bleeding from all his wounds, introduced himself with great dignity. Thus the frontier fighter learned the identity of his opponent, realized that he had defeated the French equivalent of Braddock, the enemy commander in chief, "an experienced commander, a man of high consideration in France." Rising from his bed with his wound half dressed, Warraghiyagey made Dieskau lie down and ordered the doctor to treat the prisoner first. The surgeon shook his head over Dieskau, fearing for the marshal's life, and then shook his head some more, expressing inability to remove the bullet from Johnson's hip, which had become "very painful."

Dieskau awoke from a feverish doze to see Johnson surrounded with Indians "who regarded me with a furious look and spoke to him a long time, and with much vehemence. When they had departed, I observed, 'Those fellows have been regarding me with a look not indicative of much compassion.'

"'Anything else but that!' he answered, 'for they wished to oblige me to deliver you into their hands, in order to burn you in revenge for the death of their comrades . . . and threaten to abandon me if I do not give you up. Feel no uneasiness. You are safe with me.'"

At which remark, the Indians all returned. To the anxiously watching Dieskau, the argument seemed "animated at first," but "became more moderate at the close, when, smiling, they took my hand in token of friendship, and retired."

Johnson hobbled out to the ramparts: prisoners had reported that a thousand more Frenchmen were on the way, this time with cannon. But the only force that appeared was a band of Colonials, who had been dispatched from Fort Lyman to help Johnson and had, on the way, driven the Canadians and Indians from the bodies they were scalping in the forest.

Thus ended what has gone down in history as the Battle of Lake George. The English casualties—160 killed, 103 wounded, 67 missing—were mostly suffered during the Bloody Morning Scout, and were probably slightly greater than the enemy's loss. However, the French had fled, leaving their commander in chief to be carried into a Colonial encampment that had withstood assault. The eager American public decided that this battle "wholly wiped out . . . the disgrace" of Braddock's defeat. It was indeed, a considerable victory. A large colonial army, unstrengthened by regulars and under local command (Eyre was the only English professional), had actually marched into the wilderness and stood up to a major French force, repulsing regulars and Canadians and Indians under trained command. Although the eighteenth century had half rolled away, nothing like this had happened in the eighteenth century, and for another three years of the desperate French and Indian War, the achievement was not to be repeated, as English armies consistently fled from the forests or surrendered there.

The silence after the shooting was soon broken in the Lake George camp by a great scratching of pens. Most letters expressed

admiration for Johnson's "firm steady mind during the action"—
the Massachusetts surgeon, Williams, called him "a second Marlborough"—but Lyman insisted that the second Marlborough was
named Lyman. General Johnson, he explained, had pusillanimously
nursed his wound in his tent, allowing the command of the army
to devolve on Lyman.

This contention became an article of faith for the New England
faction, and it has been enshrined in history by the great Francis
Parkman. Yet it deserves no more credence than the equally parti-
san statment of a Yorker that, as the battle raged, he had found
Lyman "behind a tree, lying on his belly with his face to the
ground." When the outraged Yorker cursed at the Connecticut
general, the "saint" lifted an ashen face to object that profanity
would draw bullets that way.

Johnson certainly was wounded early in the battle and retired
to his tent; it is equally certain that he emerged for at least a part
of the subsequent fighting. Continual presence on the line of battle
is not a necessity of command; and, in any case, the conclusive engagement at Lake George was not fought with guns, but, before
the shooting started, with belts of wampum. Due to Warraghiyagey's machinations, Dieskau had been kept without authentic
intelligence. The Caughnawagas had saved Fort Lyman by losing
the French army in the forest, and, when the fugitives from the
Bloody Scout had pelted into Johnson's camp, the Caughnawagas
had delayed Dieskau until the effect of panic had abated. The
French marshal blamed his defeat on the "treason" of his warriors.

In his own dispatches, Johnson did not dwell on forest politics;
he denied Dieskau's statement that France's Indian allies had taken
no part in the attack on the Lake George encampment. He knew
that English potentates, in their refusal to concede to the Indian
nations any sovereignty of their own, were only too inclined to
regard tribal politics as a tangle of betrayals, and "savage" armies
as too unstable to be worth employing. Warraghiyagey, so we
gather, did not wish to make any explanations that would encourage this distrust, particularly as he had to report the departure of
his own allies.

"We are all determined," the Iroquois told Johnson, "to return
to our several homes and families for the present, so farewell."

Now that war between Indians had been inaugurated, they were, he explained, afraid that their castles would be attacked. Furthermore, "they complain to me that they were sacrificed by the backwardness and flight of our people; and I fear, from the most impartial accounts, they had reason." And to top all, when they had so many dead to avenge, Warraghiyagey would not let them follow their ancient and to them honorable customs. Although Canadian priests and soldiers accepted the torturing of prisoners as a necessity of Indian warfare, Warraghiyagey had never brought himself to do so. After the Battle of Lake George, he had hurried the French off to Albany for safekeeping.*

The Mohawks had promised to return when the mourning for their casualties was over, but Warraghiyagey was soon notified that the other Iroquois nations had sent them a belt saying that "the English and French had a design to kill them all," and that, if the Mohawks continued in the war, "they would kick them from them." Hendrick was dead; Warraghiyagey could not desert his army to attend council fires. During the rest of the campaign, he rarely had with him more than a dozen Indians, and these "do not choose to go out on the scout and are of no service." To fill in the gap, Johnson recruited a band of frontier rangers, selecting as their leaders two rough young men who were thenceforth to loom large in American history: the New Hampshire counterfeiter, Robert Rogers, and the Connecticut backwoods plowman, Israel Putnam.

A cut in forest-clad mountains thirty-six miles long and up to a mile and a half wide, complicated with wooded islands and steep promontories embracing hidden bays, Lake George supplied ideal lists for the canoe-borne knight-errantry of Warraghiyagey's table round. When the French, as they sometimes did, paraded by in birch-bark might, the colonial rangers would hide behind islands or drift conspicuous, pretending to be fishermen. But, when smaller forces appeared, steering oars would churn to the maneuvering of navies of two or three canoes. Once Johnson gave Rogers two "wall pieces," tiny cannon which the major set up on the French

* Dieskau was nursed in Johnson's Albany house by Johnson's sister until the invalid could return to France, where he died in 1767 of the aftereffect of his wounds. "I cannot," the marshal had written, "too much acknowledge Mr. de Johnson's kindness to me."

shore: like a partridge feigning a broken wing, a fleeing canoe brought the enemy in range. There were also sudden confrontations on forest trails, that left green leaves a sticky red. As the French took a short step further into New York by building a fort at Ticonderoga, Rogers would watch fascinated by the hour, lying behind a log with, for camouflage, a bush held up in each hand. Such activities secured intelligence and kept the no-man's water neutral, but did not serve the object of Johnson's expedition: to drive the enemy from Ticonderoga and Crown Point.

Before an advance could be contemplated, it was necessary to transport from Fort Lyman—which Johnson now renamed Fort Edward "in honor of the second prince of the blood"—at least a week's backlog of provisions and enough bateaux to carry goods, men, and cannon down Lake George. However, the army lacked wagons and the horses were too weak to pull anything: efforts to impress from the Albanians what was needed merely encouraged them to "hide their wagons and drive away their horses." Despite Johnson's protests, the New England militia commanders darkened the crisis by writing home for reinforcements, who proved on their arrival "hungry guests," eating up the results of every improvement in supply. When Johnson finally ordered that the new levies be held at Albany, the legislatures that had sent the troops were furious.

All this played into Shirley's hands. That the governor's own slow-gathered expedition, stalled at Oswego by autumnal storms, would undoubtedly do no fighting only made him more eager to discredit his rival who had actually fought the French. In this labor, he was enthusiastically joined by the political commanders of Johnson's New England militia.* They asserted that the true hero of the Battle of Lake George was now pleading to advance, but General Johnson "pulled General Lyman back." Johnson brought this rumor, which he heard was being spread in his own camp, up at a council of war. Lyman voted with all the other officers that it was "false and groundless."

* Wraxall was adding fuel to a rising New England anger against Johnson by sending the official reports of the largely New England army only to the acting governor of New York, to be forwarded, at De Lancey's leisurely convenience, to Shirley and the other Yankee governors.

However, Shirley wrote the Secretary of State in London that, largely through New England's exertions, Johnson had been given an invincible army—yet, because he was so unenterprising, the outcome would "be dissatisfactory to all the Colonies of New England as well as myself." Snug in Boston, the Massachusetts General Court voted that Johnson should attack. Banyar warned him to do so: "You are sensible your own reputation is highly interested."

As the necessary materials for an advance amassed with an agonizing slowness, Johnson was, on October 1, "seized with an inflammation in my head which gave me inexpressible torment. I have been bled, blistered and purged which, with want of sleep and appetite, confines me in bed." At councils of war, Wraxall protected his absent chief by forcing the militia commanders into continual votes on whether the army should take the offensive. The decision was always no.

On October 29, Johnson was finally able to totter to a meeting. He agreed that the French forts could not be captured, but urged that the enemy's advance guard, which was stationed south of Ticonderoga, be destroyed in a sudden raid. This martial demonstration would "increase our influence and consequence" with the Indians and thus "probably prevent many scalping parties from disturbing our out settlements this ensuing winter." The vote continued to be no, and the New England officers continued to insist that the army's inactivity was Johnson's fault.

As a permanent contribution to colonial safety, Johnson wished to complete before winter came the forts that would seal off the two water routes into the colonies from Lake Champlain: Fort Edward on the upper Hudson, and Fort William Henry—Johnson had so named it after two more princes of the blood—on the hill overlooking the Lake George battlefield. The latter, which was further from New England, became a major source of controversy. The Council of Officers insisted that the scientific strongpoint Eyre had designed was too big—"most of the troops had an aversion to digging"—and resolved to drive some pickets into the ground. Johnson fumed until he got Eyre's plan approved, but, so he complained, General Lyman continued "a great enemy to this fort. . . . Says 'tis only beneficial to New York, will be disapproved by the other governments, who will not consent to garrison it, etc."

The Massachusetts carpenters preferred to build "huts and houses" for their own troops, and, indeed, to get anyone to work on either fort, General Johnson had to resort to a tactic with which he was completely unfamiliar: he had to plead.

In the "long, dull, and sickly encampment," the Connecticut troops threatened to go home because they lacked "sauce to their meat." When the New York and Massachusetts regiments clashed over payment for a glass of beer, the Yorkers, so wrote a captain from Belchertown, Mass., "come with swords and clubs, and come like hornets out of their nests, swearing and cursing! . . . If the devil and all he could raise had been let loose, it wouldn't look more dreadful." One New Englander was half-scalped, several on both sides wounded.

During the Revolution, Washington was to have similar difficulty in controlling the militia; and he echoed Johnson's diagnosis that the trouble lay in the election of officers by their men. Such officers, the frontiersman wrote, "must support their preeminence by unworthy condescensions and indulgences subversive to the order and very existence of an army." For his own part, Johnson continued, being "not bred to military life," he had ignored "the ceremonials and been only attentive to the essential parts of discipline"—yet he had been blocked at every turn. Courts martial were no stronger than "the fabric that occasioned them"; he had no way to enforce his authority. "The evil was too general to admit of a remedy," except the dissolution of the army and the creation of another more intelligently organized.

As Johnson struggled and got nowhere, Shirley reached the pinnacle of his ambition: early in November, he received an appointment to succeed Braddock as commander in chief. Although he had abandoned his Niagara campaign, he continued to criticize his rival for not advancing through a wilderness over which winter now frowned. Johnson, however, begged permission to "relinquish my military to attend to my Indian department." England's Indian alliances, he stated, had collapsed during his absence; it was "a critical juncture"—but Shirley "quite peremptorally" ordered him to stay with his army.

Still ailing, the acclaim of his successful battle shouted down, so it seemed, by the frustrations that had followed; warned by Banyar that Shirley was denouncing him as a cowardly general and trying to shoulder him out of Indian affairs, Johnson wrote from a frozen battlefield where he was immobilized with scheming officers and dissatisfied men, "I prefer the inward conviction of my own rectitude to every precarious salvo of applause. . . . From selfish and ambitious views, I make no court to any government, having no political schemes to carry, and resting my future on a private bottom—a lesson which mortifying experience had taught me." However, he could not resist writing the schemer Pownall that he would like to know "a little of the politics passing there now with you, for I am much in the dark here, and expect to be kept so by General Shirley and some others."

Once snow threatened to block the roads to their families, Shirley could no longer hold the homesick militia at Lake George. On December 2, Johnson was able to relinquish his command. Gladly he receded from his ranks of major and lieutenant general in the various colonial militias to the Indian colonelcy he had received from the Crown.

Shirley ordered him to come to New York for a discussion of Indian affairs, but Warraghiyagey went first to the Mohawk country to talk with the sachems. The terrible news had come that the Delawares and Shawnees were falling on the Pennsylvania settlements. He urged the Five Nations to send out belts telling them to stop. "What effect it will now have on them I can't pretend to say," he wrote Shirley, adding in implications that were all too clear that Indian affairs had been brought to this desperate juncture by Shirley's own misbehavior, first in interfering with Warraghiyagey's authority and then by keeping him at Lake George away from the council fires.

Since Braddock had given Johnson his Indian office in obedience to royal orders, Johnson assumed that his appointment came from the Crown, but Shirley reasoned that because the actual commission was signed by Braddock, he himself could, as the new commander in chief, remove Johnson and appoint a successor. He wrote the Secretary of State that he was thinking of "the noted Conrad Weiser," but when he consulted Secretary Peters of Pennsylvania, Weiser's long-time employer "laughed at the fancy" and warned that Shirley "must not risk matters with Colonel Johnson or with the Six Nations." Forced to the reluctant conclusion that his enemy was indispensible, Shirley finally sent Johnson a new commission, but on condition that he "follow my instructions." Johnson replied that he did not need Shirley's commission and would think about following his instructions.

Johnson's backers in New York City had urged him to come there for the personal interview Shirley desired; they would show the New Englander who was making his headquarters among them which general the sovereign Yorkers regarded as a hero! Finally, Johnson came. His sloop anchored six miles up the Hudson River to the cheers of "a considerable number of gentlemen" who had ridden out to escort him to the King's Arms Tavern where, so the New York *Mercury* continues, "most of the principle inhabitants" waited. Advancing down the streets, Johnson received "the acclamations of the people." Although the guns Shirley commanded at the royal fort were silent, merchant shipping paraded across the harbor under sail, firing salutes. "At night, the city was beautifully illuminated": candles quicksilvered in ordinary windows, and artists marked the occasion (and advertised their skills) by stretching across their window frames transparent paintings, lighted from behind, of such subjects as fame, in her classic nightshirt, crowning Warraghiyagey with laurels.

Shirley walked through the celebration with a smile and shrugging shoulders; he had a most unsatisfactory interview with a flushed and aggressive Johnson.* Having sent off appeals to Boston, he boarded a coasting schooner. He was more pleased than surprised to hear, as he entered his own harbor, guns saluting him from the fort and from a royal warship. The populace came out to cheer, for Shirley was as popular in New England as Johnson in New York.

---

* Having been assured by Pownall that Shirley would stop at nothing to damage him in England and intended to blame the failure of the Niagara campaign on lack of Indian support, Johnson conferred secretly at his lodgings with Pownall, Banyar, Wraxall, Claus, James De Lancey's brother Oliver, and John Watts of the New York Council on how best to arm Pownall, who was on his way to London, for the routing of Shirley. When Claus admitted that, at the height of the controversy, he had, without Johnson's knowledge, circulated a belt ordering the Iroquois to shun Shirley's expedition in favor of Johnson's, there was a great wracking of brains on how best to explain away the damaging wampum which Shirley was reputed actually to have in his possessions.

But local celebrations were toys in the battle for power compared to governmental reactions in England. As winter waves rolled, the few ships that braved the ocean moved slowly, yet in January, 1756, private letters brought to New York the rumor that Shirley was to be removed as commander in chief and that Johnson had been raised to a baronetcy.

When spring enhanced communications, it became clear that, as a Shirleyite wrote bitterly, Johnson's "mighty renoun" had "echoed through the Colonies, reverberated to Europe, and elevated a raw, inexperienced youth to a kind of second Marlboro." Despite Shirley's efforts to make it seem an inconclusive skirmish and to give what credit there was to Lyman, the English had hailed the Battle of Lake George as a great victory—"the only circumstance in our favor," as Horace Walpole wrote, "that had happened yet"—and Johnson was receiving all the credit. He had really been created America's second baronet.

An elaborate mezzotint was published in London showing the backswoodsman leaning in a tasteful mixture of armor and lace against a gilded cannon. This pleased conventional hero worshipers, but early romantics like Walpole preferred to envision a child of nature whose "extra-martinet success" would irritate the regular army. Warraghiyagey was referred to as "the heaven-taught general," and his fame, indeed, extended far beyond England. In Portugal, an enterprising publisher forged what he insisted was a first-person account of the Battle of Lake George by the victorious "Wilhelmo Gonson."

During March, Shirley was removed not only as commander in chief but also as Governor of Massachusetts; he was ordered to return to England as soon as his military successor arrived. (On his arrival there, he narrowly escaped being court-martialed for treason.) This was a most tragic downfall, for Shirley had been the soul of British preparedness in America during King George's War and again now; he had just sacrificed two sons to the British cause.

That Shirley's fortunes had received their mortal wound in his grapple with Johnson over Indian affairs puzzled politicians: How had a border-haunter managed to destroy the governor who had long been America's most powerful man? The Shirleyites refused to believe that the backswoodsman had been more than a ponderous, obtuse battering-ram manipulated by Wraxall at the orders of those sophisticated plotters, De Lancey and Pownall. The plotters themselves were worried: Even Pownall, who had secured for himself the Massachusetts governorship, found himself being "eclipsed by the new luster of General Johnson."

England had added to Sir William's baronetcy a gift of £5,000* as a reward for his achievements and to pay the governmental debts that still hung over from King George's War. Furthermore, he was sent a new Indian commission as "Colonel, Agent, and sole superintendent of the Six Nations and other Northern tribes," which stated specifically that, although he was to take orders and receive funds from the commander in chief, his appointment came directly from the Crown. No one in America had the power to discharge from his important office Sir William Johnson, Bart.

The backwoodsman's triumphs did not keep Banyar from sending frequent admonishments: "You must be sensible of the use of keeping up a good understanding with the leading men. You are fair in the saddle and must make it easy." But the only leading men Sir William bothered to propitiate wore bear's grease and feathers.

---

* Knowing that he could not resist spending any cash that he could easily control, Johnson left the gift with a banker in England who invested it in the funds.

12

Fortune My Foe

Early in 1756, as Johnson was walking the streets of Albany, the crack of a rifle was followed by a burning on his body. An incompetant militiaman had accidentally fired his gun, and the ball, so the New York *Mercury* reported, had passed up Johnson's sleeve and "grated the skin of his breast." Thus inauspicuously was heralded a tragic fighting season.

Time was demonstrating how right Johnson had been when, on undertaking the Indian superintendency, he had asked Braddock to relieve him of his military command. Forced to march away just as word of Braddock's defeat was moving through the wilderness, he had been prevented from trying to counter this blow to English prestige. While he was trapped at Lake George, the Ohio Indians had gone over to the French. Pennsylvania had felt herself safe, since between her frontiers and the Ohio Valley were the broad forests of her traditional friends, the Shawnees and the Delawares. However, these tribes were no longer friendly. Outraged over many land grabs—the Walking Purchase, the Wyoming and Ohio Valley deeds—they had joined with the Ohio Indians in raids that brought bullet, fire, ax, and scalping knife not only into Maryland and Virginia, but also into Pennsylvania where there were no stockades or defenses of any sort. Within sixty miles of Philadelphia, fat bubbled from the wounds in still-living settlers' bodies as the Indians roasted them over slow fires.

Warraghiyagey's Iroquois were crucially involved, for the Min-

161

goes, as the mixed tribes of the Ohio were called, were led by emigrant Iroquois. The Delawares were theoretically the League's subjects; and the Shawnees had refugeed from South Carolina onto Iroquois land. All the tribes fighting Pennsylvania were thus accountable to Onondaga; but they outnumbered the Five Nations. There was danger that they might force the Iroquois onto the French side.

When Governor Robert Hunter Morris of Pennsylvania urged that the League be persuaded to attack their fellow Indians in defense of Englishmen, Johnson could only mourn such dangerous ignorance in policy-makers. As Wraxall wrote, "Our Six Nations and their allies, at least the politicians amongst them, look upon the present disputes between the English and French . . . as a point of selfish ambition in us both. . . . Could the various nations of Indians form a confederacy equal to the attempt, there is reason to suppose they would unite and drive us and the French to a greater distance from their hunting grounds." Dreading the success of either, they wished the European powers "to continue destroying each other." That they regarded the English as the weaker would be, from the point of view of long-range policy, a reason for supporting them, but they were "too timorous" to outrage a people so "military, united, and active" as the French.

During February, 1756, at a full-dress council of the Iroquois sachems at his own fire, Warraghiyagey replaced six of the major casualties suffered at the Battle of Lake George by presenting the Indians with six Frenchmen captured there. ("If we want them again," he commented, he could ransom them back.) The gift was received "with the greatest marks of gratitude and satisfaction, every nation giving the shout of approbation." Did Warraghiyagey's own eyes mist as he delivered the quaking Gaul who was to replace "Tiyanoga, alias Hendrick"?

The chief sachem, Red Head, whom Johnson suspected of being pro-French, insisted that the Iroquois would not intervene to pacify the Delawares unless the English withdrew all troops from the frontiers even before the results of the mediation were known. This was of course inacceptable, but Warraghiyagey had another trump card to play. At his urging, the Crown had ordered Sir Charles Hardy, the new Governor of New York, to redress Iroquois grievances, to allow no surveys except "in the presence of the

Indians claiming a right to such lands," and to keep the more distant hunting grounds entirely free of settlement. On this basis the Sachems agreed to command the Shawnees and Delawares to stop their attacks on the frontiers from New Jersey to Virginia.

In Pennsylvania, a war party led by Benjamin Franklin was taking control from the pacific Quakers. Suspecting "that the Six Nations have privily encouraged these Indians to fall upon us," Franklin regarded "the application made through Sir William Johnson to these nations to procure us peace as the most unfortunate step we ever took." During the negotiation, Pennsylvania's hands would be tied while her people were being butchered. "In short," Franklin concluded, "I do not believe we shall ever have a firm peace with the Indians till we have well drubbed them all."

Equally opposed to Iroquois peacemaking, the French determined to alarm the Five Nations by a raid on the Mohawk Valley. At Montreal, 300 Canadians buckled on skates. They glided up the St. Lawrence to Oswegatchie, recruited some of the French Iroquois at that mission, changed to snowshoes and disappeared into the wilderness. News of the expedition reached Onondaga and was forwarded to Warraghiyagey. He galloped west along the river to German Flatts, where he was joined by 1,400 of his frontier militia. The Albany battalions refused to march.

No enemy appeared; all concluded that the alarm had been false. Johnson tried to comfort his white troops by stating that their alacrity had given "great satisfaction" to the Iroquois, and he urged the Iroquois to continue sending him warnings: "I shall be with you before they can, for I am light and my men ready always in a moment to follow me."

At another alarm a few days later, many militiamen expressed disbelief—Sir William could collect only 500—but the Indians flocked. This time, the enemy did strike. They descended on Fort Bull, a collection of storehouses surrounded with a palisade, at the carry from the Mohawk to Wood Creek on the way to Oswego. On their arrival there, Johnson's forces "found within the fort twenty-three soldiers, two women, and one bateaux-man; some burnt almost to ashes, others most inhumanly butchered, and all scalped. Without the fort, I found three soldiers scalped." The enemy had vanished.

As the early spring thaws raised the Mohawk, terrified runners reported that the French were gathering at Niagara a vast army of northern and western tribes that would capture Oswego and, if the Iroquois dared to interfere, "cut them all off the face of the earth." "I dread the consequences . . ." Johnson wrote. "So many Indians joining the French must stagger the Six Nations a good deal."

When the sachems who had, according to promise, gone to the Pennsylvania frontier* returned, they reported that the Delawares and Shawnees would change to the English side, but only if Warraghiyagey met them at Onondaga to "convince them of your desire to live with them in harmony and friendship." Close on the heels of this came word that Pennsylvania had betrayed Johnson's diplomacy. Declaring war on the Delawares, Shawnees, and Mingoes, Governor Morris had offered a bounty for Indian scalps. Any Indians who remained pro-English faced annihilation: They would be killed by the English if they stayed near the settlements, by the French if they fled westward. "How," Johnson asked, "shall I behave at the approaching meeting at Onondaga, not only to those Indians but to the Six Nations?"

And how would the Indians behave to Johnson, who seemed to have been lulling them while his fellow Englishmen prepared to strike? "For God's sake," warned a fur trader, "Don't expose yourself among the Indians!" And a Mohawk delegation urged him to stay home: "At this time, one don't know what place is safe. . . . If evil should befall you, the whole country will be open to our enemies," since only he was "active . . . ready to march on every alarm." They pointed out that, as "the bark now peals easily," the Indians who wished to see him could make canoes "and come down to you."

Although the French had sent raiders to harass English communications with Oswego and the westward forests,† and although Johnson no longer knew which Indians were his friends, he set out for Onondaga on June 3, 1756. A grenadier company and some

---

* Negotiations to stop raids from the Ohio Valley were conducted on the Pennsylvania frontier because the tribes that attacked as far south as Virginia were generally fitted out at Fort Duquesne, and, in any case, the Iroquois considered it a matter of prestige not to send their envoys chasing after unruly vassals far from the Long House.

† They were to fight an inconclusive battle at Wood Creek with a corps of bateau men under the command of Colonel John Bradstreet.

Mohawks were to protect the long, slow, clumsy line which included, as it bent through the forest, nineteen horses and so many oxen for beef that it took five men to drive them. Other Indians— perhaps allies, perhaps spies—appeared from the woods or wayside castles and joined the single-file procession. So large a party could not hope to slip along unnoticed; the oxen were belled lest they vanish in the underbrush. For ten days, the tinkling reverberated back from the tree-choked borders of the trail, and then they reached the outskirts of Onondaga.

A mile from the Castle, the party halted "to settle the formalities of the condolence agreeable to the ancient custom of the Six Nations": Red Head had died. "Then," the official record continues, "Sir William marched on at the head of the [visiting] sachems, singing the condoling song which contains the names, laws, and customs of their renowned ancestors, and praying to God that their deceased brother might be blessed with happines in his other state. . . . When they came within sight of the castle, the head sachems and warriors met Sir William . . . they having placed themselves in a half moon across the road, sitting in profound silence. There a halt was made about an hour, during which time the aforesaid sachems sung the condoling song. This being over, Rozinoghyata and several other councillors or sachems rose up and shook hands with Sir William and bid him and his company welcome to their town or castle.

"Then Sir William marched at the head of the warriors, the sachems falling into the rear and continued singing their condoling song. On entering the castle, Sir William was saluted by all the Indians firing their guns, which was returned by all the whites and Indians who attended Sir William. The sachems proceeded to a green bower adjoining to the deceased sachem's house, prepared on purpose, and, after they were seated, they sent for Sir William. When he came, they addressed themselves to him, wiped away their tears, cleaned the throats and opened the heart according to their customs."

The Delawares and Shawnees whom Johnson had come to meet were nowhere to be seen; many Seneca castles were unrepresented; and an Oneida repeated in open council a warning sent by Ohio Senecas that Warraghiyagey would "speak very fair to them . . . and make fine promises; would give them a handsome present, and at parting would drink their healths and treat them with a dram— but after they had drank it, it would throw them all into a sleep from which they would never awake."

For nineteen days, Warraghiyagey argued until he believed he had so far expelled "the French poison" that the Iroquois who were present would join a "vigorous" British attack. And the sachems finally agreed that the British might fortify the supply route to Oswego—but only on condition that, the instant the war was over, all military installations "be either demolished or put into the hands of the Six Nations."

On July 3, Johnson ended the congress with a grand distribution of presents. As rum ran free, as brave and sachem mounted to the delights of orgy, in marched a long-desired deputation of Susquehanna Delawares accompanied by some Shawnees. "There is a quantity of liquor," Johnson said, "which will prevent our doing business here." He invited them to Mount Johnson, and set out quickly lest they too get drunk.

According to the newspapers, his return journey was interrupted by three brief skirmishes with enemy Indians: If so, he preferred not to report the matter. His own record states only that he arrived home with the Shawnees and Delawares on July 7, "very much fatigued and in a bad state of health."*

A messenger soon brought a package he was expecting which combined parade, power, and magic. He held up in the light of the Council Fire a thick, beautifully lettered parchment bearing the seal of George II. Warraghiyagey and the interpreters labored to translate into both Iroquois and Delaware—the conference was bilingual—such phrases as "We also and do by these presents of us, our heirs and successors grant that the said William Johnson shall be named, appealed, called, plead, and be impleaded by the

---

* The Iroquois protection that enabled Johnson to accomplish this trip safely may have been one cause of a taunt Governor Vaudreuil addressed to Onondagas and Oneidas visiting him at Montreal: "None of your nation dare say a word to the English. Colonel Johnson's word makes all your villages tremble." The governor's complaints also reveal that the Iroquois had carried Warraghiyagey's anti-French belts to usually pro-French nations including the Montaguais (Canadian Algonquins), Ottawas, Chippewas, Potawatomis, Osages, Missisauguas, and Hurons.

name of William Johnson, Baronet, and that the style and addition of Baronet shall be put in the end of the name of the same William Johnson and of his said heirs male in all letters patent, commissions and writs and all other charters, deeds, and letters by virtue of these presents as a true, lawful, and necessary addition of dignity." Every time an interpreter paused for breath, a sachem or chief called out "Yo-hay" and the conclave "gave a loud and unanimous shout."

When the interpreters reached the end of this parchment, more verbose even than Indian oratory, everyone was very dry. "A tub of punch" was brought in. The new baronet "drank His Majesty's health and success to his arms, after which prosperity and harmony to the Six Nations and their allies." The tub was now available to all; cups and gourds dipped deep.

At the business sessions, the Pennsylvania Indians agreed to take the hatchet out of the heads of the English and sink it in the French. "My success in the treaty with the Shawnees and Delawares," Sir William wrote, "will be, I hope, of the most happy consequence to the tranquility of His Majesty's southern provinces." In his eagerness to keep Pennsylvania from pressing the Indian war which might drive all the tribes to the enemy, he exaggerated the importance of what had been achieved. Instead of specifying, as he usually did in his official reports, the number of Indians present, he used the grandiloquent phrase "Shawnee and Delaware Kings and their people." Yet there remain in the record indications that the conferees represented only a small scattering of villages.

The Pennsylvania Indians were, as a matter of fact, so disorganized that no central government existed with which anyone could treat. Thus Warraghiyagey needed to find some maneuver that, when rumored down the glades, would call individual nomads into the British interest. He decided to risk enraging the Iroquois by helping the Delawares toward their hearts' desire.

When he had urged the Five Nations to curb these dependents, he had been following established lines of forest diplomacy, yet he knew that the Delawares hated the ancient conquerors who still insisted that their braves were unworthy of the breechcloth of manhood. Here is the message the Iroquois sachems had sent them at

Johnson's request to demand a cease-fire: "Cousins the Delaware Indians: You will remember that you are our women. Our fore-fathers made you so, and put a pettycoat on you, and charged you to be true to us and lie with no other man. But of late you have suffered the string that tied your petticoat to be cut loose by the French and you lay with them and so became a common bawd, in which you did very wrong and deserved chastisement."

Since the Iroquois did not intend to beat up their bawd, this was not the right approach. The Delawares had replied sarcastic-ally that, if they were women, it was no wonder they were being seduced by the French. Indeed, one reason they were fighting the English was to demonstrate that they were men, able to hold land and declare war independently of the Iroquois.

In as audacious a political gesture as was ever made in any wilder-ness, Warraghiyagey took the petticoat of the Delawares: "I do, in the name of the Great King of England, your father, declare that henceforth you are to be considered as men by all your brethren, the English, and no longer as women, and I hope that your brethren of the Six Nations will take it into consideration, follow my example, and remove this invidious distinction—which I shall recommend to them." The Iroquois who were present—mostly Warraghiyagey's own Mohawks—made no public objection but said they could not commit the Council at Onondaga.

After the fire was "covered and an end put to all public busi-ness," Johnson sent out a flood of warnings that if the treaty of peace he had made was broken by unprovoked white attacks on the Delawares, it would "throw these affairs into a state of confusion from which I believe no person could extricate them."

To the south, all was confusion. New Jersey declared war on her border tribes at almost the exact moment when Pennsylvania de-clared a truce to start her own negotiations.

Although the Crown had appointed Sir William as the sole am-bassador to all the Indians involved, the Pennsylvanians had no intention of allowing their destinies to be determined by this out-sider. They felt themselves more capable to stop the fighting on their own borders, but they were faced with the same problem that had plagued Warraghiyagey: There was no central authority on those borders with whom to treat.

In their desperation, the Pennsylvanians escorted into history one of its weirdest figures. Born some fifty-six years before on the outskirts of Trenton, New Jersey, Teedyuscung had grown up as one of those "domesticated" Indians who had lost their forest birthright and lived by scrounging and cringing. He made brooms and baskets; tried to imbibe the white man's magic by being baptized a Moravian but proved too unstable for the Brotherhood; went at last to the forests, where he found what comfort he could in imbibing liquor. But now this Delaware proved the man of the hour because he had delusions of grandeur.

Out of the forest rolled Teedyuscung, followed by disciples and kinsmen, rumbling that he controlled ten nations, including the Delawares, Shawnees, Mingoes, and every Iroquois. Such a universal leader was so exactly what the Pennsylvanians needed that they pursued themselves into believing Teedyuscung's claims. The governor was delighted when the Indian stated shirtily that he was too influential to accept an invitation to Philadelphia: If the palefaces wished to talk to him, they coud come to the frontier. Much of the Pennsylvania government hurried to the border city of Easton, where Teedyuscung condescended to show himself. He proved "very large and portly . . . haughty and very desirous of respect and command"; and so doughty that he could drink a gallon of rum a day without getting very drunk.

Over this bibulous Indian, the ancient storm of Pennsylvania politics broke. The colony was not ruled directly by the Crown, but by "Proprietors," the Penn family, whose privileged position was under perpetual assault by the Quaker-dominated Assembly. The Quakers had a tradition of pacifism and friendship with the Indians that fitted nicely with their political interests: they opposed Western expansion which would damage their Philadelphia fur trade and, by bringing in alien populations, weaken their hegemony in the province. But the Proprietors wished to expand their colony both to increase their revenues and keep other colonies or the French from cutting in on the lands they coveted.

Thus the purchases to which the Indians objected had been made by representatives of the Proprietors and disapproved of by the Quaker party. The Assemblymen wanted Teedyuscung publicly to blame all Indian hostilities on these purchases, but the governor and his council, as appointees of the Penns, wanted nothing of the sort. They gave Teedyuscung a sensational banquet, and posted guards to keep the Quakers from talking to the great king. But the Quakers elbowed past the guards to make clear that their interests and those of the dispossessed Indians were the same.

In open council, Teedyuscung said that peace would depend on the return of stolen lands—but he was in too good a humor with himself and a world where important people considered him important to end on an unfriendly note. Although nothing much had been conceded, he promised to travel the forest and lead all the ten nations that bowed before him into the English camp. Then, having been plied with presents, he settled himself with a jug underneath a bough and meditated that the wilderness was a paradise enow. He was not so crazy as to get within ax range of the Iroquois.

As for Johnson, he was "very angry" at this violation of his exclusive authority. No sooner had he driven Shirley from the council fires than Pennsylvania trespassed in an even more disastrous manner.

By allowing the Delaware Teedyuscung to vaunt that he had bossed the Onondaga Council, the Pennsylvanians had killed what chance there had been of getting the Iroquois to soothe the Delawares by agreeing that they might exchange breechcloth for petticoat. Warraghiyagey was forced to drop that campaign as if it had turned into a rattlesnake. And nothing had been gained. Although Pennsylvania's selection of Teedyuscung as Delaware spokesman had made him a focus for tribesmen with complaints they wished to have shouted into the white man's ear, it did not raise his prestige so high that he could persuade any warriors not his immediate relations to desert the warpath. The fighting went on. Settlements that had a year before been considered far from the frontier discovered that a line of woodlots could be for marauders a quick and secret road.

An army was gathering in Albany that summer of 1756 to march on Ticonderoga and Crown Point. In recruiting warriors, Warraghiyagey received and armed at Mount Johnson Pennsylvanian braves who boasted openly of the British scalps they had recently lifted. Claus complained that "these stranger Indians" plagued him "continually for liquor, etc., with such imperiousness" that they did not behave like friends. But Warraghiyagey did not wish to seem suspicious of new-found allies.

When, in July, Lord Loudoun, Shirley's successor as commander in chief, made his belated arrival in Albany, Sir William rode down to meet him. Claus, who was left in charge on the Mohawk, sent a messenger galloping after his employer to report that an Iroquois had heard one Delaware say to another, "It would be nothing at all to scale the walls of this house and kill everybody in it without firing a gun." Then twenty-three stranger Indians had vanished "with their bundles"; they were rumored to be in the nearby woods awaiting a war band with whom they would "cut off your Honor's house. . . . I think we are really in a dangerous situation without any garrison among those savages."

Claus could hardly bear to think of the dovecote upstairs where Miss Nancy, her sister and governess, were tending their birds and reading their romances as if the world offered no dangers to purity.

In an autobiography so formal that he refers to himself as "Mr. Claus," he recorded that Sir William, on receiving his patent as baronet, had "desired Mr. Claus to ask of him anything whatsoever he had in his power to give. . . . Mr. Claus made a bow, thanking Sir William for the compliment. . . . His mind was so agitated and surprised upon the occasion that he retired to his room to sit down." Finally he rose, found his way to the ladies' garden, gestured behind the governess's back. Nancy colored and managed to come to him. However, she replied to his proposal that she was too young and that they were in the middle of a war "which was uncertain how it might turn out." She spoke of "a more convenient and quiet time."

With relief as well as disappointment, Claus had postponed speaking of his love to his fierce employer, but now that Shawnees and Delawares seemed about to storm his beloved's door, he could hardly resist patrolling there as if he had a right. If only Sir William would appreciate the crisis and come home!

Sir William had ridden to Albany with a certain jauntiness, for word had just come that England had declared war on France,*

---

* Thus England entered the Seven Years' War which was to decimate so much of Europe. That the conflict had started in America before it was declared abroad (and was to end here before it ended there) showed to how great an extent America was already a separate political entity.

making official the conflict that had started in the American forests. But his hopes that this would bring more effective conduct of the fighting with Canada were dashed when he saw the new commander in chief.

John Campbell, Fourth Earl of Loudoun, was a sandy-haired Scot whose surprisingly boyish face—he was forty-one—wore the cockiness of an unimaginative man placed by birth far along on a sure and unquestioned road to power. If the wilderness seemed different from a European battlefield, his Lordship could not help considering this an illusion, for he recognized only one kind of world, the kind he automatically controlled. Finding this commander in chief more worrisome than equivocal Delaware guests, Sir William argued and insinuated, and failed to rush home at Claus' call.

His eventual return did not end Claus' anxieties, for one dusk the murder shout sounded outside the gate. From the house where they were conferring with Warraghiyagey, from the sheds behind the house, from the arbors more than 500 braves rushed toward the messenger who announced that he had seen the head "stuck up on a pole." The Forty-fourth Regiment had, "this side of Schenectady . . . pursued and killed" an Iroquois.

"I never observed so sudden and violent a passion as they were worked into," wrote Johnson. "They foamed and gnashed their teeth." Gathering up their arms and goods, they marched angrily into the forest, whence shouts continued to freeze the quaking Claus.

Giving orders not to lock the gate, Warraghiyagey went to bed. The next morning, most of the Indians were back. Calling a council, he said that the murder had "undoubtedly been done by some drunken people." (Indians did not hold each other accountable for crimes committed in liquor.) He presented a scalp to take the place of the dead man and two other scalps, with a bundle of goods. An Onondaga spokesman responded, "We will pull up a large pine tree and bury under its roots this unhappy affair so that it may never give either of us any more uneasiness." However, the white atrocity prevented Johnson from sending a body of Indians to protect Oswego.

Then came the news he had dreaded ever since he had compre-

hended the politics and the geography of his wilderness: A French
and Indian army had sailed up Lake Ontario and was besieging
England's westernmost bastion, her only fort on the Great Lakes:
Oswego was under attack! Although suffering from "the bloody
flux" (dysentery) he climbed from his bed; he gathered 500 frontiersmen and 300 Indians; he tottered painfully on a horse to the
rescue. But at German Flatts he learned that Oswego had surrendered. The garrison were either dead or prisoners, the walls
were either burnt or battered down; the French had returned al·
most unscathed with much booty to their bases across the lake.

This catastrophe frighted the British army. Loudoun abandoned
all thought of attacking Ticonderoga. Major General Daniel Webb,
the commandant of the Mohawk-Oswego area, had shown his mettle
by sitting with a large body of regulars a day's march from the fort
while it fell unassisted. Now he found his legs: He led his troops
in a retreat down the Mohawk Valley, burning fortifications behind
him. Since Johnson did not join the flight, his personal settlement
was suddenly placed in a strategic position almost as great as that
occupied by the two scientific forts, Edward and William Henry,
which he had built to block the Lake Champlain route into the
Colonies. Johnson's mansion house was now the westernmost bastion of New York.

Since late in 1755, when Shirley had incorporated it into the
official defense system to impede a back-door invasion down the
Sacandaga River, Mount Johnson had been known as Fort Johnson, the name it still retains. But the more martial title could not
change the fact that it had been built in peacetime under a hill
which would make it indefensible if the French took advantage of
the fall of Oswego to transport cannon down the linked waterways
from Lake Ontario. Although a small blockhouse had been erected
on the overshadowing height, Sir William seems to have regarded
it only as a post for a lookout "who, upon seeing the enemy, is to
fire his piece and return to the fort." The all-obscuring woods
were so close that there would hardly be time.

At the warning shot, everyone was to dash from the other houses,
Indian sheds, and mills to the residence. French intelligence had
carefully examined that structure, and reported that two blockhouses formed with the façade a yard completed on the river side

by "a heavy swing gate well ironed." Pressed against the west wall, a one-story covered way protruded backward so far that fire from its portholes could enfilade the rear wall. All the other walls could be similarly protected by crossfire from one of the blockhouses. Most windows were either bricked up or reduced to loopholes.

To the lieutenant of a small group of regulars assigned to him, Johnson wrote, "The bastions to be properly manned, the curtains [connections between the bastions] also, there mixing some of my people with yours. The remainder of my people to man the dwelling house, and fight from thence, making use of the four wall pieces and musquetoons [blunderbusses] out of the window fitted for them.

"Whenever an alarm is given by the advanced sentry, you will order three patereroes [small cannon that shot broken iron] to be immediately fired, that being the signal I have given the Mohawks; and on their approach near the fort, when challenged, they are to answer 'George' as distinct as they can; then to be admitted if practicable.

"When there are no Indians here, the gates to be locked at eight o'clock in the evening and opened at six in the morning, first looking around to see that all is safe and clear."

For defense against an army without cannon, these measures would undoubtedly serve, and thus Indian raiders could only hope to collect by stealth or treachery the baronet's dark scalp for which the Canadian authorities were offering large sums. Warraghiyagey was told that shrewd warriors had, by presenting fraudulently labeled hair, twice collected the money. The third time?

From Canajoharie came a strangely spelled warning: "There is a leven franch Indeins in the woods about Your hous wich has a mind to take Your honour or to Schulp Your honour." One Anthony—"hee has a Peace out of his nose"—was to invite Warraghiyagey for a walk and lead him to the others. Johnson replied that he hoped he might see the assassin "squarely." Whether nick-nosed Anthony ever appeared is not stated in Johnson's dispatches which are most reticent about personal dangers.

Concerning dangers to the British cause, the prose he wrote with Wraxall's assistance flowed in a never-ending stream. Oswego had been "esteemed by the Six Nations, whenever they joined our arms, as a secure cover to them and their habitations," but now "they were open to the resentment of the French" who might at any time "fall upon their towns and cut them and their families to pieces." And, to make matters worse, Johnson's boast to the Iroquois that the Crown had ordered the redress of their land grievances had boomeranged. New York's Governor Hardy had merely handed the orders to the Assembly, which had merely expressed resentment against Sir William for initiating such foolishness. The old frauds went merrily on.

One month before Oswego was burned, Governor Vaudreuil had pleaded with the Iroquois: "Children, continue not to fear Colonel Johnson; but do not listen to his evil councils; labor only at good business; you will always be quiet on your mats." Now his interpreter boasted and threatened: "How many times have the English not told you that, compared with their power, the French were no better than ciphers? The Master of Life permitted me to pull down their pride; He wished to humble them and make them acknowledge that the French will be always victors." If the Iroquois allowed the English to re-establish even the tiniest post at Oswego or anywhere in the vicinity of Lake Ontario, the French would attack. "You can no more beseech me as formerly not to stain those lands with blood. I will not listen to you."

During the winter of 1756-57, Iroquois chiefs exchanged in Canada the medal Warraghiyagey had given them for new ones bearing the insignia of France.

13

Leave Hope Behind

The freezing weather made Lake George a dazzling superhighway down which the French walked to Fort William Henry. When Warraghiyagey heard the news, he tried to raise Indians, but not a single brave at the Lower Mohawk Castle dared carry the war belt to the Upper. For the sixty warriors in his sheds, Warraghiyagey staged a war dance; he sang his own song and then asked if they would "go with their brother." The Indians answered ominously that they "would go and see what would become of him." But his frontier militia turned out, 1,200 strong. Four days' march brought them to Fort Edward, where they learned that the French had abandoned the attack.

He was still at Fort Edward when an Oneida reported that German Flatts, the Palatine village up the Mohawk from Fort Johnson, was about to be invaded; he rode fifty miles through the wilderness in one night. Finding that the enemy had not appeared, he improvised a fort by stockading the wooden church, and connecting it by a deep trench with an existing blockhouse, which he strengthened with a ditch and covered way. The resulting dumbbell-shaped enclosure was large enough to hold all the inhabitants and their cattle.

Alarm came after alarm; cattle were herded in and out. As spring softened the ground for plowing, Sir William's militiamen had continually to drop their plows and dash for the menaced village.

However, the German settlers finally paid no attention when the bell of their fortified church cried havoc, and they expressed resentment at feeding the garrison Johnson left to protect them. Rumors were rife that, having no reason to love the English, they had employed Iroquois ambassadors to make their secret peace with Canada. (Vaudreuil was, indeed, discussing at Indian conferences the possibility of winning the Palatines to the French side.) Johnson concluded that his old friends, although not actually engaged in treason, believed that the French would spare them unless the presence of Englishmen drew scalping parties that way.

Of this, Sir William was himself far from sure. He continued to lead out his militia to German Flatts at every alarm, swimming sometimes with his gun held high through Mohawk tributaries wild with spring freshet. He began to hope that the French would actually attack, so that his frontier followers would no longer be "harassed so up and down . . . in the worst weather."

"I thank God," Wraxall wrote him, "the pain in your breast is removed. I hope your cough will soon follow. As to the rest, you deserve the scourge,* and I won't say I pity you." Yet, however much he suffered, Johnson was able to leap into action at every alarm.

In May, 1757, Lord Loudoun, not anxious to get the bare knees under his Scotch kilts scratched in the underbrush, sailed off to attack the ocean fortress of Louisburg. Since he left behind only enough troops to garrison Forts Edward and William Henry, there was no hope that England's vanished prestige with the Indians would be restored that summer by any forest offensive or even an attempt to rebuild Oswego.

Onondaga being naked to French attack, only the representatives of the increasingly pro-French upper nations—Senecas, Cayugas, and Onondagas—dared attend the spring session of the Council that ruled the League. They obeyed French promptings by declaring neutrality. The Oneidas and their Tuscarora wards were, Johnson wrote, too terrorized to oppose this decision or weaken the manpower in their menaced castles by sending braves on expeditions. Warraghiyagey could only hope to enlist in the British

* Johnson was later to write that the Indians had a specific of great efficacy in curing syphilis.

cause the Mohawks whom he himself protected from Fort Johnson and a few personal friends from other nations who found refuge in his sheds. To call out even these involved what he had so long wished to avoid—he would be flying in the face of a decision of the Onondaga Council—yet desperate situations called for desperate measures.

Again, as in King George's War, he sent against the Canadian frontier raiding parties of "Christians and Indians." In that earlier conflict, he had written jubilantly of making "the French smart by taking, scalping, and burning them in their settlements." Now his letters contain no gloating over carnage.* He no longer envisioned fighting with a young man's enthusiasm, but felt soberly its tragic overtones.

This war, however, was much bloodier than the old, particularly for the colonials. The stockades that had been driven into the earth from Georgia to New England could halt French scalping parties no more than widely separated rocks can dam a flood: The Indians flowed around all fortifications. Anxiety was for the colonials a perpetual companion wherever trees stood close and tall. Each time a man went out to hunt necessary food, he exchanged with his family what might be their last farewells. To the wife and children straining their ears from cabin or cornfield, a shot in the forest might mean venison or their protector's last breath. And for the hunter the trail home was a nightmare of suspense. "It is really very shocking," a frontiersman wrote, "for the husband to see the wife of his bosom her head cut off, and the children's blood drunk like water by these bloody and cruel savages."

At best hostile to the aborigines whose land they coveted, the frontiersmen were swept by a mighty hatred for every individual with Indian blood. When any red body, old or young, armed or defenseless, male or female, could be glimpsed through the sights of a white man's gun, the trigger was angrily pressed down. Even in his Mohawk Valley, Sir William had difficulty protecting the sachems and friendly warriors who came to and from his council fire.

* He had ceased offering bounties for scalps and prisoners, but this may have been because he had been forced to follow Shirley's more expensive precedent of paying salaries rather than offering rewards.

Nichus, one of the few remaining Oneida sachems in the English cause, led a war party from Fort Johnson early in July, but returned almost at once, not in war paint but wearing the costume of honor Warraghiyagey had given him. Piece by piece, Nichus stripped off the finery, and, when he was completely naked, he tore into shreds "a testimonial of brotherly regard for the English" which he had from Sir William four years before. His exposed body electric with rage, Nichus declared his hatred for the English and his determination to secure revenge. Two of his party, one the sachem's own brother, had been murdered as they passed through German Flatts.

After two days of argument with the naked Indian, Warraghiyagey secured a partial reconciliation; although Nichus would not pick up his own clothes, he allowed his mother to do so. Then Sir William carried his apologies to Canajoharie, where he promised that the murderer would be punished, and clothed 247 Indians "great and small." During his absence, Fort Johnson was besieged at dusk. After several shots were exchanged and some cannon fired, the enemy disappeared.

Montcalm was soon crowing that Oswegatchies and Iroquois had attacked a house near Fort Johnson, killed four men and made eight prisoners. And French intelligence from Fort Niagara reported that wandering Iroquois had repeated a forest rumor that explained English inaction in terms of Indian experience: Warraghiyagey, the great war chief, had taken to the bottle; he lay on his mat, thinking of nothing but drink. If he did not sober up by the end of the year, so the informants continued, the Five Nations would kill him and join the French.

To help matters along, the Joncaires told the Senecas that the Cherokees, Chickasaws, and Catawbas were signing agreements with the French governor of Florida, and would, unless the Iroquois joined the anti-English crusade, come up from the south to squeeze the Long House between their armies and those of Canada's Indian allies.

The southern Indians were the responsibility of Edmond Atkin, a sometime Charleston merchant who had seen in Sir William's appointment as ambassador to the northern nations a chance to obtain a similar embassy to the nations further south. By pulling strings in London, he had secured the post in May, 1756, but with

less authority than Johnson's, for he was to share his jurisdiction
with the various governors. Thus was created the southern Indian
department which continued for the rest of Sir William's career
to exist but be less powerful than his own.

On reaching America, Atkin hurried not to his Indian charges
but to Fort Johnson. Warraghiyagey told him that the Iroquois,
weakened by the falling off of their old allies and dependents,
would welcome "an alliance with the southern nations, although
too haughty to acknowledge it or take any direct steps themselves."
Sir William persuaded such Iroquois as he could still lure to his
council fire to agree that, if Atkin brought southern ambassadors
to Fort Johnson, they would confer with them.

In Pennsylvania, the fighting went on unchecked. Teedyuscung,
under the prompting of his Quaker friends, had now publicly
blamed the hostilities on Delaware resentment against the Proprietors for stealing their lands almost twenty years before in the
notorious Walking Purchase. This charge served the Quakers'
political wish to discredit the Proprietors and undoubtedly contained much truth, but it could only prolong the war for no practical way existed to accede to Teedyuscung's demand that the territory be returned to the Indians. It had been extensively settled in
good faith by freeholders whom no power could remove, and the
Iroquois, who had endorsed the purchase, would be angry if the
English now declared it illegal.

Although not consulted by Pennsylvania, Sir William drew up
his own plan for ending the war. He pointed out that the Ohio
land which the Penns had bought from the Iroquois at the Albany
Conference of 1754 had not been divided into small white claims
and could thus be renounced with a single stroke of the pen. The
Iroquois now regretted selling, and the nations who used the land
as their hunting ground—the Mingoes, Delawares, and Shawnees—
would be enchanted to have it released. To the Board of Trade,
Johnson urged that the Penns return their Ohio purchase. "I know
this land was fairly and publicly paid for, and that the Indians are
unjust and unreasonable to recant and keep the money, but if time
and policy require it, to yield will be more advantageous than to
contest."

The Penns bridled but realized in the end that Sir William had pointed a way out of their difficulties. They empowered him to take "such measures as you shall judge most expedient" to give the Indians "full satisfaction with regard to their hunting grounds" on the Ohio. With this authority in hand, Sir William invited Teedyuscung to join him and the Iroquois at Fort Johnson for a settling of all grievances. The Proprietary party in Pennsylvania, which was thenceforth to be Sir William's strong supporter, urged Teedyuscung to go, but the Quakers could not bring themselves to do so lest the Proprietors get the credit for ending the war. They played on the fears of the grandiloquent Delaware that he would be regarded by the sachems at Fort Johnson as "a very inconsiderable person" and signed with him their own treaty of peace, which failed to quiet the Pennsylvania frontier.

In the absence of Loudoun, who was still threatening Louisburg with most of the English regulars, Dieskau's successor as French commander in chief, the Marquis de Montcalm, came down Lake George with 6,000 troops and 1,600 Indians. They besieged Fort William Henry. The garrison of 2,100 called to General Webb, who was at Fort Edward with 3,432 effectives. Webb sent on the call. Sir William arrived in five days with 1,500 soldiers and 180 Indians, to hear the guns of the siege still roaring fourteen miles away.

This was the occasion when Warraghiyagey invaded Webb's chambers at the head of the Indians, demanded an advance to the battlefield where he had himself triumphed, and, when refused, led his band in imitating the gesture of the Oneida Nichus: they stripped and threw their clothes at the British commander's feet. Although reinforcements were pouring in from all the neighboring colonies, Webb considered it more politic to advise the commandant at William Henry to surrender. "The loss of the fort affected me a great deal," Johnson wrote, "as I was the first beginner and founder of it.

Montcalm had promised the garrison a safe conduct to Fort Edward, but neither he nor his subordinates were able to achieve what Warraghiyagey had achieved on the same battlefield and without making any promise. Not one of Johnson's prisoners had been maltreated by the Indians after the Battle of Lake George. However, Fort William Henry had hardly capitulated before

Montcalm's Indian allies broke into a hospital and murdered some English sick in their beds. "I saw one of the barbarians," wrote a Jesuit, "come out of the casements with a human head in his hand, from which the blood ran in streams, and which he paraded as if he had got the finest prize in the world."

When, the next morning, the garrison emerged from their fortified camp, the Indians fell on them, tearing off their clothes, and then, as a war whoop suddenly cut the air, attacking the New Hampshire men at the rear of the column. The interpreters and Indian officers were either helpless or unwilling to help; Montcalm's plea, "Kill me, but spare the English who are under my protection" was more histrionic than effective. Before order could be restored, some forty prisoners had been killed and many hundreds wounded, plundered, or carried off into the forests.

When bloody survivors staggered into Fort Edward, the militia demanded to be led to the revenge. Webb refused. Most of the militia rioted, threatened to kill any officers who intervened, and went home.

Alone among the New York troops—as even De Lancey admitted—Colonel Johnson's regiment did not mutiny. However, the spectacle of white irresponsibility was too much for Warraghiyagey's Indians. They stole horses, galloped back to Fort Johnson, turned the horses loose in Warraghiyagey's "fields of oats, corn, peas, etc.," and did much damage to the rest of his plantation. On his return, he flew into a towering rage, threatening to throw off his "friendship and regard" for the Indians.

This elicited abject apology, at least from the Mohawks, but did not change the pitiful plight of Anglo-Colonial arms, which was further emphasized by the appearance of many French scalping parties in the Valley, and by the destruction in November, when Johnson was too sick to march, of German Flatts. The inhabitants had been warned by an Oneida, but they had "laughed at me, and, slapping their hands on their buttocks, said they did not value the enemy." Eight bodies were found; 114 men, women, and children had disappeared, their arms tied behind them, into the forest.

Suffering from "pleurisy and violent stitches," Johnson could not for seven weeks even turn in bed. When he was able to sit up, he learned that the inhabitants of the Valley had "sent away all their effects or moveables and were ready to follow." Sir William summoned them in squads to his bedside. He pretended to have legal power to prosecute them if they tried to leave, and assured them that troops were on the way to garrison the Valley.

But Loudoun, who had failed to get within firing distance of Louisburg and was back at New York City in a foul temper, sent to the Mohawk not troops but threats against the Indians. If the Iroquois did not forthwith declare war on France, he would "treat them in the same manner as I do my Master's other enemies." The Mohawks, wrote the officer who always showed his vanishing backside to the French, were under his fist; the Oneidas and Tuscaroras "not so far removed from us but we can come at them likewise; nor do I think the Onondagas out of my power neither." Major General James Abercromby, Loudoun's second in command who was soon to succeed him as commander in chief, added that the Indians should be excluded from forts in their castles which Warraghiyagey had secured their permission to build for their own protection.

To those in authority on both sides of the ocean, Sir William was passionate in defense of the Indians. Although they did upon occasion make impertinent demands, the fact was that they had been most unjustly defrauded of hunting grounds. They had been implored to join the English and then left to the ravages of the enemy. Their nationals were being murdered by settlers. Since they were not "principles in the present war," their decision not to commit suicide in the English interest "is as natural as it is just." Criticisms were based on "prejudice and resentment."

The best way of winning the Indian nations to the English cause, Warraghiyagey continued, would be to authorize "a proper authority" to make a formal treaty guaranteeing that, if the tribes drove out the French, the English would make no settlements beyond a specified frontier. But Johnson felt that "this plan would be so mortifying to the great patentees and to the pestilential thirst for land so epidemic through all the provinces that I imagine it would occasion too general an opposition to be brought about." Military action against the French effective enough to impress the Indians seemed the only hope, and that possibility seemed as distant as the moon.

"Under the present situation of Indian affairs," Warraghiyagey admitted, "I can think of no measure to increase our Indian interest. To keep the little we have steady is all I can expect to do." If hostilities were undertaken against the Iroquois or if he were prevented from arming Indians he considered friendly, he would resign as "Colonel, Agent, and Sole Superintendent."

The winter of 1757-58 was for Johnson a frozen time of danger and sickness when all seemed lost. As, after the first heavy snow, he ordered his horses turned loose till spring should open the trails to their narrow feet, he said good-bye to them in his heart. To the few Indians who were still his faithful friends, he gave testimonials of their "fidelity and attachment," so that, should the English eventually triumph, they could receive credit "even after my death. . . . The life of man," he commented, "is very uncertain, and mine very much so at present."

Although he sent the official Indian records to Albany for safekeeping, he was less afraid of enemy action than of his own body. Ever since the wound and rigors of the Lake George campaign, illness had followed illness; his body had ceased to be an eager servant rising powerfully to meet his every demand. Increasingly it became his master, defeating his will with debility and anguish. He believed that, even if he lived through the winter, he would never again "be able to endure much fatigue."

14

Haven Past Hope

According to Valley legend, Johnson was trying to bolster morale on his frontier with a militia muster when a royal officer cavorted up on a highbred steed. From a clump of trees, a beautiful Indian maiden was drawn to the beautiful horse. She touched the gleaming flanks, fingered the silver bridle, and then with one light, graceful movement leaped from the ground and landed behind the officer, astride on the horse's bare back. He winked at the watchers; he made his mount gallop, turn short, rear, and leap. The girl's comely legs tightened, but she sat upright, her hands relaxed at her sides, her black hair streaming, a banner of youth and joy. The backwoodsmen flocked to admire, and the great Sir William helped the Mohawk maiden dismount. She told him her name was Molly Brant. He took her home that night and kept her as his love till death did them part.

Probably this account of Johnson's recognition of his greatest adoration is correct only in its mood of wonder. He had led Molly Brant's brother Joseph on the warpath; he had collaborated with the sachem, her father; she could not have captured his heart suddenly, as a dazzling stranger. Nor was the woman who came to him when he was sick and broken, who lifted him when he believed he was dying amid the wreck of all his hopes, an innocent child.

The major passion of Sir William Johnson's life was, of course, "handsome," "possessed of an uncommonly agreeable person," but at twenty-one or twenty-two, a ripe age among the short-lived Indians, she had seen much of her forest world, had sat at many a council fire. She was, a friend wrote, a "sensible, judicious, and political young lady of the royal blood of the Mohawks." Frontiersmen who did not like Indians came to think of her as a witch.

Since their first child was born in September, 1759, Molly's Indian marriage with Johnson probably began in 1757 or 1758. We can imagine that their love blossomed when, in that desperate time, Warraghiyagey conferred with one of the few sachems who remained friendly to the English, Nichus Brant (Aroghyiadecker). Nichus' daughter Molly (Degonwadonti) would sit quietly by until her mind's passion overcame her reticence and she interrupted with a fire that charmed and a good sense that solved the problem. As the months passed, Nichus became superfluous at the discussions, and otherwise in the way.

Molly's dark Indian eyes disguised fierce passions. She hated with violence—once she demanded the head of an enemy so she could kick it around the room—and, as a mutual friend wrote, "she loved Sir William to adoration."

Molly's move from Canajoharie Castle to Fort Johnson was not the conquest of an Indian woman by white lust or white ways: she brought with her great worldly position of her own. Her grandfather Brant (Sagayeeanquarashtow) had, like Hendrick, been one of the "Four Indian Kings" who had visited Queen Anne in London; her father was a leading sachem of the Upper Mohawk Castle. In her mother's line, down which hereditary Iroquois offices of necessity came, her blood must have been equally exalted, since she was to claim the title "elder sister of the Mohawk nation." True, she was not married to Warraghiyagey according to the white man's rites—but what did those rites mean to her? According to Iroquois ritual she was married.

Molly Brant built her fire now in a glazed room under a chimney, yet it was a true Indian fire, and for this the baronet had every reason to be grateful. He must have shuddered sometimes to think how different his life would have been had he brought home a white lady suited to his white station. Nurtured in forest freedoms, his Mohawk bride loved him without possessiveness. She did not object to his cluttering up the parlor with stuffed fish or riotous drinking companions. Nor did she deign to notice the pretty squaws or farmers' daughters with whom he sometimes dallied away idle hours. She kept her own space, her own secrets, her own integrity.

In Degonwadonti's chamber, Warraghiyagey spoke Mohawk; in Sir William's parlor, Molly Brant wore her Indian clothes. He was glad to lie at her side almost completely transmuted into an Iroquois brave.

Among Molly's many attainments was a skill at forest medicine that was to cure royal governors and pique the inquiries of the naturalists and physicians of the white world. She dosed Warraghiyagey's old wound with simples gathered at moon-dusk; and whether it was the virtue of the herbs or the love with which they were administered, he felt his corporeal winter melting in an almost unbelievable new spring. He found the strength to deal with the cataclysms of what seemed a hopeless cause.

Arming his servants for the rescue when isolated cabins went up in flames or strange shots sounded in the woods; calling for help from the Albany militia because his own frontier had emptied out; trying to enlist white rangers to take the place of his vanished Iroquois allies; receiving, with Molly by his side, the few Indians who now visited his council fire (there was gloom in the sheds that had once glowed with barbaric finery), Sir William seemed to be a stubborn captain refusing to leave a sinking ship, yet he was serving the English-speaking peoples as never before.

After the destruction of German Flatts, Vaudreuil had crowed that he had "disposed the Five Nations to attack" the Colonials, and the English high command yearned to consummate this enemy objective by attacking the Five Nations. But Warraghiyagey still loomed large enough in the wilderness—the Maréchal de Lévis considered him now the only Englishman "who has any influence with the savages"—to keep the Iroquois from agreeing on a pro-French policy; and the English generals, remembering how Sir William had helped unseat a previous commander in chief, hesitated in their aggressions against his Indian charges. Thus was won what had been in so many wars the first essential of British victory: time for the colossus to pull itself together.

The British navy had come to life and was dusting the Atlantic free of French ships. The Canadians, their own wheat crop a failure, were eating the horses they had hoped to ride in the next campaign. And no Indian goods were coming in from across the ocean.

The Canadians found themselves with nothing to barter for pelts. Western Indian nations—"naked mostly"—appealed to the Iroquois to resume their ancient activity as middlemen for the English fur trade. Gleefully, Warraghiyagey ordered his deputy, Croghan, to impress the traders with the importance of handing on to the Indians the high prices which the long-extended shortage of furs had created in the English market. A blanket that had, before the hostilities, cost a hunter three pounds of beaver, could now be sold for two.

The Canadians were as hampered in giving as in trading, and thus Johnson found himself miraculously possessed of an advantage which even in his most successful years he had never enjoyed: He could outbid his enemies for Indian favor.

Warraghiyagey's accounts of various dates reveal how he used gifts to make friends. There were parties: To entertain "the whole castle of Canajoharie" he supplied an ox, many gallons of rum and a barrel of beer. There were acts of piety: "six gallons rum to bury two women who died in the Mohawk's castle in one night." Charity was always needed, either wholesale—he clothed entire tribes—or retail—"a blanket, shirt, stockings, kettle, salt, and cash to a poor widow, mother of a young man who was killed in Canada by the French." Leading Indians were propitiated in groups —he had hats trimmed with lace a hundred at a time and bought dozens of red boxes to hold crowns—or singly: "To Hendrick's son, a banyan . . . some silver work as breast buckles, etc." Guns, axes and knives were mended; ribbons supplied to brighten braves' hair; and horses lent to help squaws with their plowing. Seed "for sweeter corn than they ever had" made furrows speak with an English tongue, and the inoculations of papooses against smallpox —fifty-four, for instance, at one time—frustrated witches and death himself.

As Warraghiyagey supplied and entertained and amused and handed out new-minted gold medals, the French medals contrite warriors delivered to him mounted to a substantial pile—yet there were grave indications that the English interest had sunk too far in the wilderness to be regained in time to save the cause.

Warraghiyagey, who had often summoned the Iroquois sachems to his own council fire, could not in that spring of 1758 even secure firm invitation to the annual Congress at Onondaga. It would be a most momentous meeting, for representatives of all the League's "former alliances and connections" had been invited. The intention was to create an Indian federation so strong that it could dictate the future; enforce neutrality on the forests; or, should the nations conclude to back either side, ensure a speedy victory. Warraghiyagey wrote Abercromby, who was now commander in chief, that, until the Congress broke up, "I look upon His Majesty's Indian interest to be in a state of suspense."

Since he believed there was a good chance that the Indians would declare for the English—and also a possibility that they would join the French; when so much depended on the tipping of so delicate a balance, he had thrust from him the despair-dictated policy of the previous summer, when he had risked offending the Onondaga Council by recruiting, without their approval, his personal Indian friends. But for once English military activity moved with embarrassing speed.

Revivified under the brilliant war minister William Pitt, the British government had poured troops into America, financed large militia levies, and ordered Abercromby to advance via Lake George to Ticonderoga. The obese British regular demanded that Colonel Johnson join him instantaneously with an Indian horde, and was given what he considered a lot of double talk about delaying while some ridiculous forest conference was going on—as though savages had politics or His Majesty's dependents were allowed to do anything but obey! If the frontier boor, whom some people considered a military genius because he had once won a battle the wrong way, could not command his despicable troops, why didn't he admit it? Although on May 28 Warraghiyagey heard that the Onondaga meeting was "still in suspense," on the 29th Abercromby gave him final orders to call out the braves.

Johnson had no choice but to paint a huge string of wampum red, thus fashioning a war belt that would carry to Onondaga his request, made in the name of the ancient Iroquois-English alliance, for an immediate Indian army. The Mohawks, who had for some time been drinking heavily, took one look at the belt and sank even deeper into "perpetual riot." When the belt reached Onondaga, the shocked sachems adjourned the Congress after dispatching a delgation to remonstrate with Sir William for trying to force their hand. Concurrently, rumors flooded into the Mohawk Valley that a major French army was on the way there: whole families, white and Indian, milled through Johnson's rooms demanding protection.

As Abercromby, storming against Johnson's disobedience, began his slow advance on Ticonderoga, the confusion at Fort Johnson heightened. The Onondaga delegation was expected but had not arrived; the local braves were drunker than ever; the settlers packing up and threatening to flee the frontier if Sir William deserted them at this moment of danger. He wrote the commander to "fix an ultimate day for joining you. . . . I hope you will be able to afford me six or seven days longer."

To Abercromby's stinging rebuke, Johnson replied, "Your displeasure adds to my perplexity." He had the "misfortune" to be "in a service which cannot, or at least which I cannot, put upon a footing of certainty and punctuality." The Mohawks, his closest friends, had stated they would not be "thus drove to war," and had threatened to turn on him if he marched before the Onondaga delegation arrived, for "it would occasion a fatal confusion in our general confederacy."

Finally the delegation appeared, accompanied by a crowd of Onondagas, Oneidas, and Tuscaroras. Sir William, so read the official record, asked "their chief men to step upstairs with him. There he acquainted them with the speech he intended to make to their whole body. They spoke with great warmth . . . told Sir William they looked upon the King's appointing him to the management of their affairs to have been done because he was the person most agreeable to them, and who knew best their customs and manners." Warraghiyagey must certainly realize that "such precipitous measures as he was now upon were in no ways consistent with the reasons for his appointment and might have bad consequences.

"Sir William told them that he was under the general's orders, which he must obey and march at all events. Upon which, he went down with them into the Council Room where the rest were assembled, and spoke to the whole body."

Glancing above the seated sachems and warriors to where Molly stood against the wall with her sister squaws, Warraghiyagey breathed deep and began:

"Brethren of Onondaga, Oneida, and Tuscarora: By the message our brothers the Mohawks brought me from you, I have impatiently expected to see you for some days past.

"Brethren: Three messengers one after another have come running to me from the general to tell me he is waiting for me and the Six Nations. . . . This order I must obey, for part of an army are already advanced to one of the islands on Lake George. The rest have their faces this way, looking out for me and the Indians, and, if we don't run all the way, they will proceed without us.

"Brethren: Now is the time for such Indians as desire to be thought friends and brethren to the English to tuck up their blankets and run with me. Brethren, there is no time to be lost nor to think of any other business. Those who go with me will, I hope, now see the English are men, and, with the assistance of the Great Spirit above, I trust we shall give the French such a blow as will oblige them hereafter to be quiet and let us smoke our pipes in peace, and I hope every Indian that goes with me will have reason to rejoice that he fought on the side of the English, and bring home with him some testimonials of victory.

"Brethren: This is the day of trial and I shall see now what Indians are my friends, for such will go with me! You who are determined to fight with me, speak!—and you shall be immediately fitted out for war. Remember, brethren, we were successful together three years ago, and I hope I shall now lead you to conquest and glory."

It was such an occasion as when Mark Antony addressed the Roman crowds over the body of Caesar. Like Antony, Warraghiyagey was trusted and loved, but spoke for a cause still unpopular. Like the Roman plebes, the Iroquois had been inwardly prepared for an emotional change. Although in their conscious minds still committed to neutrality, they had already been half-won by France's inability to supply them, and Warraghiyagey's persuasion, to active participation in the British cause. Now the spark of oratory lit explosion.

The baronet threw down red-painted wampum and the drums began. "Sir William," the report continued laconically, "danced the war dance, after which the principal men of each nation also danced."

This dance, which took place outside the regular orbit of historians and has never been reported by them, signalized what may well have been the turning point in that war which won North America for the English-speaking peoples. The fighting force which controlled the wilderness no man's land between Canada and the Colonies had definitely joined the British cause.

In his anxieties and his warnings to Abercromby, Johnson had underestimated the sudden surge to success of his long Indian embassy. The French were soon to accuse the Iroquois of "treachery," not only because they were abandoning neutrality, but because they had placed their wilderness prestige behind the peace belts Warraghiyagey sent perpetually to pro-French tribes. French oratory was failing to persuade the Caughnawagas and even the Abenakis to resume the warpath. As Montcalm prepared to receive Abercromby's attack, the Indian sheds at Ticonderoga remained empty, a situation doubly grievous because the white French defenders were outnumbered four to one by the English regulars and militia that were advancing up Lake George.

Colonel Johnson recruited a force of Indians able by themselves to defeat in the forest a considerable white army: 395 warriors. The dawn of July 8 was softening the forest gloom and streaking the far outlet of the lake when he reached with his Indian regiment Abercromby's encampment that overflowed a clearing by a waterfall and an abandoned French mill. While the English soldiers came slowly into drill-master order, the Indians crept northward past now-glowing rapids to where the stream flowed into Lake Champlain and Fort Ticonderoga stood. They opened the battle by firing at long range across the water at the enemy who, so Montcalm wrote, did not "amuse ourselves" by answering.

Too numerous to crowd into the fort, the French were busy felling trees. Some leafy trunks they piled into walls eight feet high; others, with branches pointed outward, they laid in the clearing to form the forest equivalent of a deep barbed-wire entanglement. Abercromby considered this unconventional defense laughable. Without waiting to bring up cannon, he ordered his regulars to make a frontal bayonet charge. Sir William could have told him how Dieskau had been defeated at Lake George because of a similar maneuver, but the regular scorned to consult a provincial, however "heaven-taught."

In the heat of midday, the redcoats advanced with machinelike efficiency, but the branch-entanglement pulled the machine apart. Struggling with waist-high verdure, they were like figures in a shooting gallery, and the French shot them down. When the survivors tried to return the fire, they saw only green ramparts. They fled for the sheltering forest.

Unable to accept what his entire training told him was impossible, Major General Abercromby ordered charge after charge. Six times the reformed lines advanced into the branches, tripped, fell, rose again to be more easily shot. Almost two thousand casualties remained in the leafage to sag or writhe—but none of them Indians. The Indians, who never intentionally sacrificed a fellow tribesman, watched from a safe distance in horror. The English were proving themselves "men"; but what was the use of being a man if you were also an idiot?

After six hours of slaughter, Abercromby finally admitted he had been wrong. Then his self-confidence turned into panic. Despite its losses, his force still outnumbered the French three to one; he had not even used his cannon; but he wanted to get out of these woods where a general could be punished for obeying the rules of warfare. His bugles shrilled retreat.

As the English horde blundered through the forest like barnyard cows, the French mourned their lack of Indian allies. "In the nature of those woods . . ." Montcalm wrote, "'twas impossible without Indians to engage an army that numbered four or five hundred of them." And Doriel, the Commissary of War, added that Abercromby's army could have been "entirely defeated in its precipitate retreat had M. Montcalm had 200 Indians." Once again, Warraghiyagey had, through tribal politics, saved a British general from himself.

Although this campaign hardly impressed the Iroquois with British military sagacity, it had represented English action on a larger scale than any living Iroquois had seen, and it had a fortunate result for the Long House. Having had his belly full of advances into gloomy shadows, Abercromby could assign troops to protect the Mohawk Valley. He built Fort Stanwix at the carry to Wood Creek, thus extending the English frontier into the Oneida country.

Then Lieutenant Colonel John Bradstreet, one of the few British regulars skilled at wilderness fighting, persuaded Abercromby to countenance a hit-and-run raid against Fort Frontenac (Kingston, Ontario), the link, at the joining of Lake Ontario with the St. Lawrence, between the Canadian settlements and the French bastion of Niagara. Warraghiyagey was able to supply Bradstreet with Indian scouts, but the true fruits of his diplomatic wizardry did not come plain until, on August 25, Bradstreet landed within a mile of the fort. That the enemy were taken completely by surprise showed that the Iroquois were no longer wooing French favor by carrying intelligence. (They had, indeed, lulled French fears.) And the nearby Oswegatchies disobeyed their priests, refusing to march to the defense of Fort Frontenac.

The effects of the surprise were, Johnson was notified, "incredible." The nine sailboats that were the entire French fleet on Lake Ontario were captured in the harbor, and the fort surrendered at once. In it was found a wealth of stores and ammunition (for the undersupplied French, irreplaceable) intended to strengthen Fort Duquesne and to fit out the long-planned attack on the Mohawk Valley. His home area, Johnson believed, was safe "for this year," and the enemy position on the Ohio was endangered.

British military plans for that summer had projected three campaigns. Abercromby's foolishness at Ticonderoga had left the French center intact. On the right flank, two major military figures had made their triumphant appearance: Generals Amherst and Wolfe had sailed up to Louisburg with an English fleet and captured that island fortress. The intended action on the left flank, an attack on Fort Duquesne under the command of Brigadier John Forbes, was still hanging fire.

That an effort should be made, before Forbes' army marched over the mountains into the Ohio Valley, to pacify the Indians who had defeated Braddock had been in every mind, and Sir William had

The Indian conference that was held that October of 1758 was to determine the amount of blood that would flow in the forest when Forbes marched toward Fort Duquesne, and also what flag would fly over the Ohio Valley. It opened as a political squabble between two coalitions: on one side, the Iroquois, the Proprietory Party, and the Indian Department, with Croghan as Johnson's representative. On the other side, the Quakers, their allies in the Assembly and Teedyuscung as a spokesman for the Delawares. An unsuccessful effort was made to remove Croghan by having him imprisoned for debt. When a leading Quaker characterized Croghan as "a rascal and a villain," the Attorney General of Pennsylvania offered to "slap" that Quaker "in the chops." Teedyuscung threw the Delawares' symbolic petticoat to the Senecas, "telling them to wear it," and was, in rebuttal, beaten up.

The Congress seemed about to wreck itself when the strong hands of the Iroquois sachems grasped the reins. As overlords, they declared the Delawares at peace with the English, and when Teedyuscung tried to speak, they either silenced him or left the meeting. Nor could all the praise and rum punch the Quakers administered keep their champion fighting for long. In open council, Teedyuscung admitted that the Delawares had no land of their own, and appealed piteously to the Iroquois for the Wyoming Valley: "I sit here as a bird on a bough. I look about and do not know where to go. Let me therefore come down upon the ground." The sachems replied that they would put this request before the Onondaga Council.

The Iroquois ignored Teedyuscung's impractical effort to secure the return of the Walking Purchase, but asked instead for the land on the Ohio the Proprietors had bought in 1754. Now Warraghiyagey's plan for ending the Indian war was at long last put into effect. As the Quakers watched angrily this defeat of their political hopes, the representatives of the Proprietors sold their claims beyond the mountains back to the Iroquois for five shillings. The scratching of pens on the deed made Fort Duquesne indefensible.

After a Moravian missionary, Christian Frederick Post, had advanced on the French stronghold armed with the news of England's relinquishment, the commander of Duquesne saw over his ramparts his Indian allies vanishing as if to an invisible call. He blew up his in his pocket the authority to please the tribes by returning to them the Penns' huge purchase on the Ohio. However, the Quaker faction that had succeeded during the previous summer in blocking Johnson's effort to conciliate the Indians with this shining concession were determined to block him again. As he mounted his expedition in Philadelphia, Forbes had fallen under their influence; they had persuaded him to countenance a peace conference with the Delawares called independently of the official Indian superintendant.

The belt of invitation had reached Onondaga simultaneously with Warraghiyagey's war belt demanding that every brave join Abercromby's Ticonderoga campaign. This demonstration of divided authority so compounded the Iroquois' confusion and so outraged Johnson that he gave credence to untrue rumors he had formerly discounted: It was gossip in the Iroquois fishing camps that the Quakers did not really desire peace because they were in treasonous alliance with the French Indians. Their object, Sir William reasoned, could be to kill off one of the local groups that threatened their power, the frontiersmen, and put the blame on the others, the Proprietors.

With Abercromby at his throat for warriors, he had urged the Iroquois to march with the army rather than to the Pennsylvania palaver. This persuaded General Forbes (and Parkman, who also did not understand) that he wanted no peace negotiations with the Delawares. However, as soon as the Ticonderoga expedition was out of the way, Johnson encouraged the Five Nations to confer with the Delawares at Easton.*

---

* He had also been involved in an effort to supply Forbes with Cherokee troops. That the Cherokees were hereditary enemies of the traditional Iroquois axis, including all the Indians who were now falling on Pennsylvania, made them anxious to fight Pennsylvania's battles, but created political problems. Their appearance outraged Teedyuscung and the other tribesmen Pennsylvania was trying to placate; it interposed in the way of a negotiated peace an ancient and irrelevant Indian enmity. However, various Cherokee peace missions were brought to Fort Johnson as a result of the invitation which Warraghiyagey had persuaded some Iroquois to send south in 1756. They blew soothing whiffs of smoke at the sachems from a calumet while he held the stem. This enabled him to notify the Pennsylvania and Ohio Indians that the Cherokees had entered the war not as enemies of any English-Iroquois allies, but only to fight the French and the Indians who unnaturally adhered to the French cause. However, the maneuver came to nothing, since Forbes could not get on with the Cherokees. They deserted his army in disgust.

works and fled. Then, through the defile where the bones of Braddock's Indian-slain army whitened, Forbes' army marched jauntily
and without opposition. It was, so wrote the second-in-command,
Colonel Henry Bouquet, Indian diplomacy that had "knocked the
French on the head."

15

The Siege of Niagara

A year before, Johnson had been unable to secure an invitation to the Onondaga Council, but now, in April, 1759, the sachems flocked to Canajoharie where, since there was smallpox at Fort Johnson, he had set up his headquarters in the cabin of Molly's father.

Certainly she was there, her figure softened by the baby that was beginning to stir in her womb. Lying on the straw in one of the cubicles that made up her ancestral dwelling-house, surrounded with the stir of her relations, the lovers stared at the smoke that billowed above them from the line of fires, and whispered together about tomorrow's policies.

The smiths Sir William had brought with him hammered straight the barrels of damaged Indian guns as the meeting waited for the Chenussios, "a body of the Seneca Nations," as Johnson wrote: "a brave and powerful people, and the most remote from us of any of the Six Nations." This tribe—long hosts to the Joncaires—had been the most pro-French of all the Iroquois, and on their agreement depended Warraghiyagey's scheme. When he heard they were on the way, he sent an interpreter galloping to see that they were well fed at the outlying settlements.

On April 11, sixty of these famous warriors from the Genesee marched in with three-cornered stones dangling from their nostrils, bobbing forever before their lips. With them came some Shawnees, whose scalping knives had recently dripped English blood. They "waited on Sir William and were welcomed by him as usual."

The first business of importance was the return to Warraghiyagey of five English prisoners whom the Five Nations had received for that purpose from the now-contrite Delawares. Then came a sensation: It was announced that the Tionontatis, the Miamis, the Shawnees, the Amikwas, the Chippewas, and the Missisaugas, all western tribes long in alliance with the French, were, in response to Sir William's belt of invitation, on their way to make an alliance with the English if the English would trade with them.

Encouraged by this news, the Five Nations made completely official their pro-English abandonment of neutrality. Belts kept coming in from the Caughnawagas, the Oswegatchies, and lesser groups of French Iroquois declaring they would no longer fight for the French, and then finally a pitiful message from the priest at Oswegatchie, who had mounted so many raids on the Mohawk Valley, begging the Onondaga Council to beg Warraghiyagey when he marched into Canada not to "break and destroy" the mission, "a place intended for nothing but religion and instruction of the ignorant."

It was not until an evening when a pair of oxen were boiling in five large kettles for a war dance that Sir William achieved his ultimate objective. All the sachems and warriors were squatting in two long lines facing each other across a line of fires, when "Old Belt, a great Seneca sachem and warrior," arose. He announced that the Chenussios, on whose land Fort Niagara had been built, desired the Five Nations and the English to destroy it.

The French, not wishing their enemies to take advantage of their shortage of Indian truck, were stopping the western tribesmen who attempted to traverse the Niagara pass in search of an English market. At the fort, the hunters were forced to exchange valuable furs for the almost nothing there available. In far-flung clearings, squaws shivered without petticoats, ammunitionless guns leaned against wigwam walls, and old men who had broken their jews'-harps were silent for lack of new ones. All winter long, Warraghiyagey had been pointing out to Indian delegations that Niagara would have to be kicked out of the way. Thus, the Chenussio announcement was greeted by the huge Indian audience with shouts of delight. The war dance lasted till morning.

Since only water travel was practical for carrying supplies any distance through wilderness America, should the Niagara pass fall into English control, inhabited Canada would be cut off from the French posts in the Upper Lakes and also from the Ohio River system. At one blow, the west would be conquered. Yet, as far as Johnson knew, no attack on Fort Niagara was intended by his superiors; he would have to argue the idea in white councils as he had in Indian. And he had a new superior officer to convince. While he remained irreplaceable and therefore unreplaced in the Indian Department, commanders in chief came and went. Abercromby had just been succeeded by the fifth since the beginning of the war.

Major General Jeffery Amherst was a career soldier who had entered the army at fourteen, was now forty-two, and had risen primarily in the commissariat. Reddish of hair and intense of gray eye, with a great hooked beak of a nose and a wart near the left corner of his mouth, he was efficient and determined, as ugly as he was able. However, like his less competent predecessors, he was automatically revolted by all customs not nurtured in that school of correct thought and action, the British regular army. He wrote of Warraghiyagey's Indians, "They are a pack of lazy, rum-drinking people, and little good. . . . The French are much more afraid of them than they need be." His very ability was to make Amherst the most difficult human problem Johnson ever faced.

No sooner was Amherst installed than he received letters from Johnson urging an attack on Niagara. When he reached Albany to take command of the army there, the frontiersman appeared at his headquarters to argue. Having listened with cold formality, he asked questions on "precise and circumstantial details." Then he rose and, without comment, dismissed his caller.

On the arrival of his orders, Amherst discovered that a campaign against Niagara was mentioned, although not urgently. Pitt desired primarily a pincers movement against Montreal: General Wolfe was to advance up the St. Lawrence, capture Quebec, and proceed to Montreal, where he should meet Amherst, who was supposed to have overrun Ticonderoga and Crown Point and continued down Lake Champlain. Further west, only defensive operations were laid down: Oswego was to be rebuilt, and Fort Pitt erected on the ashes of Fort Duquesne. However, Pitt urged Amherst to consider "some enterprise" against Fort Niagara "so far as the great and main objects of the campaign shall permit."

Amherst began working with his staff officers on plans for an attack against Niagara, but said nothing to the frontiersman who was still arguing for it from the forest. The regular suspected that the Indian-lover would blab to the savages, and the savages, he was sure, would blab to the French.

To lead the expedition, he appointed Colonel John Prideaux, who had just sailed in from England. Then, at long last, he notified Johnson that he had ordered the attempt on Niagara "which I proposed to myself and which was likewise hinted by you." Warraghiyagey was to go along with his Indians.*

Amherst ordered Johnson to muster and march the Indians off without giving them any conception of where they were going. To pull the individualistic braves around, as it were blindfolded, was, of course, impossible, and thus Warraghiyagey was forced to ignore the general's command. Yet one tongue-wagging warrior could have sent the whole expedition to the bottom of Lake Ontario.

As Shirley's Niagara expedition of four years before had been fatally delayed by the effort to build large vessels from raw timber, Prideaux had determined to sail in the small boats he could quickly procure. But the commandant at Niagara, Captain Pouchot, had just received a corvette, *L'Irquoise,* which could in open water eat up small boats as effortlessly as a whale eats minnows.

Prideaux left about half his army at Oswego under Colonel Haldimand to build a fort there and protect his supply line; then on June 30 he embarked his cannon and 2,200 soldiers in bateaux and whaleboats. Six hundred Indians, among them Molly's brother Joseph

---

* Amherst considered Indians useful only as scouts and skirmishers. He assigned them to what he regarded as the least important of his three campaigns because General Wolfe, who would be conveyed to Quebec by the British navy, would have little use for such irregulars; and he himself preferred to use in his projected advance on Ticonderoga and down Lake Champlain Major Rogers' white rangers, who had, since Johnson organized them in 1755, scoured that terrain.

The Indians had to be assigned in a group because few were willing to serve in small details under strange top commanders, an idiosyncrasy they shared with backwoods militia. (Thus Daniel Morgan's famous rangers refused, during the Revolution, to be divided as scouts among various commands.) Most of the warriors, indeed, would not march unless Warraghiyagey marched with them, an embarrassment when he was in bad health or engaged in political negotiation. He was perpetually trying to persuade British generals to win the confidence of the Indians by drinking and conferring with them—but always in vain.

Brant, paddled in canoes under the command of Warraghiyagey. Like an infestation of water spiders, the flotilla skirted the south shore of Lake Ontario with every eye peeled for the approach of a tall sail. On the sixth day the boats gathered unmolested in Four Mile Creek, so named for its distance from Fort Niagara. They landed without opposition. The Indians on horseback whom the sentries subsequently challenged were greeted by Sir William as allies he had sent for. Night came in as peacefully as if the stars overhead were not enemy stars. Warraghiyagey's Indians had kept their trust.

When Pouchot finally discovered and reconnoitered his English visitors, he realized that his garrison of 486 soldiers could not hope to drive them away. However, help was within call.

During the previous winter, news that Canada was in danger had moved along unmapped trails and up nameless rivers; visions of the windowed houses of their childhoods had misted the eyes of pale Indians feathered and joyous in wigwams. Their squaws had wished them many scalps and much glory; their half-breed children had admired their war paint; and, to the mingling of death shouts and folk songs, the pride and flower of Canada's wilderness skill had ridden spring freshets to the rescue. Eight hundred and fifty strong, accompanied by the Indians who were their relations, they had gathered at Presqu'isle on Lake Huron and at nearby posts to put themselves under the command of the famous forest fighters, Captains Charles Aubry and François de Lingery. Their intention had been to drive the English from Fort Pitt, thus recapturing the Ohio Valley, but, on receiving Pouchot's appeal, they embarked instead for Niagara.

Both a French regular and a wilderness veteran, Pouchot realized that the campaign was an interlocking action on a double stage. When his reinforcements arrived, there would be forest warfare; for the moment, there was a classic European siege.

Triangular Fort Niagara covered completely the point of land where the Niagara River flows into Lake Ontario. Since two sides were defended by water, it was the third at which Prideaux aimed. Here high walls, stepped, pierced, and angled by bastions, a ravelin, lunettes, a covered way, batteries *en barbette,* an epaulement, and merlons made of gabions and sandbags faced the narrow end of a rapidly widening clearing. The woods began three-quarters of a mile back, and deep in them Prideaux laid out his camp with head-quarters in the rear, the regulars in the middle, the militia on one side and his "park of artillery" on the other, while at the two extremes were clustered the bark huts of the Indians. From within the forest, royal engineers laid out a ditch, angled for protection from the fire of Pouchot's guns, which the soldiers dug so deep and wide that cannon could be submerged at one end and eventually, after weeks of delving, established within easy range of the fort.

Pouchot could do little to prevent this molelike advance, but he expected that before English batteries could be opened up near his walls and could knock them down, his wild western allies would come prancing in. That these partisans would be on that wooded battleground more than a match for Prideaux's regulars, he did not doubt—but he was worried about Warraghiyagey's Indians. The crucial need was to hustle those Indians away, and Pouchot had with him the diplomats who could do it, if any Frenchmen could.

From the fort's great main portal the river road ran to the portage around Niagara Falls. Above the falls was a fortified trading post, the command and property of Chabert and Daniel Joncaire. The "Jean Coeurs" with whom Johnson had for years sparred down the length of the Long House were now engaged with him at close range in one of warfare's strangest diplomatic duels.

The first blood was drawn by Warraghiyagey: the Chenussios, as overlords of the land, told the Joncaires they would no longer protect their settlement. Chabert and Daniel burned their stockade and retired to the main fort, taking with them a group of Senecas who were their close friends.

Although in their castles Indians could sit for days staring at a fire, once they were on the go, they liked to keep going. The slow advance of the English siege gave Warraghiyagey's braves nothing to do. Bored at last with dodging cannon balls and mocking the soldiers who dug in the ground like squaws, they became restive. The time was ripe for French embassies.

The drawbridge that blocked Fort Niagara's main portal clanked down and out came the Seneca diplomat Kaendae. Although Johnson knew that this skilled negotiator wished to subvert his Indians, he rushed to make sure that no sentry would outrage tribal sensibilities by challenging an Iroquois. For two successive days, Warraghiyagey himself called councils to hear the Seneca who publicly scolded him for embarking the Five Nations "in a bad cause." Pouchot was told that Johnson "smiled and regarded the reproof as a joke."

On the second evening, the Onondaga sachem Hanging Belt and two Cayugas returned with Kaendae from the English camp to the French fort. They were blindfolded before they were allowed to enter, led around as in a maze, and then restored to sight in the shrouded council room where hung the belts that recorded years of Franco-Iroquois negotiation. To Pouchot's delight, the newcomers presented a white belt of peace and talked of deserting the English. But, as their oratory rolled on, he began to frown. They stated that they were worried about Chabert Joncaire: lest "the kettles" (by which they meant bombs) should fall on their dear old friend, he should depart from Fort Niagara. Knowing that all the French Indians would leave with him, Chabert said he would stay.

Warraghiyagey's braves next expressed concern about Kaendae: If he were hurt, they would never forgive themselves. Pouchot countered by "covering" the Seneca's "body in advance." He placed a belt and some equipment before the Indian as they would be arranged in the grave. Kaendae was now ritualistically dead; if he were killed again, it would not call for any revenge.

The visiting Iroquois then suggested to some Ottawas in the fort that "they retire to the head of the lake and let the white people fight." Pouchot answered angrily that the Ottawas needed no advice from outsiders. Then he reblindfolded his callers and pushed them out the gate.

As the English trenches inched nearer the French walls, Kaendae continued to move between the two armies, urging the Iroquois in the English camp to go home. Through days of failure he preserved the professional cheerfulness of a trained diplomat, but his fellow Senecas inside the fort became increasingly drunken and hard to manage. Finally, Kaendae gave up. Johnson, he explained, had induced his Indian allies to remain by promising them leave "to pillage the place."

At this, the French Iroquois rushed out of the fort to Chabert's farm, where they slaughtered all his oxen and cows (which Johnson had not dared to touch), "saying they thought it better they should

LAKE ONTARIO

Niagara River

A VIEW of NIAGARA FORT,
taken by Sir William Johnson,
on the 25.th of July 1759.
Drawn on the Spot in 1758.

From a set of plans of forts in America, published by Mary Ann
Rocque, London, 1765 (Courtesy, New York Public Library)

The Cataract of NIAGARA, some make
this Water-Fall to be half a League while
others reckon it no more than
a hundred Fathom

A View of ỹ Industry of ỹ Beavers of Canada in making Dams to stop ỹ Course of ȧ Rivulet, in order to form a great Lake, about
they build their Habitations. To Effect this; they fell large Trees with their Teeth, in such a manner, as to make them come Cross ỹ I
lee, to lay ỹ foundation of ỹ Dam; they make Mortar, work up, and finish ỹ whole with great order and wonderfull Dexterity.
The Beavers have two Doors to their Lodges, one to the water and the other to the Land side. According to ỹ French Acco-

Niagara Falls with Beavers
Detail of "A New and Exact Map of the Dominions of the
King of Great Britain on the Continent of North America,"
Herman Moll, Geographer, 1715. Mr. Moll disclaims responsi-
bility by writing discreetly in a corner, "According to French
accounts" (*Courtesy of the New-York Historical Society, New
York City*)

have them than others." When they sold the meat in the English camp, Warraghiyagey undoubtedly found his share delicious.

Pouchot had lost most of his Indians, and Kaendae, as the French officer wrote in the third person "being a little intoxicated every day, teased M. Pouchot, wishing to hold sometimes the English side, and sometimes the French." Yet the commandant did not despair. The canoes coming to his rescue would blacken Lake Erie like a floating island. When Warraghiyagey's Indians knew that this vast forest force was approaching, they would undoubtedly get out of the way.

After eleven days of siege, the English engineers had their artillery in range. A ball dropped through Pouchot's chimney and snuggled up to him in bed, but it was Prideaux who was killed—one of his own shells burst prematurely. A crisis thereupon rose in the English command. It was a fixed rule that a provincial should never give orders to regulars, but Johnson insisted that his royal commission as "Colonel of the Six Nations" made him in effect a regular officer, and that by seniority he outranked all the other professionals, including the Swiss mercenary, Colonel Frederick Haldimand, who came dashing over the lake to take charge. The true regulars were uneasy—Captain Charles Lee (the future Revolutionary general) considered Johnson "a very good and valuable man" but "utterly a stranger to military affairs"—yet Sir William's popularity with the troops was so great that no one dared object.

When the news that Warraghiyagey now commanded reached Amherst, he reacted with horror. "This is unlucky . . ." he commented, "May overturn all." He hurried off to Niagara a rock-faced young staff officer, Brigadier General Thomas Gage, praying that, until Gage arrived, Johnson would "pursue the same plan as Mr. Prideaux."

But the tone of the Niagara command had changed. "The general," Prideaux had written in his official orders, "is determined to put any officer in arrest who does not perform to a title what his orders express." Johnson wrote, when he was disobeyed, "The general is not a little surprised," and added that he would be glad to redress any legitimate grievances.

Respecting the skills of Prideaux's engineers, Johnson encouraged them to open up more and closer batteries. The French were forced to chink broken ramparts with the Joncaires' valuable furs, but the walls did not come tumbling down. Sir William was far from sure that he could wait. Oswego had been attacked and, although the defenses there held, the expected convoys of supplies were kept from going up the lake. Running short of food and ammunition, he ordered the building of ladders for an assault over the walls: "I am determined to take the place if possible."

Then four western tribesmen appeared in Johnson's camp. They called together his Indians, and, in his presence, expatiated on the approach of Aubrey's force of partisans and Indians. It was fortunate, they continued, that these invincible conquerors had no quarrel with the Iroquois, who could save themselves by getting out of the way.

This message delivered, the emissaries asked Warraghiyagey to send them on with a flag of truce to the enemy commander, for whom they had dispatches. He did so. In the fort, they gave Pouchot a letter from Aubrey and his fellow officers requesting intelligence. Sure that Warraghiyagey would see what he had written but not stop his dispatch, the Frenchman was guarded about his defensive plans but described in detail the British position. Out the drawbridge the Indians came and back to the English camp for some rum and a little entertainment. Warraghiyagey kept a benign face but was worried. The emissaries' loud repetition that more than a thousand Indians were on the way with the French partisans was visibly cowing his 900 braves.

The Canadian foresters were in high spirits as they watched Lake Erie narrow into the Niagara River, drifted down to the portage, disembarked, and climbed over hills on a fine road between "very beautiful and open woods . . . the trees are all oaks and very large." The voyageurs sang to the slithering quicksilver of the falls, laughed that they could not make themselves heard over the roar, and soon came on some English soldiers guarding bateaux, whom their Indians efficiently killed. A dozen English heads were waved on poles for the edification of the Iroquois who came to investigate the sound of shooting.

The confrontation set off a frenzy of forest diplomacy. Neither Indian group wished, in the face of the growing white menace, to reduce total Indian power by fighting the other in a white man's war. Each group urged the other to desert its European ally. Working as never before, Warraghiyagey managed to dissuade a delegation of western braves from returning to the French who had sent them. This was encouraging, especially as all the Iroquois ambassadors came back to him from their parlays in the enemy camp. However, only a few of his warriors were willing to join in the defensive preparations against the arriving army.

Since he had to guard his encampment, artillery, stores, and boats from attack by the garrison in the fort, Johnson could not detach a large force, nor did he wish to separate his army more than was absolutely necessary. Thus he arranged his ambuscade of the portage road at La Belle Famille, an area of woods so close to the clearing that Pouchot, as he leaned over his bastions, could see mysterious movements at the rear of the trap.

Sir William ordered that the road be blocked by the point of a V-shaped rampart which, as it widened through the woods toward the approaching enemy force, became invisible, for it was built of foliage so newly cut that the still-living leaves blended into the underbrush. Behind this defense, Colonials squatted, while about a hundred Iroquois wandered around in back of them, excited and perplexed. The rest of Warraghiyagey's warriors were fidgeting in their camps, also waiting for events to determine what part they would play in the impending battle.

When their Indian delegation failed to return to them, the French commanders decided to permit no more negotiation among the tribes: They ordered the attack. At this, some chiefs demanded a further delay "until," so a Frenchman interpreted, "they had spoken to the Iroquois to oblige us to make peace with the English." Aubry and de Lingery waved their swords, called to the Indians, and ran toward the enemy. But the war-painted horde vanished into the forest, leaving with their French allies "only thirty of the most resolute."

Many of the *couriers de bois* were also feathered and painted; they advanced into the English trap "with a very great noise and shouting"; but the Iroquois saw at a glance that these were not real Indians whom an Indian should hesitate to slay. The warriors on the flanks joined in the burst of English fire, and messengers brought the rest of Warraghiyagey's braves from their encampments at a run.

The French made several attempts to fight their way over the breastwork, to a junction with Pouchot's troops in the fort. Then they turned and fled down the road and through the woods. Chewing on bullets to prevent thirst, the Iroquois, as Johnson wrote, "pursued them very briskly and took and killed great numbers of them." It was a holocaust of statesmen: Every enemy who fell tore another hole in French wilderness influence.

Pouchot heard the sounds of carnage but, as he craned over his ramparts, he could see only branches curtseying to midsummer zephyrs. In hopes that Johnson had engaged so many troops that the English camp was exposed, he ordered a sortie toward the artillery, but "the whole trench at once appeared full of men who showed themselves stripped to the waist, with companies of grenadiers at the head of the trenches. We fired some cannon, which quickly made them re-enter, and our sortie did not take place."

"At two p. m.," so wrote a soldier in the French garrison, "we heard by a savage that our army was routed and almost all made prisoners by the treachery of our savages. When immediately the English army had the pleasure to inform us of it by summoning us to surrender." Refusing to believe, Pouchot sent an officer to the English camp, where he saw many of Canada's most famous partisans lying wounded, and heard from their lips the tale that left the fort without further hopes of succor.

So, on July 25, 1759, Fort Niagara bowed to Sir William Johnson, Bart. Like his first, his second major command had ended with a resounding victory. He gave credit to the Indians: "By having so many on our side, we gained Niagara with the weakest force and the most insignificant train of artillery that was ever sent so great a distance against so regular and respectable a fortification."

The drawbridge groaned down flat. Sir William and his suite marched over to see, lined up to receive them, the French garrison. As Colonel Johnson accepted and graciously handed back Pouchot's sword, his mind was certainly half concerned with the officers who stood behind the French commandant, wondering which were his ancient enemies, the brothers Joncaire. Pouchot finally introduced them, and then, with a bow, invited the Englishmen to join his staff in the fine dinner his chefs had prepared as their farewell to the flag of France.

While Burgundy and brandy circulated, the forest men had much to discuss; they laughed over bounties one had offered for the hair of another; compared stratagems each had initiated with results the others had seen; drank to the charms of mutually admired squaws. But under their hilarity they were all conscious of the sounds outside.

Johnson had promised the garrison protection from his Indians, but he had promised the Indians that they might eventually plunder the fort. Unable to wait, some 500 warriors had swarmed over the walls. They were taking the hinges off doors, fighting over bales of furs, breaking open barrels of brandy which they lapped from the ground. As the saturnalia mounted, everyone wondered whether the French prisoners could in fact be protected. Would there be reenacted in reverse the tragic scene at Fort William Henry where, despite promises similar to Johnson's, Montcalm had been unable to guard the surrendered English garrison?

As at Fort William Henry, the crucial moment would come when the captives left the fort on their way to internment. Johnson agreed they could keep their guns in this moment of danger, but Pouchot warned against the use of weapons. If molested, the soldiers should give the Indians "a good kick in the bowels or strike them with the fist in the stomach," as "it is of no consequence to an Indian to be struck in this way. The others would not take his part as if he were hit by a gun, sword, or bayonette."

The surrendered garrison marched out with drums beating, muskets on their shoulders, and two large cannon, the matches lighted, at the head of the column. On each side, solid ranks of Englishmen made a breakwater, holding back twin seas of Indians. The only casualty was one of Johnson's officers, who was cut with a knife by a disappointed brave, but the Frenchmen were happy to drop their guns on the shore and leap into the bateaux which cast off the instant they were filled, although Lake Ontario was troubled with high waves.

Warraghiyagey, who regarded the battle with Aubry's partisans at La Belle Famille as a separate Indian victory,* could not sum-

---

* This annoyed Lieutenant Colonel Eyre Massy, who wrote Pitt, "As I hear the Indians have got credit by that day, in Europe, I think I would not do justice to the regiment I had the honor to command if I would allow the savages, who behaved most dastardly, to take that honor which is deservedly due to such of his Majesty's troops as were in that action."

marily take from his allies the human spoils captured there. For £160, he ransomed the twenty-five captured officers, but he divided the ninety-six enlisted men and 150 scalps among the participating tribes. Whether any of the Frenchmen who were carried away by the Indians in canoes riding deep with plunder were eventually tortured, history tells not, but certainly none were tortured in War-raghiyagey's encampment.

The conquest of Niagara was the greatest English military victory so far achieved on the American mainland during the French and Indian War, and its effects were incalculable: It won the west. In their headlong flight, the survivors of Aubry's wilderness army burnt the French forts of Presqu'isle, Le Bœuf, and Fenango before they holed in at Detroit, which was now as completely isolated from central Canada as central Canada was from Louisiana. General Stanwix could build away at Fort Pitt without worrying about any danger. The French could not get at him, and the tribes were finally convinced that the English would win the war.

In New York City, the favorite toast was "Johnson forever!" and in London Horace Walpole wrote a member of Parliament that, since England's ally Frederick the Great of Prussia did not seem a match for Austria's mighty General Daun, "I believe that the future of the world will come to be fought for somewhere between the north of Germany and the back of Canada between Count Daun and Sir William Johnson."

16

The Fall of Canada

From Fort Niagara, English soldiers streamed to view Johnson's most spectacular contribution to the British Empire. Correct citizens of the eighteenth century, who considered untamed nature anything but beautiful, eyed it with "secret horror," but that early romantic, Charles Lee, was ecstatic: "Had I a throat of brass and a thousand tongues, I might attempt to describe it!" In his journal, Johnson wrote simply, "I went to see Niagara Falls."

He was more concerned with repairing the fort for winter occupancy, constructing gunboats to keep the supply line with Oswego open, procuring rum for the troops "who are much fatigued," and taking in the forests political advantage of his victory. The western chiefs whom Aubry had sent to seduce his Iroquois now exchanged the silver medals the French had given them for English medals and agreed to carry to their tribes an invitation that every hunter come to Niagara or Oswego to trade. As a result, many "nations on the overside of the Lakes and elsewhere" made their peace with the English power.

Leaving a garrison behind, Johnson sailed on August 4, 1759, for Oswego, where the new fortifications were still abuilding. "I hope," he wrote Amherst, "to receive your Excellency's orders concerning the next step." Instead, he received Brigadier General Gage. His new superior brought Amherst's official congratulations on the Niagara capture, which awarded promotions to several regular officers but did not even mention Johnson's name. When the Indian colonel asked what orders Gage had brought, he was not answered.

Gage, who was to be the British commander in chief over whom the American Revolution exploded, was on his first independent command. He was unhappy about his orders, for Amherst had commanded that, in addition to finishing Fort Oswego and keeping a garrison there, he lead what troops could be spared down Lake Ontario into the St. Lawrence, where he was to capture and occupy the fortified island of La Gallette, (now called Chimney Island) which, now that Niagara had fallen, was the westernmost outpost of central Canada. Such an advance, Gage believed, would be feasible only if Wolfe and Amherst were converging according to plan on Montreal, from which La Gallette could easily be reinforced. Wolfe was battering, it seemed vainly, at Quebec's high towers. Although the French, outnumbered and deserted by their Indians, had obligingly abandoned Ticonderoga and Crown Point to Amherst, he was strengthening these forts and improving his supply lines without moving forward. Much of Canada's remaining power was free to gobble up the expedition Gage had been ordered to undertake.

In his perplexity, Gage yearned to lean on the older and more experienced Johnson, yet he felt that an English brigadier should not demean himself by confiding in a provincial. Not until his anxieties got the better of his training did he explain his orders. Having added, in Johnson's paraphrase, that "his honor was as dear to him as General Amherst's could be to him, and he did not understand running his head against a wall," he was overcome with a sudden shame and strode off to his headquarters.

However, something that Johnson had said kept coming back to him: While agreeing that La Gallette could not safely be occupied, Johnson had suggested that the fortress could be destroyed in a hit-and-run raid. After hesitating for two days, the commander invited the provincial to dinner, went over the matter a hundred times, and finally agreed to a quick attack. He ordered Warraghiyagey to summon his Indian allies, who had gone home after Niagara's fall.

When they arrived along paths or floating in hollowed tree trunks, the Iroquois were loud with protests: since La Gallette was near Oswegatchie, any movement against the French fort would endanger French Iroquois. Although Warraghiyagey breathed pretended fire, he had no actual intention of hurting the Oswegatchies. His true objective being to frighten them into changing sides, he agreed at last that the attack should be delayed until the Iroquois could send their brethren a warning.

Gage was glad of the respite, for the future commander at Bunker Hill remained far from sure that an advance down the savage lake, however brief and sudden, would not be an invitation to disaster. Around the half-built fortifications, past his comforting but uncomfortable regulars, through all the confusion that characterized an Indian and also a militia encampment, the brigadier paced unhappily. With rueful amusement, Johnson noted in a journal that the superior to whom his own actions were tied changed his mind on all matters several times a day. In the evening, Gage would expatiate with pleasure on the number of his Indian soldiers, and in the middle of the night storm into Warraghiyagey's tent to shout that the hungry horde was eating his campaign into destitution. The Indians themselves were sullen, insisting that any hostilities toward Oswegatchie would terminate the English-Iroquois alliance.

Into this confusion came a letter from Molly saying that she would like to join her man. Although she would be of great help in handling her Iroquois brethren, Johnson could visualize the expression on Gage's face at the arrival of the Indian beauty, now large with the baronet's child. He wrote Molly not to come, and tried to escape from it all by going with some of his Indian friends on a camping and hunting trip along the shores of Lake Ontario.

After Johnson had returned, Gage finally found the courage to sit right down and write Amherst that he could not possibly obey orders by moving on La Gallette. For three nights, he slept with the soundness of a man who had made up his mind, and then came Johnson's turn to wake him. The Oswegatchies, the Indian colonel shouted at the sleepy general, had sent a message stating "in the most solemn manner that they would not only quit the French, but on our approach meet and join us, and show us the best way to attack the enemy. . . . They desired we would make all the haste possible."

There drifted through the door of Gage's tent the unmistakable sounds of a war dance: the news from the Oswegatchies had inspired a complete about-face in the policy of the Iroquois, whose diplomats had for years labored to close the schism with their pro-French brethren. And when word came that the other emigrant nation, the Caughnawagas, would also join an English army, the Six Nations' desire to attack became a fever. Scouting and scalping parties went out in waves.

Gage, so Johnson wrote, "vowed he was at a loss what course to take." On one hand, Warraghiyagey insisted that an advance was now of crucial importance, since it would, by winning over the French Iroquois, open to easy conquest the Canadian heartland; on the other, French prisoners stated that "the enemy were strongly entrenched" at La Gallette, "their numbers superior to ours." (The French garrison actually numbered 1,800 white troops, while Gage could detach only 1,000 from Oswego.) Warraghiyagey feared no white army now that he had unanimous Indian support: he told his friends that he would ask Gage for permission to advance himself with his Indians and 600 volunteers. Warned of his subordinate's intention, eager neither to refuse nor approve the request, Gage went into hiding. Once he incautiously left the door of his tent open. Johnson came to the door and stood there, but Gage pretended not to notice.

Equinoctial storms screamed along Lake Ontario. After "the severest night I can remember for wind and rain," Sir William found a drunken sentry tucked comfortably away in his tent. Hoping that no regular officer would notice, he sobered up the deserter and slipped him back to his regiment "not as a prisoner." He himself had felt the need of many nips that inclement evening.

On October 8, raiders returned from La Gallette with scalps, prisoners, and the first word to reach British territory of one of the eighteenth century's most famous events: Wolfe and Montcalm had met below Quebec's high walls; both had been killed; but the citadel of Canada had fallen to British arms. For some reason, this news gave Gage the courage to announce that he had absolutely no intention of leading or permitting any large-scale attack on La Gallette.

To the Indians Warraghiyagey explained that the season was now too far advanced. And then, in full council, he warned the delegates of the Oswegatchies and the Caughnawagas that if their tribes engaged in any further hostilities against the English, "I never would speak a word in their favor, but advise the general to cut them to pieces." He supped with his friends among the British regulars, "when all the company were very merry," and returned to Fort Johnson.

A new thin wailing filled the house, for in September Molly had presented him with a son, whom he named after his most famous relation: Peter Warren Johnson.

Now that the capture of Niagara had driven the French front line back from the Great Lakes into the St. Lawrence, now that the pro-French Iroquois were too afraid of British power to obey their priests, the Long House and the Mohawk Valley were safe from attack. Like a medieval baron, Sir William had brought security to his own land and people. More than ever, he was idolized by the settlers and the Mohawks. But rumors reached him that in the cities it was being said that he had usurped power at Niagara, since a royal commission to command Indians did not make him a regular.

To Amherst, Sir William sent pleas that he be put on the regular payroll as a colonel. He even called on the commander to enforce his request. But, in arguing for rank, the heaven-taught officer did not cite the victories he had won. He stated, so Amherst remembered, "that he did not wish or pretend to be a military man" and only wanted his rank acknowledged "because some people talked as if he had no rank at all." This amused Amherst, who was sure that Warraghiyagey could have no rank within the pales of civilization.

When the commander in chief visited Fort Johnson, he was horrified to see a handsome squaw in residence, doubly horrified by her half-breed baby whom the frontier baronet had named after a British admiral and Knight of the Bath. "Several Indians there living on him," was Amherst's comment. One of his staff officers gave six pence—which he charged to the Crown—to "a little Indian boy," perhaps William of Canajoharie.

As the spring of 1760 came in, Amherst conspicuously failed to confide in the victor of Niagara any future plans. Sir William could only guess that, since heavy cannon were moving from Albany to Schenectady, "the greatest affair will be this way." That was correct, although Amherst intended to converge three armies on Canada's last major stronghold, Montreal. One would go west up the St. Lawrence from Quebec, and the second north down Lake Champlain from Crown Point, but the third was to be the largest. Under Amherst's personal command, it would cut the Canadians' escape route to the wilderness by going east from Oswego.

Amherst's force, as it advanced down the St. Lawrence, would have to pass Oswegatchie and Caughnawaga, traverse rapids where white soldiers in small boats would be almost helpless against guerilla attack. Yet Amherst was unsympathetic to Warraghiyagey's attempts to woo the French Iroquois into the English camp. All the bitter experience suffered by English armies had failed to convince him that "savages" could damage regulars. He wished to have the Oswegatchies who accepted Johnson's invitation to trade at Oswego driven away as possible spies.

Only Warraghiyagey's willingness to disobey what he considered silly orders stood between the British and the last great menace to the conquest of Canada. The French power had been so drained by blockade, so wounded at Frontenac and Louisburg and Niagara and Quebec that it could not by itself escape the *coup de grace*. But the Indian power was intact, and French agents saw in Canada's very weakness a chance to bring down on the English an almost unanimous horde of those warriors who were Mars' darlings wherever the woods were thick.

The Joncaires were still interned, but Pouchot had been exchanged and was now in command at La Gallette, where he was erecting a new scientific construction, Fort Levi. However, he had less interest in piling dirt and wood and stone than in talking to warriors. He pointed out—as did every other Frenchman who could find an Indian ear to speak into—that the tribes were in desperate danger of losing forever their profitable role as makeweights in the balance between Canada and the Colonies. Had they forgotten "the necessity of putting France and England under obligation to seek them, and consequently to prevent one from prevailing against the other?" If they had forgotten, woe to them, for the English were trying to get France out of the way so that they would have the Indians at their mercy! By innumerable council fires French hands dropped the largest belts they could in their penury procure to emphasize the message that the Colonies were only

Major General Jeffery Amherst, the British general who was
Sir William's enemy and the Indians' bane, by Sir Joshua Rey-
nolds, who depicted Amherst as a noble knight in armor (*Mead
Art Museum, Amherst College*)

published 6 April 1782 by C Bretherton

A considerably different depiction of Amherst by Thomas
Pownall, Johnson's sometime political advisor, who labeled
this caricature "The Cautious Commander"

awaiting the final conquest of Canada to turn on their Indian allies.

Some chapter and verse could be given: Rhode Island selected this crucial moment to repeal all laws that protected Indian land, and in the south the Cherokees were engaged in battles with the frontiersmen which Warraghiyagey had to admit were caused by white rapacity.

But Canadian voices sounded at the council fires as thinly as the wind through winter branches; like leaves left over from autumn, their wampum belts fell unheeded to the ground. Jesuits no longer could call their worshipers to mass. At La Gallette and what other military installations the French still controlled, the Indian sheds remained empty.

For this final disappointment of that last hope of New France, the Indians' passion for the balance of power, Pouchot blamed one man. "Johnson alone," he wrote, "was able to quiet them and make them forget their ancient political system in this war."

Johnson himself commented that in their fear of a total English victory the Indians would have "greatly protracted" the war "but for the great pains I have been constantly at in dividing them and preventing their unanimity." While beckoning all Indian groups into the English camp, he encouraged their ancient distrusts of each other. Thus the various confederacies found themselves vying for the favor of the white nation which, because they could not agree among themselves, seemed likely to dominate the continent.

Warraghiyagey was using the confidence which the Indians felt in him to further a policy which he knew was contradictory to their long-range interests. However, there is no evidence that he was bothered by any conflict of loyalties. The sachems understood that he was an emissary of the British Crown, and welcomed the services he rendered in that capacity. To his white correspondents, he boasted of how he was dividing the tribes. His basic loyalty could not help being, as he put it, "our own": the Anglo-American world. He could only hope to avoid the Indians' future dangers, which the French so lyrically described, by using his personal power to secure for them from the Crown the rewards they would so justly merit after they had played a crucial part in the defeat of Canada.

Johnson's Indians were to join Amherst on the advance down

the St. Lawrence. To the meeting place at Oswego, he brought some 700 warriors. While Amherst drilled his troops and checked his ordnance, the Indians sat around their kettles and Warraghiyagey talked. He talked to western chiefs he had impressed by capturing Niagara, to Oswegatchies and Caughnawagas, to chiefs from the nine Abnaki nations that lived near Montreal.

On August 10, a great armada embarked. The first European impediment to the invasion was Pouchot's Fort Levi at La Gallette; the first Indian impediment was Oswegatchie. While Amherst prepared to fight Pouchot, Warraghiyagey delayed the section of the army which was to advance on the Catholic Iroquois so that it would not, by arriving in the dark, appear unfriendly. The next morning, "some Indians run off for fear of us," but those that remained "received us kindly."

Pouchot, however, was bristling his little guns like a hedgehog defying huge hounds. Amherst felt it would be too condescending to mount a formal siege: He ordered his gunboats to float down the river and blow Fort Levi out of his passage. In this maneuver Warraghiyagey's Iroquois had a particular interest, for Amherst had condescended to name the gunboats after their various nations. When, from a vantage point on the river bank, the warriors saw the *Oneida* and the *Seneca* run aground under French fire, they "made furious cries"; and, when the *Seneca* supinely surrendered, the painted soldiers yelled to where Amherst stood: "A Frenchman's fist has made you cringe." Amherst was not amused.

Under a more careful siege, the fort fell. "Agreeable to their customs," as Johnson put it, the Iroquois wished to make the prisoners expiate the insults their own ancestors had received from the French since the first settlement of Canada. This Warraghiyagey forbade. He was in the habit of softening such refusals by comforting the Indians with captured spoils, but Amherst wanted all the spoils for the regulars. He ordered that no Indians be allowed in the fort. Some ran over the walls, and, before they were ejected, saw grenadiers "plundering and pillaging."

Finally, Amherst admitted his allies, but only on condition that they "not take the least thing that was not given them." When the tribesmen were finally pawned off with £30 worth of goods, 506 of Johnson's 691 braves went home. Seeing them go, the Indian colonel hoped they would get out of reach before the general was notified. Sure enough, Amherst expressd rage that he could not catch the braves and punish them as he would have punished English deserters.

The crucial moment of the campaign was now at hand, for Amherst's army had to traverse that "most terrifying navigation," the rapids where, so Johnson pointed out, a few warriors "joined with other troops might act with great advantage." As the British boats flew foaming one by one between the rocks, Johnson and the almost 200 Indians left to him patrolled the shore. Eighty-four British soldiers were drowned, but not one was even scratched by enemy action: No enemy appeared.

That the French did not even attempt to make use of the last great natural barrier in Canada seemed to an English diarist "amazingly unaccountable." The diary of the Maréchal de Lévis, the French commander, gives the reason. Two days before Amherst took to white water, Lévis had summoned to La Prairie, near Montreal, the Indian tribes that had for two centuries lived in the Canadian heartland as Canada's closest allies. Lévis was importuning them to help their old friends in a final, crucial stand, when an Indian embassy that had been sent to Warraghiyagey stepped out of the forest. For once the tribes, forgetting decorum, turned from a speaker. The ambassadors announced that they had signed a peace with the English. The warriors vanished, leaving Lévis with a belt of wampum dangling uselessly from his hand.

On hearing this news, the Canadian militia also vanished: They feared that the Indians who had always been their right arm would join the enemy and be their executioners.

And so the English advanced unmolested. At Caughnawaga, some 500 of the Mohawks with whom Johnson had warred and treated for so many years stood on the banks of the St. Lawrence unarmed. Warraghiyagey hailed them as brothers and, to show his trust, allowed five of them to row his whaleboat to the island of Montreal.

The other two British armies had also met only token resistance; they were awaiting Amherst before the French capital. Hopelessly outnumbered, Vaudreuil surrendered Montreal and with it all

Canada. Thus, one of the determining changes in American history was accomplished.

"Sir William Johnson," Amherst wrote, "has taken unwearied pains in keeping the Indians in humane bounds, and I have the pleasure to assure you that not a peasant, woman, or child has been hurt by them, or a house burned, since I entered what was the enemy's country." This negative credit was all that was given by the commander in chief to Johnson. Amherst admitted no significant contribution toward victory from the Indian warriors.

Without (as he tactfully put it) "in the least derogating the bravery of our troops," Johnson claimed that "had it not been for the greatest pains taken to prevail on some Indian nations to act, some to neutrality, and to divide others in their councils," Canada would not have "fallen under our dominion." That the Indians had indeed played so determining a role would, down two centuries, have been indignantly denied by almost every historian, by none more firmly than Parkman.

To find a tenable position in this disagreement, we must recognize that there were several theatres of war, widely separated in geography and in basic principles.

There was to begin with the ancient rivalry between England and France, a confrontation that seemed so alien to British-Americans that they resented the successive conflicts with Canada as having been foisted on them irrelevantly by the British Crown. Involved were the economies of the two European powers, governments three thousand miles away from the American fighting, and battles fought on traditional terrains according to traditional tactics. From this theatre of war there came to the combatants in America funds and supplies, troops led by regular officers (the French proved more adept at wilderness fighting than the English), and administrative orders. That Britain eventually (although well after the war had been won in America) achieved victory on a global scale reveals that in the European theatre, which fed the American, the odds were on the British side.

A second theatre was the Atlantic Ocean. It could be contended that it was on blue water that the crucial battles of the French and Indian War were fought. The triumphs of British seapower prevented Canada from being adequately supplied. But this advantage would have come to nothing without effective action in America.

Louisburg and Quebec, being easily accessible to the British navy, were conquered in campaigns unconcerned with Indian power. But there were, during the seven years of fighting in America, no other such campaigns. On land, where Indian power was, there lay victory.

Major fighting was inaugurated when Braddock's two regular regiments crumbled bloodily to the earth under Indian fire. Johnson and his Indian allies defeated Dieskau at Lake George. As the British regulars cowered from wilderness hazards, the French and their Indians captured Oswego and Fort William Henry. Then, Johnson's diplomacy was given wings by the inability of the French to supply, reward, and arm their Indian allies. Only a few miles from where the flesh of Braddock's regulars had rotted, the French were abandoned by the Indians and in turn abandoned Fort Duquesne. Niagara fell to Johnson. And Amherst, who had found himself bogged down on the Lake Champlain route, was suddenly able to move as if clogs had fallen from his feet. Cradled along by Indians many of whom had previously been pro-French, he took now helpless Montreal without bloodshed, thus bringing to a triumphant end the French and Indian War.

PART THREE

Peace and Indian Rebellion

17

A United Continent

Because of Johnson's contributions to the capture of Canada, a movement began in London to make him Royal Governor of New York. He was, he commented, "extremely obliged . . . but, as I am sensible of my inability for the execution of so important a trust, and the settling of my lands requiring my presence and daily encouragement in these parts, it would not at all answer for me. Besides, as I have hitherto had the most fatiguing and disagreeable service, I now propose to retire and spend the remainder of my days more tranquil, which I am convinced in that station I never could."

Sir William was so eager for the arts of peace that he tried to ignore new dark towerings in the Indian sky. During the first winter after the surrender, a friend wrote him from Albany, "I don't know where you live, for I can neither see you nor hear tell of you." He was in the wilderness, laboring to make it blossom like a rose.

He boasted that "although my lands lay on the frontiers here, and much more open to the incursions of all the enemy's parties than any other, I nevertheless, at considerable expense, established over 100 families thereon during the heat of the war, furnishing them with cattle, provisions, and money to encourage them to remain thereon, at a time when all the neighborhood were abandoning their settlements, which they would have left to a man to the

223

great detriment of the province, if not induced to the contrary by my own example and that of my tenants, for which purpose I spent all the time in which I was not on the public service in a small lodge in the wild woods amongst them." He named this lodge Castle Cumberland after a younger son of the King. It seems to have been close to where he later built the village of Johnstown and his own mansion, Johnson Hall.

His brother Warren Johnson, who visited him from Ireland, noted that "Castle Cumberland and about it is very fine, deep, rich black soil," so fertile that tree stumps which should have died pushed out roots year after year, making so strong a tangle that the settlers had to hitch "two bullocks behind and one horse before the plough." Here Sir William created his favorite toy, a prodigy for any wilderness, a garden of "two acres and a half without root or stump." In it he erected a summer house and planted strange trees and flowers collected for him in Canada, beside the Great Lakes or the Ohio. Over all presided an English gardener who, as a pair of Canadian geese Sir William was trying to domesticate hissed at his heels, wondered whether his "£30 a year, meat and drink" could compensate for grotesque animals and seeds from which you could expect only the unexpected.

To the old New York families, Sir William seemed like a snag that would not sink to the bottom. When he had relinquished the fur trade, they had been delighted, but their relief had been short-lived: He had merely turned his energies to settlement. And now that war no longer distracted him, he was drawing into the Mohawk Valley a flood of aliens which, unless damned, would surely overwhelm the Dutch control of Albany County. Even the Germans, whom the Albanians had fought and despised, now seemed preferable to the new immigrants, particularly the compatriots of the hated baronet.

In January, 1761, an Irish settler was killed at Schenectady by a Dutch mob. When a Dutch court let the murderers off with small fines, Sir William wrote that "the English [for so the Irishmen called themselves in opposition to the Hollanders] must have recourse to something else." His brother Warren noted, "The Dutch are more afraid of Sir William than any man living: he is the only person can keep them in order. . . . Sir William has had many escapes from them, being often waylaid by numbers of them, and had at one time at Albany eight lusty dogs of them upon him, of which he got the better by the assistance only of one Irishman, and almost destroyed them."

His Irishmen might be able to lick four times their weight in Dutchmen, but they were not yet an electoral majority. When he recommended for sheriff one of his Hibernian retainers and the appointment went to Hermanus Schuyler, he commented bitterly, "We must submit to those of greater consequence and interest, and have things go in the old Dutch channel."

The backwoodsman had made no effort to hold the political coalition that had gathered behind him to defeat Shirley. That a faction under Livingston family leadership had risen in the New York Assembly to oppose the formerly all-powerful De Lanceys did not encourage Sir William to join either party or maneuver between them for power; both parties agreed that he should get no further land that they could block. Since he wanted quantities of land, he had been naïve in repudiating so summarily the movement in London to make him royal governor: as long as that threat remained, his enemies would not have opposed him too hard.

Although the Provincial Council controlled the first and last step in purchasing Indian territory—granting a license to purchase, granting the patent—Sir William practically never traveled to the city to take his seat on the Council. He preferred to further his land ambitions through his personal control of the essential middle step: securing an Indian deed.

Johnson especially desired a tract which adjoined his settlements on the west and which he estimated publicly at 40,000 acres, privately at about 100,000. Opposite Canajoharie Castle and behind existing patents that hugged the north river bank, it extended back from the Mohawk, between East and West Canada Creeks, for some thirteen miles. He suspected that the politicians would not grant him a license to purchase so princely a domain, but noted that the land laws contained no provisions about gifts.

In January, 1761, in response to an Indian summons—or so he wrote Banyar—Warraghiyagey made a perilous crossing of the Mohawk that was full of floating ice, and lodged in Molly's father's house "on a straw bed before the fire." At a formal council, the Mohawks "let me know that they had unanimously resolved to make me a present of a considerable tract of land"; the deed was signed by every respectable Indian in the castle. It was a gift, not a purchase, Sir William insisted, though he later admitted that he had responded with gifts of his own: £1,200 in cash and "a handsome present to their families." Molly's brother Joseph received personally $50.

Since James De Lancey had died and Governor Hardy had gone home, Colden was acting governor: He wrote the Board of Trade that his old friend was trying to circumvent regulations "under the pretence of a deed of gift." And Banyar notified Johnson that there were prior claimants to the same land, who would undoubtedly receive the Council's license to purchase.

Let them try, Johnson replied, to add to that license the necessary Indian deed!

As Warraghiyagey and the Council could each block the other, the result was a stalemate. Why not, Banyar suggested, divide the tract fifty-fifty?

Sir William's indignation against "trifling and little low means used by some people" was not tempered when Banyar acknowledged that he and Colden were among the rival claimants. Johnson was convinced that, whatever the letter of the law, he had a moral right to the land. The Indians wanted him to have it and it was theirs to give. Furthermore, there would be no white settlements on the Mohawk, only fields choking up with second growth, had he not protected and held together the frontier during the late war. As it was, land on the Mohawk belonging to other big holders was usually left unimproved, but wherever Warraghiyagey had bought there soon flourished a happy community dedicated to the arts of peace. If he gained money from his settlements, he had a right to that too, since he had made tremendous financial sacrifices for the public good. After his abandonment of the fur trade, his income had "never been half what it was before"; he had lost money on his triumphant military campaigns because Amherst had refused him his pay as regular colonel. And he was again, in this new peace, paying out of his own pocket for Indian presents lest His Majesty's Indian service suffer.

Warraghiyagey admitted that before he advised the Indians to sell any land, he insisted that the prospective purchasers give him a share: "I look upon this to be the principal advantage arising from the office I sustain." However, he felt that the Council was not justified in levying a similar tribute for granting licenses and patents; they had made no such contributions, no such sacrifices.

"I am ashamed," so he concluded one of his many tirades to Banyar, "to say so much about it, but I am vexed." He was so vexed that he persuaded the Mohawks to go on a selling strike. Since all the land that New Yorkers coveted belonged to that nation—the rest of the Long House was too deep in the wilderness —this put, as Colden complained, "an entire stop to Indian purchases."

That the Mohawks would thus support Warraghiyagey's claims leaves no doubt that the sachems did not agree with the colonials who criticized him for securing from his Indian charges such quantities of land. The Mohawks were in a situation like that of the New England natives whose ancestral acres pass into the hands of summer residents. The New Englanders' land could no longer be profitably farmed, even as the Mohawk's civilization-surrounded territory was no longer much use for hunting. In each case, the owners resented their plight but had no better use for their soil than to sell it.

The Indians had an additional problem: Their new neighbors could easily prove inimical to the point of considering it a virtue to murder them. Naturally, the Mohawks did not wish to sell to people with whom they were "not acquainted." Naturally, they were outraged that Warraghiyagey was kept by a government they did not acknowledge from receiving what they wished him to have and he had paid for, while strangers stole their lands with the approval of that same government.

New fraudulent deeds were emerging from old strongboxes; and the most disturbing encroachment of all sprang up with new menace. When Indian military co-operation had been desperately needed, William Livingston had renounced his pretensions to the Canajoharie Castle and its surrounding fields—but he had signed nothing. Now, he secured an extremely active partner in George or Ury (christened "Johangurgh") Klock, the black sheep of a respectable Palatine family long established near the Castle.

Bibulous, unscrupulous, tenacious, and able, Klock deserves a nod from history as the only yeoman who dared, year after year, tweak the mighty Johnson's tail. During King George's War, he had defrauded drunken Indians of the equipment Warraghiyagey had given them for use against the French. Now, he served in Livingston's name dispossess notices on white farmers who, as the Indians' tenants, cultivated the Canajoharie flats.

The Mohawks, Johnson wrote Colden, were "more alarmed and uneasy than ever before; I never saw people so enraged." The trouble, replied Klock's partners, was that Sir William wanted to keep his Canajoharie henchmen near his residence, and therefore by "imposture," by "threats, frauds and false promises," prevented them from moving into the further forest from the lands they had legally sold.

All Johnson's representations that the Indians were being defrauded were open to the interpretation that he was merely serving his private interests, so Banyar warned him, as long as he kept the Indians on a selling strike to force on the Council acceptance of his Canajoharie "gift." This argument, plus the continuing impasse, made Sir William agree in the end to divide the tract with other members of the Council. If he expected thanks, he was disappointed: Banyar's reaction was to object to the location of the lots offered him and also his share of the cost.

Under such provocation, Sir William described himself as a "plain, rough-bred rustic" shocked by the perfidious machinations of the *"beau monde"*—but he lived extremely well. He ordered Claus, who was in Montreal as his deputy to the Canadian Indians, to buy the household plate of some fleeing Frenchman if it were fashionable and not above £100; to send a blooded horse or a shaving case. When Sir William's Negro slaves were sickly—Kitchener dead; Quacko ailing; "I fear it will thin my flock"—Sir William decided to fill in with Panays, agricultural Indians of the West whom the more warlike northern tribes enslaved and sold in Canada. However, Claus thought £50 to £60 for young girls was "too extravagant a price to give." Soon Claus was asking at Indian councils about a Panay Johnson already owned who had disappeared northward into the forest.

Claus was assiduous, for he was preparing a letter on which his whole future depended. It reached Sir William early in April,

1761, at Castle Cumberland. To Claus' request for a loan of £800 so that he could buy a captaincy in the regular army and "secure me a genteel certainty for life," Sir William nodded agreement: his young friend had already been promised help. But the letter continued: "I always had and ever shall have a sincere regard and esteem for Miss Nancy, your elder daughter, who likewise was kind enough as not to discourage me therein, wherefore I should before now have asked your consent and approbation to marry her, had it not been for the troublesome times we hitherto sustained, but that period being at last come, I embraced this opportunity for doing it now, and from your natural goodness flatter myself a favorable answer."

Sir William was amazed, nor was his anger appeased when he discovered that his companions at Castle Cumberland had been conscious of the romance. Unwilling to admit himself blind to his daughter's emotions, he assumed that the young couple had blabbered to everyone but him. This gave him "a bad impression of my daughter's regard for and duty towards me." How could she expect, when she acted thus "independent," not to forfeit her expectations of a great inheritance "as well as parental regard"? So he fumed, but he did not gallop to Fort Johnson to upbraid or question Nancy, nor did he answer Claus' letter.

Claus sent his superior three reports on Indian affairs in which he made no further reference to his proposal. Once he added "recommending myself to your patronage," but recopied the letter, omitting even this oblique appeal.

After a month, Sir William wrote his subordinate. First he said that he would put up the money for Claus' commission; then he discussed the business of the Indian department. Finally: "I have always had a regard for you and believe you are sensible of it, from the notice I have on all occasions taken of you. That alone, should have weighed with you or any man of honor, and be a bar to prevent the carrying on any private intrigue in my family. . . . I have not yet spoken to her on the subject, but intend it as soon as I go to the house, and when I find out her sentiments or inclination, shall be able to say more to you on the affair. In the meantime am, sir, as usual, William Johnson." He added a p. s. showing concern for Claus' professional welfare.

Twelve days after sending this letter, Sir William visited Fort

Johnson and at long last spoke to Nancy, but his next letter to Claus dealt altogether with business.

As soon as the mails allowed, the lover came to the defense of his lady: "I always discovered in her a profound love and duty to her parents. . . . If my having a great regard and esteem for, and her being kind enough to retaliate it with compliance and civility may be called carrying on private intrigues in your family, I only must submit to your interpretation. . . . I assure you, sir, with truth, that I never had nor expected any positive answer from her" until "after obtaining your consent." He made no further request for that consent.

Johnson replied that Claus' explanation had removed "the ill-impression . . . which I shall now think no more of, and only add this, that I would not have you make any advances that way until your arrival here, whenever it may be." His duties, the father then implied, would probably keep him in Montreal for a long time.

Johnson did buy Claus a commission, but in the many letters that continued to pass back and forth between the two men, Nancy is not again mentioned; Claus did not even put her name among those to whom he sent regards. It is hoped that the lover found some way of communicating with his lass that did not violate his highly developed "scruples," for almost a year intervened before the rising tempo of crisis in Indian affairs allowed him to reach the Mohawk Valley. Then events moved rapidly. On April 13, 1762, Claus was married to Nancy by the only minister available, a Lutheran, according to the rites of the Church of England.

Two weeks before, Sir William had foreshadowed a dream by heading a letter from his new settlements not "Castle Cumberland" but "Johnson Hall." He ordered from England blue glazed tiles and a silver crane, sought "a good brickmaker" in Pennsylvania, and wrote in February, 1763, "I am swallowed up to the head and ears in mortar, stone, and timber, which are all intended for the house I propose building next summer. I have had, for this month past, thirty or forty sleds bringing the same, so that it cannot be said I was without some kind of company. We have snow here now about three feet deep and more daily falling, which, although a gloomy prospect, makes the country alive with their sliding, flying machines."

The Clauses settled in the farmhouse Johnson had built when

he first crossed the river from Warrensburg. This they now named Williamsburg (a discourtesy to future scholars who, whenever they have found a letter so headed, have assumed that Claus had made a sudden leap to Virginia). The bridegroom sold his commission to remain his father-in-law's Canadian deputy. He used some of his own money to renovate the house, but Sir William kept the title to the property, as seemed suitable to everyone concerned.

That Nancy should marry one of her father's retainers was inevitable since Johnson, himself uneasy in cities, had erected for his daughters a life that introduced them to few outsiders. He did send John to the academy Franklin had founded in Philadelphia, but not until the boy was in his middle teens. John proved, as a report stated, "backward in writing and ciphering because he has not hitherto been much put to it." Tiring of trying to catch up, he soon returned to the frontier.

Within a year after Nancy's marriage, Mary, then twenty, married her cousin, Guy Johnson. Guy had appeared unexpectedly at Boston in 1756, a rough Irish lad of sixteen. Using his uncle's name, he had borrowed the money—which he forgot to repay— that carried him on to Fort Johnson. He was welcomed, given instead of a formal education a militia commission, and eventually pushed upward to a lieutenancy in the regular army. In 1762, Johnson had appointed him a deputy superintendent in the Indian department.

"You cannot imagine," Guy wrote when stationed at a wilderness outpost, "how disagreeably I spend my time here, having not one single person to converse with." He loved "to dance and caper," the adjectives "jovial" and "jolly" automatically associated themselves with his name; but he had a certain ability to work if he were not pushed too hard (then he became "haughty" and "harsh"). Pleased with the marriage of his nephew to his daughter, Sir William built for the couple near Fort Johnson a mansion called Guy Park (it is today maintained as a museum).

Astute readers may have noticed that, in defending his Nancy before they were married, Claus wrote, "I have always discovered in her a profound love and duty to her parents," using a plural which implied that he had seen the girl in company with her mother. Other documents indicate that Catherine Weisenberg had reappeared, the earliest being the account book of Daniel Campbell of Schenectady, where Johnson's account is billed, on June 28, 1756, two shillings ninepence for "one pair of gloves for Mrs.ˢ. [Mistress?] Caty."

One of her grandchildren was to state that Catherine died in 1759. This is corroborated by the fact that in April of that year (as he was preparing for the Niagara campaign), Sir William bought from Campbell crepe and twelve pairs of white gloves for a funeral. Wraxall wrote from New York, "When I left you, I thought there appeared little hope of Miss Katy's life. I condole with you thereupon, and hope Miss Nancy's management of the house will supply the loss you have sustained." The tone of this letter, which seems to regret the loss of an upper servant rather than a beloved consort, seems strange, but no stranger than other information we have on the position in the Johnson household, where her children moved grandly as heirs, of Catherine Weisenberg and also of her mother.

That in the voluminous Johnson archives for the 1750s Wraxall's letter alone mentions Catherine or her demise makes it clear that she was not introduced as an equal to his correspondents. A similar silence about her mother (whose name even is undiscoverable*) was only broken when a trip of John's to Europe in the early 1760s inspired written communication between the chil-

* A seeming clue to information on the Weisenbergs was supplied by the transcript of a sworn statement by Barnabas Kelly, German Flatts, June 28, 1778, in which a Tory "Captain Service" (Servis, Servos) is called "Sir John Johnson's uncle." However, extensive researches made for this writer by Katherine M. Strobeck in family, official, and religious records have failed to connect the name Weisenberg to either of the Captain Servises to whom Kelly might have referred: Christopher married Anna Clara Grieff, daughter of Jacob Grieff of the vicinity of Johnstown; Peter married a Magdalena whose last name is unrecorded.

Miss Strobeck points out that both these Captain Servises were uncles of another John Johnson who was unrelated to Sir William. Their sister, Elizabeth Servis, had married a Colonel John Johnson who was killed at the siege of Niagara; they had a son named John, a suspected loyalist who seems to have been referred to earlier in Kelly's statement. The possibility exists that the scribe who took down what Kelly said—the witness was himself illiterate—added "Sir" before "John Johnson" out of careless habit.

Simms referred to Peter Servis as a relation of Catherine Weisenberg, but this may not be a separate bit of evidence, as Simms may have seen Kelly's statement. Johnson's own correspondence with members of the Servis family signals a paternalism no more intimate than he then exhibited to his other leading neighbors.

dren. Claus reflects her unexalted status by stating, when she was quartered in the same house with a bibulous overseer, "I wish he mayn't abuse Granny." John mourned that she had suffered too many "of the cares and troubles of this world," to which he had added by "my too frequent and passionate behavior to her, which I heartily regret." He sent "my tenderest love to Granny," and when she died in 1766, wrote, "I not only feel for myself, but for my sisters, whose distress on that fatal occasion I can easily form an idea of." Johnson's own comment on the grandmother's demise was in the unemotional tone of Wraxall's comment on "Katy's": "The Old Woman was just buried as we arrived yesterday. I found all well everywhere."

Catherine Weisenberg had come to William Johnson as a house-keeper; she had borne his children as a housekeeper; and, so it seems, he laid her as a housekeeper in her grave. This was consistent, logical according to feudal mores, even admirable as he had taken good care until the end not only of his old mistress but also of her mother.

However, her illegitimate children had not moved for long on the conventional track which would have carried them, under the distant benevolence of their natural father, to inconspicuous but solid prosperity as yeomen. Never bringing himself to make a marriage that would yield legitimate heirs, the frontier baronet changed his mind about his housekeeper's children. Baptised Weisenbergs, John and his sisters became Johnsons who could look forward to succeeding their father as the rulers of the Mohawk Valley.

Since "Katy" and the "Old Woman" failed to make a similar transition, we gather that their appearance and manners must have remained lower class. The children could not have been altogether sorry that their father buried them in social shadow—yet the women who were kept apart from their friends were by blood and natural sentiment inextricably entangled with their being.

The date of Peter Johnson's birth indicates that his mother was living at Fort Johnson for a year or more before Catherine died. It was certainly no novelty for Sir William's former mistress to share the house with younger successors—but Molly Brant was not like the other beauties that had come and gone. In that bi-racial household, the Mohawk stateswoman wielded greater prestige than was ever possessed by Catherine (or Catherine's mother, whose residence with the family was to overlap Molly's by many years). How the Weisenberg women reacted to being thus overshadowed by an Indian no records indicate, but evidently the children and sons-in-law felt spite. Claus wrote as an old man that Molly had been ugly and pitted with smallpox (and also implied that she had had a military lover before Johnson). After their common father's death, Catherine's children tried to rob Molly's.

What did John and his sisters think of the question of their own legitimacy? Their mother seems to have worn a wedding ring —a granddaughter claimed to have inherited it—and certainly no one at Fort Johnson knew of the little brown book in which the Rev. Barclay had recorded their fatherless baptisms.* Yet during 1760 Johnson's close friend Banyar, in a letter that ignored the claims of John and the girls, urged the baronet to marry so that he could produce heirs.

The two sons-in-law must have believed that there was at least a chance that their wives were legitimate, for in 1776 Claus wrote John, "Guy and I were at the Herald's office in London, and found your late father's title entered in print in a book of heraldry, but not his arms for want, it is said, of knowing his descent, his marriage, and lawful issue." They urged John to send, with other documents, his parents' marriage certificate: "it will be a very convenient voucher for yourself and posterity." The certificate was never sent.

Historians and legend makers unfamiliar with English law have tried to resolve all conflicts by stating that at some time after the birth of their children—at Catherine's deathbed, the story usually runs—William married the housekeeper in order to legitimatize the offspring. Had such a marriage taken place the dated certificate would have been the most destructive of boomerangs, since children born out of wedlock could not be thus legitimatized until the humanitarian twentieth century. Better for Sir William to take

* When Johnson's tomb was opened in 1862, there was found among his remains a plain gold ring bearing the inscription "June 1739. 16." Sentimentalists have argued that this was "Lady Johnson's" wedding ring, but Barclay's record proved that Catherine and William were not married in 1739. The significance of the ring remains obscure.

no action, show no documents, insist that his children were legitimate as he did in his will, and hope for the best. Better for the
children—but we do not know what they really thought the situation was. Could they believe that, despite her continuing lower
social station, their mother had once been their father's bride?
Or did they prefer to ask no questions?

Unless his father made a belated marriage that produced a truly
legal heir—or someone stirred too deeply in baptismal records—
John could look forward to inheriting the baronetcy. Sir William
was generous to the boy and his two sisters: they could all expect
princely legacies—that is, unless Molly (or some new love) should
machinate the property away for her own progeny. The dynastic-
ally-minded Indian Superintendent was training no young assistants who could succeed to his influence with the Iroquois except
Claus and Guy. Catherine Weisenberg's children seemed headed
for exalted destinies, but they could never be altogther sure.

In the meanwhile, their father's hold on life appeared precarious.
During 1761, at the age of about forty-six, he had suffered the
first attack of a malady (probably cirrhosis of the liver) which
"put me to the most excruciating torture, during which I become
delirious. Its duration was about four or five days, since which
time I have had several returns of the like, sometimes thrice in a
year but at very irregular and uncertain periods. It seems seated
near the stomach, which swells much during the paroxisms of the
disorder attended with a jaundiced countenance, the eyes being
particularly discolored." Each time that he felt the fit coming on
he feared that he might not survive, yet he seems to have suffered
from no active worries about the competence of his heirs to encourage his settlements, control and protect the Indians, carry
through the next generation what he had created. If the equivocal
offspring of his housekeeper lacked strength and tranquillity, he
was as blind to that as he had been to the courtship, under his
very nose, of Claus and his Nancy.

18

Rumors of War and Love

When it occurred in 1760, the surrender of Canada could not be recognized as a determining historical event. Since the peace was only local—the Seven Years' War ground on in Europe—a new French army might sail in to revive the fighting. Or during the final peace negotiation, Canada might be returned to France as Louisburg had been after King George's War. (A powerful party in England wished to exchange the chilly American North for Guadalupe.) And wars between England and France were perennial: a new one might well tread on the heels of the old.

Amherst quickly established British administration in central, inhabited Canada, but before the French forts in the forest could be taken over, they had to be reached. Boats carried an English garrison to Detroit, where Croghan made with the Indians of the neighborhood a tentative peace for Sir William to ratify.* However, the French posts on the upper lakes and Fort de Chartres on the Illinois were left (with the Indians that surrounded them) as undisturbed as if no war had been lost.

The French traders and Jesuit missionaries who alone among white men knew the paths and watercourses that led to the castles of the western nations had no desire to open the leafy tangles, the wide savannahs, the dusky rivers, and the glowing lakes where

* The formerly pro-French Indians near Detroit offered Warraghiyagey as a personal peace offering what he called "a fine island, eight miles long and three broad." Perhaps because it was too far away, perhaps because of scruples, he refused what as Grosse Isle is now one of Detroit's most fashionable suburbs.

236

they had so long brooked no rivals, to British traders and Protestant divines. They warned their Indian friends that the English were tricky and hungry for land: listening to an English embassy was like inviting a serpent to curl up at your council fire.

If chiefs from those distant forests found their way to Warraghiyagey's fire, he could give them lace coats with which to cover the to him inexplicable painting on their bodies, he could hand around peace pipe and rum ladle, but not he or any of his interpreters or any Indian he trusted could speak in any language that would create images behind the eyes that regarded him with distrust. Often he could not even identify the nations these ambassadors represented.

On the nearer tribes in his enlarged department—the Oswegatchies, the Caughnawagas, the various nations living near Montreal —Warraghiyagey cast his usual spell, but he realized that the task he faced on a continental scale would require resources beyond any he possessed. He wrote Amherst urging that his department be enlarged both in manpower and funds.

To persuade the general that the Indians constituted a major military threat, Johnson wrote that, "without derogating the known bravery of our troops," it was provable that the English could not have won the French and Indian War had the Indians not backed them: "I flatter myself that I could in a short conference render this clear to Your Excellency."

As a result of the victory, Amherst was now Sir Jeffery and Governor General of all British America. How could he believe that he was beholden for these honors to a parcel of undressed savages?

Having not reached the American mainland until Warraghiyagey had neutralized the pro-French tribes, Amherst had never experienced an Indian attack; and the only campaign in which he had served with many Indian irregulars had been the final advance on Montreal, when at Fort Levi the braves had taunted his regulars with military incompetence and had then gone home because they were not given the rewards they thought they deserved. Convinced that the Indians were despicable people of no importance, he was delighted to conclude that the fall of Canada had, by depriving them of European allies, left them completely at the mercy of English arms.

Far from expanding the Indian department to meet its expanding problems, Sir Jeffery ordered Sir William, in the name of economy, to discharge most of his officers and discontinue the age-old custom of giving presents at annual congresses. He saw no reason, as he put it, for "purchasing the good behavior of the Indians." They should barter furs for everything they needed, which would keep them constantly hunting and out of mischief. But he had no intention of letting them have ammunition to hunt with, lest they use the bullets against Englishmen.

Wherever Amherst saw military expediency, he overruled Indian rights. Although, when he had wanted warriors, he had specifically promised the contrary, he seized the most important pass in the Seneca Country, the Niagara Carrying Place, and granted it to some of his friends "to keep up communication with the upper posts." Sir William's protests were unavailing, as were his objections to a blockhouse erected on Indian land where the Sandusky River joins Lake Erie. "I must and therefore will—say what you will—have one at that place," wrote Amherst.

"The Indians," so Sir Jeffery interpreted his policy, "may be assured that I shall always use them as they deserve: reward them, as far as is in my power, if they merit it; and punish them if they deserve it."

By the spring of 1761, his policy was bearing increasingly bitter fruit. Denied ammunition, the tribesmen were forced to hunt with bows and arrows, a skill so lost that the emaciated corpses of whole families lay in the underbrush, or survivors staggered pitifully to English forts, having eaten some of their children. What pelts the hunters did secure would buy practically no necessities, for the traders who had followed the peace into the wilderness were profiteering unchecked. And Warraghiyagey, his royal funds cut off, could relieve with his private purse only the Indians around Fort Johnson. At Montreal, he complained, all the tribes had not received during the winter gifts totalling what the French would have given four families.

That the Connecticut pretenders to the Wyoming Valley were laying out townships in the territory which the Iroquois and Pennsylvania had declared a permanent refuge for the Delawares made Pennsylvania officials fear "an Indian war in the bowels of this poor province." On the South Carolina and Georgia borders, the war with the Cherokees, which Sir William conceded to be the white man's fault, raged on. Amherst urged Johnson to broadcast through the forest news of every Cherokee setback, but Johnson was trying to play the conflict down. It raised, he wrote, "great suspicion and jealousy through all the nations."

Rumors reached him that a rising tide of Gallic voices was crying through the wilderness that what they had prophecied had come true: The English, no longer afraid of French intervention in the Indian's behalf, were trying to crush their former allies. But the Indians, so the voices continued, should not despair. Warriors should sharpen their hatchets so that they would be ready to join an army that was being sent to their rescue by their father, the King of France!

Sir William found that the management of Indian affairs had become "so very difficult and disagreeable that I heartily wish I was clear of it." When the Indians pointed out that every promise that had been made to secure their military co-operation was being broken, Warraghiyagey could only reply that Amherst was a passionate man who had become offended when the warriors had deserted the march on Montreal. All he could advise was patience.

Johnson's protests to Amherst were as loud as his warnings. In June, he presaged the Indian war that came to be known as Pontiac's Conspiracy. He was, he wrote, "very apprehensive that something not right is brewing, and that very privately among them. I do not only mean the Six Nations. I fear it is too general whatever it be."

What cost the Crown nothing and did not strengthen the Indians, Amherst was willing to do: he agreed that if Johnson would set fair prices for furs, he would order the commandants of the various military outposts to enforce them. Recognizing "the expenses and risks" of wilderness travel, Sir William drew up a list that allowed a 50% profit at Oswego, 70% at Niagara, 100% at Detroit, and on upward further to the west. He also provided that no trader should operate without a license from his department. To make all enforceable, he enunciated a policy he was to fight for during the rest of his career: merchants should not be allowed to set up shops in Indian villages or at wilderness cross-trails where their activities could not be supervised. All bartering with the Indians was to be conducted under official eyes in a British fort.

The plan, Johnson wrote later, was "satisfactory to the Indians whilst adhered to, but there was as yet no establishment for officers to inspect the trade." Since the military had other duties and the traders were—or so Sir William asserted—"the very dregs of people," the rules remained unenforced and the cheating of the Indians went on.

Now, almost a year after the surrender of Canada, Amherst ordered Major Henry Gladwin with 300 men, to "explore in the best manner you can" Lakes Huron and Michigan, and take over the French posts in that region. Johnson was to go as far as Detroit to hold the promised official peace conference with the western Indians.

In contrast to many colonials whose Indian influence was tiny compared to his, Warraghiyagey was a hug-the-hearth. His trips around the Long House and his expedition to Niagara when he captured it made up almost the total of his wilderness travels. Now he was to go hundreds of miles further west than he had ever been.

He had hardly started in July, 1761, when word came from Amherst that Detroit was fortifying in the face of a rumor that the Five Nations had invited all the Indians "from the Bay of Caspé to the Illinois" to join them in a simultaneous surprise attack against every Englishman on the frontiers. This dispatch was followed by a sound of panting and Molly's brother, Joseph Brant, appeared at a run with two other Canajoharies to report the same plot and say that the bad belts were being sent out by those powerful Genesee Senecas, the Chenussios. Presenting their own belt, the Canajoharies begged Warraghiyagey not to risk his life by going on. He answered that he "hoped by his timely arrival [at Detroit] to be able to put a stop to or frustrate" all "such wild, wicked designs."

If Johnson dreamed that the ominous news would make Amherst reflect, he was doomed to disappointment. The Indian plot, the general wrote, "never gave me a moment's concern, as I know their incapacity of attempting anything serious." Should the Indians misbehave, he would "punish the delinquents with entire destruction . . . extirpate them root and branch." He was more determined than ever to deprive them of ammunition and presents, kindness and trust.

The belts Warraghiyagey sent asking the Seneca sachems to meet him at Niagara were ignored. He found awaiting him there only some inconspicuous braves. When they presented a belt that asserted their nation's complete innocence, he scorned to accept it, yet—how Amherst would have frowned—he gave the Indians he distrusted some ammunition so that they could hunt, fill their bellies, and be less discontented.

As he awaited the boats he needed for Lake Erie, Johnson learned that a "malignant fever" was killing many at Canajoharie, and all Molly's family except her mother were ill. However, he could not return.

Warraghiyagey set out on August 18, his flotilla of twelve army bateaux and one Mohawk canoe hugging the savage north shore of the lake. The forest man worried about "the sudden winds that rise there" and noted in his journal that the little fleet moved for hour after hour under high sand banks "where there is no harbor or even landing for boats in bad weather." Afraid that "the high, short seas" would break the groaning back of his vessel, he longed for a good thicket. The final misery was supplied by the boat that contained the liquor, which fell far behind. A good Samaritan, Warraghiyagey shared his private stock with the Mohawks, and then he had none. It was a great relief when, on the fifteenth day, he was able to "eat some melon" at "a fine house" near Detroit.

On a clear, cold, windy afternoon, he advanced up a sun-spangled Detroit River into a most surprising break in the wilderness. He passed the neatly whitewashed houses of a French suburb, and saw on the shore Croghan surrounded with Indians that deputy had brought up from the Ohio. Beyond were three great Indian castles: the Potawatomis and the Hurons facing each other across the river, and then the Ottawas. Ahead, the fort loomed tremendous: pickets fifteen feet high surrounding a whole town that showed over the walls pitched roofs and church steeples.

The commandant of the English garrison, Captain Donald Campbell, proved to be fat, clumsy, and nearsighted, but his heart

beat as high at the sight of a pretty girl as if it were not soon to be
torn from his body by a Chippewa chief and eaten while still
warm. He explained to Johnson that the male French inhabitants
did not amount to much, but the women—ah, the women—they
"surpass our expectations."

All the principal men came nervously to call on the most important English official ever to visit their half-hidden world. They
expressed "respect" and asked "protection." Sir William, as he
wrote, promised them "His Majesty's protection while they continued to behave as good subjects. Then gave them rusk and shrub
[cakes and fruit punch] in plenty, which they made good use of,
and went away extremely well pleased—their priest at their head."

Campbell invited Detroit's twenty leading sorceresses to a ball
so that "I may see them." Johnson noted in his diary that he
opened the dancing with "Mademoiselle Curie—a fine girl."

The name which Warraghiyagey, his ear unattuned to French,
thus shortened was Angélique Cuillerier dit Beaubien: and the girl
was as strange a combination of characteristics as the baronet himself. She was beautiful: two centuries later her dark eyes still burn
in Detroit legend. She was a lady, but unlike any that civilization
grew. Although she shone among the stunners at the ball like a
comet among fixed constellations, her little feet were less familiar
with the dance than with Indian trails. She commonly spent her
nights in the flicker of council fires, throwing to ritualistic shouts
the belts that created forest policy.

"A fine scholar" and "the best interpreter of the various Indian
languages" at Detroit, Angélique was the daughter of the fur trader
and forest politician whom Johnson considered the principal
French inhabitant. Antoine Cuillerier had built his mansion outside the fort so that breechclothed hunters and feathered embassies
could come easily and go unobserved. Fascinated by Indian politics,
the great belle had at twenty-six found no white man interesting
enough to marry.

Now she floated from the ballroom on the arm of the fabulous
frontiersman. The beauty was unfamiliar with English, the baronet
with French. Pacing the midnight quiet of the walled town, they
flirted in Iroquois, which he spoke with a Mohawk intonation, she
with a provincial Huron twang.

Johnson Hall at Johnstown, New York
Sir William's second and grander mansion where Indians were always welcome, and from which he presided over his efficiently planned agricultural communities. The block house, intended for defense, is one of the two that flanked the Hall. (*Courtesy, NYSPIX-Commerce; New York State Department of Commerce*)

LA RIVIERE DU DÉTROIT
Depuis le Lac Sainte Claire
jusqu'au Lac Erié
Echelle de Deux Lieues Communes

Riv. Rouge

Village de Poutéouatamis

Ruisseau des Brais

Ecorés de Sable

Ruisseau de Ruin

Fond de Sable

DÉTROIT

Village des Hurons

Ruisseau de la Vie

Habitations

Rivière aux Dindes

Dindes

Rivière aux Ecorces

Pointe Monguago

Riv. de la Carrière

Isle aux Dindes

Petite Isle aux Dindes

la Carriere
Belle Pierre
de Grais

la Grande Isle

RIVIERE
DU

Rivière de la Presqu'Isle

Rivière aux Canards

Isle a la Pierre

Chenal
de la
Presqu'Isle

Prairie
Mouillée

Isle aux
Bois blancs

Pointe de Sable

Rivière
aux HieFons

Pointe
Mouillée

la Presqu'Isle

Riviere
aux Signes

LAC ERIÉ

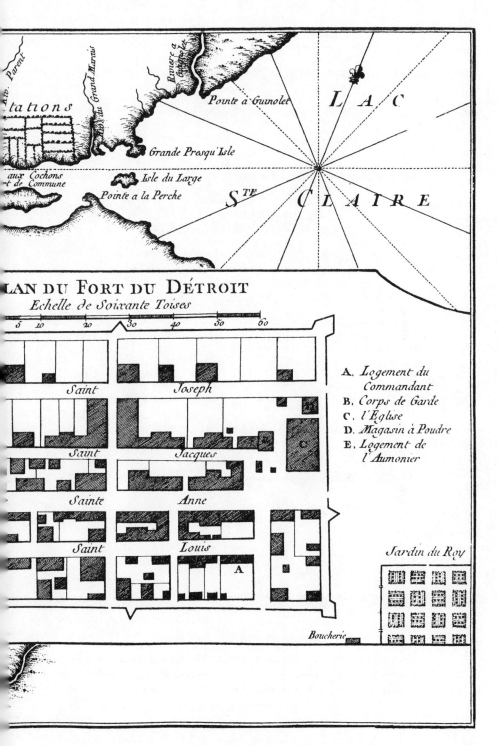

Aᵛ Parent

Rivière à Guillaumes

Rivière du Grand Marais

tations

Pointe à Guinolet

L A C

Grande Presqu'Isle

aux Cochons
t de Commune

Isle du Large

Pointe a la Perche

Sᵀᴱ C L A I R E

LAN DU FORT DU DÉTROIT

Echelle de Soixante Toises

5 10 20 30 40 50 60

Saint Joseph

Saint Jacques

Sainte Anne

Saint Louis

A. *Logement du*
   Commandant
B. *Corps de Garde*
C. *l'Église*
D. *Magasin à Poudre*
E. *Logement de*
   l'Aumonier

C

A

Jardin du Roy

Boucherie

A morsel of France deep in the wilderness, where Sir William
was almost lured into contracting a Christian marriage (*Clements Library, University of Michigan*)

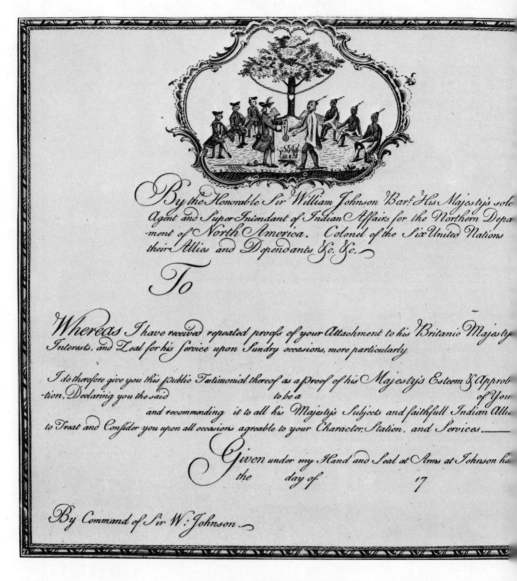

By the Honorable Sir William Johnson Bart: His Majesty's sole Agent and Super Intendant of Indian Affairs for the Northern Depa-ment of North America. Colonel of the Six United Nations their Allies and Dependants &c. &c.

To

Whereas I have received repeated proofs of your Attachment to his Britanic Majesty Interests, and Zeal for his Service upon Sundry occasions, more particularly

I do therefore give you this public Testimonial thereof as a Proof of his Majesty's Esteem & Approb -tion, Declaring you the said   to be a   of You and recommending it to all his Majesty's Subjects and faithfull Indian Alli to Treat and Consider you upon all occasions agreable to your Character, Station, and Services.____

Given under my Hand and Seal at Arms at Johnson ha the   day of   17

By Command of Sir W: Johnson

Sir William's Indian certificate

This document was intended to enable Indian allies to pass British military lines, and also to protect them from white persecution and random violence (*Courtesy of the New-York Historical Society, New York City*)

A slight, short, blond young man certainly stared anxiously after them. John Johnson knew his father's weakness for girls who were also Indian politicians, and whatever doubts he had as to his legitimacy must have risen to his mind in a bitter flood. Angélique was no doxie for his father to enjoy outside of marriage: supposing she became Lady Johnson and had a son? Who would then be the second baronet?

We can hear John sigh with relief when the couple returned from the darkness—but the two fierce, bold, dark, and charming heads remained close together in the light. Surely Catherine Weisenberg's son found the hours long before the dance broke up at 5 a.m.

When the great Indian council was called out of doors, "there being no house here half large enough to meet in," the French lady negotiator watched critically what the English forest-master would do after he had smiled at her over the sachems and warriors: Hurons, Saquenays, Ottawas, Chippewas, Potawatomis, Miamis, Delawares, Shawnees, Mohicans, Mohawks, Oneidas, and Senecas including many Chenussios.

Following strict rules of formality, the Huron speaker intoned thanks to "our brother Warraghiyagey who has now brought peace to our country which was in a tremor, and has fixed our hearts in their proper places which before his arrival were fluttering and knew not where to settle. We now take him by the hand, as all the nations have done, with a certainty that nothing can separate us. We give him now this bunch of green wampum which has the power to dispell all darkness."

At her own family council fire, which was the very center of French intrigue against the English, Angélique had heard very different sentiments from the same Huron lips. With no expression in her eyes that indicated more than polite interest, she looked across to see whether Sir William was being fooled. His eyes expressed only polite interest.

Although they certainly had not mentioned it to each other, they had both been excited by the presence among the Senecas of Kyashuta. Both had private information that this Chenussio had co-operated with a half-Indian son of Chabert Joncaire in sending out the "bad belt" calling for united action against the English that had so alarmed Detroit. Angélique could not help being impressed with Warraghiyagey's ability to manipulate Indian conferences when, in answer to his question, "Who sent that belt hither?" the Huron speaker obediently pointed to Kyashuta.

The Chenussio (who was to be more responsible for "Pontiac's conspiracy" than Pontiac, who was sitting silent) "stood up," so Warraghiyagey noted in admiration, "and with great oratory and resolution endeavored to clear himself." This produced countercharges from the Huron, who was seconded in his accusations by an Ottawa. Sir William permitted "a great deal of altercation," and then "I got up and desired that they would not go to too great lengths, being now joined in stricter friendship and alliance than ever. Left them liquor, and broke up the meeting."

Sir William stated publicly that he was working to establish an "even and broad" road of peace "as far as the setting of the sun"; but he realized that, until Indian grievances could be rectified, such a road might carry thousands of warriors against the frontier settlements. Better to have the Indians disagree among themselves. "I did all in my power in private conferences," he later admitted, "to create a misunderstanding between the Six Nations and western Indians, and also between the latter and those of Ohio."

He called Kyashuta to him. Knowing that the Seneca would laugh if threatened with the British troops Amherst believed could "extirpate" the Indians, Johnson warned that, at any further Chenussio misbehavior, "the western and other nations" would "revenge our quarrel, they being easily inflamed against the Senecas." If Kyashuta ran through his mind the name of Pontiac, an Ottawa who hated the English and had great influence with western nations, he did not mention it. Promising to "reform and repent," he accepted a large string of wampum, two strouds, two pairs of stockings, and a swig of liquor.

Warraghiyagey realized that more would have to be done to neutralize the Chenussios, whose "late ill-behavior is occasioned in a great measure by our ill-treatment of them," yet he felt—and Angélique did not disabuse him—that those western tribes that were centered on Detroit were "extremely well disposed. . . . Unless greatly irritated thereto, they will never break the peace established with them, and there now only remains to complete everything by calling down [to Fort Johnson] the Six Nations," in order to induce Onondaga to put further pressure on Chenussio.

Sir William gave a dinner for "the principal inhabitants" at which "the French gentlemen and the two priests who dined with us got very merry." There was applause when he "invited them all to a ball tomorrow night, which I am to give for the ladies."

The following evening, "the ladies and gentlemen all assembled at my quarters, danced the whole night until seven o'clock in the morning. . . . There never was so brilliant an assembly here before." Naturally, Sir William made advances to his Angélique. Fingering the cross that hung from a throat designed for lovers' kisses, she coyly but expertly brought the conversation around to marriage. He remained importunate, eager for favors today, decisions to-morrow, yet his every amorous sally somehow brought him closer to the landing net. We can visualize John watching with burning eyes, regretting each time his embattled father stepped from the fray to fill his glass and return again, more eloquent, more heated. But the baronet was too experienced a lover, too expert a drinker, not to sober up when he reached the jumping-off place. As he noted in his journal, he "promised to write Mlle. Curie as soon as possible my sentiments."

In the bright morning which had overtaken the dancers, Sir William and the young beauty went their separate ways—yet he was not sure what his sentiments were. For the first recorded time, Johnson was seriously considering matrimony.

The trip homeward along the south shore of Lake Erie was for him a long hangover shot through with perplexity. He was hardly in his bateau before he began swallowing medicines. He swapped guns with a Chippewa; drilled a buck to the shorebound barking of the three wolves who had driven it into the lake; he did some exploring—but always his mind tumbled in a search for his senti-ments. He coughed and coughed; his old wound spoke "with pains in my thigh and downward, so that I could not walk or stand up without help nor sleep a wink." Word came that "all were well at my house" and "Molly was delivered of a girl." Dear Molly! But also, dear Angélique!

The weather had turned cold, with "a smart, white frost" after sundown, when Sir William rode up to Fort Johnson with the anxious solicitude of a lover who knows he has not been faithful. "I found all my family well. So ended my tour, *Gloria Deo Soli* [Glory to God alone]."

To be with Molly again was happiness, but for an aging, ailing man a new young love seems a talisman against the thin, descending years and their inevitable end. If Angélique came to him, would it not be the realization at long last of an old dream? More than Catherine Weisenberg, the housekeeper, or even Molly Brant, the Indian; more certainly than all the strange women he had briefly loved, she personified the visions of the lady he would marry that he had nurtured as an Irish lad, when forests were unknown to him—and still Angélique was not out of place in forests. Yet there was a look in those fine dark eyes of hers that hinted freedom's end. She would want to redecorate Fort Johnson; she would lecture his drinking companions; and she would not put up with Molly, any more than Molly would welcome a queenly white bride. And if Molly left, what would happen to his heart?

He probably soon guessed that he would not take on this cataclysmic new love, yet to feel that the chance still existed eased the growing weakness in his body that even Molly's herbs could not cure. From month to month, he postponed sending Angélique his sentiments.

The following June, he received a letter from Captain Campbell: "I gave a ball on the King's birthday where a certain acquaintance of yours appeared to great advantage. She never neglects an opportunity of asking about the general. 'What,' says she, 'is there no Indian councils to be held here this summer?' I think, by her talk, Sir William had promised to return to Detroit. She desired I would present you her best compliments."

Still a year later, Angélique called herself again to Sir William's attention through a letter from the new commandant at Detroit, Henry Gladwin. Then he dashed her hopes with a cold reply. But he added with the nostalgia that comes with the passing of years and the nonpossession of beauty, "I have not forgot the powerful effect of the charms of the lady who honors me with a place in her remembrance."

19

A Lighted Fuse

In Europe, the Seven Years' War expanded. England declared war on Spain, giving France's remaining American colony of Louisiana a new ally: Spanish Florida. Northward up the crisscrossing trails came the propaganda-inspired rumor that the hour of glory would soon be at hand: French and Spanish armies would relieve the Indians of the cruel British yoke. At Niagara, starving tribes were eating the fish cleanings thrown away by the soldiers, and Croghan, his staff cut again, could only be kept from resigning his deputy superintendentship in Pennsylvania by Sir William's pleas. The regular officers stationed at the wilderness forts were frightened into complaining to Warraghiyagey of their commanding officer: Amherst's repressive policies, they grumbled, were nurturing an Indian war.

Sir William's cries of alarm had been heard in London, and on March 11, 1762, he received a copy of orders sent to all the royal governors that no further grants of Indian land should be valid until approved in England by the Board of Trade; and that all squatters on Indian land and insisters on dishonest claims should be prosecuted by the Crown in the colonial courts.

The first provision enabled Johnson to write Banyar and Colden that, since the Council had lost the power to give him a patent for his Canajoharie gift, he was cutting them out of his deed—yet he was far from sure that the ruling was a wise one. By creating a major impediment to the securing of new grants, legitimate as

247

well as illegitimate, the need for English review increased the value
of old grants, however fraudulent: Land speculators would be more
determined than ever to enforce the dishonest claims that so enraged the Indians. Redoubled pressure would thus be put on the
provision that existing grievances be righted—but it was framed in
a useless manner, since it depended on the action of colonial courts.

Under Johnson's very nose, the Livingston partner and agent
Klock was cooking up the most perfect and irritating proof of this.
That "yeoman . . . of evil name and fame and dishonest conversation" started a small revolution in the Canajoharie Castle by
carrying off to his own land nineteen braves, who, "in love with
him for some rum," signed papers confirming the old Livingston
steal of the Canajoharie heartlands. In complaining to Warraghiyagey, the sachems "threw" not belts of wampum but whiskey
bottles picked up outside Klock's house. And, indeed, when Sir
William stayed near Canajoharie with Klock's respectable brother,
"by singing and dancing and other noise" the revelers kept the
Indian Superintendent awake all night.

Klock argued that Warraghiyagey was defrauding the Indians
of the rum and money they could get from selling to the Livingstons because he wanted to secure the disputed land for himself at
no cost. That Molly's father, old Brant, led the anti-Klock party
gave color to such tales and proved truly embarrassing when it
developed that many years before Brant had himself signed the
much-denounced parchment on which the Livingston claim was
based. The sanctimonious sachem was forced to tell the sots, "I
was young and did not mind such matters. . . . It is probable that
I might have formerly signed it, when in liquor." (On the document his mark, a crude drawing of a deer, is defaced by a huge
blot.) This explanation produced whoops and then threats. Molly's
parents, so Warraghiyagey was told, would have been murdered
were it not for the intervention of an heroic Oneida called
Cowcake.

"By heavens," Johnson burst out to Banyar, "were you and the
people sensible of the villainy used in this dispute by the opposite
party from the highest to the lowest, you and they would be as-
tonished beyond measure. In short, I have not words nor knowledge of villainous ideas sufficient to expose their roguery."

Under the new royal decree, the Attorney General prosecuted Klock for attempting to defraud the Indians, but the Livingstons were influential in the court, and what other leading family did not have in its strongbox deeds they would prefer not to have questioned? The case was thrown out on the grounds that matters of equity could not be considered at common law. However, a chancery suit was impossible, as not all the parties were in the province. "A patent," Johnson commented bitterly, "however fraudulently obtained, is a claim superior to all justice and reason." He was at a loss what to tell the sachems.

In Pennsylvania, local politics continued to exacerbate already irritated Indian nerves: The Quaker party had set Teedyuscung on his feet again, and was encouraging him to keep Delaware public opinion outraged against the Penns' old Walking Purchase. From London, the Privy Council had ordered Johnson to determine the validity of the Indian grievance, but the Quakers had blocked his efforts to do so.

The issues had not changed since the matter had been brought up during the French and Indian War. Since the Iroquois had backed the purchase, they would still be annoyed if the Delawares were placated, and, since the settlers long established on the land could not be displaced, any award to the Delawares could still only add to the broken promises which all the Indians regarded as English treachery. The Quakers, however, continued to consider these matters secondary to abstract justice and the wonderful opportunity which the continuing ruckus over the Walking Purchase gave them to discredit the Proprietors who had perpetrated it. They had encouraged Teedyuscung's reluctance to expose himself to the Iroquois at Warraghiyagey's council fire. And so the issue remained an open wound, irritating the Iroquois and souring the Delawares.

Finally, the ailing baronet decided that if Teedyuscung would not come to him, he would go to Teedyuscung: He journeyed to Easton, Pennsylvania, probably his longest trip southward through the forest. A Quaker effort to head off the Delaware failed, and on June 14, 1762, the two champions were in the same town. This was so tense a situation for the self-styled king of all the Indians that he reached for his bottles and remained dead drunk for five days, while the Quakers spent half their time trying to sober him up and the other half in anguished conclave. It was only too clear that they had placed their campaign to annul Pennsylvania's proprietary rule in the hands of an alcoholic who dared not stand up to Sir William. Their only hope, they decided, was to discredit the result in advance by making the Indian Superintendent seem an overbearing violater of Indian rights. As they painfully lifted Teedyuscung to his feet, they whispered in his ear.

A trap was hidden in the Delaware's first formal speech: He asked authority to appoint his own clerk who would "take down whatever I have occasion to say," so that his grandchildren would have something to show in writing as well as the English. The Quakers were delighted when Sir William replied that a court could not have two official records. The Indian secretary, Witham Marsh, had been appointed directly by the King; he could be counted on to "write everything fairly down." However, Charles Thomson, who was to be the secretary to the Continental Congress, inscribed minutes for the Quakers.

After the Proprietors' case had been presented, Teedyuscung assured Warraghiyagey that he had understood everything which had transpired, but at the next session he presented a paper, obviously prepared by the Quakers, which said that he had understood nothing and feared, as he had been denied his own clerk, that Warraghiyagey "did not intend justice." Asked to explain the contradiction, the poor Indian receded miserably into his hangover.

At this the Quaker leader, Isreal Pemberton, sprang up and "with great warmth and indecency"—so reads Marsh's official but hardly nonpartisan report—insisted that Johnson was putting words into Teedyuscung's mouth. Referred to the official minutes, Pemberton replied that they "were not fairly taken." He would complain to the government in London.

Sir William then pointed out that the Crown had appointed him sole arbiter of the matter: By what right did Pemberton interpose? Pemberton replied—"insolently," the record reads—that he was a freeman. Then three other Quakers, Fox, Galloway, and Hughes, "made another attack on Sir William," who responded with such heat that it was rumored he drew his sword. Finally, to end "so much noise and clamor," he adjourned the meeting.

Teedyuscung soon presented another paper as his own, but when Warraghiyagey asked if he knew its contents, he replied, so continued Marsh's report, "My cousin wrote it. . . . I did not come to have any difference, but to settle matters on a good footing. I did not come to put my hand into your purse or to get clothing. I give up the land to you and the white people."

Desiring only to take his headache to some dark, silent glade, Teedyuscung stated on the next day that he had been convinced by the Proprietors' evidence that he had been misinformed by his ancestors: The land had been legally bought. Thereupon, to make the Delawares "perfectly easy," Sir William ruled that the Proprietors should give them £600 in addition to the usual presents.

Informed that the Quakers were sending charges to the government in England, Richard Peters, the Proprietary Secretary of Pennsylvania, urged Johnson to retain in London an agent to come to his defense. Although the anti-proprietary agent who would lead the attack was Benjamin Franklin, Sir William hired no agent. He had in London no personal representative except his banker, but his dispatches went directly to the most mighty. In these, he lambasted the "great impropriety" of the Quakers' "meddling."

Despite Franklin, the Indian policy of the Quakers, who had for so long claimed to be the best friends of the tribes, was discredited. The Board of Trade decided to regard as fact Teedyuscung's denial, testified to by Sir William, of the Quaker charges against the Proprietors. This convicted the anti-proprietary party of making trouble for their own purposes in the forest; and even those who disapproved of Johnson felt that the reflections cast in the presence of the tribes on the integrity of His Majesty's Indian representative tended "to promote the worst consequences from persons so irascible." The Friendly Association, which was the Quakers' organ for dealing with the Indians, collapsed. Again Warraghiyagey had driven rivals out of his domain, but it was like holding back the sea with a broom. There were always more.

From the Indian point of view, the approval of the Walking Purchase gave added importance to the Wyoming Valley which had, in conjunction with that purchase, been set aside by Pennsylvania and the Iroquois as a haven for the Delawares. But Connecticut speculators still claimed the Valley.

Warraghiyagey sent to Hartford an Iroquois deputation which forced Governor Fitch of Connecticut to proclaim, under the new orders from England, official disapproval of the settlements—but the speculators paid no attention. One night, all the Delaware houses in the Valley went up in flames: among the ashes lay the charred remains of Teedyuscung. His son, Captain Bull, sharpened his hatchet.

To England, Sir William's warnings flowed on. Some method would have to be found to obtain reasonable equity for the Indians in some type of white court. His department needed power to stop trade abuses, which continued because there were no teeth in the regulations that Amherst had allowed him to draw up. He needed authorization to give the Indians the presents they annually expected, and "above all" he needed to be allowed enough officers and interpreters to smooth discord when it first developed on the local level. All this would be expensive, but cheaper than an Indian war.

Lest Amherst's vaporings about Indian helplessness before the regular army lull English fears, Johnson prophetically described the tragedy that was on the point of breaking. However short they were kept under peace, the Indians would not in war lack for ammunition as they would capture military supply trains in the woods and find powder in the frontier houses they overran. Nor could warriors used to living off the woods be starved out by any blockade or strategic cutting of their supply lines. The forts on which Amherst relied to hold them back would, if not captured, simply be by-passed by the war parties that would "cut off and destroy a number of families, destroy their houses, effects, and grain, all within the compass of a very few hours, and then return by a different route to some of their places of rendezvous. . . . The surviving inhabitants, together with all those near them, immediately forsake their dwellings and retire with their families in the utmost terror, poverty, and distress to the next towns, striking panic into the inhabitants who then become fearful of going to any of the posts. Trade becomes at once stagnated, nothing can be carried to any of the posts without an escort and, unless 'tis a very strong one—which is not always to be procured—the whole may fall into the hands of the Indians. . . . This picture of a state of a country under an Indian war, however improbable it may seem, will be found on due examination not to have been exaggerated."

In November, a trader and his servant were murdered in the Senecas' country by two Indians from Kanestio, a village, so Johnson wrote, of "profligate fellows from several nations . . . Senecas, Shawnees, and a few Delawares." The Seneca sachems freed a third colonial, whom the Kanestios had captured, and sent belts of condolence to Johnson Hall.

Murders had, since the fur trade began, happened in the forests (as they happen everywhere), and they had always been forgiven by French or English authorities after such apologies as the Senecas had just made (even as the Indians forgave colonial murders of their own nationals). But Amherst ordered Johnson to demand that the Indian culprits be surrendered to him for a white man's trial. (He would never have surrendered a white killer to the Indians, but could see no parallel.) Otherwise, "I will give immediate orders for the march of a body of men to take revenge on the nation or village."

The village was under the protection of the Chenussio Senecas, who were already far from friendly to the English. Any effort to attack these Senecas would bring all the Iroquois to their defense, and in such a quarrel the Iroquois could count on the assistance of every Indian who could reach a Colonial scalp. Warraghiyagey sprang into the breach to keep Amherst from precipitating a general Indian war.

He sent belts to the Chenussios demanding in the commander's name the delivery of the murderers, but with the belts went reports that he himself was "of a contrary mind" from Amherst and "trying to mitigate matters." To Amherst he wrote that, since the Indians "never bring an offender to punishment in cold blood," the Onondaga Council was "entirely at a loss what step to take." He threatened both the general and the Indians with his resignation if either pursued extreme policies.

The Onondaga Council sent messages westward—"you have really shook us by the head so often," a Chenussio stated publicly, "that we have not a hair left"—but they put no teeth in their requests that the murderers be delivered to Amherst. The only result was that the culprits, at first "not the least concerned at the mischief, but rather boasting about their manhood," were finally forced to flee to the woods so that the Chenussios could say that they could not find them. Thus, month after month, the precarious peace was preserved.

But there were disturbing reports of religious hysteria in the forests. A prophet among the Delawares wept continuously as he urged his hearers to cleanse themselves for a crusade with emetics, sexual continence, and by renouncing every art and object that stemmed from European contact. The Onondaga speaker told Warraghiyagey that one of his people had been visited by the Great Spirit who told him in a vision that, if the white people did not stop "squabbling and fighting for these lands which he gave the Indians," he would exterminate the white people, "although their numbers were ever so great."

Warraghiyagey replied, "Brother, your romantic notions, custom of dreaming and seeing visions, however usual amongst you, cannot but appear in a very ridiculous light to white people, who will consider it only a scheme set on foot by some designing persons to answer their purposes."*

From Chenussio, Kyashuta was sending out war belts demanding a wide alliance against the British. Like a snowy sounding board, the forest echoed rumors that winter of 1762-63. A synchronized signal, Warraghiyagey heard, was to be given by the frogs. When from damp places everywhere the peepers raised the love songs of spring, every Indian hatchet would cleave a white man's skull.

Although the peepers sang in peace, the tension remained. Amherst wrote Sir William to keep pointing out to the Indians how "contemptible" they would make themselves "by violating the most solemn promises of friendship without the least provocation on our side." Johnson listed the Indians' grievances to anyone who would listen, and insisted that in redressing them "the honor of the Crown and the credit of the British nation appear to me to be concerned."

Outside Detroit, Pontiac was excited by the promise relayed through Angélique's sweet lips that, if the Indians would only

---

* It was common with Indians, when they wished something, to state that they had dreamed it was given them. Thus Sir William noted in his accounts, "To Peter, a Mohawk warrior, to fulfil his dream, a silver band, £1.12.0." This custom inspired a stock frontier story of a white man who outdreamed an Indian, which was ascribed to various individuals including Johnson. Hendrick, so one version goes, described a dream in which Johnson gave him a scarlet uniform. The uniform having been produced, Johnson said that in one of his dreams Hendrick had given him 500 acres of good Mohawk land. Sadly signing the deed, Hendrick stated, "I will never dream with you again."

start a war, the French would come at once to their support. The Ottawa chief had received and sent on so many Seneca war belts that, as he later told Johnson, if they were gathered together it would take more than one man to carry them. However, he had himself sent out only one belt, and that was a reply to the Iroquois. Unlike Kyashuta, he did not envision a synchronized attack against all reachable English holdings. He decided that he would lead the local tribes in an uprising that would restore Detroit to the control of its French inhabitants. He promised Angélique's father that he would appoint him military governor.

On May 5, 1763, the Frenchman and Indians determined that in two days Pontiac and his Ottawas would pay a seemingly friendly visit to Detroit but, once inside the fort, they would exterminate the English. Although Angélique had helped prepare for this dread decision, she felt that one enemy had to be saved. After dark, she slipped into the walled town to the Irish fur trader, James Sterling, who had taken Sir William's place in her heart. She was credited, ten years later, with having given "the best information," but other reports seem to have come to English ears. Pontiac had made a fatal mistake in assuming that in the three-sided community of Indians and French and English, two groups could keep so dire a secret from the third.

Since the forewarned officers frustrated Pontiac's ruses, the fort could not be taken by surprise—but the Ottawas were too excited to return to secret plotting. On May 9 they attacked such Englishmen as they could find outside the walls. The three death halloos that sounded over the mangled corpses of Mrs. Trumbull and her sons signaled the outbreak of what has been called "Pontiac's Conspiracy," but could more accurately be called "Amherst's War."*

* Angélique's reward for protecting her virtue from Sir William and for saving Sterling's life would not pass in a Sunday School tract. Sterling eventually married the beauty, but only, as he boasted to a friend, for her dowry and to supply his fur business with an interpreter who did not have to be paid. Her priest soon reported to his bishop that tears flowed from her fine eyes as, under the tyranny of her husband, "an absolute master who must be obeyed," she got Indians drunk in order to steal their merchandise. When asked if she had been forbidden to go to mass, she replied, "He has not said so yet." Sterling sent Johnson his wife's compliments, and asked in her name (but vainly) that he be employed in the Indian service.

20

Pontiac's Conspiracy

" 'Tis an old saying," wrote a Yorker, "that the devil is easier raised than laid. Sir Jeffery has found it so with these Indian demons."

Its gates bolted shut, Detroit was impregnable to Indian warfare, but the wild was equally impregnable to the garrison. No English messenger could warn the other forts, but Indians ran free.

The news that fighting had started kindled Indian resentment in an ever-enlarging arc of forest—and the trick Angélique had helped frustrate at Detroit worked elsewhere. As Indian social callers passed through fortified gates and changed suddenly into executioners, every other wilderness fort except Fort Pitt fell prey to the tribes.

Travelers, traders, and military detachments at large in the forests learned of the war an instant before they tasted death or capture. The borders from New Jersey to Virginia were suddenly loud with shouts, lurid with fires. The surprise, indeed, was as total as the Japanese were to achieve at Pearl Harbor.

Warraghiyagey had foreseen trouble but, as he explained, "Indian alarms are aften repeated before the blow is struck, the time of which can never be certainly known." But once the blow fell, he never doubted of its seriousness. "Without any exaggeration, I look upon the northern Indians to be the most formidable of any uncivilized body of people in the world."

His first thought was for his own Valley. He reinforced Oswego with his personal followers, and, in order to be among his outer tenants, moved from Fort Johnson some twelve miles deeper into the forest to the yet uncompleted Johnson Hall. Surrounding the gaping mansion with "a good stockade, well-flanked," he encouraged the erection of other strong points.

When, in New York City, Amherst received the first incomplete reports, he fumed at the "ingratitude" of the tribes, but was convinced that any posts "commanded by officers can certainly never be in danger from such a wretched enemy as the Indians are." At word that posts were actually falling, he cried out to Johnson that "the whole race of Indians" should beware or he would "put a most effective stop to their very being." For this purpose, he relied on his regulars.

Reinforcements reached Detroit by boat, but were partially destroyed when they sallied to where the Indians could get at them. Another detachment under Colonel Bouquet marched for Fort Pitt. The battle they fought at Bushy Run is written down as a great victory for the white man: more than four hundred and sixty regulars actually managed to fight off ninety-five Indians with the loss of only sixty soldiers! This triumph got the survivors into the fort, where they did little but stare out again over the walls.

Fought in a green immensity by extreme individualists, white and Indian, the war was an irrational patchwork of personal tragedies. Only at Detroit, where Pontiac tried naïvely to stage a European-style siege, was there a definable line of battle. The typical engagement was a fusillade shocking the forest silence, sometimes toppling an Indian in his canoe, twenty times more often a white man at his plough. A few wigwams went up in flames, but hundreds of settlers' cabins, for the Indians had the advantages of woodcraft, mobility, and surprise. It was a rare frontiersman who could sport an Indian scalp as a tobacco pouch.

Most Indian prisoners the Colonials took did not survive long enough to appear in records. Although the tribes exterminated whole colonial families, they also led hundreds of survivors over long trails. The captives were treated with a mixture of kindness and savagery hard for modern minds to fathom. If one tottered under his pack, the Indians would add the burden to their own, but, if the sufferer continued to fall behind, they would kill him and proceed cheerfully with his scalp. Female prisoners were, on reaching their conquerors' castles, accepted without any racial intolerance by their red sisters and married as complete equals to warriors. All male captives had to run the gantlet; after that their fates hovered for a queasy period between two extremes. Some were in the most horrible manner tortured to death as tests of their fortitude and offerings of revenge; others were adopted to take the place of Indians recently deceased. Since these white men had been ritually made over into Indians, they were armed and given complete freedom. Many a captive returned to civilization boasting of his sagacity in murdering, as they trustingly slept, his Indian "brothers" and "sisters."

There were alarms in the Mohawk Valley—after two female slaves had seen an Indian skulking around Johnson Hall with a lance, "I had all my people under arms the whole night"—but, as the political situation became clear, tension dropped. Warraghiyagey's influence had proved strong enough to exempt from "Amherst's War" not only his own home territory but the whole New York frontier as far west as Oswego. The eastern Iroquois nations had remained pro-British, forming a neutral zone which no other nation dared invade. The Senecas, who alone among the Iroquois were active in the fighting, could not attack down the Long House: they forayed north to the Niagara pass and along Lake Erie, or south to raid Pennsylvania with the Mingoes, Delawares, and Shawnees.

Warraghiyagey's first political objective was to make the Senecas change sides: his ace in the hole was the very nation that had during the French wars been the enemy's trump card. The Caughnawagas now loved Sir William and the English with all the ardor of new converts. Into a meeting of as many Iroquois sachems as he could lure to Johnson Hall—the Senecas were conspicuously absent—he inserted a delegation of the formerly pro-French Iroquois, who scolded the traditional allies of the English for having let slip the ancient covenant chain.

Then, to the horror of the sachems, the show began. The Caughnawagas gathered "in the summer house in the garden, and ten of their warriors, being naked, painted and feathered, one of whom had a drum on his back made of a keg covered with skin, marched in slow order in two ranks, singing their song according to the Ottawa custom, Tom Wildman [chief] in the rear rank beating the drum with one stick, and the rest accompanying it with notched sticks, which they struck in good time on their axes. In this manner they proceeded to the house, where they entered, when Tom Wildman advanced before the rest and sung his war song, which he twice repeated, after which Sir William gave them liquor, pipes, tobacco, and paint, whereupon they returned back in the same order. The occasion of this ceremony was to show Sir William that they had approved of what he said and had taken up the axe against our enemies."

The threat of military action tugged hard at Iroquois diplomacy. If the Caughnawagas really marched against England's Indian enemies, they might be joined by the Mohawks and Warraghiyagey's personal friends in other nations. If England's enemies still included the Senecas, the ancient League would dissolve in fratricidal war. Should the Senecas, however, reverse their policy and join the campaign, a united Iroquois army could, in conjunction with the Caughnawagas and the English, return the Delawares and Shawnees to subjection, break up the Mingoes who were luring away Iroquois nationals, and perhaps even chastise once more the Iroquois' ancient opponents, the Hurons, Ottawas, etc. When, Warraghiyagey asked, had there been such an opportunity to reassert the ancient prestige of the Five Nations?

It was a clever maneuver, but its success depended on Amherst's acceptance of Indian allies. Sir William did not write the general, as he did the Board of Trade, that a few braves "would do more mischief and create more uneasiness among our enemies" than a hundred regulars, but he did warn Amherst that regulars who attempted an unaccompanied invasion of the Seneca country would probably not get out alive. Sir Jeffery only expressed amazement that Sir William would place any trust in any Indians whatever after "such perfidious treacheries."

Warraghiyagey answered that the Senecas had "as sufficient causes for falling out from us as many people in Europe had to quarrel with another." Why did not Amherst admit his mistakes, remedy injustices and give the Indians presents as of old? It might "appear a disagreeable circumstance to purchase their favor, but what can we do? Can we destroy them all?" The best that could be hoped would be, "after much expense and loss," to "drive those who are nearest to take shelter with the Western and Northern Indians, which will but increase their power and hatred, and which our Colonies will frequently feel the effects of."

Amherst's reaction was to state that after "the savages" had been "sufficiently punished" he would "think of giving them peace." To a military subordinate, he suggested annihilating "this execrable race" by presenting them with blankets infected with smallpox.

While the commander in chief snarled at Warraghiyagey, the Board of Trade implored him from London for help: "We have little other immediate hope of comfort than what arises from our reliance upon your ability and activity."

To the Board, Johnson wrote fatefully, "I humbly conceive that a certain line should be run at the back of the northern Colonies beyond which no settlement should be made until the whole Six Nations should think proper of selling part thereof. This would encourge the thick settlement of the frontiers, oblige the proprietors of large grants to get them inhabited, and secure the Indians from being further deceived. . . . The thirst of making distant settlements is very impolitic, as such frontiers are too weak and remote to oppose even an ordinary scalping party, and therefore it will be time enough to advance our settlements when the large tracts already patented are thoroughly inhabited."

The siege of Detroit was going badly. Devoid of cannon, innocent of engineering, prevented by their lack of large boats from stopping the supplies that sailed to the enemy, Pontiac could do nothing but quarrel with his allies and await the French army, skillful at battering walls down, he had been promised. But during June there arrived instead dispatches stating that the Seven Years' War was over and that France had ceded to England all North America east of the Mississippi except the area immediately around New Orleans.

But Pontiac suspected a propaganda lie. For correct intelligence and to demand immediate aid he sent ambassadors to the nearest French post, Fort de Chartres (Randolph County, Illinois). The commandant there was buried so deep that he had heard nothing; he sent on to New Orleans for facts. Having floated down the Mississippi, the messengers had to paddle laboriously up again. It was October 23 when Pontiac was finally handed a letter from the commandant at Fort de Chartres. "What joy you will have," the Frenchman wrote, "in seeing the French and English smoke from the same pipe and eating out of the same spoon and finally living like brethren!" Pontiac could crumple the letter in his hand but he could not change the fact that the Indians had been betrayed.

To the British commandant Pontiac wrote, "All our young men have buried the hatchet." He would forget "what you have done to me," as he was sure the English would forget what he had done to them. Then he lifted the siege and with his followers departed unmolested to a winter camp on the Maumee. He intended to try in the spring whether appeals at Fort de Chartres would not, despite European diplomacy, elicit French support.

Paradoxically, Pontiac's great reputation as an Indian general is based on what made him a poor one: That he foolishly besieged a fortress pleases the military prejudices of white historians. Actually, the effective Indian fighting was being done in the aboriginal manner. Although their names have mostly been forgotten, the guerilla chiefs needed no European help; they were not halted by the Anglo-French peace. During the winter of 1763-64, fountains of smoke sprang suddenly skyward deeper and deeper into Virginia and Pennsylvania. At the Niagara Carrying Place, Senecas drove a convoy of men, horses, and wagons over the brink of Devil's Hole into the roaring depths below, and, when regulars were sent from the fort to the rescue, decimated these also.

British arms were achieving little, but in London statesmanship was on the move. Amherst was recalled to be succeeded by General Gage. And the Board of Trade leapt at Warraghiyagey's suggestion that a hard and fast boundary be established between the colonials and the Indians. They fixed on the line easiest to define: the top of the Alleghenies. Everything west of the heads of streams that flowed into the Atlantic was, "for the present and until our further pleasure be known," reserved for the tribes.

This did not, of course, put a stop to all purchases, since the Indians still controlled extensive territories east of the Alleghenies.

Rescinding their former ruling that all new grants had to be approved in England, the Board of Trade now provided that Indian purchases be made only in the name of the Crown at public councils by a royal governor or the commander in chief (who would then hand them on to private buyers). The same officials were severally to license fur traders. No provision was made for rescinding fraudulent deeds then on the books or for giving presents to the tribes. Although the Indian department was not even mentioned, Johnson wrote that, as the rulings promised to prevent some future grievances, he would use them to show the Indians that the King had, at least, a "gracious and favorable disposition to do them justice."

As Amherst sailed for England, he urged his successor to "punish" the Indians before he permitted Warraghiyagey to treat with them. But among Gage's first official acts was a trip to Albany seeking Sir William's advice. The officer who had longed to lean on Sir William three years before at Oswego but had been afraid it would compromise his dignity had gained in maturity and was now able to lean without embarrassment. Furthermore, as commandant at Montreal he had learned to respect the Indians, even sneaking them ammunition against Amherst's orders. Now Gage gave Johnson permission to recruit warriors.

Warraghiyagey instantly began conspicuous preparations to send the Caughnawagas and his own Iroquois friends against an enemy that included, so he announced, the Senecas. This brought Senecas popping out of the forest. Shepherded by mediators from other Iroquois nations, they filed into Johnson's clearing.

During December, he gave the Senecas "the most severe reprimand in the presence of the rest." In January, 1764, he received in the bedroom where he lay ill two Chenussios who he was warned had come to murder him. Fixing them with his eye, he denounced the "so vile and unnatural conduct of their nation," and added, "unless a proper atonement be made for the blood of our people which you so unjustly spilled, the general will take such revenge as the heinousness of the crime deserves."

Sir William was walking a hairline. Should he receive the Senecas as friends while their axes still reeked with unavenged blood, he would damage English prestige in the forests. Yet any action which would tear the Iroquois League apart would, even if feasible, be the worst possible disaster for order in the forests. He could threaten, but he would in the end have to satisfy the other Iroquois nations by making peace with the Senecas.

He planned therefore to send his warriors against the Shawnees and Delawares—many a sachem agreed they needed a good scare—and against Kanestio. Although that polyglot village, which still harbored the Indians who had in 1762 murdered two Englishmen, was under Chenussio protection, conservative Iroquois statesmen would welcome its destruction as discouraging the growing tendency of their nationals to mix with subject tribes.

On January 25, 1764, the Iroquois warriors at Johnson Hall "took up the war belt, which they had painted red and feathered for that purpose, and sung their war song with great spirits," after which Sir William thanked them "and ordered a barrel of cider and a runlet of rum to their camp to drink the King's health, and a large roll of tobacco." The next day he gave them clothing, paint, and ammunition; and the following two days "they spent in drinking and feasting and dancing their war dance." On the 29th, "they delivered in their numbers by a parcel of red-painted sticks from every tribe"—roughly a hundred—and set out with some white woodsmen and officers against the Delawares and Shawnees. Warraghiyagey had offered "out of my own pocket" bounties for two Delaware chiefs, Long Coat and Squashcutter, but had stipulated, remembering how often hair had been sold to the French as his own scalp, that he would only pay if handed "the whole head."

All negotiation on the Pennsylvania frontier having been drowned out in gunfire, Croghan's crack interpreter, Henry (Andrew) Montour was at Johnson Hall. This son of a French mother and a Delaware father led another party—over 200 warriors—toward Kanestio. As they refreshed themselves in an Indian village near the main branch of the Susquehanna, there was a stirring in the forest, and out came seven enemy Delawares led by Teedyuscung's son, Captain Bull. This chief was described by an English officer as "quite the fine gentleman . . . the best looking Indian I ever saw." Johnson found him "very likely and remarkably active . . . full of prevarication . . . and a villain of the first rank." Bull squatted down gracefully among the massed pro-English braves, lit his pipe, and explained that he and his friends were on their way down the river for a little peaceful hunting. But Montour suspected that his visitors intended "to burn, kill, and destroy, being noted for murdering, notorious villains." The atmosphere became increasingly tense and finally Montour's party, after some little resistance, bound Captain Bull and his party "hand and foot." Montour then led his force against a nearby encampment of Bull's followers. They captured eleven sleeping braves, eight squaws, and three papooses.

After the prisoners were delivered at Johnson Hall, Bull dared boast to the great Warraghiyagey that "he had with his own hands killed twenty-six English since spring." Sir William was given a squaw to replace his father—Christopher Johnson had just died in Ireland—and the warriors, including Bull, were sent in irons to a New York City jail. Their incarceration as for all practical purposes hostages, Johnson stated, did much to tame the Delawares still at large. But in London Amherst, who was fighting for his political life against Sir William's charges that he had fomented the Indian war, insisted that the whole incident proved that his critic and the evil Indians were in cahoots: Bull had permitted his party to be captured in order to make it look as if Sir William were initiating and winning battles.

The Delawares themselves nursed a grievance which the missionary John Heckewelder recorded a half-century later. He was told that the Iroquois (Senecas?) had urged the Delawares to fall on the English, and then, when persuaded by Johnson to stop the war, "instead of conforming to the ancient custom of the Indian nations, which was simply to take their war hatchet back," they fell on the "unsuspecting" Delawares, taking prisoners whom Johnson confined in irons. "This cruel act of treachery," the Delawares told Heckewelder, they would "never forgive or forget."*

However, the Iroquois violation of "ancient custom" did not extend to truly sanguinary warfare. Although one Delaware brave was killed in the very act of singing his war song, the advance of

---

* Captain Bull's capture was profoundly to affect American literature, for Cooper based on Heckewelder's account his belief that the Iroquois were characterized by treachery and had conquered the Delawares only by tricks.

Warraghiyagey's war parties along what is now the boundary between New York and Pennsylvania continued to be practically
bloodless. As the nearby Chenussios looked the other way, as the
Delawares and mixed tribes who inhabited the region withdrew,
Montour, so he reported to Johnson, "destroyed three large towns
[one was Kanestio], besides all their little out villages and inhabitants [habitations] to the number of 130 very large and well-built
Indian houses in the most beautiful country that I ever see. . . .
The warriors here sends their love to you and says they hope you
are well satisfied with their behavior."

Warraghiyagey was both satisfied and worried. The captives, the
enemy retreat, the smoldering villages, all reflected a shift in the
wilderness balance, but the villages could be quickly rebuilt, and
the captives would have to be returned. ("Such," wrote Johnson,
"are their notions of clemency, they will become our most inveterate enemies hereafter.") What the hostile Indians really cared
about, their manpower, had not been touched.

Although Pontiac was dashed by his continuing inability to
procure assistance from Fort de Chartres, his forces were wandering
around the Illinois country unscathed. The Pennsylvanians had, it
is true, made a few successful raids on Indian encampments near
their frontier, but Gage complained that the English had not done
enough to make it clear that "every puny tribe" could not "insult
us with impunity." This promised "continual broils."

Since Indians would not kill Indians, Sir William urged action
by white troops that would give the tribes "a good opinion of our
abilities." He called for 400 rangers "acquainted with woods and
furnished with snowshoes"; but Colden wrote him that what
"humor" there had been for chasing after Indians through forests
had abated. To make up the lack, Johnson sent out his son John
at the head of an army of his own retainers, but they achieved
nothing. The only effective white action of the winter of 1763-64
was against a group of unarmed, Christian basket-makers.

Rather than seek out the strongholds of their enemies—"murderers," Johnson commented, are "generally cowards"—the Paxton
Boys, a gang of Pennsylvania frontiersmen, turned on some Moravian Indian converts who lived peacefully nearby, killing six in
cold blood. Other friendly Indians were hurried to Lancaster for

safekeeping, but the frontiersmen marched, broke open the workhouse, and slaughtered fourteen men, women, and children as they knelt in prayer.

Terrified for the safety of the 140 converts at Bethlehem and Nazareth, the Moravians spirited them in the dark—the sick and blind in wagons, the rest on foot—to Philadelphia and hid them in a church. When the news came out, the frontiersmen marched on Philadelphia to murder the Indians, and were only stopped by Franklin's persuasion and a display of force by British regulars. The refugees begged to be sent to Sir William Johnson, who was eager to receive them, but the New York authorities refused them admission lest their pitiful plight give a "bad impression" to the Iroquois. Warraghiyagey insisted that he had plenty of influence with the Iroquois to overcome any such impression, but he could not prevail on the timid city men. Gage finally housed the refugees in royal barracks guarded by regular troops.

In February, 1764, Warraghiyagey allowed the other Iroquois nations to persuade him to receive a formal peace delegation from the Senecas. They expressed eagerness to fight "the Shawnees, Delawares, and others—His Majesty's enemies—declaring their sorrow for what was past and their readiness to make any satisfaction, if forgiven." To establish that this was an English victory, Warraghiyagey set peace terms that would hurt. The Senecas would have to "deliver up the two murderers of Kanestio [and] all our people among them, whether prisoners, deserters, Negroes, etc.; and cede to His Majesty all the lands from Niagara to the falls on both sides of the strait." After the signing of the treaty, they were "to leave their chief men hostages for the performance of the several articles." The Seneca delegates promised that they would urge their sachems to accept these terms formally at a great peace conference which Warraghiyagey had scheduled for Niagara for July.

As the spring of 1764 feathered a million branches, Mohawks appeared in every inhabited clearing as far west as the anti-English turmoil had extended. They carried the red-painted belts with which Warraghiyagey threatened to exterminate his enemies, and other belts inviting all disposed to peace to meet him at Niagara.

To the Detroit Hurons, who had already abandoned the fighting, the Mohawk Peter said that Sir William Johnson "looks on every side and finds himself struck from all parts, and is so covered with blood that he can scarce see, and that he knows not for what reason, and said he deserved pity—but on reflection said, 'No!', when it is in his power to extirpate you and all those who do him ill." It was the Hurons who needed pity, and he would give it them "notwithstanding your ingratitude to him."

The Huron speaker replied, "We see that the eyes of our brethren are shut with blood by means of the strokes they have received from all sides, and we think to wash them a little." They would hang the war ax up in the air where only God could reach it.

But Big Jaw, the chief of the Hurons at Sandusky, replied to a similar embassy that the English might have "as many men as there were leaves on the trees; but we look upon one Indian as good as a thousand of them, and, notwithstanding we are but mice in comparison to them, we will kick as much as they can." He added that "they were very sorry that Sir William Johnson was coming here as they imagined by that he wanted to have [leave] his bones here."

Alexander Henry, a trader stranded by the war at Sault Ste. Marie, described how his Chippewa hosts, when given Johnson's alternatives of coming to Niagara or facing a hostile army, clamored for the advice of the Great Turtle. A large forum was quickly built and roofed over, and a mooseskin tent raised within it on ponderous, solidly planted poles. At nightfall, the tent was almost surrounded with a ring of fire and the nation assembled. A painted priest began to crawl under the skins. No sooner was his head inside than the massively beamed tabernacle rocked as in a tempest. Then the skins fell behind him, and from within numerous voices sounded, "some yelling, some barking as dogs, some howling like wolves, and in this horrible concert were mingled screams and sobs, as of despair, anguish, and the sharpest pain. Articulate speech was also uttered, as if from human lips, but in tongues unknown to any of the audience." The congregation heard some of the voices with indifference, but hissed those of "evil and lying spirits which deceive mankind."

The cacophony was followed by silence, and then there came "a low and feeble voice, resembling the cry of a young puppy. The sound was no sooner distinguished, than all the Indians clapped their hands for joy, exclaiming that this was the chief spirit, the turtle, the spirit that never lied." When the turtle was asked if the nation were really in danger from an English invasion, the tent rocked so violently it seemed about to fall and "a terrific cry announced with sufficient intelligibility, the departure of the turtle."

Everyone sat in silence for a quarter of an hour and then the turtle was heard to return. His puppy whines told the priest who translated to the people that he had, during his brief absence, crossed Lake Huron and gone to Niagara. He had seen few soldiers there, but when he sped on to the St. Lawrence he found a huge army already afloat "to make war upon the Indians."

Rising in great perturbation, a chief passed a libation of tobacco through an aperture in the mooseskins, and asked, "If the Indians visit Sir William Johnson, will they be received as friends?"

The puppy whined to mounting anxiety. Finally the priest translated that Johnson would "fill their canoes with presents; with blankets, kettles, guns, gunpowder and shot, and large barrels of rum, such as the stoutest of the Indians will not be able to lift." Furthermore, every man would return in safety to his family. On that, there was a great clapping of hands, and a hundred voices exclaimed, "I will go too! I will go too!"

Henry accompanied the delegation of sixteen that was finally sent. When they happened on a rattlesnake, they surrounded it, "all addressing it by turns, and calling it their grandfather, but yet keeping at some distance." They ceremoniously lit their pipes and blew tobacco smoke at the snake who, so Henry noted, "as it appeared to me, really received it with pleasure. . . . After remaining coiled and receiving incense for the space of half an hour, it stretched itself along the ground in visible good humor. Its length was between four and five feet." The Indians beseeched it "to be pleased to open the heart of Sir William Johnson."

21

Calmed by the Rattlesnake

On the waterways leading to Niagara bob what might seem to a distant eye floating clusters of flowers. Since black-painted nakedness is the investiture of war, the tribes are trying to reassure Warraghiyagey by wearing their brightest paint, their most resplendently dyed porcupine quills and feathers. Yet as they near the fort, the paddles shake in their hands and at their feet loaded muskets lie hidden.

In the clearing behind the ramparts a city appears without hammering: a silent lifting of the wedge-shaped, oblong, and round-domed houses native to widely separated forests. Fires lighted according to half a hundred rituals flicker on the largest Indian fighting force ever assembled: 1,700 warriors, the equivalent of four eighteenth-century British regiments. That few squaws or children have come to sit at the Englishman's kettle is a prodigy for Indian conferences and reveals tension. Themselves given to smiling on enemies until the ax falls, the warriors wonder what lies behind Warraghiyagey's smile.

Although ordered to take no visible precautions that would heighten Indian suspicion, the garrison of the fort worry perpetually about the priming of their guns, and Sir William admits in private that he is "greatly alarmed." Indian rumor reports that the Chenussios, 400 strong, are hidden in the nearby woods with 100 Delaware refugees from the towns Warraghiyagey had ordered

269

burned. He fears that, should the hoverers attack, "many of the Western Indians might be tempted to join them."

The uneasiness is so great that the smallest incident might ignite explosion, yet Johnson's every action is slowed down by crowds; he is like a man trying to walk shoulder-deep in an agitated ocean. Individual braves, he notes, "always have something to say as well as to ask, and would be greatly disgusted if I did not give them a hearing at any moment they please." And the many white captives who were being turned in by their Indian owners usually needed succor. "I was received by Sir William," Henry, the rattlesnake's friend, wrote years later, "in a manner for which I have ever been grateful to his memory and person."

The Chenussios, it transpired, had been stopped on their way by the singing of "bad birds" who told them Warraghiyagey intended to kill them. They finally came in, without Delawares, 179 strong.

When the council finally got under way on July 11, 1764, most of the nations there represented insisted that they had never damaged an Englishman. Johnson was often skeptical, "yet the impossibility of making a more strict inquiry or punishing some without bringing on fresh troubles" induced him, in every case where guilt could not be clearly proved, to renew the old peace on condition that all Frenchmen be expelled from Indian territory, all prisoners be released, and indemnities be paid to any traders who had been robbed.

With the Detroit Hurons, who had already negotiated with Croghan, and the Chenussios there were provisional peace terms to ratify. The Hurons made no difficulties, but the Chenussios, whose delegates had expressed at Johnson Hall an eagerness to fight Delawares, now admitted that the Delawares who had been displaced by Warraghiyagey's offensive were "under our arm." The Seneca speaker tried to mediate an immediate peace for these belligerents, whose good behavior the Chenussios could guarantee, they "being liable to be squeased by our arm whenever they misbehave."

The Delawares, Sir William replied, would despise the English "if they had peace for the asking." The two war chiefs, Squashcutter and Long Coat, whose disembodied heads Warraghiyagey had vainly tried to buy, would have to be surrendered "to be disposed of as the General [Gage] shall think proper." In the mean-while, the mediating Senecas should leave two of their own chiefs as hostages for the Delawares' compliance. Since the Chenussios insisted that they could not deliver up the Kanestio murderers— one had died, the other fled—Sir William forgave them this obliga-tion, but insisted in doubling the land around the Niagara portage they were to cede to the Crown. All was agreed to, and the treaty signed that made the Iroquois unanimous in the British orbit and paved the way for peace with one group of Delawares.

That many hostile tribes had stayed away from the peace confer-ence Johnson blamed largely on their fear of revenge: "Pontiac is now with about 300 men some distance up the Miami River, but has expressed his desire of making peace. . . . The Shawnees and Delawares of the Ohio . . . are now up the River Scioto watching our motions, but I imagine that the transactions of the Congress will bring all to reason, in case we are not able to effect anything against them."

On August 19, Warraghiyagey was back at Johnson Hall, being, as was now the case after every strenuous exertion, "a good deal indisposed." The next step, which was to carry an olive branch on a sword, involved linked military campaigns. An army under Colonel John Bradstreet was to sail from Niagara along Lake Erie to the Sandusky, and up that river on their way to the Scioto Valley and the enemy encamped there. A second army, under Colonel Bouquet, was to go from Fort Pitt down the Ohio and then up the Muskingum to the southerly Delaware and Shawnee towns, whence his force could march northward to meet Brad-street's coming down from above. Sir William would supply Indians for both armies, and also send Caughnawagas out on independent forays. The preparations were to be as warlike as possible, but the peace movement had gone so far that Warraghiyagey neither ex-pected nor wanted any fighting. A tribe damaged in battle would flee to the western nations, spread hatred against the English, and prepare to resume the war; but an already frightened tribe further impressed by a show of power would stay within reach, sign and keep a treaty.

While Bouquet was still stalled at Fort Pitt by the slow arrival of militia levies, Bradstreet set out with 1,200 soldiers and 300 Indians. For years he had sought what he called "great honor," and now he saw his chance. Only a man who hated his own destiny, he believed, would obey Gage's order to send all Indians who sued for peace to Johnson. The whole world would see how John Bradstreet ended wars!

When he reached Presqu'isle, ten Indians appeared from the Scioto. Their objective was a little polite spying, but Bradstreet assumed that they were ambassadors, and the imaginative braves seized gleefully on this opportunity to halt by guile the threatened invasion. Their main difficulty was that they had with them only two tiny strings of wampum, quite unsuited to the great negotiations they intended to improvise—but they threw the wampum with an air, and Bradstreet was too enchanted with the usurped role *he* was playing to notice anything strange. Without (as Gage put it) asking "the least satisfaction" for "the many horrid murders," he signed, in the name of George Rex, a treaty of peace. He agreed to abandon his own invasion of the Scioto, and hurried off a messenger to Bouquet saying it was no longer necessary for him to march. The Iroquois Warraghiyagey had sent with Bradstreet understood, of course, that he was being immobilized by braves who could commit no nation to anything, but they let the colonel "go on as he pleased, as he did not think worthwhile to consult us."

In a haze of self-congratulation, Bradstreet advanced to Detroit, where he summoned the neighboring nations to a peace conference. To outgesture the Indian orators, he chopped up a belt of wampum with an ax, so heinous a violation of parliamentary decorum that the tribesmen could hardly believe it possible, even for a barbarous Englishman. To outbargain Sir William, he demanded that the Indians declare themselves "subjects" of George III. There being no way to express this conception in Indian languages, the interpreter translated that they should call the King "father" not "brother." The tribesmen were not so discourteous as to refuse.

When he received the record, Warraghiyagey trembled for the consequence if someone explained to the Indians the English meaning of what they had signed. "The very idea of subjection," he wrote, "would fill them with horror," nor would they "ever consider themselves in that light, whilst they have any men or an open country to retire to." They had "no other ties amongst themselves but inclination. . . . Suppose that it's explained to them that they shall be governed by the laws, liable to the punishments for high treason, murder, robbery, and the pains and penalties on actions for property or debt. Then see how it will be relished, and whether they will agree with it!" The frontiersman who himself resented any interference with his own will, concluded happily, "They cannot be brought under our laws for some centuries."

For Bradstreet the honeymoon was soon over. He had sent, in response to assurances from the bogus ambassadors, a subordinate to accept the surrender of Pontiac and the Illinois tribes: The subordinate was grateful to get back still wearing a scalp. The peace terms Bradstreet had accepted were violated under his very eyes, and he received from Gage a blistering dispatch that blamed new attacks against Pennsylvania on his foolishness, and commanded him to advance at once against the Scioto Valley. He considered the water in the rivers too low, and, in his confusion, allowed the water of Lake Erie to destroy half his bateaux at a stupidly selected anchorage. Retiring with his regulars to Niagara in what vessels remained, he left his provincials and Indians, "without an ounce of provisions," to find their way home as best they could. In mid-December, braves were still staggering into Johnson Hall, "naked and almost famished," whom Sir William clothed, comforted, and medicated with all the enthusiasm of an amateur physician.

In the newspapers, Bradstreet, as Johnson put it, tried "to puff and bluster away a sort of reputation amongst the vulgar." Not daring to blame his troubles on Sir William, he insisted that the Iroquois had treacherously frustrated his peacemaking because while the war continued they profited from mediation. Johnson belabored him mightily in his dispatches, and soon the voice of John Bradstreet was heard no more.

The Caughnawagas and Iroquois Johnson sent to Fort Pitt arrived too late to join Bouquet, but the tide toward peace ran so strongly that autumn of 1764 that the English army advanced without opposition to the Muskingum River where Bouquet made a preliminary peace with Shawnees, Delawares, and Mingoes from the Ohio. He reported to Sir William that they delivered over 200 captives and left fourteen hostages for their future peaceable behavior and for the appearance at Johnson Hall of a delegation that would "ratify and execute all the conditions of the treaty you will make with them."

Bouquet's campaign brought a virtual stop to Indian hostilities against the colonials, but Warraghiyagey would have to arrange many treaties (Pontiac, for instance, had so far agreed to nothing) before *finis* could be officially written to "Amherst's War."

Seeking a permanent basis for peace, the Lords of Trade had made use of Sir William's suggestions to draw up a comprehensive plan for Indian policy which, on July 10, 1764, they sent to him for comment. The two Indian superintendents, Sir William and the southerner John Stuart,* were to be responsible directly to the Crown and, to enhance their local power, were to sit as ex-officio members on the provincial councils of all colonies abutting on the frontiers they ruled. (This, Franklin concluded, would seat Johnson at the councils of "Nova Scotia, Quebec, New Hampshire, Massachusetts, Connecticut, New York, New Jersey, Pennsylvania, Maryland, and Virginia.") The superintendents alone would be able to call Indian congresses, deal politically, determine war and peace. Although the governors and the commander in chief would be empowered to license traders, the instant the traders stepped into Indian country they would be under the jurisdiction of the superintendents. Commerce would be kept under strict supervision by being limited to designated military posts where prices would be established and enforced by commissaries appointed by the Crown but responsible to the superintendents. The superintendents would appoint deputies, interpreters, and blacksmiths to mend Indian arms. The Society for the Preservation of the Gospel would be asked to send Anglican missionaries.

The Indians were to sell land only at general councils called by the superintendents, and only to a governor or the commander in chief. Tribal representatives were to attend and approve all surveys.

When drawing up this plan, the Board of Trade had intended to continue their ruling that no settlements be made beyond the Alleghenies, but Croghan, who had been representing Johnson's Indian department in London, had insisted that this boundary

---

* Stuart was a Scot who had come to South Carolina in 1748, when he was almost fifty, and had struck up a friendship with the Cherokees. After his appointment as Superintendent of the southern Indians in 1762, he demonstrated marked ability, although he never rivaled Johnson's power and prestige. When the two men clashed over which should have jurisdiction in the Illinois country, Stuart was routed.

could not possibly be enforced, since both Virginia and the Crown itself had already made grants beyond it which it was a practical impossibility to rescind.* Assured over and over again that a realistic border was "close to Sir William's heart," the Board of Trade had finally empowered the superintendents to "ascertain and define" with "the consent and concurrence of the Indians" a "precise and exact boundary."

On paper, the new plan gave Sir William the exclusive English power in the northern and central wilderness he had so long desired. Yet he felt the provisions for enforcement were inadequate.

The Board of Trade had provided that the officers of the Indian department should be justices of the peace who could decide civil cases, but only up to £10—appeal being to the superintendent—and commit criminal offenders to the colonial courts, where larger civil cases were also to be tried. In a reversal of existing colonial law, Indians were to be accepted as witnesses.

Sir William objected that Indians could not be punished for perjury, and only the Christianized understood the meaning of the oath. Furthermore, Colonial interest was so strongly opposed to Indian interest that the Indians could expect no justice in white courts. He wished that the superintendent, "assisted with the governor or some other person or persons of the province concerned," would be empowered "to determine in a summary way such disputes relative to claims or titles."

How little could be achieved for the Indians on the Colonial level was emphasized by the reaction of the New York Assembly to a request of the Board of Trade that they void one of the most conspicuous land frauds, the Kayaderosseras Patent,† on which Johnson blamed much Indian uneasiness. The Assembly replied

---

* George Washington expressed the common colonial opinion when he described the Allegheny line as "a temporary expedient to quiet the mind of the Indians," and concluded, "any person, therefore, who neglects the present opportunity of hunting out good lands and in some measure marking and distinguishing them for his own, will never again regain it."

† Since he had first become a Mohawk, Johnson had been protesting this patent. He asserted that, during the reign of Queen Anne, an Indian sale of enough land for three farms had been expanded in the English deed to "all the lands then unoccupied between the Hudson and the Mohawk River to certain places on both those rivers, containing by estimation about 800,000 acres of land, which included the most valuable part of the Mohawks' hunting ground."

with a resolution aimed at legalizing all the deeds that waited in strongboxes until Indian witnesses should die and Indian oral records become dim.

There was, of course, no possibility that the Colonies, all less interested in protecting Indians than robbing them, would appropriate the money needed to put into effect the Board of Trade's Indian plan. Nor could the English taxpayer be expected to assume this altogether American expense. The obvious solution was a tax levied in America by the English Parliament. Thus, the Board wrote Johnson to ask whether the proposed Indian administration could be supported by imposts on the fur trade.

In his reply, he estimated that there were 10,000 hunters in his department, "exclusive of the Sioux, with whom we have had very little intercourse"; that each hunter had one woman. One Indian out of ten would buy a blanket every year, one out of five a pair of stockings; an annual pound of beads would serve twenty, an annual gallon of rum would serve two and a half. Calculating thus, estimating the consumption of the children at one-half what the adults consumed, he guessed the value of the northern Indian trade at £179,594 sterling a year. He urged an all-over five percent duty, with an additional five percent on liquor, arms, ammunition, and sales made not in the Indian country but on the frontier. This would bring in £10,963, about £100 more than his estimate of the costs of his department.

Although from a purely financial point of view the tax was feasible, its enactment, on which the Board of Trade's Indian plan depended, was a political matter that had to be decided by Parliament. Against an enabling law, an outcry instantly arose.

The governors of the colonies whose frontiers would be comprised in Sir William's department complained that he would be made a governor within their governments. The business communities shuddered at the thought that he would become a virtual dictator of fur trade and western expansion. Merchants saw the authority Johnson would be given to set prices as a reaffirmation of the old governmental conceptions of financial control which were under fire from advocates of free trade. Americanism was also outraged. In London, Benjamin Franklin prepared a brief against the plan, pointing out, among other things, that it raised the question—to become historic under the catchwords "no taxation without representation"—whether Parliament had the "right to lay duties in America."

As the English government awaited a diminution of controversy before enacting the tax that would make their Indian plan operative, Sir William went ahead with the negotiations he had been empowered to undertake that would draw, for royal approval, a tentative boundary between white and Indian America. Since the Crown had not so ordered, he ignored Gage's advice that he call in the governors of the colonies whose western limits he was planning to define. As for the non-Iroquois nations involved, he was convinced that they had no legal right to the territories from which they would be displaced. The Mingoes on the upper Ohio lacked a national entity that entitled them to hold land under Indian communal law. The Delawares and Shawnees were Iroquois dependents whose lack of a homeland had been demonstrated when, "several times since I came to America," the League had moved them from one assigned place of residence to another. The Cherokee's claim to the lower Ohio had been, he insisted, extinguished by Iroquois arms. Thus Sir William felt that the intended partition of much of North America could be worked out exclusively between himself, as the King's representative, and the Iroquois, as the owners of the land.

When, in April, 1765, he sat down with the sachems at a great congress held at Johnson Hall, he found them determined to alienate no land in the Long House: No agreement could be reached on a boundary north of Owego on the east branch of the Susquehanna. However, from Owego southward, through territory the League did not itself occupy, a line was soon amicably drawn. It followed the East Branch of the Susquehanna southeast to the West Branch (thus leaving on the Indian side the embattled Wyoming Valley), and then jogged northwest along the West Branch, cut over to the Allegheny River, went down the Allegheny and the Ohio to the Tennessee River, and up the Tennessee to its head. If, as Johnson now recommended, this grant were approved by the Crown and paid for, it would add to the colonies west of the Allegheny line of 1763 the Ohio Valley to within thirty miles of the Mississippi, all of present Kentucky and West Virginia, much of western Pennsylvania and Tennessee, and a bit of northern Alabama.

That summer, Sir William completed the peace treaties that the Senecas had been mediating with the Upper Delawares and that Bouquet had begun with the Lower Delawares, Shawnees, and Mingoes. Into the treaties he wrote agreement in advance to whatever land arrangement the Iroquois and the English should finally make. That the non-Iroquois nations, although they signed the treaties, were far from pleased served Johnson's political ends: The land provision was further punishment for war against the white men, and, by encouraging resentment against the Five Nations, it helped keep the Indians divided.

The treaties also dictated an exchange of prisoners. As Captain Bull and his Delaware companions were ferried up the Hudson from a New York City jail, they were afire with eagerness for freedom in the forests. Through those forests down eastward-running paths a pale-faced group was advancing under Indian guard: Many hung back, shedding tears that were duplicated in the eyes of the red men who conscientiously hustled them along. Let white chauvinists meditate Colden's statement that although there was no record of a captured Indian ever wanting to stay with the colonials, many a white captive had to be driven from Indian loves and rites to "liberation."

Sir William soon had on his hands two white women about sixteen or eighteen years of age, each with a half-breed baby in her arms, who could not remember where they had been captured or what their English names had been. Another white girl knew only that she was called Esther. More than a dozen small children, surrounded with faces that were strange though colored like their own, wept for the squaws who were the only mothers they could remember. Johnson advertised in the newspapers for relatives. He took one of the waifs under his care, named him Simon Clark, and eventually gave him a farm. A nubile girl (or so the story goes) married Sir William's half-Indian son, Brant Johnson. She seems to have been the Peggy Johnson who made herself useful to the Canajoharies as an interpreter.

Early in the negotiations, the Delaware ringleaders Longcoat and Squashcutter had delivered themselves to Johnson Hall, where they were lodged with two Seneca chiefs outside the walls as hostages for Delaware compliance with Warraghiyagey's conditions. Before they were released from their parole, Squashcutter died of the white man's smallpox, and Warraghiyagey had many conferences with the more important Seneca hostage, Gaustarax. The warrior admitted freely that he had struck the English, but said that if the Indians were thenceforth treated with justice, he would "use his utmost influence to preserve peace hereafter." Sir William had immediate use for Gaustarax, whose "very great influence" was reputed to extend to the Illinois, that last center of active resistance, where Pontiac still lurked and the French still reigned supreme.

An Eden in the wilderness, the Illinois was separated from the nearest English settlements by a bristling of branches 500 miles deep. Where three great rivers—the Mississippi, the Missouri, and the Ohio—met to form an irregular cross, fields bloomed with French husbandry. An annual churn of paddles carried voyageurs away through the autumn blaze, and with the adolescent green of spring they returned, laden with furs, to the permanent farming population of about 2,000. Over all frowned the high walls and gaping cannon of Fort de Chartres. This secret interior paradise had, by the scratch of a European pen, been surrendered to the English with the rest of the territory east of the Mississippi, but in the more than two years that had passed no Englishman had been able to penetrate there. The Illinois continued to market its furs through French channels, sending them down the Mississippi to New Orleans.

Johnson had long been convinced that the inhabitants of the Illinois were stoking Indian unrest. When France, as part of the territorial adjustments after the Seven Years' War, had ceded her North American possessions to Spain, the switch to a new flag had had little effect; the anti-British propaganda was inspired not by European policies but by local rivalries for furs. The French inhabitants were as anxious as ever to keep the forests between the Illinois and colonial fur traders closed with a deep entanglement of anti-British warriors.

And so the flagpole at Fort de Chartres continued to await the English flag that should by treaty fly there. In the spring of 1764, the authorities at New Orleans allowed a party of 400 British regulars to embark on the Mississippi for the Illinois, but they had hardly begun the long, upriver paddle when they were turned back by Indian gunfire.

The next plan was to drift an army a thousand miles down the Ohio from Fort Pitt, but even if they managed to fight their way through the successive barriers of tribes, what would be gained? To escape English jurisdiction, the French needed only to cross the Mississippi—already they were building on the west bank a trading post which they named after St. Louis—and the Indians, their hatred for the English confirmed by renewed warfare, would certainly follow them. This, Johnson pointed out, would remove from the English economy "the best hunters in America."

Sir William's solution was to send not an army but a single colonial. After Croghan, assisted by the belts Warraghiyagey had persuaded Gaustarax to send, had won the Illinois tribes with diplomacy, an army might comfortably follow to occupy Fort de Chartres.

Croghan was at Fort Pitt early in May, 1765, preparing for his dangerous mission, when a convoy of almost a hundred horses loaded with about £3,000 of "Indian truck"—supposedly for the use of the Indian department—set out from Philadelphia addressed to him. A murmuring arose among frontiersmen who believed that redskins should be killed not pampered, and near Paxton ruffians with blackened faces appeared whooping from the forest, pinioned the guards, stole or destroyed all the goods.

Sir William was prepared to amplify Croghan's already loud screams of protest, when he learned that most of the goods in this "official" convoy had not only belonged to private traders but were being smuggled into the Indian country without the required license from the Governor of Pennsylvania. To Croghan he wrote that, unless the matter could be cleared up, "the enemies of the department may possibly carry it some length." Croghan, and the firm of Philadelphia merchants involved—Baynton, Wharton, and Morgan—replied that, realizing the importance to Indian relations of bringing English trade to the Illinois the instant that region was opened, they had patriotically shipped goods before all horses were engrossed by harvest. But, of course, they had never intended to make sales until they had the governor's license.

The smugglers had stood to gain from getting their goods into the Illinois well in advance of any colonial rivals, but Croghan, outraged at the suggestion that he was seeking personal profit, haughtily offered his resignation. This placed Johnson in a quandary. He had always known that his deputy was considered dishonest—the ill-bred woodsman reached out for graft which in the eighteenth century was considered the exclusive province of the well born and highly placed—yet he needed Croghan. In his own person, Warraghiyagey had little contact on the local level with the nations outside the Long House—it was indeed impossible to be simultaneously an Iroquois and a trusted national of other tribes—and Croghan was an indefatigable forest traveler whose skill in Indian negotiation rivaled Warraghiyagey's own.

Defending his subordinate in public, Johnson wrote privately to Gage that he doubted Croghan's innocent professions. The commander in chief would, of course, be within his province if he investigated ruthlessly, but Johnson would find it difficult to replace Croghan with "a man at all calculated for the employment" who would not take even more advantage of his office. Gage let the matter drop.

Having charmed some Shawnees into accompanying him, Croghan set out from Fort Pitt on May 13. Three weeks later, as his party of fourteen entered the Illinois, they were attacked by eighty Kickapoos and Mascoutens, who killed three Shawnees and two white men. "I got the stroke of a hatchet on the skull," Croghan wrote, "but my skull being pretty thick, the hatchet would not enter, so you may see a thick skull is of service on some occasions."

Bleeding, rounded up with his companions as a prisoner, Croghan felt "very grave," but conversation between victors and vanquished quickly reversed everyone's roles. The attackers were horrified to discover that, in killing Englishmen, they had also killed Shawnees, neighbors whom they had considered England's enemies. This unbelievable situation made them give credence to Croghan's statement that, in addition to the Shawnees, the Delawares and all the Iroquois were now in alliance with the English and would be only too happy to chastise the miscreants who had murdered the associates and broken the head of Warraghiyagey's deputy.

Although nominally still a prisoner, Croghan made a triumphant progress through the Illinois, where the French and Indians saw equally the necessity to conciliate a man who represented so potent an alliance. He moved north to Detroit, followed by an ever-increasing band of tribesmen who whinnied for friendship. Now, at long last, Pontiac entered again the council room he had tried to capture by strategy. Handing Croghan a pipe, he asked that it be sent "to Sir William Johnson that he may know I have made peace." After that, as Warraghiyagey had foreseen, the English marched without firing a shot to the Illinois, where the French commander courteously handed over to them Fort de Chartres.

The next summer, in July, 1766, Amherst's War was brought officially to an end at Oswego under a canopy of green boughs when Pontiac joined Warraghiyagey in blowing smoke to the four corners of the world from a calumet with an ancient head of stone. This was no abject surrender, for Pontiac had come fully armed through Indian-controlled forests with his undefeated warriors around him. He stated, "Since you have been so good as to bury everything that might be disagreeable to us, we shall reject everything that tends to evil." He threw "a string of four branches" and declared, "You may be sure by this string that I shall fulfill this promise." To the Board of Trade, Johnson wrote that he hoped he himself would be enabled to keep "the reasonable promises of justice and favor which it was my duty to make them on the part of the Crown."

From the military point of view, Amherst's War—or, if you please, Pontiac's Conspiracy—had been won by the Indians. Their casualties and property loss had been negligible, while, according to Croghan's estimate, the braves "killed or captivated not less than 2,000 of His Majesty's subjects, and drove some thousands into beggary and the greatest distress." Colonial property loss was tremendous. Yet the very fact of military success demonstrated the tragic weakness of the tribes: Their triumphs had not damaged but only "insulted"—to use Gage's word—the ability and determination of European civilization to surge westward.

Perhaps the Indian war had most profited Sir William Johnson. His ability to insulate the New York frontier from attack, to mount an Indian army, to restore peace, had carried his prestige to the apogee. The British government was moving to make him a legal dictator in the northern wilderness. Amherst's recall as commander in chief and replacement by Gage, who bowed to Warraghiyagey in all matters Indian, had ended forever the long succession of officials, royal and colonial, who had down the years challenged Johnson's forest rule. His word west of the well-established frontiers was now law—as far as there was any law.

Yet the area over which he ruled was too vast and too rich ever to lie easily in his hand. He was soon struggling with what he considered anarchy, a random upsurge of self-willed men, but what was actually part of a yet hardly glimpsed revolution against the royal power on which all his policies were grounded.

PART FOUR

Power and Creation

22

The World Sir William Made

With the tapering off of Amherst's War, Johnson had turned his mind increasingly to the arts of peace. As much as any American who ever lived, he fashioned the world around him as he wished it to be, yet many things he dreamed of he did not achieve.

Sir William was certainly in his own generation and probably in the whole history of western expansion the most able frontiersman. He was no land speculator or merchant or soldier or territorial governor who made forays into the forest and then returned to bases in the civilized centers. He practiced all these callings and more; he determined imperial policy and shaped the continent, yet he lived his whole effective life in the wilderness and saw the world in forest terms. It was not in his temperament to formulate theories. However, his pleas and suggestions to government, his official acts and his personal actions reveal his basic conceptions concerning the quicksilver line that was to slide across the continent, where forest and field, Indian and white man met.

Most vexed of the problems with which he wrestled and involved in them all was the future of his Indian friends, who were, he wrote, "really much to be pitied." He tried to protect them for the present through effective administration, but realized that long-range planning for their welfare revolved around the question (still unresolved on twentieth-century Indian reservations) of how far the Indians should hold on to their own culture, how far abandon it to become like white men.

287

With the end of the French and Indian War, missionary activity had burgeoned in the Mohawk Valley. Johnson gave at least qualified support to the efforts of the proselytizers to teach the squaws "housewifery," to make the braves drop their guns, take the plough handles from their women and delve as God had instructed Adam to do. But he soon wrote that the whole matter required more "serious consideration."

Molly's influence was undoubtedly strong in his final conclusion that efforts to Europeanize the Indians should wait until "they discover superior advantages in our way of living than in their own, which, as yet, they do not." The forest nations, he wrote, did not find reassuring the example of New England's "domesticated tribes" who had become Christianized and "in some measure civilized. . . . They are poor, abject, full of avarice, hypocrisy, and in short have imbibed all our vices without any of our good qualities, and without retaining their former abilities for gaining a subsistence in the only way they conceive that Nature intended they should." He would rather, he added, "trust twenty Ottawas in a room with my plate than one of them."

To readers of Cooper, the conception of "the last of the Mohicans" was to have a romantic sound, but it gave Kaysoakamake, the Mohican chief, no pleasure to speak to Warraghiyagey as follows: "We are now in tears; we have lost everything. The Patroon has got all our lands, and we have nothing for them, and, being old and helpless. . . . We beg that we may have some provisions and a little clothing to cover us."

When the Indians abandoned their military skills, they abandoned their ability to protect themselves from white men who wished to rob and destroy them. Five hundred warriors made in the forests a redoubtable force that could speak to England's king as a nation; five hundred Indian farmers would be an insignificant minority in a colonial county. Their "apprehension," as Johnson wrote, that adopting civilization "would be followed by their annihilation as a people cause them to be extremely jealous of any endeavors to promote such a design." The ability of the tribes to fight was, indeed, Sir William's principal weapon in his battles for their rights and safety: he threatened the Board of Trade so often with an Indian war that they must often have suspected—although they could never be sure—that he was crying wolf to enforce his policies.

The chase kept the warriors in training. "They say," Warraghiyagey reported, "that it appears to them ordained from the beginning that the white people should cultivate the arts and themselves pursue hunting; that no other way of life is agreeable to them and consistent with their maxims of policy." If they abandoned the chase, Sir William continued in his own voice, they would no longer benefit from the fur trade, and white men, better qualified for other occupations, would have to take their places lest the crop of pelts cease. Furthermore, the French had demonstrated "that a civilized member of society and an Indian hunter are not incompatible characters." The Canadian tribes were "as orderly a people as any of our lower class are."

The rapidity with which the white men were to pre-empt the continent depended on matters unforeseeable: steam travel, immigration, and the drop in infant mortality that created such a bumper crop of aggressive palefaces. Believing that the forests would not be annihilated for "at least a century to come," Johnson urged that the Indians prepare for future changes through slow evolution. "The motion must flow from themselves."

The tribes eagerly welcomed smiths to their castles and would probably welcome carpenters. If these mechanics were by government supervision "confined solely to their trades" and kept from enraging the Indians by engrossing land and furs, "some of the Indians would doubtless be allured in a little time to apply themselves to arts so useful to themselves, and their proficiency in one or two arts, beyond which we should not go in the beginning, would prepare them to receive others which are at present not necessary for their manner of living." Even farming would be absorbed, when it became essential, without doing violence to Indian strengths and virtues.

Warraghiyagey felt that the Indians had, under white influences, evolved so far from their aboriginal state that it was "extremely difficult, if not impossible, to trace their customs to their origin or to discover their explication." Yet he advised Samuel Kirkland, as that missionary wrote, "by no means to ridicule any of the traditions of their fathers till I was master of their language, and then I might take them up gently and on rational grounds."

Religion was the aspect of European culture to which the Indians took most kindly, and thus the catalyst that might lead to the acceptance of all the rest. In Johnson's time, the colonial group most interested in proselytizing the Indians were the New England disciples of the Great Awakening. Their prophet, Jonathan Edwards, considered Johnson "a man of not much religion" but counted on his support, as did the Rev. Eleazar Wheelock, who established at Lebanon, Connecticut, Moor's Charity School (that grew into Dartmouth College) to train Indians and missionaries to the Indians.

The most successful of the missionaries was Kirkland (subsequently the founder of Hamilton College). Assigned at the close of Amherst's War to continue the pacification of the Senecas, he describes in his journal the "extraordinary attentions" he received from Sir William, who "would have me come [to] his house and make it my home till I proceeded westward"; who briefed him on "the general character of almost every chieftain in the Six Nations, their talents and prevailing dispositions"; and who carefully selected the best Senecas to guide the tenderfoot into the distant forests and sponsor him there. When Kirkland was adopted into the nation, he was sworn to secrecy concerning the tribal rights, but told that he might nonetheless speak with complete frankness to Warraghiyagey. After almost a year, the emaciated missionary returned for a visit to Johnson Hall. Sir William received him at the door, cried out, "My God, Mr. Kirkland, you look like a whipping post!" fed him, and lent him a new blanket "on condition I would never return it."

Kirkland's adopted Seneca brother and sister-in-law had accompanied him to the Mohawk, where the squaw died. Sir William sent for her husband and "appeared so affected himself" that he had to leave the room for a time to master his emotions. He gave the Indian mourning for himself and all the children.

Although Johnson supported Wheelock's missionaries, he viewed them with some distaste. The New Englanders, he complained, tried "to abolish at once their most innocent customs, dances, and rejoicings at marriages, etc.," which seldom bettered the aborigines but increased "the misanthropy of the splenetic" and exchanged natural "morality for a set of gloomy ideas." From the Congregationalists, the Indians "imbibed an air of the most enthusiastical cant . . . intermixed with the greatest distortion of the features and zealous belchings of the spirit, resembling the most bigoted Puritans, their whole time being spent in singing psalms amongst the country people, whereby they neglect their hunting and most worldly affairs, and are, in short, become very worthless members of society."

The tribes, he believed, would respond best to missionaries who, although "detached at least in appearance from all worldly concerns," had "a knowledge of the world" and were "as distant from gloominess as from levity." Since, "the Indians are fond of pomp and ceremonies . . . that religion in which they most abound is most likely to succeed among them." Catholicism was, of course, that religion, but the church of Rome was, on the frontier, identified with the cause of France. Sir William plumped for the Church of England, not only because it was urbane and possessed ritual, but because it was "the best support of monarchy," and thus "a force for peace and order in America."

Resolving to revive an Anglican prayer book issued during 1715 in a phonetic rendering of the Mohawk language, Johnson entrusted the revision and expansion to several missionaries, and ordered 400 copies of "a handsome small octavo," twenty specially bound with gilt lettering for chiefs and sachems. The printer complained that because there were so many g's, k's, and y's in Mohawk, he was obliged to borrow letters from fellow printers to set even a half-sheet, but in 1769 the volumes, still smelling of fresh ink, infiltrated the forest.

Anglican books could be distributed more easily than Anglican priests. The New England "enthusiastics," Johnson wrote, "being often idle and illiterate," were able to live with the Indians without a grievous drop in their standards of living, but "our clergymen are all men of regular habits, bred in a land of luxury [England]." They found that residence in an Indian castle involved "too many sacrifices."

And whatever ecclesiastic Warraghiyagey sponsored was likely to discredit religion with the Indians by his example. That squaws were to be had for the asking inspired bachelor clerics to ardors that made the tribes laugh at their hypocrisy. And even the most respectable reverends lusted for Indian land. Thus, after he moved on to Trinity Church in New York City, the Rev. Barclay outraged the Mohawks by insisting that the glebe on which the Indians had placed him as missionary at Fort Hunter remained his personal property.

Sir William wished in the long run to replace missionaries with Indian teachers who, as personal possessors of Indian tradition, would skillfully graft new ideas on the old. That this was not easy is revealed by an Anglican missionary's report of a Mohawk objection: "You Christians were so wicked as to crucify your God, and now he is angry with you, and therefore, to pacify him, you endeavor to persuade us to serve him, but why would we? We never heard of him till Christians came here. He is not angry with us. We never did him any hurt."

Early in 1761, Warraghiyagey sent to Wheelock's school three suspicious Mohawks, who kept their horses ever ready for a galloped retreat from Connecticut's white clapboards. Two, Wheelock noted, were almost naked; "the other, being of a family of distinction, was considerably clothed." This was Molly's brother, nineteen-year-old Joseph Brant. Although he had for years frequented his sister's rooms in Johnson Hall, he could speak only "a few words of English."

Wheelock considered him "of a sprightly genius, a manly and genteel disposition, of a modest, courteous, benevolent temper." He took well to instruction, but after he had been in Connecticut off and on for two years he got a letter from Molly, written in Mohawk and ordering him, as he told Wheelock, "to come directly home; that the Indians are displeased with his being here at school." Molly had heard that her brother was being forced to disgrace his manhood by working on the minister's farm. Despite Wheelock's efforts to get Sir William to intervene, Joseph did go home—but without hard feelings. His house remained "an asylum for the missionaries in the wilderness."

Joseph Brant grew into the outstanding exemplar of the new Indian Warraghiyagey was trying to create. The *London Magazine* could describe him as "gentle and quiet," adding that "to those

Joseph Brant, by Gilbert Stuart
Stuart's painting style is so suave that his depth of character
study may be overlooked. Much can be deduced from the face
of Warraghiyagey's brother-in-law, the most celebrated Indian
of his generation, who exemplified Sir William's hopes for Indian character in a white world (*New York State Historical
Association, Cooperstown*)

Hopothle Mico, or The Talafsee King, drawn by John Trumbull
(*Smithsonian Institution*)

With the exception of Gilbert Stuart, John Trumbull was the
ablest artist to depict an eighteenth-century Indian. We
have here tragic character studies of an imperilled race.

Hysac, Or the Woman's Man, drawn by John Trumbull
(*Smithsonian Institution*)

Sir William Johnson
Copy after a lost portrait painted by Thomas McIlworth at
Johnson Hall in May, 1763. A sterner likeness than the others.
(*Courtesy of the New-York Historical Society, New York City*)

who study human nature, he affords very convincing proof of the tameness which education can produce upon the wildest race." He even owned a prosperous farm—yet during the Revolution he was a great commander and personal hero. He carried the sword in one hand and the prayer book (his own Mohawk translation) in the other. He swept Indian councils with traditional eloquence, and yet was competent at white councils. Thus, Joseph Brant became one of the most famous Indians in the American story.

As a nation, the Mohawks were molded by Warraghiyagey for some thirty years. When New York's then governor, William Tryon, visited the Valley in 1772, he wrote that the Indians there "appear to be actuated as a community by principles of rectitude that would do honor to the most civilized nations. They are, indeed, in a civilized state." Like Brant, they were showpieces of Johnson's Indian management. Their population, seriously wounded by a hundred casualties in the French and Indian War, had returned under healthful conditions to its former figure of about 420. These few individuals had kept enough of their Indian power to shake a continent, yet they had learned the arts of husbandry. Not only were they themselves farmers and, so Tryon tells us, good ones, but they had white tenants on some of their lands.

When pillaged during the Revolution, the Mohawk castles proved to be "abounding in every necessity. . . . Their houses are very well furnished with all necessary household utensils, great plenty of grain, several horses, cows, and wagons. . . . These Indians," concluded Colonel Marinus Willett of the militia, "live much better than many of our Mohawk Valley farmers." They were also more literate, since almost all could write very well.

To allow other Indian nations to achieve a similar evolution, Johnson wished to abolish the first destructive wave of pioneers who penetrated the forests in advance of stable settlement, that thin line of violent men who slashed the trees and Indians down and then moved to new solitudes as an influx of homesteaders created around them law and order. Sir William would have been torn between laughter and indignation at the picture, so dear to later American legend, of noble log-cabin dweller and Indian slayer. Only if the aboriginal owners of the forests are thought of as rattlesnakes to be exterminated can this type of pioneering take on a moral tone. Otherwise, we must agree with Warraghiyagey that it was armed banditry grounded on murder. Indeed, many of the white men who fled to the danger and squalor of the further forests were misfits in civilization, psychopaths, such men as are found today in prisons, alcoholic wards, and the skid rows of big cities. The western bad man lived on eastern river banks as well as in mining towns, and to him the only good Indian was a dead Indian.

Johnson's dream was to carry civilization and its laws into the Indian country hand in hand with settlement. To achieve this, he relied basically on such boundaries between land open to the whites and land reserved to the Indians as the one he had just drawn with the Iroquois; he pressed in letter after letter to England for its approval. He realized that as time passed other boundaries would have to be drawn, successively further westward, but he hoped that each would be enforced until all the land behind it was filled with flourishing communities.

He visualized a boundary as a dam that would hold back the little ragged streams of settlement, combining and raising all into a great placid lake that would reflect the glories of European civilization. On it, Indians would paddle their canoes in safety, and, beyond it, they would work out their evolving destinies in forests where they remained supreme.

An immediate problem was created by the Illinois that was too far west to be on the colonial side of any rational border, but which had already been settled by the French. The voyageurs there continued to channel furs down the Mississippi to New Orleans and stir up their Indian neighbors against the English. Johnson admonished the Indians to ignore such "barking of a cross dog, for which we can always find a switch when we are much vexed"— but where would he find a switch that would silence the French interest, not just concentrate it across the Mississippi on Spanish territory at St. Louis?

In January, 1766, Croghan, newly returned from the bison-drenched plains of the Illinois, persuaded Sir William that French influence could be drowned by establishing there a new English colony. Croghan had sounded out the Indians, who had agreed provided they were well paid; and he proposed that they be paid by a private company which would establish the colony at no expense to the Crown and at great eventual profit to themselves.

Since the proposed colony promised not only to squelch French troublemakers, but also to establish a stable government that would protect Indian rights, Johnson concluded that, as usual, public policy and his private interest could be made to work together: he took an eighth share in the speculation. Like the other most influential partners, Governor William Franklin of New Jersey and through him his father Benjamin Franklin, he agreed that he could serve the good cause most effectively by hiding his personal financial interest. It was thus as a seemingly disinterested official that he backed to the Secretary of State a petition, signed by the nonsecret partners, for a colony considerably larger than the present state of Illinois in which the projectors would be given 100,000 acres "to be located in one or more places as they may choose." From London, where he was discreetly pushing the scheme, Benjamin Franklin wrote Johnson that he was glad to be in touch at last with "a man whose character I have long esteemed and to whom America is so much obliged."

A new colony and fixed boundaries for the old promised to solve only in part the problem of white ruffians in the wilderness: there were still the fur traders. Their control, through licensing and an inspection system that limited trading to British posts, had been provided for in the Lord of Trade's plan which Warraghiyagey had suggested and enthusiastically endorsed. He urged on the Crown final approval of the plan.

In the meanwhile, Sir William was showing, through his own holdings in the Mohawk Valley, that the application of planning, capital, and paternalism could create a happy meeting ground between Indian and settler—and also make a fortune for the promoter.

However much land he personally possessed, he always felt that he needed more on which to build; preferably not the distant acres with which many speculators burdened their estates, but soil immediately improvable. At the heart of his yearning was the Canajoharie's huge gift behind Little Falls which the New York Council had refused to grant him while they still had the power. He now wished it granted by the Crown.

However, although he mentioned his desire in passing to the Board of Trade, he postponed from year to year presenting a formal petition. His political friends explained this as "modesty"; wrote that he was "a good and diffident man who cannot speak out when it is for himself"; but the explanation could be that he was too proud to beg favors, even of the King.

Thomas Penn, one of the grateful Proprietors of Pennsylvania, finally intervened and insisted that Sir William send a petition. Doing so in 1766, he leaned over backward to be pitiful, as proud men sometimes do when they abandon their pride. The great landowner made it seem as if his disinterested zeal to serve the Crown as soldier and Indian Superintendent had carried him to the verge of destitution.

When Penn asked that the petition be backed with an actual survey of the land he desired, he sent one covering 66,000 acres. It crossed on the ocean a letter from Penn stating that the Board of Trade was willing to grant 100,000. Rushing off a new survey, this time for 130,000 acres, Johnson stated—did he for the moment so believe?—that its approval would "satisfy me in regard to land for all the days of my life."

Several years passed, and then, in June, 1769, he received as a personal gift from the King "in acknowledgement of your services" a deed to 99,000 acres (154 square miles), the annual quitrent being set poetically at two beaverskins. He proudly named his princely domain Kingsland or the Royal Grant.

Previously, Johnson had promoted a purchase which revealed that settlement was finally filling up the Mohawk chamber in the Long House. He bought from the Oneidas 200,000 acres (it surveyed down to 123,000) slightly west of German Flatts on his beloved north bank of the Mohawk. The partners included Gage; the British statesman, Lord Holland; Sir Henry Moore, then Governor of New York; and Johnson, whose 25,000 acres were discreetly granted to a group of his dependents headed by Peter Servis.

At about the same time, he took large shares, totalling 27,000 acres, in two patents—N. Byrne; Lawyer and Zimmer—some twenty miles south on Schoharie Creek. Further southwest, he secured in 1770 some of the lands on which he had originally dreamed of making his major settlements: a tract twenty miles long and one mile deep on both sides of the Charlotte River. Northeast of Johnstown and Kingsland, he extended his holdings, as the years passed, to the far bank of the Sacandaga and along that river to its junction with the Hudson. This involved shares in the Sacandaga, Mayfield, Duncan, Stuart, Northampton, Glen and Vrooman, and Achilles Preston Patents, as well as purchases into such older grants as Wilson and Abeel.

Johnson sent Banyar lists of friends, dependents, tenants, and indentured servants whose names were to be put on his part of the patents, and Banyar checked with him periodically to make sure the men were still available and willing "to sign the instrument." (One, for instance, had to be scratched out because he had run away.) This was, of course, too usual a procedure to excite any comment. It was also usual for eighteenth-century officials to use their positions within reason to feather their nests, but there were those who accused His Majesty's Indian Superintendent of being unreasonably greedy.

To charges that he was engrossing all the best land, Johnson replied that he was doing the public a service because he instantly —sometimes even before the patent was actually granted—placed on his acres settlers of whom he took personal care.

His early hatred of absentee landholders was increased by his wilderness years: they profited, he wrote, from trouble on the frontire. Only too often their land titles had been dishonestly secured. Unconcerned with the "lives of such ignorant settlers" as became their first tenants, and having not made personally any improvements that disorder could destroy, they were enchanted if their greediness started an Indian war. The tribe they had defrauded might "be driven to despair and abandon the country," which would silence Indian protests against their crooked deeds.

Even if not grounded on fraud, absentee landlordism discouraged settlement: homesteaders saw no reason to support speculators who would do nothing for them and would eventually take title to anything they did for themselves. Thus was created a deep and ragged frontier, the eastern part broken with speculator-owned patches of virgin forest, while settlers were driven into the Indian country, where, being out of the reach of the law, they squatted on land stolen from the outraged Indians.

The disorders in Pennsylvania convinced Sir William that the alternate land system to New York's, that of encouraging on the frontier a mosaic of small freeholders, was wasteful and dangerous for the aborigines. It is, of course, basic to the American legend that unimproved bits of forest were genii's lamps that with only a little rubbing brought prosperity to the poor. However, first and even second settlers commonly lost their acres, after several years of labor, to capitalists behind the frontier. (Such failure, not romantic dreams of untouched wilds, was too often the reason that homesteaders moved several times in a lifetime further west.) Even after a bit of wilderness had been paid for, before the land could be cleared and a crop raised, cash or credit were needed to secure guns, ammunition, axes, ploughblades, seed, food, and clothes, to say nothing of such luxuries as nails, mattresses, medicines, books, a horse or a cow, a little liquor to make the fierce toil bearable. Moneylenders became in effect the absentee landlords of so-called freehold frontiers.

Small independent settlers brought to the wilderness as their own possessions little more than their own angry muscles, wives who soon grew scrawny and often died, children who grew up far from church and school. The freeholders hated the Indians with the blind bigotry of the suffering, the insecure, and the unlettered. Thus was created what Johnson called "a total want of men of spirit, capacity, and interest on the frontiers or in the Indian country, capable of doing any material service, of gaining any influence, or of obtaining any just or necessary information."

What a man of "spirit, capacity, and interest" could achieve on the frontier Sir William demonstrated. His tenants might farm the bottoms of narrow shafts in a gloom of branches but they had no need to close their cabin doors at night except to keep out mendicant skunks. Their Mohawk neighbors were less likely to lift their scalps than, out of love for their landlord, lend them horses.

For Johnson's tenants, not only fear of the Indians but every other rigor of the frontier was eased. They had, it is true, to clear the heaviest woods from their acres, since their land had been selected to be the most fertile, but before a single tree fell, they were part of a functioning economic unit. The wilderness privation that usually extended from first ax-blow to first harvest, when all food had to be bought except game that finally choked in the mouth, was banished by Sir William's foresight in clearing, before each group of tenants came, communal fields on which they might sow and reap until their own farms were ready. He would supply seed and even horses and cows on the easiest terms. Nor was isolation ever a problem. Roads (the settlers would have to labor on them an allotted number of days a year) already connected the unimproved farms with the outside world, the gristmills and sawmills which the proprietor erected before he settled each new section of his expanding estate.

The lack of specialization normal to the frontier, which encouraged farmers more handy than their neighbors to practice a wide variety of crafts when not too busy in their own fields, seemed to Johnson to encourage waste and incompetence. He advertised in big-city newspapers for "tradesmen and artificers" who would make goods for the settlers or process the raw materials the frontier produced. Although he discouraged a goldsmith, he welcomed a sword-maker, a hatter (some of whose beavers were exported to New York to be trimmed for the city trade), a breeches-maker, an indentured shoemaker, a tanner, a wheelwright, a collar-maker, a surveyor, etc., etc. One of his cronies used the endless ashes created by the clearing of fields to make potash, and Dr. John Dease, a nephew recently arrived from Ireland, lived at the Hall and was the neighborhood physician.

As a center for his artisans, in 1765 Sir William "made choice of a good situation within a small mile of my house" where he laid out and began to build his personal capital of Johnstown. By 1766, there were ten houses; five years later there were twenty arranged on the blocks created by the intersection of four north-and-south streets with four that ran east and west. "The town," he wrote in January, 1771, "is a mere thoroughfare, every day full of sleds . . . which really makes the place more lively than Albany or Schenectady, who are suffering from the want of snow."

Up at the Hall was a private agricultural experimental station where farmers were always welcome. The old settlers in the Valley, Sir William noted, "neglect husbandry." His own tenants were "in too low circumstances to seek on their own anything but subsistance," yet he intended to help them set a good example. He claimed that, when he first came to the Valley, wheat had been the only crop, although it was a drug on the market and cash had to be paid to New England for other necessities. He had introduced hay—"before I set the examples, no farmer on the Mohawk River raised so much as a single load"—and sheep—"to which they were entire strangers till I introduced them." He promoted hemp and peas—for the latter, he built splitting-mills—and tried out everything from Canadian grapevines to peanuts from the West Indies: "Shell or hull and roast them moderately and they are very good," a friend wrote. Johnson conducted, in addition to a weekly market at Johnstown, two annual fairs, at which he personally offered and awarded prizes for the best vegetables and livestock.

For civilizing the settlers he relied, as with the Indians, on religion and schools that were, in the eighteenth-century manner, church schools: religion, wrote the man who had abandoned Catholicism as a block to ambition, was "so useful an institution." Although personally sympathetic to priests and laymen of his ancestral religion, for political reasons he would not permit the Scotch and Irish Catholic among his tenants to organize for worship. He summarized his attitude: "I have equal charity and inclination to serve all denominations of the reformed church; at the same time, I think it my duty to offer any services in my power to the Church of England."

One of his first acts in colonizing the Johnstown area was to give his Dutch and German tenants glebes for Dutch Reformed and Lutheran parsonages. The settlers did not build the parsonages. They were, he concluded, so "ignorant," had so "very little acquaintance with any religion . . . that the first church which goes on successfully and without interruption must attach them all."

Wishing his settlements to "become zealously attached to our constitution in church and state," he appealed to the Anglican Society for the Propagation of the Gospel for ministers and schoolteachers. That high-sounding organization, being often unable to supply them, blamed Blackstone, whose recently published *Commentaries* had emptied England's theological seminaries by making "the study of the law easy and agreeable, instead of being dry, disgusting, and intricate as formerly." Johnson had to recruit ministers through his friends, and schoolteachers through newspaper advertisements. What salaries the inhabitants and the Society did not pay, he made up himself.

During 1765 and 1766, he built at Johnstown St. John's Episcopal Church and "a snug house for a clergyman." It took only five years for the community to outgrow the church, and in 1772 he erected a new one—Judge Jones considered it "one of the genteelest in the province"—to accommodate about 1,000 souls. He himself described it as "a handsome stone building, near ninety feet in length with the steeple and chancel, to which I have lately added a neat organ that cost me £100 sterling." The main entrance was to the north, but much of the western wall folded open so Indians could squat on the ground and listen. To the right of the pulpit, a pew under an elaborate canopy was reserved for the King: it remained forever shut, a silent symbol of imperial power. To the left, a similar pew was reserved for the man who had built and still owned the church, for Sir William and his heirs.

St. George's Anglican Church at Schenectady was completed in 1769 with Sir William as principal patron (his pew there was marked by "a handsome canopy supported with pilasters"). He kept the Queen Anne Chapel at Fort Hunter staffed and under repair. After the Indians had themselves collected a hundred dollars for a church at Canajoharie Castle, Warraghiyagey contributed the rest of the cost and perhaps the design. A tall, gracefully proportioned box on an empty hillside, this final shard of a vanished Indian city still points its wooden steeple accusingly at the white man's sky.

In 1769, Johnson opened free schools at Fort Hunter—30 pupils —and Johnstown—45. As his settlements opened out, he added other schools.

Not only was the Johnstown institution interracial, but Molly's children, who combined both races, were treated, as one fellow pupil remembered bitterly, "with kind partiality and pointed indulgence" by the usually fierce Irish pedagogue, Edward Wall. Sir William boasted that Wall had "received a liberal education in Europe," but his scholars only recalled his brogue, his perpetual wrath, and his insistence that whenever he was addressed the child should accompany the words with a "bow, a backward motion of the right hand, and drawing back upon the floor of the right foot."

Woe to the wilderness child who scraped indecorously with the left!

The children learned manners, the three R's, and tolerance.

Johnson, of course, combined paternalism with self-interest. Although he had lands on his Schoharie and Charlotte River grants for sale to settlers who did not want help, in his heartlands, the Fort Johnson-Johnstown-Kingsland-Sacandaga area, he followed the established New York custom of not selling but, as a complainant put it, exacting "a certain tribute annually and forever." His leases were long, usually for two or three lives.

The first five years, when woods were being changed into farms, were given rent free, and the next ten at a reduced rent. Sir William insisted on keeping the rights to all ores; he liked to take a percentage of the value of improvements if a lease were sold, and to forbid the building of mills to compete with those he himself built and rented. Various feudal services, which one objector summarized as "customs and carriages," were asked for by Johnson but not always insisted upon.

He was known as "so generous a landlord"; his terms were considered "easy"; and his lands were, as he boasted, "both with respect to situation and quality very valuable." His acres filled up so fast that by 1772 he no longer found it necessary to advertise for tenants. His settlers varied from individual households to groups: a flock following an Anglican pastor expelled from Congregational Litchfield in Connecticut; Catholic Scottish Highlanders led by their tribal chiefs.

When forty Scotch families had to be settled at one time, he wrote that they were "a heavy burden on me and full as much as I can bear. But should they prove industrious and get forward, it could heighten my happiness, there being nothing upon earth delights me more than to see the rude woods made cultivatable, and afford sustenance to the poor and distressed."

He boasted during 1771 that the road to "the extensive meadow of the Sacandaga, a branch of the Hudson's River fourteen miles from hence" had three years before run "through an entire wilderness but is now one continued chain of settlements. . . . The progress of industry, to which I flatter myself I have in some degree contributed," had spread far beyond his personal holdings. "Two new churches are built at Canajoharie, two more at German Flatts, and some settlements are begun far beyond it and near to Fort Stanwix." It was with "pleasure" that he surveyed "the dawnings of improvement and infant cultivation of arts in this country of forests."

It was all so expensive that Sir William was forced to dip into the £5,000 which the government had given him many years before and which he had invested as a backlog in England.

However, although he sometimes lacked for cash, he never lacked for luxury as he defined it. He felt that his enjoyment of good living was another of his virtues, since he believed his example would "stir up a spirit of industry amongst the people here." Too often "content with the mere necessities of life, they don't," he complained, "choose to purchase its superfluities at the expense of labor, neither will they hazard the smallest matter for the most reasonable prospect of gain."

No bolted gates protected the baronet's demesne; the peasantry were always welcome and they saw much to emulate. Sir William seems to have designed the Hall himself: Certainly he sent plans to the builder, Samuel Fuller of Schenectady, rather than asking for them. The result was, as a Connecticut physician wrote, "truly grand and noble," yet Johnson Hall (it still stands as a state-owned museum) was not, like the mansions being built by Sir William's economic peers, a different order of house from more modest American dwellings. The paneling, that was freely (but not lavishly) applied to the walls, displayed simple combinations of rectangular moldings that could be found in many a prosperous farmhouse. The elaborate neo-classical forms that the fashionable were importing from England did not trouble the architectural frontiersman: no detailed carving complicated his mantles, no Adam tracery his ceilings, no intricate lathe-work the strong banister and balustrades of his stair. The "elegance" on which even the sophisticated commented was inherent in proportions which exhaled calm, light, and cheerfulness, made every dimension seem larger than its physical scale.

Sir William's favorite room was the blue parlor which contained prints of the King, Queen and Royal Family, seven large pictures in gilt frames (one probably the fleshy *Susannah and the Two*

Elders he had been given), twenty-four freemason pictures, three fiddles and a flute, a mahogany and walnut table with thirteen leather-bottomed walnut chairs, two silver-mounted small swords and one silver-mounted hangar, a short, basket-hilted sword without sheath and a steel-mounted long sword, two silver-mounted whips, a display of Indian artifacts over the mantle, two backgammon tables, a spyglass, some maps, plate valued at £291.2.0, fifty-eight drinking glasses, and seven quart decanters.

Across the 15-foot-wide hall through which, as has been pointed out, a horse and cutter could have been driven, was the white parlor, which seems to have doubled as a dining room. Probably because the bullet in his thigh made it hard for him to navigate the stairs, he shared the two back rooms on the ground floor with Molly: one was their bedroom, the other the nursery. The four chambers on the second floor were for guests. Throughout were spread Indian souvenirs and animal skins; and everywhere there were sleeping accommodations—cots in the parlors, and in one bedroom, for instance, the following: a straw bed, two feather beds, two four-posters, and two buffalo skins.

The kitchen and the butler's room were in the cellar. Such other servants as lived in the house were undoubtedly quartered in the huge attic without central beams that was like the inverted hull of a ship.

Though one of Johnson's tenants kept "an excellent inn at Johnstown"—he went bankrupt—Sir William invited the visitors who came to his capital "from all parts of America, from Europe, and from the West Indies . . . to repair to the Hall," where, so wrote Sir William's friend, Judge Jones, they "all were equally and hospitably entertained. . . . The gentleman and ladies breakfasted in their respective rooms, and, at their option, had either tea, coffee, or chocolate, or if an old rugged veteran wanted a beef steak, a mug of ale, a glass of brandy, or some grog, he called for it, and it always was at his service. The freer people made the more happy was Sir William. After breakfast, while Sir William was about his business, his guests entertained themselves as they pleased. Some rode out, some went out with guns, some with fishing tackle, some sauntered about the town, some played cards, some backgammon, some billiards, some pennies, some even at nine pins.

Thus was each day spent until the hour of four, when the bell punctually rang for dinner [the dinner bell weighed 100 pounds] and all assembled. He had besides his own family, seldom less than ten, sometimes thirty. All were welcome. All sat down together. All was good cheer, mirth, and festivity. Sometimes seven or eight or ten of the Indian sachems joined the festive board. His dinners were plentiful. They consisted, however, of the produce of his estate, or what was procured from the woods and rivers, such as venison, bear, and fish of every kind, with wild turkeys, partridges, grouse, and quails in abundance. No jellies, creams, ragouts, or sillabubs graced his table. His liquors were Madeira, ale, strong beer, cider, and punch. Each guest chose what he liked and drank as he pleased. [He now ordered limes by the thousand.] The company, or at least part of them, seldom broke up before three in the morning. Everyone, however, Sir William included, retired when he pleased. There was no restraint."

As the wilderness baronet presided over Gargantuan consumption of food, punch, and wine, John Kain, a blind Irish harper he had imported, sang ancient eddas. Kain finally drifted away to Philadelphia, where he committed a murder. He was replaced as castle musician by a tiny and chirpy violinist called Billy, who grimaced as he played duets with a bewigged Indian able to scrape European tunes "tolerably" out of a fiddle. Among the applauders was a man famous—or notorious—in musical literature. Richard Shuckbaugh, a physician who preferred drinking to doctoring, long Johnson's friend and after 1765 official Indian Secretary, is said to have convulsed a festivity at Albany during the French and Indian War by setting to a tune either orginal or traditional—how the musicologists argue!—a jingle—ah, fatal act!—mocking the New England militia and called *Yankee Doodle*.

Flanking the rear of Johnson Hall were two freestanding stone blockhouses built during "Amherst's War," large enough to shelter his immediate community. They were connected to the Hall by tunnels. One was used as Negro quarters; the other, which was over the wine cellar, was probably Johnson's private study. The bowmaster (overseer) had a stone house of one room. There was a blacksmith's shop, a red coach house, stables, a coop for the peacock and his hen, a cage for the monkeys, kennels, a large framed barn, more slave quarters, "a good saw and gristmill," and "many little buildings for the accommodation of the Indians." Nearby were a large, thriving orchard, flower gardens where "a West Indian bird called a flamingo" drank from the fountain, and the 500 acres Hall farm "chiefly enclosed with board fence and hedges."

The farm, so Valley gossip remembers, was worked by some fifteen slaves who were dressed like Indians except that their blankets were stitched into coats. The many household slaves obeyed a very active German butler called Frank. Two dwarfish looking waiters, both named Bartholomew, were squawked at by the parrot in the entrance hall. An Indian boy in livery handed around tobacco. So effective were what Croghan called "the fertile loins of your estate" that when the children needed shoes, the order overflowed Johnstown and had to be farmed out among several Schenectady shoemakers.

Years before, as he was building Mount Johnson, William had written his brother Warren for a coat of arms he could legally cut in stone. By means of genealogical legerdemain, Warren claimed the arms of the ancient Irish royal family of O'Neill. When the proper authorities spurned this pedigree, he protested. (William's descendants were to revive the argument and finally get Burke's *Peerage* to allow them the O'Neill arms in 1912). For his part, William put coats of arms out of his mind until he actually needed one as a baronet. Then he did not appeal to the College of Heralds for something conventional. He himself concocted a design (first published in 1762 on a map of his Niagara campaign) which expressed his personal career but confounded the language of heraldry. In describing the fur skirts of the two Indians holding up Sir William's shield, the author of the *Encyclopedia Heraldica* wrote that they were "wreathed round the waist with leaves vert"; and he spoke thus of their feathers: "crowned with fleurs-de-lis." Sir William adopted the modest motto *Deo Regique Debeo,* I owe God and the King.

To white travelers, Johnson Hall was a center of hospitality, but to the Indians it was an international capital. For every white visitor there were ten to a hundred Indian guests. The tribesmen who thronged at will from their own quarters into the house did not step aside to let any belaced lord pass; and when great ladies

Coat of Arms of Warrighagey, Baronet,
probably sketched by himself for the Engraver

He used the arms primarily on book plates such as that here reproduced. William Berry's *Encyclopedia Heraldica*, 1828, gives the following description: "Arms, gu. on a chev. betw. three fleurs-de-lis ar. as
many escallops of the field.—Crest on a wreath, a cubit arm in armour,
holding in the hand an arrow in bend sinister ppr. point downwards.
Supporters, two North American Indians ppr. wreathed round the
waist with leaves vert crowned with fleurs-de-lis." The motto translates
into "I owe God and King."

in silks and powder stared at squaws in porcupine quills and bears' grease, the squaws stared just as curiously back. If a brave decided to go to sleep in the front hall, everyone stepped over him until he chose to awake.

The South Carolina patrician, Ralph Izard, wrote, "Sir William continually plagued with Indians, generally 300 to 900. Spoil his garden; keep his house always dirty." And Lord Adam Gordon, son of a Scottish duke, added, "No consideration should tempt me to lead his life. I suppose custom may in some degree have reconciled him to it, but I know no other man equal to so disagreeable a duty." Aristocratically minded visitors did not regard the baronet as representing their way of life.

However, the middle-class precursors of the romantic movement wished to cast him as their kind of hero, as is shown by Charles Johnstone's international best seller, *Chrysal, or the Adventures of a Guinea, wherein are Exhibited . . . Interesting Anecdotes of the Most Noted Persons . . .* (London, 1766). Johnson is brought into the story when the piece of money, whose wanderings from hand to hand give what unity it has to the narrative, comes into his possession. He is described as exemplifying "the unaffected ease of natural liberty," and hating all restraints not in accord with "the the light of natural reason." In particular, he was philosophically opposed to any hampering of "the strongest passion that rules the human heart"; *i.e.,* sex. "He had enforced his precepts so powerfully by example that there was scarce a house in any of the tribes around him from which he had not taken a temporary mate, and added a child of his own to the number."

The author visualized Johnson Hall as surrounded with "little cottages" each inhabited by a woman and her children. The concubines, who "often amounted to hundreds," never suffered from jealousy, "so equally" did their potent lover "dispense his favors among them." Every morning he made the rounds, keeping them faithful to him—he imposed no artificial restraints—"by the unaffected tenderness with which he enquired about their welfare and returned their caresses." They could look forward to frequent "idyllic games" at which Sir William served healthful "milk and broth."

The early romantics, who were charmed by this vision of freedom restoring purity to sex, would have been horrified to discover that Johnson's attitude was suited to Rabelais. The screams of a tavern keeper's wife when forcibly thrown onto a roisterer's bed seemed no less funny to Sir William and his companions than the inebriate's alcoholic inability to finish what he had started. Male impotence was an endless source of joking. Thus Johnson wrote Banyar (the passage is suppressed in the printed *Johnson Papers*), that he would introduce him to a rich and handsome girl, "provided I could be assured of your paying her more civility than you did to the lady I showed you in Albany, and discharging the necessary duty which men of years and infirmities are seldom capable of."

Far from staging romantic fetes enlivened with milk and broth, Sir William entertained his neighbors, white and Indian, first at Fort Johnson and then at Johnson Hall, with games that went back to the pre-history of Ireland. Greased hogs, that could be held only by the tail, were the prize of anyone who could catch them, a feat which was once achieved "amid the jeers of the laughing multitude," by a very old lady who had prepared herself with a handful of sand. "Half a pound of tea," so a local chronicler continues, "was awarded to the individual who could, by contortion of feature, make the wryest face. . . . Two old women were sometimes heard scolding most vehemently, the successful one to be rewarded with a bladder of Scotch snuff." Johnson's "ingenuity was taxed for new sources of merriment, and various were the expedients adopted to give zest to the scenes exhibited on those gala days."

Years later, grandmothers tried to hush down the fact that as young girls they had, to the amusement of Sir William, who was watching with his friends from a platform, wrestled with squaws "for some gaudy trinket or fancy article of wearing apparel." How could they explain to their nineteenth-century granddaughters that they had not demeaned themselves by playing the fool before the baronet because he would not hesitate to play the fool before them? He was as amused as anyone to hear it told how, on his way home from a convivial evening at Schenectady, he had staggered into the house of a peasant to say that he had heard the cry of a strange animal—which proved to be a bullfrog.

Sir William's manner was not that of an aristocrat shedding

bounty but of a tribal chief protecting and chiding his own. As one acquaintance wrote, he was remarkable for "gentleness," for "a temper of sympathy and friendship," for "modesty" as opposed to "ostentation and arrogance." He could refuse a favor with "infinitely better grace" than most people could grant one.

Letter after letter thanks him for "fatherly acts," for "paternal kindness." He would help anyone who would be grateful, not only the poor and industrious who appealed to his moral sense but the scapegraces who appealed to his heart. He was perpetually paying men's debts to get them out of prison; he was continually lending people farms to get them closer to the plough and further from the bottle. Although he had no objection to domestic or neighborly conflicts as long as they were kept within bounds—a bloody head, he felt, hurt nobody—he would intervene if things became serious; he provided for the children of separated couples and personally horsewhipped a man who had beaten his aged father.

When he agitated to have his estate made into a manor like those of the older New York landholding families—this would have given him his own appointed representation in the Assembly and personal judicial power—Colden replied that "the King cannot now erect a manor since the abrogation of feudal tenures." Which was ironic, for feudalism was aflame in the Mohawk Valley.*

De Tocqueville might have been describing Johnson and his followers when he wrote of times long past, "The nobles, placed high as they were above the people, could take that calm and benevolent interest in their fate that the shepherd feels towards his flock, and,

---

* Here and there in the American colonies there remained huge land holdings which had been granted, in a semi-feudal manner, during the early years of settlement. The Fairfax family owned the Northern Neck in Virginia, gradually alienating the land through sales or gifts. In Pennsylvania, the Penns stood between the Crown and the inhabitants, as in Europe great noblemen sometimes did. In Johnson's New York, grants made by Holland, when the area was New Amsterdam, had established on the banks of the Hudson "manors" where the "patroons" enjoyed governmental privileges and rented to small farmers.

However feudal in conception, these hangovers from former times had slipped into considerable conformity with more modern practices. The tenants of such great New York families as the de Lanceys did not bear arms for their overlords as Sir William's did, nor did the owners feel any patriarchal obligations to their dependents whom they (like the absentee landlords Johnson had hated in Ireland) regarded as impersonally as mere tenants to be bled to the landlord's advantage.

without acknowledging the poor as their equals, watched over the
destiny of those whose welfare Providence had trusted to their care.
The people . . . received benefits from them without discussing
their rights."

That medievalism could flourish on the frontier, which historians like to argue was the very spawning ground of democracy,
is not surprising, for the frontier was an historical anachronism
which recreated many of the conditions from which feudalism had
originally grown. As a physical environment, the wilderness was
certainly more like vanished forests of northern Europe than the
later world of roads and cities that fostered, first centralized aris-
tocracies, and then the middle classes with their equalitarian ideas.

In his epoch-making essay, *The Frontier in American History*,
Turner wrote, "Complex society is precipitated by the wilderness
into a kind of primitive organization based on family." Although,
as Turner pointed out, such an organization tended to be "anti-
social" (and thus open a path through anarchy to individualism)
this was the case only in so far as family thinking failed to extend
beyond small groups of blood relations. In the Mohawk Valley,
the clannishness deepened and coalesced into a socially responsive
super-family embracing the whole community under a patriarchal
leader.

Only clan feudalism could make it possible for a rich and powerful man like Johnson to live on the frontier and dedicate his
life to its concerns. (Aristocratic and bourgeois leaders—kings,
courtiers, and senators, merchants, and land speculators—had to
ground their power in the centers.) And the economic interests
of the frontier were almost opposite to those of the cities, for the
forest turned naturally to barter rather than buying and selling,
to voluntary co-operation rather than hiring for wages. Money,
the lifeblood merchantile democracies, was for the settler in his
own clearing largely an instrument of oppression.

A feudal frontier could perhaps have been the rule rather
than the exception had the wilderness been, like the Scotch Highlands, a broad, coherent, and stationary area. However, as an extended, narrow ribbon that was always on the move, it was forced
to feed in segments on the middle-class areas that followed it along.
Even if a pioneer resented being exploited by a mercantile so-

ciety inimical to his needs, he was usually irrevocably entangled in it.

The entanglement was not only physical, for the frontier was both plagued and exalted by a sense of impermanence. The pioneers might be living in a miraculously reconstituted middle age, but that would be gone tomorrow. Towns would rise, bringing lawyers; roads would improve, bringing trade; for those settlers who did not move on to new forests money would become a convenient instrument for the control of those who did. Thus, in the foreseeing minds of many frontiersmen the bourgeois democracy that might make them or their sons rich overshadowed the feudalism that was more suited to their immediate state of life.

In Sir William's case, the antimedieval restlessness inspired by perpetually impending change was to affect his heirs' rather than his own power. His settlements did not attract the more democratically minded pioneers, who went to other areas where they could secure land as full freeholds. Johnson's tenants and neighbors did not normally come from democratic communities in Europe or more easterly America. Except for his enemies, the Albany Dutch, the inhabitants of the Mohawk Valley were preponderantly recent arrivals from places—Ireland, Germany, the Scotch Highlands—where the medievalism Johnson had himself imbibed in Ireland was still a contemporary force. Although the settlers had fled aristocratic tyranny, they proved highly receptive to the benevolent feudalism that was, in so many ways, to their immediate advantage.

The world Sir William made was a frontier society developed on the frontier in frontier terms, and strong enough to keep out the money-changers of the cities and also the equalitarianism that was the golden result, for those who could profit by it, not of the forests but of a trading economy. That his world was feudal Sir William certainly did not know or care—the word "feudalism" certainly never came from his pen. He had met the problems of the wilderness one by one, as they appeared and as he thought best. So naturally did it grow from his temperament and his wilderness that he never wondered whether he had raised in middle-class America an exotic if ancient flower.

23

Sir William Draws a Boundary

The plan for Indian affairs which the Board of Trade had drawn up under Johnson's guidance involved the costs not only of Indian administration but of the frontier forts to which all trade with the tribes was to be restricted and where it would be supervised. Since colonial assemblies could not be relied on for the necessary funds, taxes would have to be applied directly by Parliament. While holding in abeyance the tax on the fur trade that was specifically to support Johnson's department, Parliament voted in March, 1765 (while the negotiations to end Pontiac's Conspiracy were still in progress), a stamp tax intended, among other things, to pay for the wilderness posts and their garrisons.

Naturally, Sir William hailed this first step toward a unified imperial system that would protect the interests of his Indian friends. "Their reliance," he wrote, "is and has been entirely on the Crown"; they had experienced "the utter impossibility" of receiving justice at colonial hands. As for the Colonies, "A proper consistent support of the privileges of the Mother country are the surest prop to our liberties here against the future encroachments of the ambitious in America."

When the Stamp Act riots began, Johnson blamed them on "a few pretended patriots" who "have propagated their republican principles amongst an ignorant people." In depressed moments, he could dimly foresee the Revolution, write that rabble rousers had "kindled a fire which all their engines may not extinguish," but when he looked out of his own windows he saw no radicals and no liberty poles: certainly the Crown could do what he could do. Firmness, he was certain, was all that was necessary to make the Sons of Liberty—he considered their "patriotism" a cloak to hide evil personal ambitions—return to the hovels from which they had come.

"The Parliament," Gage wrote Johnson, "will probably have too much other business on their hands respecting America than to settle matters concerning your particular department, but the King and his ministers will have that confidence in you as to approve any steps you take." Thus Johnson was able to announce at his final peace conference with Pontiac—this was the spring of 1766—that "men of honor and probity are appointed to reside at the posts, to prevent abuses in trade, to hear your complaints, and such of them as they cannot redress they are to lay before me." There were to be interpreters and also smiths "to repair your arms and implements."

Gage put up the money, and attempted to limit trade to the supervised posts, but Parliament pusillanimously repealed the Stamp Act. This British retreat, which implied no tax on furs and thus no permanent establishment for the Indian Department, made Johnson write to London that the tribes had been counting on the Board of Trade's plan. He could not stop abuses "with my little powers." If abuses were not stopped, another Indian war would certainly ensue.

To Gage, Johnson exclaimed that the "weakness" of the English government and "strong prejudices of the people here render it unsafe for me to continue my assurances of redress, for where will this redress come from, or will it come at all?" Arriving from the westward, belts told of squatters on the Indian lands beyond the Alleghenies that were still the legal boundary; and from the eastward letters with official seals told how gubernatorial proclamations and even action by the regular army had failed to unseat illegal settlers on the Ohio. Murder after murder, Johnson complained to the Crown, was committed on Indians by "these frontier people as licentious as the most savage nations"; and when the killers were arrested, mobs freed them. A man who was successfully hanged for "an unparalleled murder against two squaws"

Lord of the Mohawks

declared "at the gallows that he thought it a meritorious act to kill heathen whenever they are found." This, Warraghiyagey mourned, "seems to be the opinion of the common people."

The tribes, he continued, valued the life of one Indian more than the colonies valued the lives of ten white men; and, being not familiar with "the niceties of the law," expected "justice." All in all, the Indians had been amazingly long-suffering; they had "retaliated in a very few instances, though I know the contrary is too often represented."

When in the summer of 1767 Warraghiyagey fell to the floor of Johnson Hall in one of his deathlike paroxysms, elderly sachems who had long been his supporters and friends hurried from the wilds to his bedside. They would show him, they said, a magic, healing spring many days' march in the forest, but first he should protest again to the English Crown. For if he were to die before order was established on the frontiers, no force would remain to keep the Colonies and Indians from war.

And so, Sir William sent Lord Shelburne, who occupied the newly-established post of Secretary of State for the Colonies, as much of the old story as he had strength to write. The sachems, he warned, scorned the settlers as "not fighting people but traders who would do anything for money"; they "saw their own present strength and capacity to ravage the frontiers . . . whilst we can distress them very little."

The letter sealed and dispatched, the Indian senators watched while braves moved Warraghiyagey from his bed onto a boat. The whole party—certainly Molly came too—drifted down to Schenectady. The sick man was placed gently on a litter, raised to strong Indian shoulders, and carried into the wilderness. For days, he dozed on his back, lulled by the smooth motion of trail-wise feet, by the monotony of the full-leafed branches under which he glided. At night, he was laid in a newly built house of boughs and bark, where in the firelight ancient sachems ceaselessly watched his face. Torches in the forest revealed young men digging for medicinal roots. "There are," he wrote, "many simples in this country which are, I believe, unknown to the learned, notwithstanding the surprising success with which they are administered by the Indians."

In the banks of a stream that steamed with heat and nitrogen, a Massachusetts outcast, John Wadhams, slammed shut the door of his lone cabin at the sudden appearance of many Indians carrying high what seemed a sacrificial figure. To his surprise the figure stirred and proved the greatest man in all the forests.

At what is now New Lebanon Springs, New York, an aromatic pool, confined by Indian doctors in wood walls calked with clay, bubbled to the very edges of a small clearing. Here Warraghiyagey bathed, drank the waters, and rubbed them on his wounded leg, while hunters brought in food and the sachems chanted incantations to strength and sprightliness. But his cure was cut short by new rumors of grievous unrest in the western forests.

To his many warnings and complaints, Lord Shelburne responded by beseeching "in the strongest manner" that he soothe the Indians until some plan could be worked out to give them actual satisfaction. This was not, as it might seem, a vain plea, for Warraghiyagey had in himself many resources. Although he never spelled them out in any consistent form, they may be reconstructed from his thousands of letters and reports.

Basic were personal alliances which reflected his personal growth. The Mohawks, by whose castles chance had dropped him, were still his closest collaborators. Gradually, he had pushed his power westward across the Long House: to Onondaga during the French and Indian War; to the furthest Seneca country during Pontiac's Conspiracy. The Chenussio Kyashuta now represented Warraghiyagey to the Mingoes he had once led against the colonies. Sir William relied for the support of his own and England's policy primarily on the Five Nations.

Statistically this policy would seem madness. As he wrote in 1773, the Mohawks numbered hardly more than 400, and the entire League with its population of 10,000 (2,000 fighting men) was a small minority in his department, which contained, he estimated, 130,000 Indians (24,420 fighting men). However, he pointed out that the Mohawks, whom he used as a nation of ambassadors, were traditionally the leaders of the Five Nations. He admitted that the western Indians were "very sensible of their present superiority in numbers" to the League as a whole, but added that they had all been conquered by the Iroquois at one time or another, and "could not divest themselves of awe before them, and considered them people of superior skill." The Hurons, "the most polished and sensible people to the westward," who had "much influence over the rest," spoke almost the same language as the Mohawks with whom they were closely connected. Furthermore, the Caughna-wagas and Oswegatchies, now allied to the Iroquois in politics as well as blood, were "greatly esteemed for their abilities by the western Indians." Add to this that all the western nations consid-ered "the Six Nations as the door (as they call it) to their country, by which they might receive the surest intelligence concerning the designs of the white people"—and Warraghiyagey felt him-self justified in grounding his policy on an Iroquois alliance.

In 1756, when he had taken the petticoat off the Delawares, he had experimented with supporting revolutionary pretensions against the Iroquois. Due to the intervention of the Quakers and the buffoon Teedyuscung, this policy backfired before it had been given a fair trial, but Warraghiyagey did not try again. From then on, he considered the Delawares and the closely related Shawnees as inferiors and dependents, insisted they "would not undertake any public act without the privity and consent" of the Five Na-tions, particularly the Senecas. He entrusted their management to Croghan, who was accountable to him as he considered them ac-countable to the Iroquois.

To weaken the Mingoes and strengthen the Five Nations, War-raghiyagey urged the emigrant Iroquois who lived with Shawnees and Delawares on the Ohio to return to the Long House. This policy, which was as popular with the sachems as it was unpopular with Shawnees and Delawares, was the subject of many partially successful embassies during the last years of Sir William's life.

His solution for the Indians "who are now surrounded by white inhabitants" also contributed to Iroquois strength. These "domes-ticated" tribes were being perpetually robbed of what little land remained to them: their appeals to Sir William were endless and lachrymose. He wrote that they were undoubtedly suffering wrongs. However, since they had given up hunting and martial exercise to be loafers, fishermen, or laborers for the white men, he could not frighten their oppressors with the possibility that they would start a war: "I despair of obtaining any redress."

Without seeming to recognize the long-range contradictions, Johnson, who sought a panacea in encouraging his Mohawks to farm on
the edge of settlement, viewed with scorn the "domestic" tribes
whose hunting grounds had already become engulfed in the advancing wave. Their warriors having become "women," the Indians
were helpless to protect what had become farmland from rapa-
cious whites. Warraghiyagey believed that they needed to be reformed by a return to the rigorous forest. Again and again, he
urged the Iroquois to take into the League—giving them such a
partial membership as the Tuscaroras had long enjoyed—such of
the white-corrupted tribes as dared reassume the breechcloth of
manhood. He helped settle in the Long House Montauks from
Long Island; Mohicans from Connecticut; Wappinger, Esopus,
and Catskill Indians from the Hudson Valley; some Delawares;
and Nanticokes and Conoys from Maryland.

Since some fighting was necessary to keep the Iroquois sharp,
Warraghiyagey welcomed the ancient war with the Cherokees
which sent braves down the long trail behind colony after colony
for a comfortably distant harvest of scalps. Getting the worst of it,
the Cherokees begged the Virginia government to intercede. The
Virginians, who wished to placate the Cherokees to keep them from
revenging on Virginia murders committed by white men, appealed
to London to put pressure on Warraghiyagey. Warraghiyagey protested that his previous efforts to stop this war had convinced him
that a permanent peace could only be established if the Cherokees
admitted their country conquered and themselves the Iroquois'
slaves. He did not wish to "meddle." But Lord Shelburne was
shocked by the idea of Indians killing each other; he ordered
Johnson to halt the war. The result was two years of negotiation
that, in 1768, produced an armistice.

To win Indian approval for his policies Warraghiyagey relied
primarily on "the principal Indians" with whom he argued "in private. . . . From my own experience," he wrote, "I well know that the
modesty and good sense of an Indian is not proof against a great
weight of favor and courtship." During the French wars, he had
wrestled with the Joncaires to influence the appointment of
sachems. In 1767, he explained, "I have always made use of a few
approved chiefs of the several nations, whose fidelity I have had

occasion to put to the test on many occasions for above twenty years past, who have never yet deceived me, and from whom I have obtained timely advices of almost everything of importance in agitation. . . . I have made it to their interest as much as I believe it is to their inclination to be faithful, and have gratified their predominant passion by seeming to ask their opinion and to communicate matters to them which are of no importance, though it is a high compliment to them."

To talk at Warraghiyagey's Council Fire became the ambition of rising young orators. He could win the love of a future statesman by telling him that he went through a complicated ceremony "very prettily."

Since the tribal leaders ruled altogether by securing popular agreement at every step, Warraghiyagey needed popularity with the Indian masses. His methods would not seem strange to the boss of a modern municipal political machine like Tammany Hall. He distributed largesse to the poor, not officially, not institutionally, not self-righteously, but fast, affectionately, and on the basis less of worth than need. And he was perpetually available to all Indians, however humble. "Any person," he wrote, "who chooses to engage their affections or obtain an ascendancy over them must be the greatest slave living."

After a policy had been established, it had to be enunciated at a grand council. Warraghiyagey labored to keep the Indians sober during business sessions, but a great drunken party was the inevitable and relished climax. This horrified Moravian and Congregational missionaries, not only because of the fights and accidents that resulted—braves killed each other or stumbled into their own fires—but because, when the intoxicated warriors flourished axes "as if evil spirits were let loose," the missionaries felt it necessary to hide under rocks. Warraghiyagey was often annoyed at Indian bibulousness, but never expressed fear for his own safety. "Whenever any of them get drunk," he advised in a manner that must have seemed to the missionaries fatuous, "the only way is to disarm and tie them."

That the Indians were as a group driven mad by liquor has been explained as due to lack of ancestral conditioning or to some peculiar chemistry of their bodies. More probably, they were alcoholics for the same reason white men are: because the world had put them in a situation from which they could discern no escape.

They liked to blame their drunkenness on the white man who kept them, as a Tuscarora complained, "up to their lips in rum, so that they could not turn their heads anyway but it ran into their mouths." Yet efforts at prohibition were resented. How dare the white man, asked an Oneida, try to deprive them of the "rum we want for christening, weddings, dreams, burials, etc.?" If liquor could not be bought legally, it was bought illegally from unscrupulous traders who took every advantage of the drunken Indian. Sir William recommended that the sale of rum be permitted under proper inspection at the supervised posts. "The Indians," he explained, "value it above anything else," would be universally discontented without it, and could, unless they bore the cost of liquor, satisfy their needs so easily that the fur trade would suffer.

Guy Johnson, whose official duty it was to assume many of his father-in-law's round-the-clock labors, lived several hours' ride away (and was, indeed, not trusted by his self-sufficient father-in-law with the key to the Indian records). It was Molly who, as the fierce delegations filed in, sang to them, "Welcome from the long trail of the fleeing deer." Now that her man ailed more and more, she bore the brunt of the endless palavers by which Indian policy was made. She could feel that in serving her lover and England she was also serving her nation and the Iroquois League, for Warraghiyagey had linked their power all together. Pan-forestism was as alien to Indian thought as pan-Europeanism was to white, and thus she had no reason to feel guilty about furthering his policies by sometimes encouraging cleavages between tribes. On such cleavages Indian statecraft had always been grounded.

Molly was torn between the two races infinitely less as a politician than as a mother: how were her children, who were also the children of a powerful baronet, to be reared? Neither parent favored indiscriminate mixing of the two cultures.

It is an indication of white writers' fundamental condescension to the Indian that Sir William is praised in text after text because—so it is said—he permitted Molly to play hostess at his dinner table and insisted that his white guests treat her as politely as if she were not an Indian. Actually, Warraghiyagey scorned to subject his aboriginal princess to curiosity.

Although any Indian might grasp Molly by the elbow in greeting, few of the white guests at Johnson Hall who watched her pace by in her Mohawk robes achieved an introduction. She condescended to meet the most highborn of Sir William's English visitors—the daughter of the Earl of Ilchester found her a "well-bred and pleasant lady"—and at least once she got enough involved in a drunken party to make Warraghiyagey scold his cronies for going off without wishing her good-bye. But Molly is usually mentioned in the Johnson papers only in ill-spelled missives from Indian castles. When one of her babies died, Johnson's formal correspondence contained no messages of condolence, yet word came that the Senecas had wept in the forest.

Warraghiyagey allowed most of his half-Indian children to be brought up as pure Indians in their mothers' castles.* Before Molly had come to him, he had only broken this rule for William of Canajoharie, the boy who had remained at Mount Johnson after his Mohawk mother had vanished. The result was not encouraging.

When in 1765 William, then in his teens, was sent to Wheelock's school, tensions instantly developed. Wheelock's son, for instance, ordered William to saddle a horse for him, and William replied that he would not because his father was a gentleman.

"Do you know," sneered young Wheelock, "what a gentleman is?"

"I do," replied William. "A gentleman is a person who keeps race horses and drinks Madeira wine, and that is what neither you nor your father do. Therefore, saddle the horse yourself!"

Although Wheelock yearned mightily for Sir William's patronage, he was finally forced to ask the father to rebuke his son for

---

* In 1766, the *Scots Magazine* reported, "By letters from Fort Johnson we learn that eighteen young white women have lately been married to as many Indian chiefs, and that Sir William gives all possible encouragement to intermarriages." This was fiction. Although his one-time secretary Wraxall and the Board of Trade played with the idea of intermarriage as a way to increase English influence in the forests, Johnson never made any such suggestion. He wished the children of white men and Indian women to belong wholeheartedly to their mothers' clans. But he felt that the children of white women and Indian men, whose clan situation was less secure, were better off if removed, even forcibly, from the Indian world. Thus, at the end of Pontiac's rebellion, he favored Bouquet's insistence that the Shawnees and Delawares deliver to the English all children of white women, as "that mixed race, forgetting their ancestry on one side," became (probably in their eagerness to reassure themselves as to their Indian status) England's most "inveterate" enemies.

"pride and violence of temper." Instead, Johnson called William home. He sent the boy on to Lancaster, Pennsylvania, as a boarding pupil in one of America's most intellectual families: William's preceptor was Thomas Barton, naturalist and Anglican minister; his preceptor's wife was the sister of David Rittenhouse; his much younger playmate, Benjamin Smith Barton, was to become an even more famous naturalist.

However, Lancaster was a frontier metropolis where buckskinned thieves of Indian land boasted of the Indians they had killed. To his preceptor's horror, William "challenged almost every person he met with, and boxed half the young Dutchmen [Germans] in town." Persuaded at last that cracking heads was less constructive than study, William developed "a thirst for knowledge that carries him rather to excess in his diligence and application." He exhibited, alas, little "quickness" or "genius." At Barton's table, where he was invited when there were no guests, he revealed "something of the sullen, reserved, and unsociable."

Eventually William seemed to relax. He played happily with his preceptor's children, and then news of a new outrageous murder of braves too drunk to stand, defenseless squaws, and sucking babes filled the frontiersmen of Lancaster not with shame but the desire to rescue the murderers from jail and kill any Indians who dared resent the outrage. Suffering on the streets "lawless, insolent behavior," William no longer offered to fight back, but he abandoned his studies. He lurked in the parsonage, "the most dissatisfied, sullen, careless creature imaginable." Finally, he fled for the Mohawk Valley and his father.

Then his drunkenness began. His father gave him "repeated admonitions"; he replied with "assurances of amendment" that came to nothing. Sir William threatened "to take no further notice of him," but that too came to nothing.

Peter Johnson, Molly's eldest and for many years her only son, was in all probability brought up in his infancy under his mother's tutelage. This would mean that the nursery was organized in the Iroquois manner to encourage "liberty in its fullest extent." Clothes were not worn lest they warp the body, chiding outlawed lest it dull the sense of honor. Much in this regimen appealed to Warraghiyagey's love of freedom, but the boy could not spend all his time in his mother's part of the house or in the Indian sheds where he was revered as a great crown prince. Sometimes Peter had to come to the parlor where his father's white visitors drank, or Claus and Guy watched him play with their pale-skinned children. Warraghiyagey watched too, and saw in the eyes of the white men expressions that were hardly reassuring.

At the age of seven, Peter was taken from his mother to study with the Anglican minister in Albany. His teacher was soon complaining that he was kept home too long at vacations, and, when he was twelve, he was sent far away to Montreal.

Sir William was less interested in having his half-Indian son secure "school learning" as—the father took a flier into French—*"un petit air dégagé."* The boy was taught French, which he learned to speak "with the greatest ease and elegance," given fencing lessons, and sent to the Assembly carrying two pairs of dancing shoes, yet he remained homesick for his mother and the Indian life she led.

After sixteen months, he was allowed to come home, but his father instantly shipped him off again to Philadelphia to learn business, not the wholesale buying and selling of bourgeois merchants, but what was needed for a gentleman to handle his estates. Peter begged to be allowed to return to the Valley; comforted himself, but only "in leisure hours," with his fiddle; worked hard at his accounts; and requested "an Indian book, for I'm afraid I will lose my Indian tongue if I don't practice it more than I do." He was "a very good, sober lad," unusually ready to accept what directions he was given, but the black eyes that peered from his narrow face over the tremendous hook of his Indian nose were sad and puzzled.

Molly's younger children—Elizabeth, born 1761; Magdalene, 1763; Margaret, 1765; George, 1767; Mary, 1769; Susanna, 1771; Anne, 1773—were educated in their father's school at Johnstown. As they grew older, they took more and more to the European clothes which their mother refused to wear. For the girls, this was a protection against insult. Gossip records how several of them were almost raped when in Indian costumes by officers with whom they later haughtily refused to dance when swathed in white silk at a ball.

In the state of nature, Indians could not protect themselves from white rapacity, and to protect them was an eternal and often discouraging task. Sir William's efforts to keep fur traders under supervision at army posts pleased no one, not even Gage who, as he compliantly tried to enforce the plan, insisted it was unenforceable. To Indians who had enjoyed the convenience of having French traders spend the winter in their villages, Warraghiyagey argued that fair prices were worth a trip through the wilderness. To Governor Carleton of Canada, who argued that not being allowed to "go wintering" worked a great hardship on the former voyageurs who were now British subjects, Sir William replied that, once out of sight, the Frenchmen would spread sedition. To the British government he wrote that he did not know which most to fear: the superlative skill with the Indians of the French or the superlative greed and incompetence of the English. Both served to make the Indians hate the conquerors of America. To the protests of colonial businessmen against what they called interference with personal liberty and freedom of trade, Johnson answered that the thief never loves the policeman, particularly when he believes his victims created by God to be bilked.*

Thus the arguments ran for two years until all was decided by money. The Townshend Acts, Parliament's new efforts to make America pay for services to America, were broiling up nonimportation agreements, which were bankrupting English merchants, and decreasing rather than augmenting royal revenues. Lord Shelburne, who was sympathetic with western planning, was succeeded

---

* Johnson's policy was greatly embarrassed by Robert Rogers, whom he had twelve years before "raised," as he wrote, "from the lowest station because of his abilities as a ranger." Rogers had gone to England where, in the great rooms of country houses, he had played so successfully the early-romantic role of a natural hero that he had returned with orders to Gage that he be appointed military commandant and administrator for the Indian Department at Michilimackinack. Johnson protested that Rogers lacked "understanding or principles," would "stick at nothing" to make his personal fortune. Sure enough, he spent huge sums, which he wished the Indian Department to reimburse, to serve the ends of partners in the fur trade who disobeyed the regulations he was supposed to enforce. When Johnson sent Benjamin Roberts to curb Rogers, Rogers imprisoned Roberts. The former ranger was soon caught in suspicious correspondence with the French and arrested for treason (a charge never proved or disproved). The unsavory controversy, which implicated the Indian Department although Johnson denounced Rogers, was carried to England, where Rogers denounced Johnson to his highborn friends.

at the head of the American department by Lord Hillsborough, who visualized the frontier primarily as an itching belt that would keep the unruly colonials scratching. On April 15, 1768, he promulgated a new Indian policy with the preamble that, since the French had been defeated, friendship with the Indians was no longer of much importance. Although the two Indian superintendents were continued in charge of political relations, their annual budgets were cut to £3,000 apiece, and the control of the fur trade was returned to the individual colonies. Any real system of inspection was made impossible by the abandonment of all western forts except Niagara, Detroit and Michilimackinack.

Sir William protested, but could not believe that the new trade regulations would last for long. Were he not so without self-love, he wrote, he would regard the change with "malicious pleasure," since the failure of the policy supported by his critics would in the end "enlarge" his own reputation. And the British government, while taking power from him with one hand, had given him much desired power with the other. Before Shelburne had been removed from office he had at long last empowered Sir William to make a final settlement concerning the boundary between white and Indian territory which he had tentatively drawn with the Iroquois three years before.

By wampum and by letter—this time he asked representatives of the colonies involved—Johnson sent out invitations to a great council at Fort Stanwix. Near the half-marshy carrying place between the Mohawk and Wood Creek which the fort guarded, carpenters fashioned from tree trunks "a large arbor for a council house, seats, etc." Every white man's room in the fort and its environs was repaired and cleaned (the Indians would build their own temporary houses). Squaws and settlers' wives strung beads into wampum; cattle and sheep to feed thousands arrived and were soon lowing or baaing from improvised pens; firewood cutters and haulers were organized for perpetual motion; casks of rum were rolled out of bateaux and locked in the strongroom beside the carefully tilted pipes of Sir William's wine. (He warned the converging colonial commissioners not to taste the stuff they would be served in the taverns along the river.)

On October 24, 1768, Sir William opened the official council.

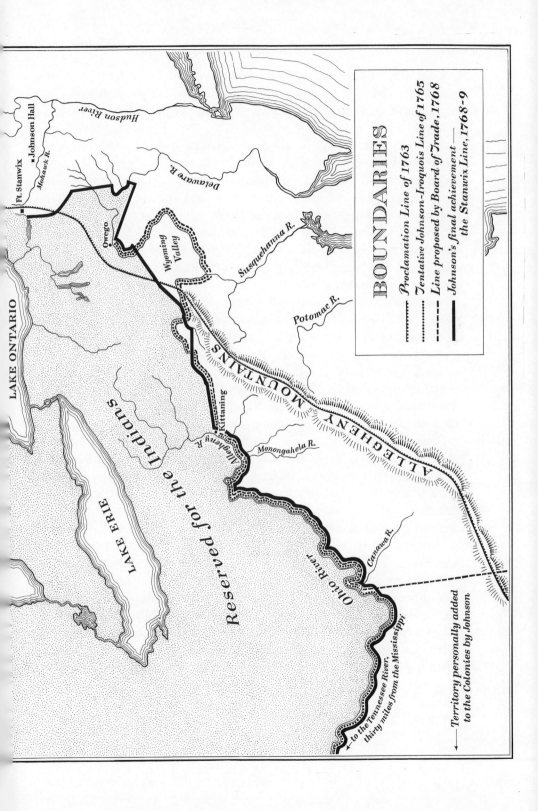

BOUNDARIES

.... Proclamation Line of 1763
———— Tentative Johnson-Iroquois Line of 1765
·········· Line proposed by Board of Trade, 1768
━━━━ Johnson's final achievement—
          the Stanwix Line, 1768-9

Territory personally added
to the Colonies by Johnson

LAKE ONTARIO

LAKE ERIE

Reserved for the Indians

Hudson River

Johnson Hall

Ft. Stanwix

Mohawk R.

Delaware R.

Owego

Wyoming Valley

Susquehanna R.

Potomac R.

ALLEGHENY MOUNTAINS

Kittaning

Allegheny R.

Monongahela R.

Kanawa R.

Ohio River

to the Tennessee River,
thirty miles from the Mississippi

Present were Governor William Franklin of New Jersey, commissioners from Pennsylvania and Virginia (Sir William doubled as representative from New York), various white men on private missions, and some 3,000 Indians: Iroquois, Mingoes, Shawnees, and Delawares. Although all these nations hunted over territory which Sir William wished to secure, he intended to make this final boundary, as he had made a tentative one, by exclusive negotiation with the Iroquois who, as overlords, would receive the total purchase price. The other tribes, he wrote, should be grateful to be "loaded with presents to which they have no right." If, instead, they felt resentment against the Iroquois over the sales, that would still serve Warraghiyagey's policy of protecting the Colonies by keeping the Indians divided.

Johnson's orders, which told him exactly where the boundary should go, followed with one major exception the line he had previously drawn, but he had changed his mind about several matters, and he did not at all like the exception. He was sure that he knew more about the forests than any Englishman, however highly placed. Acting in George III's name, but exerting over the Indians his own personal influence, he again and again disobeyed His Majesty's commands.

Since the Johnson-Iroquois boundary of 1765 had jogged around the Wyoming Valley, the Crown's orders included the jog. However, Johnson was now convinced that the Wyoming had become such a plague-spot of controversy that it would be best to pay the Indians for the land and establish a clear white title. And the Penns, anxious to squash the Connecticut claim once and for all, had offered to make a separate treaty acquiring the Wyoming from the Iroquois for 10,000 Spanish dollars. This sale Johnson intended to consummate.

Connecticut, whose pretensions to the Wyoming would thereby be denied, officially boycotted the conference, but her Congregationalists intervened. Wheelock had long had an understanding with the New England claimants that if he brought them success with his religious prestige they would give him three or four townships on which to place his school and tenants to support it. When he had broached this combination of God and land speculation to Johnson in 1762, Johnson reacted with anger, but Wheelock had continued his agitation. Now his horror at the report that Johnson was going to frustrate the Congregationalists by buying the Wyoming for Pennsylvania was increased by the false rumor that Sir William intended to conjure from the Indians a princely tract for the support of what every low-church Protestant considered an abomination: an Anglican bishopric in America.

Off to Stanwix and to the rescue Wheelock sent a ghostly ambassador, the Rev. Jacob W. Johnson, who had never conversed with Indians but held daily conversations with angels. (He was, according to his descendants, to prophesy to the second the time of his own death.) Wearing a hair shirt in imitation of John the Baptist, Jacob arrived to denounce the Antichrist of the wilderness. However, he was at first charmed: "I must confess that Sir William has and does treat me and mankind in the most handsome and genteel manner imaginable, which has endeared him to me very much. Though he has not Grace, he has no small share of lovely humanity."

But Warraghiyagey proved foolhardy. When Jacob's voices told him that the persons who purported to be Seneca delegates were really painted "Popish priests" come to murder all Protestant divines, Sir William merely smiled at the intelligence. "As I am a seer," Jacob protested, "I may be knowing to some things your Excellency possibly may not. . . . I can't think but it is time to be serious, if there be any such time." Sir William did take it seriously when Jacob refused to drink to George III except according to his own formula: "The King of New England's health; the health of the King who hears New England's prayers."

However, Johnson did not really explode until Jacob interfered in the business of the congress, trying to persuade the Indians to sell no land unless much of it went to the Congregational church. Then the baronet's bellows were heard all the way to Connecticut, whence Wheelock sent messengers to recall Jacob, state that his behavior was not authorized, explain that he was a madman. Far from placated, Sir William complained to Gage and the home government, insisted that any man less mild than he would have confined Jacob in irons for interfering with the King's business.

The major result of all this was the founding of Dartmouth College. Johnson closed to Wheelock the Iroquois country, forcing him to move his school to the New England frontier. And, partly because Warraghiyagey now kept his Indians home, the Indian part of the school shriveled away, leaving a white college.

Despite Jacob and all his attendant angels, the Iroquois took Warraghiyagey's advice and sold the Wyoming Valley to the Penns.

Since the Iroquois had been unwilling to alienate land in the Long House, the tentative boundary they had drawn with Johnson had not gone north of Owego on the east branch of the Susquehanna. Although the Crown had accepted this in its draft of a final line, Johnson insisted that if the boundary were not now extended all the way to Lake Ontario "the Indians will not be secure and the affair of the boundary will be defeated." However, the former causes of contention remained. New York could not abandon Oswego, and any line that included that port would alienate both the Mohawk and the Oneida homelands. Warraghiyagey argued and argued, "obliged," as he wrote, "to sit whole nights, generally in the open woods, in private conferences with the leading men," and in the end closed half the gap. A line was drawn from Owego roughly east to Tionadhera Creek and then north to touch but not cross Wood Creek, halfway between Stanwix and Oswego.

It was, of course, not according to the Crown's instructions that Sir William bought as a royal official extensive tracts in trust for his personal friends. He thus strengthened an Indian deed Croghan had secured to 100,000 acres between Lake Otsego and the Unadilla River. (He regretted that, without opening himself to charges of self-interest he could not also write into the treaty his own Canajoharie gift, which had not yet been confirmed by the Crown.) The most important of his private purchases was based on the agreement of the Indians after Pontiac's Conspiracy to make restitution to the traders who had lost goods in that conflict. Now, over the protests of the Virginia commissioners, Johnson secured for a syndicate of these "suffering traders," headed by the Philadelphians Samuel Wharton and William Trent, 2,500,000 acres in what was to become northwestern West Virginia. Although Johnson had no personal interest in this grant, he later admitted that his "friendship" for the merchants might have made him "serve them with more warmth than others might have done."

In his role of a semi-independent wilderness ruler, who only obeyed George III's orders when he agreed with them, Sir William had been weighing the one major change the Crown had made in his tentative boundary. That line, by continuing southwest to the junction of the Ohio and the Tennessee, would have opened for settlement territory 700 miles inland from the Atlantic Ocean. His Majesty's government had, however, concluded that to permit settlements so distant from where their navy rode would encourage sedition, since England's chastening hand might not be able to stretch over so much forest. Thus the government resolved to stop western expansion at the confluence of the Ohio and the Kanawha, a point only 300 miles inland.

A plausibly noble explanation being beloved of statesmen, the ministers discovered within themselves a sudden love for the rights of the Cherokee. They had written Johnson that since these southern Indians, not the Iroquois, owned the territory beyond the Kanawha, any truly legal boundary would have to be negotiated with them by John Stuart, the southern superintendent. Stuart was ordered to draw a line which, far from penetrating westward almost to the Mississippi as the Johnson-Iroquois boundary had done, would turn sharply southeast in what is now West Virginia and run directly to the Allegheny Mountains. Stuart had quickly carried out his orders, but Warraghiyagey was not so docile.

His letters and reports give no indication that he understood the imperial policy behind the Crown's determination to bar settlers from the distant West. He seems to have taken at face value the ministry's explanation that they were concerned for the rights of the Cherokee—and he considered those rights poppycock. As an adopted Iroquois married to a beautiful Mohawk, he could no more than his clan brothers accept without outrage the ruling that the despicable southern enemies owned land which the League claimed and had agreed to sell.

And the Virginia commissioners at Fort Stanwix, angry at having their colony cut off at the Alleghenies, pointed out that the Crown's boundary was completely unrealistic, since much land beyond it had been legally granted and, indeed, settled. Sir William could only agree that it would not bring peace to draw up a treaty that would be violated by the colonials the day it was signed. His whole policy, as he wrote, depended on a border that could be enforced, and for this it was necessary to give the settlers so much room that the Indian territory would be "well known and secured by laws before there would be occasion to invade it."

And so Sir William did exactly what he had intended to do before the English government had tried to intervene: He sent the Colonial boundary driving down the Ohio to the Tennessee. In the name of George III, he bought from the Iroquois a vast expanse of the American West which the Crown had specifically ordered him not to buy.

Sir William paid the Iroquois £10,470.7.3 of the British treasury's cash,* and he gave to all the tribes present gifts also chargeable to the Crown worth £2,328.5.0. Each, so he complained, eating as much as two white men, the Indians consumed goods worth £758.4.5. The total cost, £13,156.14.1 seemed to him very small for what he had bought for the Crown.

Blithely assuming that the British government wished to secure "as extensive a cession as practicable," Sir William was very pleased with himself and expected his superiors in England to be equally pleased—but Lord Hillsborough was furious. How had the wilderness baronet dared to draw his own limits for His Majesty's Colonies!

"The obtaining of so large an additional tract of land in that part of the continent," the minister wrote Johnson, "was upon political and commercial principles . . . only of disadvantage and embarrassment" to the government. Hillsborough would lay the matter before the Board of Trade, but urged Sir William in the meanwhile to tell the Iroquois that His Majesty refused the additional cession, not because he doubted the Iroquois' right, but because in his love for the League he wanted them to reserve the land for their posterity. Johnson asked Gage what the Iroquois would think if, after he had made this touching speech, the Vir-

---

* Silver dollars became more plentiful in the wilderness than seemed believable, which inspired the rumor that Sir William had distributed pewter counterfeits. Selling rum to the new-rich Indians, traders made their fortunes; and the commandant at Fort Ontario wondered, as the Five Nations enjoyed one of the greatest binges in history, whether he could hold on to his scalp till the money ran out. The Indians had no facilities for storing money or any way of investing it for future profit, nor did they, in their communal societies, have any use for it in their dealings among themselves. Its only utility was for immediate purchases from the whites.

ginians—as they certainly would—settled on the land so sentimentally returned to the tribes?

Since Hillsborough had been supported by his government when he had originally ordered that the boundary turn east at the Kanawha, he expected to be supported in his indignation—but it is one thing not to ask for a gift, and another to refuse it when it is actually offered. In the cabinet, land hunger overcame policy.

Hillsborough was allowed to save what face he could by roundly denouncing the special purchases which Warraghiyagey had made for Croghan and the suffering traders. But on the lands beyond the Kanawha, he was forced to eat crow. If Johnson, the peer wrote him on May 13, 1769, should believe that to insist on an alteration of the line to which the Iroquois had agreed would "excite jealousy and discontent; in that case, His Majesty, rather than defeating the important object of establishing a final boundary line, will, upon your report of this matter, give the necessary directions for the confirmation of it as agreed upon at Fort Stanwix."

Sir William had defeated His Majesty's Secretary of State for America and singlehanded added to the territory open to settlement what is today a corner of northern Alabama, most of West Virginia, much of Tennessee, and all of Kentucky.

24

The Inevitable Hour

Sir William Johnson now rivaled Benjamin Franklin as the most powerful American. Sachems and warriors admitted him "the chief of all the Indians," and Colden, the historian of the Five Nations, wrote that "his greatest abilities and singular disposition enabled him to acquire and hold a greater influence among the Indians than any other Englishman ever had."

Experts in British imperial politics echoed this verdict in another direction: no other American, one wrote, "hath such influence" with the government in London. In the Colony of New York, Johnson could, a lawyer believed, "carry anything he pleases both with the Governor, Council, and Assembly." He was rich and he ruled the Mohawk Valley as a paternal figure who could not be gainsaid. The Irish immigrant had come far in the thirty years since he had appeared in America as Warren's poor relation.

He had operated as a politician only among Indians in the wilds. Although he grounded his white power on London, he wrote his bookseller not to send him the political pamphlets that abounded there: he was only interested with "works of reputation," primarily history. That Lords Hillsborough and Shelburne, who alternated in the American department, held opposite prejudices about the frontier he was often told, but he assumed equally in dispatches to both that every sane man would wish orderly expansion and peace with the Indians. To suggestions that he could strengthen his influence if he personally visited London, he turned a deaf ear. His

Majesty's most influential official in America showed no desire to set eyes on His Majesty or any royal minister.

Sir William's seat in New York's Provincial Council remained vacant for years at a time. When Acting Governor Colden had, during the Stamp Act riots, begged him to strengthen by his presence the royal party in the Council, he had replied, "I have little inclination and much less time to enter into these affairs." He would rather "remain quiet and leave it to time than to incur the trouble and abuse with which every man who differs from the rest is loaded."

His favorite panacea for American unrest was a show of power from England; his next, "patronage and protection" for the Anglican church, that "best support of monarchy." The Anglican leaders knew Johnson was not a deeply religious man; they knew about his morals—Solomon, one of them wrote defensively, had built a temple although he was also "eminent in his pleasures with the brown ladies"—but nonetheless the Society for the Propagation of the Gospel, as its secretary wrote, "have turned their eye on you as the principle patron of their cause in America." Their objective was to secure an American bishopric that would make unnecessary sending young Anglicans abroad for ordination. The best place for an American Canterbury, they wrote, would be Albany under Sir William's wing. He offered, should the Crown approve, to secure from the Indians land that would support such a bishopric, but begged that his offer be kept secret. Anglicanism was anathema to the patriots, so much so, indeed, that he was never called on for the land: The crown was having enough trouble without establishing an American bishop.

From colonial politics, Johnson wished merely the power to rule his own area. When demanding the right to make all local appointments, he wrote that he could not be accused of "selfish motives" since "for many years past, I have so little interfered in any matters of a provincial nature that I have no favors to solicit or obligations to requite with anyone. . . . Whatever I do, it shall not be prostituted merely to party." Since his career-long opposition to the Albany Dutchmen grew out of issues seated on his frontier—and also personal distrust—he considered that it had nothing to do with party.

As the Mohawk Valley had filled out, Johnson had come, as he had foreseen, to control an increasingly large electorate, yet he was kept from running his own candidates for political office by a liability which he thus described. "We have, as yet, few or none of any talents hereabout." While waiting for his own son to grow to maturity, he used his influence as a threat. Thus, in 1750, he had summoned to him two Albanians who had announced for the Assembly, Philip Schuyler and Hans Hansen, "and told them if they would do their best for the good of the country, we would not set up anybody against them now, but if they would not do good now for the country, we would set up others next time."

Eighteen years later, he was supporting another Philip Schuyler, the future Revolutionary general, when the rumor grew strong that he would now send to the Assembly his own son, John. Schuyler responded with a bill to bar members of the Council from interference in elections, and, so Sir William was informed, tried to stir up low-church resentment against him by stating that he had misrepresented the conduct of Wheelock's missionaries at Fort Stanwix.

Johnson wrote Schuyler, "It is not without some concern that I have been given to understand by sundry persons that you have at New York taken such liberties with my character and animadverted on my conduct in such a manner as (if the proof is well founded) I cannot help taking notice of. . . . It is neither my inclination to suffer any man to treat me ill with impunity, nor too readily to admit such a charge against a person for whom I have had an esteem. . . . The candor and plainness with which I have mentioned this matter to you, will doubtless induce you to satisfy me as soon as possible."

Schuyler's "exculpatory" letter did not altogether satisfy Sir William, yet, as he wrote sadly, "My son does not at all incline to a seat." He was forced to continue his support to Schuyler, who was from then on more careful not to cross the frontiersman.

What Sir William wanted most, now that he had been denied a manor, was to have his own area made a separate political unit from Albany County. Most of the assemblymen "seemed pleased to have an opportunity to serve and oblige you," and, on March 12, 1772, Tryon County was established. It included all or most of the following modern counties: Delaware, Otsego, Herkimer, St.

Lawrence, Jefferson, Franklin, Hamilton, Fulton, Montgomery, and Schoharie. Johnstown was, of course, made the capital. Sir William personally expended the funds appropriated for erecting a courthouse and a jail, adding money of his own to make them more handsome. With the exception of the county clerk and the sheriff, all the civil officers he recommended received appointments. As assemblymen for the new county he nominated his son-in-law, Guy, and a dependent, Hendrick Frey. "The election of our representatives," he soon wrote, "was unanimous, and will, I hope, always be such, as making parties or divisions among the inhabitants can never be for their interest."

For all practical purposes Johnson had now appointed two assemblymen, and he could also "direct the election of the Albany and Schenectady members as he pleases." (This made the modern historian Carl Becker conclude with scholarly caution that in New York before the Revolution Johnson's "influence was perhaps the greatest of all.")

Guy, the leader of Sir William's parliamentary forces, reported during his first term in the Assembly, "The members look queerly at the time which the House has already given to my bills and which is without precedent." What the Johnsons were swinging their big stick to achieve were provisions for public buildings in Tryon County, improved roads and controlled ferry service, curbed "filthy" swine, exterminated "hungry" wolves and panthers. Sir William was still using colonial politics altogether for local ends.

Gradually, he had succeeded in clearing up all the land squabbles in his neighborhood between colonials and Indians. He had used the terror created by Amherst's War to force the Livingstons to make binding in a legal document their long-violated promise that they would abandon their claim to the Canajoharie Castle. Klock, it is true, had refused to sign, but he had shrunk from an active menace to an angry voice shouting up insults from below the high turrets of Sir William's power.

Since land speculators, as long as Johnson publicly protested their grants, could get no one to rent or buy farms; and since a New York deed, however fraudulently obtained, kept the Indians from enjoying their land or selling it, there was always pressure on both sides to reach a decision. Again and again Johnson served as arbiter. Sometimes, after examining documents and hearing testimony, he decided summarily for the Indians, sometimes for the colonials. Or he would work out a compromise, as he did in 1768 on the Kayaderosseras confusion: The proprietors relinquished to the Mohawks much of the enormous tract and paid for the rest $5,000. That Sir William's personal land ambitions were often involved in his rulings was recognized, although he liked to deny it. However, white claimants could find no way to get around him, and the Indians accepted his decisions.

In 1767, Sir William had been appointed brigadier general (subsequently he became major general) of all the New York militia above the Highlands. In this office, he demonstrated that his own landed wealth had not made him feel any community of interest with his fellow great landowners, the long-established patroons of the Hudson Valley. John Van Rensselear (whose uncle had initiated Johnson to New York by cheating him over horses) wished to strengthen the family's manorial claim to land around Claverack by being made colonel of the regiment raised there, but Johnson kept the regiment under control of the small freeholders who were opposing the jurisdiction of Rensselaerwyck Manor.

That the militia was Sir William's personal organ is revealed by the roster of officers: His son and two sons-in-law each commanded a regiment (John had the elite horse) and Guy doubled as adjutant general.

When Johnson became a freemason in 1766, he quickly took over the movement in New York, founding his personal lodge, St. Patrick's, at Johnstown; becoming master of the older Union Lodge in Albany; making his son John Provincial Grand Master. Boats were named after Sir William, scapegraces pretended to be his relations, sheriffs asked his permission before arresting his friends; merchants were ruined by rumors they had lost his favor; and in Albany, once the stronghold of his enemies, no magistrate was appointed without his approval.

But he cried out in a moment of depression, "Riches, titles, and everything are nothing without health . . . the most valuable thing on earth to all people!" The bullet in his hip was so "troublesome" that he "could rarely attempt to sit on a horse or take my usual exercise." If his barber nicked him with the razor, he bled with frightening profuseness. As for his paroxysms of "most excruciating torture," the doctors diagnosed them variously—dropsical, scorbutic; they prescribed variously—a mixture of horse-radish, mustard, and scurvy grass cooked "anyways as may be pallitable," or water especially dredged up by captains from the Gulf Stream—but all to no avail. "As the cause remains fixed," he wrote, "I must expect severe returns which I fear can only be palliated."

Seeking health, he automatically turned his back on civilization, made trips into the wild: a green voyage to the columns of steam in the forest that became the famous spa of Saratoga Springs; pilgrimages to sea water and sea air during which he avoided the curiosity of even the smallest villages and was content at Montauk Point in "an empty Indian house with scarce a table to set down to."

Since he could no longer ride, he built a carriage road fourteen miles from Johnson Hall into a landscape that contrasted sharply with the wooded Mohawk Valley where every year his settlers' axes opened up more low-rolling vistas. Here a huge marsh stretched flat and treeless to the distant blue semicircle of the Mayfield Hills. On a spit of solid earth which he called "Pleasure House Point" (it was so known until inundated a few years ago under the Sacandaga Reservoir) he built "Mount Joy," a neat cottage suited to his aching bones. In spring freshets, the marsh became a lake, and the point an island: from an armchair on his porch he could pull from gleaming water gleaming fish. In fall, all was brown rustling, and his spaniels, as they sought the birds he brought down with his Pennsylvania rifle, ran whimpering through reeds. Vlaie Creek was now a sharp, blue line through the soggy land. Four miles down that waterway was "Fish House" (a village still commemorates the name), a wild camp, unfurnished and unglazed, which he had built as a healthier hunter. When he was helped into a canoe to drift there, he took along a feather bed.

About two miles down Vlaie Creek, he fired two shots in the air, and instantly quick footsteps in a wilderness cabin were followed by the rustling of silk. Susannah Wormwood was "a beautiful girl of middling stature, charmingly formed, with a complexion fair as a water lily, contrasted with which she had a melting dark eye and raven hair." Sir William had tried to do the right thing by her several years ago. Before their son appeared, he had married her to one Dunbar, and solaced himself with her sister Elizabeth, who was a younger and darker version of Susannah. But Susannah could not take to Dunbar after what she had known—and now the sisters took turns hurrying to Fish House at Sir William's summons.

The girls' parents often could not resist following whichever of their daughters was so fortunate as to be enjoying the good food and wine. When the father complained to a neighbor, Mrs. Shew, that his arm was paining him, she said, "Pooh! You have made it lame by sleeping on the floor again at Fish House."

"No I haven't," she remembered that he replied. "I slept on a good bed, for Sir William brought down from the point a very nice wide one which was plenty large enough for four."

"Four! Pray how did you manage to sleep four in a bed."

"Oh, easy enough. Susannah made it up very nicely on the floor, and then Sir William told us how to lay. He first directed the women to get in the middle, and 'Now,' said he to me, 'you get on that side and take care of your old woman next to you, and I'll get in on this side, and try to take care of Susannah.' No, I didn't make my arm lame by sleeping on the floor *last* night."

Sir William limited what an early writer called "Solomonic lust" to the dark hours; he wanted no girl in waders along with him when he fished. His days were male days, enlivened with bottle, oath, and physical joke. Two streams in Fulton County still bear names based on the duckings of Johnson's friends. How John (Han) Coyne landed in "Han's Creek" is not clear, but Sir William always insisted that he was trying to catch trout with his hands. At the mouth of "Daly's Creek," Dr. Daly was encouraged by the baronet to leap, painter in hand, into a drift of autumn leaves that seemed to his rum-blurred eyes a sandbar.

Wherever Sir William was, belts and letters found him out. The Stanwix boundary—he had formally signed the treaty with the Iroquois at Johnson Hall in July, 1770—was, it is true, doing everything for Indian-white peace that could be expected of it as an isolated phenomenon: there was little encroachment on the hunting grounds beyond the new line. However, between it and the old line at the Alleghenies, where the Indians still controlled much land, confusion reigned. Unable to handle their colonials as effectively as Warraghiyagey handled his Indians, the Crown did not even attempt to make any provision for administering the territory that had just been opened. The area was neither established as a separate political entity nor officially divided among the Colonies. Pennsylvania and Virginia arrested each other's officers around Fort Pitt; Connecticut settlers continued to push into the Wyoming Valley.

Under the circumstances, any colony that tried to curb its fur traders, land speculators, and settlers would only have handicapped them in competition with their rivals from colonies that had established no controls. And when the New York Assembly tried to call a conference that would establish a general policy, the plan was vetoed in London as a dangerous step toward American unity.

Thus, the establishment of a new, strongly administered colony west of the Alleghenies seemed to Sir William doubly important. Although the old Illinois scheme had died, the special grant Johnson had secured at Stanwix for the "suffering traders" had mushroomed into a syndicate, led by the London banker Thomas Walpole and including among its seventy-two shareholders Johnson, Franklin, and many leading politicians on both sides of the water. In 1772, this company was granted 23,000,000 acres in the Ohio Valley in return for repaying the exact cost to the Crown of all the land ceded at Stanwix. The Indians, Johnson reported, were pleased when notified of this new government that would bring them protection—but the scheme did not survive the "rage against America" in the British government once the Boston Tea Party had taken place.

In the meanwhile, traders were carrying into the forests little but rum; debauched Indians, their guns sold, starved to death amidst a plenty of game; and such murders occurred as that Johnson described to Hillsborough in 1772. Banished from Fort Niagara, the "unruly" David Ramsay cheated some Chippewas and Missisaugas "a considerable distance from any fort or place of inspection or control." Their efforts also to banish him "occasioned a quarrel between him and some of them who were in liquor, of whom he killed three." He moved to another spot on Lake Erie, where, so he claimed, some Missisaugas "laid hands on him and bound him." Having succeeded in killing three men, one woman, and an infant, he carried the scalps triumphantly to Niagara where the unsympathetic commanding officer clapped him in jail.

It was Ramsay's defense, so Johnson continued, that "he was told that a war had been actually commenced between the English and the Indians, and that in his hurry and confusion the woman and child were killed." But Johnson insisted that he had been inspired by "wantonness and cruelty. . . . The Indians, whenever they meditate mischief, carefully avoid liquor, whereas it appears that they were very much disguised, and, though apt to use threats and quarrel at such times, yet incapable of putting them in execution, as is evident from the number he killed of them; and in the next place, he could have but little temptation to kill the woman, and not the least inducement to murder the child, but what has arose from sentiments of barbarity superior to the most cruel savage, who seldom puts an infant to death."

Fearing an Indian war, traders fled out of the forests to the frontier towns (it was this hysteria that ended William of Canajoharie's education at Lancaster); but Ramsay held court in jail for admiring frontiersmen to whom he stated that Johnson "would forgive an Indian for killing a white man, but not me for killing an Indian." Had Ramsay killed a hundred Indians, Johnson commented, no white jury would convict him.

As for the Chippewas and Missisaugas, their leaders converged on Johnson Hall. Rumor in New York City reported that they had "attacked your house and burned it," but Warraghiyagey managed to cover up the eight graves "with a large and handsome present and with proper messages and belts to their nation." The Indians departed, their resentment dimmed from a blaze to a smolder.

Indian anger at atrocities was given a dangerous focus by authoritative rumors that England was on the point of renewed war with Spain and France. The tribes, Johnson wrote, were gleefully foreseeing "a time when they shall be restored to their former consequence and independence of us." He too would have welcomed such a European war as an opportunity to drive from the Mississippi Valley the French traders who, he believed, were trying to join the Wabash and Illinois tribes with the Shawnees and Delawares and some wavering Senecas into a coalition strong enough to overawe the Iroquois.

In Europe the peace was not broken. However, there are indications in the Johnson papers that the English authorities would not have objected, at moments of stress with their obstreperous colonials, if the Indians had created a diversion by burning the frontiers and scalping the settlers. The most outspoken suggestion was made by Gage, who wrote Johnson in November, 1767, when the opposition to the Townshend Acts was at its height, that if the Indians should revenge white atrocities committed against them beyond the Alleghenies, "and confine their hostilities to those spots only, though the killing of people must be shocking to humanity, I could not answer giving any assistance or to begin any hostilities against the Indians till the whole affair should be laid before the King and that I should receive His Majesty's orders thereupon."

Thus Gage invited Johnson to start a war that would have changed the flow of American history. It could not have been limited to the far side of the Alleghenies. It would have been much more destructive than Pontiac's Conspiracy. Not only would the Colonies have lacked the protection of the regular army—at least for the months it took to get orders from England—but the approval Gage asked Warraghiyagey to give would have added to the anti-colonial hordes that force, the Five Nations, which had done the most to curb the previous rebellion.

Would this have touched off the American Revolution in the late 1760s as a conflict between the Colonies and such an Anglo-Indian alliance as the patriots feared in 1775 but which, after Johnson's death, England's Indian agents were never able to achieve? Or would the Colonies have accepted, in return for British help, Parliament's right to tax, thus postponing the Revolution, perhaps until there was no more need?

For Sir William to start the war would only have been to carry to the ultimate recourse his policy of an Indian-Royal alliance. Had his heart beat, as has sometimes been charged, solely for himself, the Indians, and the Crown, he might well have painted his wampum red.

However, he had lived for thirty years on the frontier without once returning to the Old World. He was the most effective colonizer of his American generation. He could not promote what he called "the total ruin of those settlements which industry and peace have added to the Colonies."

Warraghiyagey taught the Indians to reverence the King as their friend—Joseph Brant, on a visit to London, was shocked at the way Englishmen criticized His Majesty—yet, during the Stamp Act riots, Sir William reported to the Board of Trade that he minimized in forest conferences all lack of unity among the King's subjects lest the Indians "interest themselves in the affair, or fall upon the inhabitants in revenge for old frauds."*

Sir William saw nothing as he rode through his personal world to make him realize that everything he had created was menaced by onrushing Revolution. An expert organizer, by nature expansive, by inclination generous, amused by eccentricity and eager to encourage ability, he violated the theories of liberty but gave his Valley much of the substance. There were rent riots on the neighboring manors but never a recorded murmur on his estates (when the Wormwood girls whispered to their lover of the rights of man they were not anticipating Thomas Paine). At every high point of colonial dissatisfaction, liberty poles rose in many places, but never, while Sir William lived, on the banks of the Mohawk.

In 1772 New York's then governor, William Tryon, visited the baronet's domain. General Johnson treated him to three musters of militia regiments "amounting," as Tryon noted, "in the whole to upwards of 1,400 effective men. . . . The land on the Mohawk River is extremely fertile and under the highest cultivation, producing as good wheat and peas as any in the old countries. . . . An industrious people, and not less seemingly pleased with the presence of their governor than he was with them. I heartily wish the eastern parts of the province were as peaceably settled."

Although Tryon had his annoying times in New York City, even there the drift toward civil conflict was not clear. The repeal of the Stamp Act had raised a new wave of love for the Crown, and the New York merchants had not resented the Townshend Acts in any tangible form until an administrative decision entangled this new legislation with an ancient issue of paper currency. Then the Colony did come into line with New England's nonimportation agreements, but it had eagerly dropped most of them again when,

---

* Kirkland, it is true, charged that Johnson had prejudiced the Indians against the New Englanders by saying that they had killed their king—*i.e.*, Charles I. However, this accusation was inspired by Congregational-Anglican rivalry, and, under questioning, the Congregational missionary withdrew the charge.

in 1770, the Townshend duties were withdrawn on everything but tea. Writing in 1771, only four years before Lexington, that "a calm seems to have taken place on this side of the water," Johnson expressed an opinion commonly held. New York's class organization built an opaque roof over dissatisfaction. Only the conservative part of the population could vote; having no voice in the Assembly, the Sons of Liberty could not shock its decorum.

It was the Boston Tea Party that, on December 16, 1773, sounded, after years of distant, ambiguous rumbling, the thunderclap which at long last warned astute upper-class observers of the coming revolution. New York's colonial politics were still dominated by rival factions under the leadership of the Livingston and De Lancey families. The De Lanceys stood pat, but the Livingstons, although more conservative (if less royalist) than Johnson, appeared at meetings called by the Sons of Liberty. They wrested the steering wheel of the dangerous movement out of radical plebeian hands, preparing the way for the moderate leadership that in New York protected property and vested interest all through the War of Independence.

Sir William had his settlements to protect and also the interest of the Indians which he had so long linked with the influence of the Crown. However, he was, as Guy wrote, "sensible of the approaching end. The violent return of his disorders renders it but too apparent." The patriarch was relinquishing the helm. If his feudal but effective world were to ride out the American Revolution, it would have to be under the leadership of those he appointed to succeed him.

In January, 1774, he drew up his final will. He referred to Catherine Weisenberg as "my beloved wife," and took every opportunity to make her children seem legitimate,* even to pointing a contrast by calling Molly his "housekeeper" and Molly's offspring "natural." As the second baronet, John was to inherit Johnson Hall, Fort Johnson, Mount Joy, most of Johnstown, and the lion's share of the other inhabited estates. The Clauses and the Guy Johnsons were to receive considerably more than Molly or any of

* He requested that Catherine's body be deposited with his own in the grand tomb he had built for himself in the Johnstown church, "if not done before my decease." Neither he nor her children ever thus honored her bones.

her children, but in this second family primogeniture was again observed. Peter was bequeathed valuable farms and functioning mills that overshadowed the considerable legacies to his full brother and sisters, and the rent-producing land Molly received was to revert to him. Probably because she intended—as, indeed, she did—to return after Warraghiyagey's death to her clan house at Canajoharie, she was left no dwelling, but her body slave "Jenny the sister of Juba" was assured to her. Her children were to have "one fourth of my slaves and stock of cattle of every kind." All were given substantial cash legacies.

In an emotional passage, Sir William named six "guardians and trustees" for Molly's children, conjuring them in the name of their "close connection" with him and his own "long, uninterrupted friendship" with Molly "to observe and execute this my last charge to them, the strong dependance on and expectation of which un-burdens my mind, allays my cares, and makes a change the less alarming." Whom he suspected of wishing to rob his half-Indian brood is perhaps indicated by the fact that from the trustees of their safety he conspicuously omitted John, Claus, and Guy. (He was hardly dead before John's lawyer was whittling away at Molly's children's share.)

However, it pleased him to think that the heirs of all the white and half-Indian children he acknowledged would live side by side forever. He entailed the Royal Grant and put them on contiguous tracts. Molly received "lot number one," which would revert to Peter; John 50,000 acres; Claus and Guy 10,000 each; Peter 4,000 plus a strip lying closest to the river; Molly's other children 3,000 apiece with the exception of Elizabeth who got 2,000 in considera-tion of another valuable legacy; Brant Johnson and William of Canajoharie 1,000 apiece.

Of his distant acres Johnson provided for keeping only the property at Onondaga which had been given him because of its political significance and could not be sold without outraging the Indians (he willed it to John). All other outlying tracts, including his lands on the Charlotte River and his share in the Oneida Pur-chase which adjoined the Royal Grant to the west, he wished to have sold for the benefit of his Irish relations. To his friends, re-tainers, tenants (and the mass of his illegitimate children) he left almost no bequests, preferring "most earnestly [to] recommend it to my son to show lenity to such of the tenants as are poor . . . which will, upon reflection, afford more satisfaction and heart-feeling pleasure to a noble and generous mind than the greatest opulency."

The responsibility of steering Sir William's settlement through the Revolution would fall on John. To mellow his provincialism his father had sent him during 1765, when he was twenty-three, to England. If considered a baronet's legitimate son, he had an automatic right to a knighthood; this, to Johnson's relief, George III instantly bestowed. Lord Adam Gordon, who had visited at Johnson Hall, tried to interest John in high society but was soon complaining, "His modesty conceals his merit." The young man longed for what he called "the sweet, enchanting banks of the Mohawk," and, as soon as his father would let him, hurried home eager to show his cronies what he had acquired: an English butler, an English coachman, and luxuries on which the freight alone came to £55.13.9.

After Sir William had moved to Johnson Hall, John had taken over Fort Johnson. Here the son of Catherine Weisenberg established a mistress of his own. The teen-age daughter—she was born in February, 1751—of an Episcopal German family long settled in the Valley, Clarissa Putman presented her "warm and somewhat whimsical" lover with a new William Johnson and then Margaret, named after John's sister. As titles cannot be passed along illegitimately forever, Sir William wished John would marry a suitable lady, but "I would lay no force on a young man's inclinations."

Sir John shrank from the beauties of New York City offered him as a great inheritor. "The finest race of young women I ever saw!" exclaimed one matchmaker. ". . . Polly Watts, Hannah Vanhorne, Betsey, her sister (an angel!), Sukey Vanhorn: if I were two and twenty, I would not wish for more than her and 6,000 bottles of her father's old wine." In 1773, John finally sent Clarissa and her children into exile and married the rich and nervously irritable Polly Watts, but he still avoided every other kind of responsibility.

Sir William's nephew and son-in-law was the family man of affairs. Warraghiyagey arranged with the Indians and urged on the

Crown that Colonel Guy Johnson succeed him as Indian Superintendent, and, as we have seen, sent Guy to New York as the Johnson leader in the Assembly. Guy would have to report back, if anyone did, the strange new revolutionary handwriting on the wall. "The poor colonel," John's father-in-law wrote of Guy, "would be more alert with less bulk." (When he tried to look impressive, as in Benjamin West's famous portrait of him with an Indian standing behind him, he looked overstuffed, his eyes hazardously popping.) He was later to explain that he had gone "to one of the people's meetings, which I found had been called by an itinerant leather-dresser, and conducted by others if possible more contemptible. I had therefore little inclination to visit such men or listen to their absurdities."

Thus it happened that Sir William was still able to write on April 17, 1774—exactly a year and a day before the Battle of Lexington—that "tumults and disorders have given place to tranquility." He added in May that the troubles in Boston "are not so formidable at bottom as is, I believe, imagined by some people in England."

Sir William was avoiding all activities "which in my present low state would exhaust my spirits," when a wave of murders forced him to pull his dying body upright. Captain Michael Cresap had killed three peaceable Indians near the Ohio. This inspired his neighbors to invite some Mingoes in for a drink, and, when the Indians were too drunk to defend themselves, chop mortal holes in the guests who included a brother and sister of the great Cayuga chief, Logan. Bald Eagle, an aged Delaware chief, proved, as he paddled along in a canoe, an inviting target; his scalped body was sent drifting down the river, a bloody Lady of Shalott. The Shawnee chief Silver Heels was added to the casualties by some traders on whom he was paying a social call.

These most politically explosive of murders induced the Delawares, Shawnees, and Mingoes to fall on the Virginia frontier in what is known as Cresap's War. When Logan appealed to the Onondaga Council for official Iroquois support in his revenge, the sachems picked up their blankets and hurried, with some 600 followers, to Johnson Hall.

Considering the situation very grave, Sir William wrote, "I shall persevere. The occasion requires it, and I shall never be without hopes till I find myself without that influence which has never yet forsaken me." But what was more basic forsook him: life itself.

As, scorning an interpreter, he addressed the sachems on July 11, 1774, in the arbor behind his house under the hot summer sun, he became "apprehensive of the fit coming on from a sense of compression and tightness across the stomach." However, he continued to speak, as an eyewitness noted, "with all the spirit, activity and energy" of an Indian. Beginning to totter, he gave his last charge to the warriors and squaws and children who had so long been his friends: "Whatever may happen, you must not be shaken out of your shoes."

He ordered "pipes, tobacco, and some liquor for the Indians," and was then "obliged to call for assistance to get to his room." He "drank some wine and water, sat himself down in an elbow chair, reclined his head against the back of it, and expired without a groan."

At Fort Johnson, John had been notified that his father was stricken. He galloped his "English blood horse" so fast that the animal expired on the road. John was running when the death wail suddenly filled the air from innumerable Indian throats.

To the speed of pelting moccasins, the wail moved westward through the wild, following a sun that set in bloody splendor over a dying world.

Epilogue:

The Drowned Lands

The procession took a long time to weave down the hill from Johnson Hall to St. John's Episcopal Church at Johnstown. First came all the clergymen of the Mohawk Valley. Next, the coffin flapping mourning cloths, marked with silver nails, "W. J. aet. 60 years." Sir William's remains were borne on the shoulders of civic leaders: Governor William Franklin who had hurried up from New Jersey; Robert R. Livingston, Sr.; James Duane, Robert Morris, Banyar, and others. Next came the chief mourners: Sir John, now writing himself down "Bart."; Claus and Guy. As self-important as if they had not failed, the physicians paced along. Then, in deepest mourning, Johnson's two acknowledged white daughters with their babies, Molly and her eight children, Brant Johnson, and William of Canajoharie. Wrapped in black blankets, wearing crepe on their hats, and inky gloves, the Mohawk sachems led in procession every living Mohawk, infants too small to walk staring to the rear from boards strapped to their mothers' backs. After Warraghiyagey's tribe had passed, more than 2,000 settlers in their Sunday best crowded behind the high sheriff of Tryon County. They were followed by delegations from the remaining Iroquois and many other Indian nations, each singing a death song acclimated to a different forest.

More literally than anyone in the long line could realize, the bell that tolled for Sir William Johnson tolled for every one of them. In five years, they would all be dead or scattered.

The Indians provided as best they could for the future by ritualistically making Guy Johnson over into their beloved friend who had died: "The heavy clouds which have hung over you and us have prevented us from seeing the sun; it is therefore our business with this string to clear the sky which was overcast. And we likewise with this string put the sun in its proper course that it may perform the same as before, so that you may be enabled to see what is doing and pursue the good works of peace." Chiming in, the Crown officially made Guy Sir William's successor as Indian Superintendent, with Claus his first deputy and Joseph Brant as secretary. John stepped into his father's shoes as leading landowner and major general of militia. And then the Revolution broke.

A few months after Sir William's death, there arose in the Mohawk Valley at long last a Committee of Safety which explained its late appearance by stating that Tryon County "has for a series of years been ruled by one family." John tried to ignore the rising tidal wave, Guy to fracture it with upper class sneers. Eventually, all of Sir William's white heirs deserted his settlements, fleeing to Canada with as many of their tenants as still accepted their lead. John, Guy, and Claus took command in Warraghiyagey's name of His Majesty's Indian forces.

In actuality, that part of Sir William's Indian influence which did not die with him descended less to his white heirs than to Molly. When at the flaring of council fires, she wept tears of passionate sorrow for her dead lord and affirmed that he had "so often declared to live and die a firm friend and ally of the King of England," she was among George III's best recruiting agents in America. "One word from her," Claus admitted, although he hated Molly, "goes further with them than a thousand from any white man, without exception."

According to the minute book of the Tryon County Committee of Safety, William of Canajoharie "came from Johnstown accoutered with two pistols, a gun, and a broadsword on his side, saying, 'I am a King's man, who dare say anything against it? I have killed so many Yankees at Fort St. John's with this sword of my father! They are no soldiers at all! I kill'd and scalp'd and kicked their arses; and the damned committee here have gone too far already. I will show them better and will cut some of their heads off by and by. I only pity the wives and children, for I shall come with 500 men which I have ready, to cut off the whole river, and burn their houses this fall yet."

William of Canajoharie flourished his father's sword so conspicuously that legend reports his demise at several different battles; we only know for certain that he did not survive the Revolution. A lieutenant in the British Indian service, Brant Johnson did survive to bring up four daughters.

Molly's darling oldest son, Peter, put an end to the first patriot attack on Montreal by capturing Ethan Allen "with his own hand." General Tryon considered Peter "intrepid and active," wrote that he had been chosen by the Indians as their war chief and should be commissioned a general. But the half-Indian sailed for England, where he exchanged his chieftainship for the lowest commission in the British regular army. As an ensign in Lord Adam Gordon's regiment, the 26th, he returned to America, and died ingloriously of disease in 1777.

John, Guy, and Claus had their opportunity to prove that they were as effective Indian leaders as Sir William when, in the summer of that year, the British planned a two-pronged invasion of New York from Canada. The main army, under General Burgoyne, was to advance by the Lake Champlain route, while a second force under Colonel Barry St. Leger was to come from Oswego via the Mohawk Valley and meet Burgoyne at Albany. Sir William's successors recruited their father's Iroquois to march with St. Leger against their father's settlements.

While Burgoyne was advancing toward the upper Hudson, St. Leger besieged Fort Stanwix at the carry to the Mohawk. The displaced and returning heirs circulated threats that unless the defenders immediately surrendered, they would be unable to restrain the Indians from killing every man, woman, and child still in the Valley. But the actual British triumph of this campaign was due to the Brants. Molly sent word that the patriot militia were advancing under General Herkimer to the relief of Stanwix. Joseph Brant was the personal hero of the ambush at Oriskany where

John Johnson, the son Sir William pretended was legitimate, and his socially correct wife. The portraits, by unknown artists, hang in Johnson Hall (*Courtesy, Johnson Hall*)

Guy Johnson, Sir William's nephew and son-in-law, by Benjamin West (*Courtesy, National Gallery Of Art, Washington, D.C.*)

many a tenant Sir William had coddled lost his scalp, and the militia were routed.

The Valley seemed doomed but, as Stanwix tottered under the advancing siege, the Iroquois became restive and talked of going home. Sir William's white successors were eager to make them persevere but were outmaneuvered at this critical juncture by a man who brought to Indian negotiation only his native wits. The still-loyal patriot General Benedict Arnold sent to St. Leger's encampment a semilunatic settler, whom the Mohawks regarded as a seer. The madman so encouraged the misgivings of the warriors with stories of advancing patriot might that, as John, Guy, and Claus looked on helplessly, the Indians rioted, forced St. Leger into retreat, and even attacked his regulars. This reverse left Burgoyne unsupported and contributed to his surrender.

Burgoyne's defeat terminated orderly British operations in northern New York. However, Molly, who had been forced after Oriskany to flee to Canada, stoked Iroquois resentment against the patriots who she felt had betrayed the policies of her man. She called for scalps, "embraced every opportunity during the war to insult or injure captive Americans," and—or so said gossip— avenged herself on General Schuyler by using tribal pressure to drive his Mohawk mistress from his bed. With Joseph Brant often serving under him as war chief, Sir John led pro-British Indians and the Scotch Highlanders who were his most faithful and martial tenants in raiding parties that killed his father's old dependents and friends, burned the farmhouses Sir William had seen erected with such pride. The Mohawk Valley became the Revolution's bloodiest cockpit. It has been estimated that two-thirds of the inhabitants were killed and that of the survivors 380 were widows and 2,000 fatherless children. Seven hundred buildings and 50,000 bushels of wheat were destroyed. By the end of the conflict, hardly a human voice sounded in the world Sir William had made.

Warraghiyagey's Indian allies fared little better. The patriots confiscated the Mohawk castles, destroyed Onondaga, and brought fire to the Seneca strongholds on the Genesee. Forced to flee to Canada, the Five Nations lost forever their historic Long House.

All the extensive estates Sir William had willed were expropriated and sold. Since his heirs never dared show their faces again where he had been so beloved, his bloodline was officially represented in the Valley only by his doubly illegitimate granddaughter, Clarissa Putman's child by John Johnson, who claimed and was assigned his baronial pew, under its ornate canopy, in St. George's Episcopal Church, Schenectady.*

For two centuries historians have speculated on what would have happened if Johnson had not died in 1774, but had lived well into or all through the war of the Revolution. It seems certain that the conflict would have followed so radically different a course that the ultimate outcome might have been greatly changed—or even reversed.

Sir William would without doubt have been a loyalist. This did not imply any attitude inimical to white America: Warraghiyagey had labored, often to the disadvantage of the Indians, to protect the frontiers. Loyalists truly believed the Colonies would benefit from continued rule by the Crown.

It is one of the fascinating aspects of Johnson's career that the Irishman, whose family had under English law suffered serious disabilities because they were Catholic, had become so determined a supporter of the Church of England and the Crown. The evidence shows no doctrinal zeal behind either choice: both were pragmatic.

Johnson's appearance in the Mohawk Valley and his drawing settlers there; his fur trading activities; the influence he developed with the Indians; his land acquisitions and his power to control the land acquisitions of others, had all put him at loggerheads with the rul-

---

* Sir John, who had proved the most energetic of Sir William's heirs, replaced Guy as British Indian Superintendent. He received from the Crown, as compensation for his losses, large sums and an estate in Canada on which he lived out the rest of his life. He died in Montreal, January 8, 1830. The baronetcy has continued to the present day under the designation "Johnson of New York."

Guy's wife, Mary, died while fleeing to Canada. The better to press his suit that he be reimbursed for his confiscated property, Guy went to London where he died, somewhat alcoholically, in 1788.

The Clauses also went to England in hope of restitution. Claus died at Cardiff in 1787; his wife, Nancy, lived for another eleven years. Their son, William Claus, fought for the British in Canada as a colonel in the War of 1812.

Molly received for her services to the Crown during the Revolution valuable Canadian lands and an annual pension of £100. Until her death—she was buried from the Episcopal Church in Kingston, Ontario, on April 16, 1796— she was consulted on Indian affairs by the governors of Upper Canada. Her son George (a farmer, schoolteacher, and tosspot) remained single, as did her daughter Mary. The four other girls married socially correct Canadians.

ing families of New York. He was also highly unpopular with speculators from New England through Virginia. His power, of course,
depended on the Indians, and throughout Colonial history the
Crown, seeking warriors to fight and recognizing the value of the
fur trade to British merchants, had been friendly to the Indians, in
contrast to land-hungry and trigger-happy settlers. Furthermore, orderly Indian administration had of necessity to transcend the boundaries and interests of individual Colonies, an objective that only the
Crown had jurisdiction to achieve. Add that the maltreatment the
Indians received from the white men they encountered in their own
forests encouraged Johnson to set up, as a white power worthy of
Indian alliance, the King of England. It was from the government
in London that he himself received his own official power. Even his
military triumphs, that were resented on American shores by regular
generals and New England militiamen, were more recognized in
England than at home.

The Crown stood for a society organized from the top down for
the greatest good of the whole nation. Even if this ideal was being
violated by Great Britain, it was Sir William's ideal, and to his mind
vastly superior to middle-class pursuit of profits. He had seen in
Ireland what happened when landlords became businessmen, and
he was not edified by the financially inspired squabbling in American legislatures. As for the doctrines expounded by the theorists of
the American Revolution, they sounded in his ears as if in an unknown language. Johnson believed in taking care of his own people
benevolently but in his own way.

The Church of England was regarded by most Colonial patriots
as an organ of British propaganda, and it was certainly so used by
Sir William. The Irishman who had in his youth suffered from
religious persecution did not bar his valley or the forests to Congregationalists and other such sectarians, even those who favored
democratic ideas. But he gave all the encouragement he tolerantly
could to Anglicans. He felt that their missionaries could best rival
the Jesuits in the wilderness. The Indians, who had their own religious beliefs and styles of oratory—and who knew no English—were
less susceptible to the sermons and theological hairsplitting of the
low churches than to high Anglican ritual.

Before the Revolutionary War raised its own group of soldiers, Sir

William was among Americans the most skillful, successful, and experienced military commander. It took even George Washington more than a year and a half to learn how to cope, as he was forced to do, with the British regular army, but Johnson had all the know-how he needed for the kind of warfare to which he would have been called. He was expert (a skill his heirs did not inherit) at raising Indian armies and bringing them into successful cooperation with white troops. True, he was about sixty when the fighting started, old for a combat general even had he been in the best of health, but it is not necessary for a triumphant commander to lead into actual combat the forces he has organized, directed, and inspired.

Although there can be no doubt as to which side in the Revolution Sir William would have taken, it is not clear at what point in the developing situation he would have swung into active support of the Crown. Always, he had preferred to strengthen his own power bases without entering other arenas of political affairs. Before the actual fighting had begun he had labored to keep the Indians uninvolved, and he was too dominant in the Mohawk Valley for revolutionary agitation to raise its head there. He would probably have left the revolutionaries alone until they bothered him. They would surely have preferred not to stir him up for as long as they could— but it could not have been very long. As soon as the war exploded, there would have been no way to maneuver around him. There were no more strategic areas on the continent than those he controlled or could easily control.

One of Washington's first official acts as commander in chief had been to set in motion an invasion of Canada. The main patriotic force, under Schuyler and Montgomery, was to go down the Lake Champlain route; a secondary force, under Benedict Arnold, was to aim directly at Quebec via the Kennebec. As it actually happened, both armies reached their destinations. Had Warraghiyagey lived, Schuyler could not possibly have fought his way through the Mohawk-haunted territory. Arnold, being further north, might possibly have got through, but had his smaller army arrived without Schuyler's in Canada, it would certainly have had to surrender there. The chances are that, with Sir William's shadow in the way, the invasion would not have been undertaken. This in itself, since the effort failed, could have been an advantage to the patriot cause, but the power of a living Warraghiyagey would soon have brought much greater disadvantages.

In mid-1776, the British, having evacuated Boston where they were in a *cul de sac*,* captured what was to remain throughout the war the main British base: New York City and its environs. From this highly defensible bastion the Hudson River ran north to Albany at the edge of the wilderness. It was a seductive enemy dream and a corrosive patriot fear that the British would somehow capture Albany, enabling them to use the intervening water, which was navigable to ships of the royal navy, as a rampart cutting the rebellion in half. The British never secured Albany, but Sir William, with his white retainers and his Indian allies, could easily have captured that city. Furthermore, the fertile Mohawk Valley farms, which were in historical fact destroyed by Indian raids and civil conflict, could, under Sir William's protection and control, have gone far toward feeding any English forces that cared to operate in and from upstate New York.

As it turned out, the British could never use Canada as an effective base for the invasion of the rebellious Colonies, because their armies would not penetrate the intervening wilderness. Had Warraghiyagey lived, the forests and lakes and watercourses would have been kept open to them. This would have done more than give them domination of the Hudson River. They would have been allowed an interior back door to the rebellion. New England could have been squeezed between simultaneous attacks from its back counties and the ocean. And no Burgoyne's surrender would have taken place and encouraged the French to join the war on the American side.

Warraghiyagey had divided the Indians to keep them from attacking the settlements as a unified power. Had he used the same skills to join them again, the whole western frontier of the revolt would have gone up in flames.

As events actually transpired, Sir William was a major founding father of the United States. The victory over the Canadian French

* The British were hurried out of Boston when Washington placed cannon on Dorchester Heights, overlooking the city. Had Warraghiyagey lived and cared to intervene, Washington would never have had the cannon, since they were captured (Fort Ticonderoga) and then transported through Mohawk-dominated territory.

which he had done so much to achieve, had made feasible the War of Independence. And Warraghiyagey's policy of keeping the Indians divided, which his heirs lacked the influence and skill to reverse, frustrated their efforts to summon united Indian power. When, to the best of their ability, they entangled the Five Nations in the English cause, all the other tribes from the Great Lakes to the Illinois and the southern frontier, whom Warraghiyagey had encouraged to fear and distrust the Iroquois, were pushed toward the inactive role so many of them played. (Few Indians could be induced actually to fight for the land-stealing colonials.) Thus, to take one example, George Rogers Clark was able to shunt his tiny army around the Illinois as if the forests Pontiac had once haunted were now inhabited by nothing more dangerous than bears.

During the Revolution, the Iroquois themselves never showed true unanimity and determination in their English alliance. Unwilling to prepare them for an active role in the arguments between the Colonists and the Crown, Warraghiyagey had urged them to live at peace with white men; and he had encouraged them to believe that it was possible. Long after he was buried, his protégé Joseph Brant labored by trust and by treaty to re-establish with the United States the equitable friendship which had once flourished under Sir William Johnson's rule in the Mohawk Valley.

It is an amazing tribute to Johnson that, despite the devastation caused there by his heirs, his Valley preserves in its folk tales love for its founder. As one drives today along the Mohawk, one sees improvements that would have made his eyes widen (and perhaps his heart fail because they are so ugly). But here and there, not only in the many houses he built that are reverently preserved, but wherever progress has left a little of the old intact, Sir William's spirit lives. Deer fly from his rifle through that shred of forest; lovely women rise from under those gravestones at his call. The water enslaved now by the New York State Barge Canal still creases on stormy nights under his paddle, and the Indian beads which insensate bulldozers jangle cry out the strange syllables "Warraghiyagey." You cannot pause to look at an antiquity but an old man will hurry down the new road to say, "Yes, Sir William Johnson was once here."

Acknowledgments

I am grateful to the New-York Historical Society and its director, Dr. R. W. G. Vail, for much hospitality and help. Other institutions which have kindly given me assistance include: the Albany Institute of History and Art, the Burton Collection of the Detroit Free Library, the Clements Library, the Hamilton College Library, the Historical Society of Pennsylvania, the Library of Congress, the Montgomery County (New York) Archives, the National Archives of Canada, the New York Public Library, the New York Society Library, the New York State Library, the Princeton University Library, the Public Records Office in London, and the Wisconsin State Historical Society.

I am particularly indebted to Dr. Milton W. Hamilton, the current editor of the *Johnson Papers,* who has answered many queries. Miss Katherine M. Strobeck has generously undertaken researches at my request in the Mohawk Valley. Mrs. Isabel Kelsay, who is preparing with rare scholarship a life of Joseph Brant, has called to my attention much important material about Johnson's family affairs.

I wish also to express my gratitude to Peter Anderson, Wayne Andrews, Miss Geraldine Beard, Miss E. Marie Becker, Arthur B. Carlson, Mrs. Catherine S. Crary, Miss Betty E. Ezequelle, Dr. William Fenton, Louis H. Fox, Miss Joan Gordon, Dr. E. G. Hamilton, Dr. James J. Heslin, Leroy Hewlett, Louis C. Jones, Robert D.

Lord of the Mohawks

Kazlow, Dr. William K. Lamb, Wilmer R. Leach, Miss Janet R. MacFarlane, Sylvan W. McHenry, Edward O. Mills, Miss A. Rachel Minick, Dr. Howard H. Peckham, John Pell, Dr. Walter Pilkington, Marvin D. Schwartz, Sylvester Vigilante, Nicholas Wainright, Dr. Paul A. W. Wallace, Dr. Gurt Wallach, Dr. Chilton Williamson, and Miss Juliet F. Wolohan.

Note for the Revised Edition

In 1976, Dr. Milton W. Hamilton, who had edited the final volumes of the *Sir William Johnson Papers,* published what was announced as the first volume of a biography: *Sir William Johnson, Colonial American, 1715–1763* (Port Washington, New York). No subsequent volume has appeared. Dr. Hamilton was able to convict me of a few factual slips, mostly misspellings. These have been corrected in this edition.

No other works than Dr. Hamilton's have appeared, subsequent to the publication of *Lord of the Mohawks,* that I believe should be called to the attention of the reader.

In preparing this revised edition, I have added a new foreword. Throughout the text, I have made changes where I felt literary effect could be enhanced. To broad historical interpretations and discussions, I have added whatever further understanding I have acquired during two more decades of research in American beginnings. Most importantly, I have recast many of my summations of Johnson's deeds and achievements. More than twenty years ago, when almost no one was deeply concerned with Indian rights, I was, despite my great appreciation of and sympathy for the tribes, less upset than I am now by the white man's selfishness. That Warraghiyagey was so much less guilty than others seemed to me then, more than it does now, a justification for his sometimes betraying the confidence and reliance of the Indians. My new insights bring into the book a deeper note of tragedy, since it becomes more clear that the Indians, who needed to depend so importantly on a man whose greatest loyalty was as they realized elsewhere, were in a hopeless position—doomed.

359

Sources

THE JOHNSON PAPERS

Most of Sir William Johnson's personal archives that survived the Revolution came into the possession of the New York State Library at Albany. In 1849-51, a selection from these were published by E. B. O'Callaghan in *Documentary history of the State of New York*.* A few years later O'Callaghan printed many of Johnson's official dispatches that had been gathered from English archives in *Documents relative to the colonial history of the State of New York*. In 1865 William L. Stone quoted in his life of Johnson various documents including diaries kept by Sir William at Niagara and Oswego in 1759, and on his trip to Detroit.

Early in the twentieth century, many of the Johnson manuscripts in the New York State Library dated between 1738 and 1760, as well as a few from between 1760 and 1762, were put in type but not published. In 1909, a calendar of the entire collection was brought out by Richard F. Day. Then the State Capitol burned, destroying many of the originals.

In 1921, the Division of Archives and History of the University of the

* Full references to the books here mentioned will be found in the Bibliography.

State of New York began publication, under the title *Sir William Johnson Papers*, of the material from the state archives that still existed in original or in printer's proof. As the project advanced under various editorships, documents from other collections were increasingly inserted in the chronological sequence which reached Johnson's death at the end of Volume VIII (1933). The publication was resumed with Volume IX to include, with a few indicated exceptions, all existing papers signed by or addressed to Johnson not printed in the earlier volumes of the series, in the *Documentary history*, the *Documents relative to Colonial history*, or Stone's life. This series came to an end, under the editorship of Dr. Milton W. Hamilton, with Volume XII in 1957.

A few additional papers that were discovered too late to be included in the second chronological sequence may be consulted in the office of the compilers in the New York State Library. There is also available there a detailed account book kept by Sir William's business manager. A scattering of further Johnson material keeps coming to light: If enough accrues, a supplementary volume may be printed. An index to the *Johnson Papers* is planned.

The Johnson archives, which run to about four million words, constitute one of the most important sources for the history of mid-eighteenth-century America. This book is the first effort to use them in their entirety.

MANUSCRIPT MATERIAL

In addition to almost all Johnson's papers, many original documents used in this volume have been published in various compendia (see Bibliography).

The most important relevant unpublished collections, the Claus and Haldimand Papers, are in the National Archives of Canada. The New-York Historical Society, the New York State Library, and the Historical Society of Pennsylvania contain much collateral material. The Clinton Papers are at the Clements Library and the Kirkland Papers at Hamilton College. At the New York Public Library I found especially valuable the transcripts of Loyalist claims against the Crown. The Lyman C. Draper Papers at the Wisconsin Historical Society (consulted by me in a microfilm belonging to the Princeton University Library) contain much factual and hearsay material about Johnson's Indian family.

BIBLIOGRAPHY

This list is intended primarily to give fuller titles to users of the Source References. However, I have included, whether or not they are there cited, all book-length biographies of Johnson, and a few of the most important among the hundreds of books I consulted to secure background material. Newspapers and periodicals cited in the Source References are not listed here.

Alden, John R., "The Albany Congress and the creation of the Indian Superintendencies," *Miss. Valley Hist. Rev.*, XXVII (1940), 193-210.

———, *John Stuart and the southern colonial frontier*, Ann Arbor (1944).

———, *General Gage in America*, Baton Rouge (1948).

Alexander, William, *The conduct of Major General Shirley*, London (1758).

Alvord, Clarence Walworth, "The British ministry and the treaty of Fort Stanwix," *Proc. State Hist. Soc. Wis. for 1908*, Madison (1909), 165-83.

———, *The Mississippi Valley in British politics*, 2 vols., Cleveland (1917).

American Antiquarian Society, *Calendar of the manuscripts of Sir William Johnson in the library of the Society*, Worcester, Mass. (1908).

Amherst, Jeffery, *Journal,* ed. by J. Clarence Webster, Chicago (1931).

Andrews, William; Barclay, Henry; Oglivie, John, *The order of morning and evening prayer . . . translated into the Mohawk language*, New York (1769).

Anonymous, "Life of Joseph Brant," *Christian Recorder* (May-June, 1819), transcript, Draper Papers, I, 105.

Atkin, Edmond, *Indians of the southern colonial frontier*, ed. by Wilbur R. Jacobs, Columbia, S. C. (1954).

Bald, F. Cleaver, *Detroit's first American decade*, Ann Arbor (1948).

Bartram, John, *Observations . . . made . . . in his travels from Pensilvania (sic) to Onondaga, Oswego, and the Lake Ontario*, London (1751).

Becker, Carl, "Nominations in Colonial New York," in *Am. Hist. Rev.*, VI (1900-1), 260-75.

Billington, R. A., "The Fort Stanwix Treaty of 1768," *N. Y. Hist.*, XXV (1944), 182-94.

Blodget, Samuel, *A prospective plan of the battle near Lake George . . . with an explanation thereof*, Boston (1755).

Boyd, Julian P., ed., *Indian treaties printed by Benjamin Franklin*, Philadelphia (1938).

Buell, Augustus C., *Sir William Johnson*, New York (1903). Substituting imagination and spurious quotations for fact, this book has misled many later writers. For discussions of its inaccuracies see Hamilton, Milton W., "Myths and legends of Sir William Johnson," *N. Y. Hist.*, XXXIV (1953), 3-26; Hart, Albert Bushnell, "American historical liars: Augustus C. Buell," *Harper's Mag.*, XXXI (1915), 726-35.

Carse, Mary Rowell, "The Mohawk Iroquois," *Bull. Archeological Soc. of Conn.*, XXIII (1942), 3-53.

Chase, Frederick, *History of Dartmouth College*, 2 vols., Cambridge, (1891-1913).

Chauncy, Charles, *A second letter to a friend, giving a more particular narrative of the defeat of the French army at Lake George*, Boston (1755).

Claus, Daniel, *Narrative of his relations with Sir William Johnson*, New York (1904).

Clinton, George, *Public Papers*, 10 vols., New York and Albany (1899-1914).

Colden, Cadwallader, *History of the Five Nations of Canada*, 2 vols., New York (1902).

———, *Letter books*, 2 vols., New York (1877-8).

———, *Papers*, 9 vols., New York (1918-23, 1937).

Davis, Matthew L., *Memoirs of Aaron Burr*, I, New York (1852).

De Kerallain, René, *La jeunesse de Bougainville*, Paris (1926).

De Tocqueville, Alexis, *Democracy in America*, I, New York (1954).

Documentary history of the State of New York, ed. by E. B. O'Callaghan, 4 vols., Albany (1849-51). Citations are to the 8vo edition.

Documents relative to the colonial history of the State of New York, ed. by E. B. O'Callaghan, VI, VII, VIII, X, Albany (1855-8); index, Albany (1861).

Dwight, Timothy, *Travels in New-England and New-York*, 4 vols., New Haven (1833).

Entick, John, *The general history of the late war*, 5 vols., London (1766).

Fenton, William N. and others, *American Indian and white relations to 1830*, Chapel Hill (1957).

Fenton, William N., "A calendar of manuscript materials relating to the history of the Six Nations or Iroquois Indians in depositories outside Philadelphia," *Proc. Am. Philos. Soc.*, XCVII (1953), 578-95.

Flexner, James Thomas, *The traitor and the spy*, New York (1953).

Fox, Edith Mead, *William Johnson's early career as a frontier landlord and trader*, microfilm, Ithaca, New York (1945).

Franklin, Benjamin, *Writings*, ed. by Albert H. Smythe, 10 vols., New York (1905-7).

Frothingham, Washington, *History of Fulton County*, Syracuse (1892).

Gipson, Lawrence Henry, *The British Empire before the American Revolution*, IV-IX, New York (1939-56).

Grant, Mrs. Anne, *Memoirs of an American lady,* 2 vols., New York (1901).

Griffis, William Elliott, *Sir William Johnson and the Six Nations,* New York (1891).

Gundy, H. Pearson, "Molly Brant," *Ontario Hist. Soc. Papers and Records,* XLV (1953), 98-108.

Hamilton, Milton W., "Sir William Johnson and Pennsylvania," *Penna. Hist.,* XIX (1952), 52-74.

———, "Sir William Johnson's wives," *N. Y. Hist.,* XXXVIII (1957), 18-28.

Hanson, Willis T., *A History of St. George's Church in Schenectady,* 2 vols., Schenectady (1919).

Heckewelder, Rev. John, "An account . . . of the Indian Nations," *Memoirs of the Hist. Soc. Penna,* XII (1876).

Henry, Alexander, *Travels and adventures,* Chicago (1921).

Hill, William H., *Old Fort Edward,* Fort Edward (1929).

Hindle, Brook, "Cadwallader Colden's extension of the Newtonian principles," *Wm. and Mary Quart.,* XIII (1956), 459-75.

Hodge, F. W., ed., *Handbook of American Indians north of Mexico,* 2 vols., Washington (1907-10). Whenever possible, I have followed this work in the spelling of Indian names.

Hunt, George T., *The wars of the Iroquois,* Madison, Wis. (1940).

Johnson, Frederick C., *Reminiscences of the Rev. Jacob Johnson,* n. p. (1910).

Johnson, Warren, "Journal," *The Galleon,* nos. 12-13 (1953).

Johnson, Sir William, *An account of conferences held and treaties made between Sir William Johnson, Bart., and the chief sachems and warriors of the . . . Indian nations . . . at Fort Johnson . . . in the years 1755 and 1756,* London (1756).

———, *Papers of Sir William Johnson,* I-III ed. by James Sullivan, Albany (1921-2); IV-VIII, ed. by Alexander C. Flick, Albany (1925-33); IX, ed. by Almon W. Lauber, Albany (1939); X-XII, ed. by Milton W. Hamilton, Albany (1951-7).

———, *Proceedings and treaty with the Shawanese, Nanticokes, and Mohikander Indians . . . negotiated at Fort-Johnson . . . by the Honourable Sir William Johnson, Bart.,* New York (1757).

Johnson, Sir William, attrib. to, *Relaçaõ de huma batalha succedida no campo de Lake Giorge . . . [translated from a letter by] Coronel Guilhelmo . . . ao general Wensvort, governado da nova Hampshire,* Lisbon (1757).

Johnstone, Charles, *Chrysal, or the adventures of a guinea*, III, London (1765).
Jones, Thomas, *History of New York*, 2 vols., New York (1879).

Kellogg, Lucy, C., *History of . . . Bernardstown . . . Mass.*, Greenfield (1902).
Klingberg, Frank J., *Anglican humanitarianism in colonial New York*, Philadelphia (1940).
Knox, John, *Historical journal of the campaigns in North America for the years 1757, 1758, and 1760*, ed. with appendix by Arthur G. Doughty, Toronto (1914-16).

Lafitau, Joseph, *Moeurs des sauvages amériquains*, 2 vols., Paris (1724).
Lee, Charles, *Papers*, I, New York (1872).
Lévis, François Gaston, duc de, *Collection des manuscrits du Maréchal de Lévis*, 12 vols., Montreal (1889).
Livingston, William, attrib. to, *Review of the military operations in North-America*, New York (1757).
Long, John Cuthbert, *Lord Jefferey Amherst*, New York (1933).
Lydecker, John W., *The faithful Mohawks*, Cambridge, Eng. (1938).

Mante, Thomas, *History of the late war in North America*, London (1772).
Mark, Irving, *Agrarian conflicts in colonial New York*, New York (1940).
McCallum, James Dow, *Eleazar Wheelock*, Hanover (1939).
——, *The Letters of Eleazar Wheelock's Indians*, Hanover (1933).
Mereness, Newton D., *Travels in the American colonies*, New York (1916).
Miner, Charles, *History of Wyoming*, Philadelphia (1845).
Moravian journals relating to central New York, ed. by Wm. M. Beauchamp, Syracuse (1916).
Morgan, Lewis Henry, *League of the Ho-dé-no-sau-nie or Iroquois*, Rochester (1851).
Munsell, Joel B., *Annals of Albany*, 10 vols., Albany (1850-9).

National Archives of Canada, "Calendar of the Frederick Haldimand papers," *Report on Canadian Archives*, 6 vols., Ottawa (1884-9).
New York (Colony), *The colonial laws of New York*, III, Albany (1894).
New York (Colony) General Assembly, *Journal*, II, New York (1766).
New York State Library, *Calendar of the Sir William Johnson manuscripts in the . . . Library*, compiled by Richard E. Day, Albany (1909).
New York (State) Secretary of State, *Calendar of New York colonial manuscripts endorsed land papers*, Albany (1864).
New York State Historian, *Annual report*, II, New York (1897).

O'Conor, Norreys J., *A servant of the Crown . . . based on the papers of John Appy*, New York (1938).
Ontario, Bureau of Archives, *Reports for 1903 and 1904*, Toronto (1904-5).

Paré, George, *The Catholic church in Detroit*, Detroit (1951).
Pargellis, Stanley M., *Lord Loudoun in North America*, New Haven (1933).
———, *Military affairs in North America, 1748-1765; selected documents from the Cumberland Papers in Windsor Castle*, New York and London (1936).
Parkman, Francis, *Conspiracy of Pontiac*, 2 vols., Boston (1933).
———, *Half-century of conflict*, 2 vols., Boston (1893).
———, *Montcalm and Wolfe*, 2 vols., Boston (1903).
Pearson, Jonathan, *History of the Schenectady Patent*, Albany (1883).
Peckham, Howard H., *Pontiac and the Indian uprising*, Princeton (1947).
Pennsylvania Archives, 1st series, I-IV, Philadelphia (1852-3).
Pennsylvania Colonial Records, III-X, Philadelphia (1851-2).
Pitt, William, *Correspondence . . . with colonial governors and military and naval commissioners in America*, 2 vols., New York (1906).
Pouchot, Pierre, *Memoir upon the late war in North America*, trans. and ed. by Franklin B. Hough, 2 vols., Roxbury, Mass. (1866).
Pound, Arthur, *Johnson of the Mohawks*, New York (1930).
Putman, Eben, *History of the Putman family*, n. p., II (1908).

Recum, Franz V., *The families of Warren and Johnson of Warrenstown, County Meath*, New York (1950).
Reid, W. Max, *Mohawk Valley*, New York (1907).
———, *Story of old Fort Johnson*, New York (1906). Both of Reid's volumes should be consulted with the greatest caution.
Robertson, John Ross, *Diary of Mrs. John Graves Simcoe*, Toronto (1911).
Rogers, Robert, *Journals*, ed. and with additions by Franklin B. Hough, Albany (1883).

Severance, Frank H., *The old frontier of France*, 2 vols., New York (1917).
———, *Studies of the Niagara frontier*, Buffalo (1911).
Seymour, Flora W., *Lords of the valley, Sir William Johnson and his Mohawk brothers*, New York (1930).
Shirley, William, *Correspondence*, ed. by Charles Henry Lincoln, 2 vols., New York (1912).
Simms, Jeptha R., *Frontiersmen of New York*, 2 vols., Albany (1882-3).
———, *History of Schoharie County*, Albany (1845).
———, *Trappers of New York*, Albany (1871).

Smith, James, *Remarkable occurences . . . during his captivity with the Indians*, Cincinnati (1870).

Smith, Richard, *A tour of four great rivers*, New York (1906).

Smith, William, *History of the late province of New York*, II, New York (1830).

Sonneck, Oscar, *Report on the Star-spangled Banner . . . Yankee Doodle*, Washington (1909).

Stone, William L., *Life of Joseph Brant*, 2 vols., New York (1838).

Stone, William L., Jr., "King Hendrick," *N. Y. State Hist. Assoc. Procs.*, I (1901), 28-34.

————, *Life and times of Sir William Johnson, Bart.*, 2 vols., Albany (1865).

Thayer, Theodore, "The Friendly Association," *Penna. Mag. of Hist. and Biog.*, LXII (1943), 356-376.

Thwaites, Reuben Gold, *Jesuit relations and allied documents*, 73 vols., Cleveland (1896-1901).

Tilghman, Tench, *Memoir*, Albany (1876).

Trumbull, James R., *History of Northampton*, II, Northampton (1902).

Tryon County Committee of Safety, *Minute Book*, New York (1905).

Turner, Frederick J., *The frontier in American history*, Madison (1894).

Van Doren, Carl, *Benjamin Franklin*, New York (1938).

Volweiler, Albert T., *George Croghan and the westward movement*, Cleveland (1926).

Vosburg, Royden W., *Records of St. John's Episcopal Church in Johnstown, New York*, New York (1919).

Wallace, Anthony F., *King of the Delawares, Teedyuscung*, Philadelphia (1949).

Wallace, Paul A. W., *Conrad Weiser*, Philadelphia (1945).

Walpole, Horace, *Letters*, ed. by Mrs. Paget Toynbee, Vols. III-IV, Oxford (1903).

Washington, George, *Writings*, ed. by John C. Fitzpatrick, Vols. I-III, Washington (1931).

Wheelock, Eleazar, *Narrative for 1762*, Boston (1890-?).

Wraxall, Peter, *An abridgement of the Indian affairs transacted in the colony of New York . . . 1678 to the year 1751*, ed. by Charles H. McIlwain, Cambridge, Mass. (1915).

Young, Arthur, *A tour of Ireland*, II, London (1780).

Source References

Citations comprising only volume and page numbers refer to the published *Johnson Papers*. The abbreviation *"J"* means Johnson; "D" means *Documents relative to the colonial history of the State of New York;* "DH" means *Documentary history of the state of New York*. Full titles for all volumes cited will be found in the bibliography.

The following abbreviations have been used to connote manuscript collections: "CL": Clements Library; "DP": Draper Papers; "HSP": Historical Society of Pennsylvania; "NAC": National Archives of Canada; "NYHS": New-York Historical Society; "NYPL": New York Public Library; "NYSL": New York State Library.

FOREWORD

J AND WEBB: De Kerallain, *Bougainville,* 199.

CHAPTER 1

BIRTHDATE: N. Y. *Gazette,* 7/25/1774; Simms, *Frontiersmen,* I, 310.
FAMILY BACKGROUND: IV, 897-8. NYSL, *Calendar,* 383; Recum, *Families.*
HOME: Lease, Christopher J & Earl of Fingal, 1/22/28, copy NYSL.
IRISH ENVIRONMENT: Fox, *J,* Chap. 1 & 2.
APPEARANCE: Portraits; *London Mag.,* XV (1756), 432.
NEGLECTS PARENTS: I, 258.
BUTLER'S PURCHASE: VIII, 958; Smith, *History,* II, 31.
WARREN'S MARRIAGE: N. Y. *Gazette,* 7/31/1731.
WARREN RECRUITS *J:* DH, II, 825.

CHAPTER 2

CONFERENCE WITH WARREN: Warren to J, 11/20/1738, NYSL; J's accounts, Warren Papers, no. 18, NYHS; I, 930; IX, 1; D, VII, 671; DH, II, 936; Stone, *J*, I, 63.

FIRST IN ALBANY: VIII, 922-3; Stone, *J*, I, 63.

TRIP TO WARRENSBURG: Smith, *Tour*, 19-23.

WARRENSBURG DESCRIBED: Surveys, Warren Papers, NYHS; I, 907.

FORT HUNTER AND TEANTONTALOGO: Lydecker, *Mohawks*, 32, 37-8, 40, 50; Flexner, *Traitor*, 36.

INDIANS HARD TO KNOW: DH, II, 946-7.

SETTLEMENT STARTS: Warren to J, *op. cit.*; Warren Papers, nos. 18, 19, 27, 38, 40, 55, 60, 74, NYHS; I, 4-8; Fox, *J*.

INDIAN TRUCK: I, 384; II, 898-900; III, 334-5.

J'S FARM: Warren Papers, no. 18, NYHS.

BUYS ACROSS RIVER: I, 4-6.

BEGINS FUR TRADE: I, 7; IV, 556-7; D, VII, 953.

TRIP TO OQUAGA: DH, III, 1039-46; Smith, *Tour*, 65-7.

CATHERINE: Register of Baptisms, etc., Fort Hunter, 1734/5-1745, NYHS; I, 14; VII, 213; Simms, *Frontiersmen*, I, 204.

SEX MORES: I, 44; Warren J, *Journal*, 9; Young, *Tour*, II, 127-8.

TO MOUNT JOHNSON: *Loyalist Transcripts*, XLIII, 399-400, NYPL; I, 8.

CHAPTER 3

HISTORICAL BACKGROUND: Colden, *History*; Gipson, *Empire*, V, 64-112; Morgan, *League*; Hunt, *Wars*.

MOHAWKS FRIGHTEN NEW ENGLAND: Colden, *History*, I, xviii.

MOHAWKS ACCUSE ALBANIANS: Wallace, *Weiser*, 226.

DEBTS TO WARREN: J to Susan Warren, 5/11/1741, HSP; Warren Papers, nos. 18, 19, 33, NYHS; I, 907-8; DH, II, 825.

DOESN'T KEEP ACCOUNTS: I, 410-1.

FRIENDLY WITH GERMANS: *Gentlemen's Mag.*, XXV (1755), 426.

BUSINESS DEALINGS: I, 6, 44, 239, etc.; Jones, *History*, II, 362-3; *London Mag.*, XXV (1756), 432; *Moravian Journals*, 134-5.

J RESEMBLES INDIANS: D, VI, 741.

HENDRICK DESCRIBED: Portrait engravings; Grant, *Memoirs*, II, 58; Dwight, *Travels*, III, 164; Stone, *Hendrick*.

LEARNS IROQUOIS: Colden, *History*, I, xxxv-vi; *London Mag., op. cit.*; Stone, *J*, II, 485.

ADOPTION CEREMONY: Smith, *Remarkable*, 14-6.

MEANING OF WARRAGHIYAGEY: Warren J, *Journal*, 5.

ALBANIANS ATTACK J: J to ?, 10/23/1743, Burton Coll., Detroit Free Library; I, 19, 305; Jones, *op. cit.*, 363; N. Y., (Colony) *Laws*, III, 241-62.

CHAPTER 4

CLINTON DESCRIBED: Livingston, *Review*, 25; Smith, *History*, II, 83, 191.

DE LANCEY DESCRIBED: Livingston, *op. cit.*, 25, 37, 39.

1745 INDIAN CONFERENCE: Boyd, *Treaties*, 309-11, N. Y. Assembly, *Journal*, II, 79-80; *Penna. Colonial Records*, V, 7-26; Stone, *J*, I, 162-72.

MOHAWK RIOT: Wallace, *Weiser*, 226-8; Lydecker, *Mohawks*, 56-7.

EFFORT TO BLAME J: Barclay to David Clarkson, 5/11/1745, affidavit, Peter Migironne, 5/9/1745; deposition, Daniel Horsmanden, 10/?/1745, NYHS.

HENDRICK RESPONSIBLE: Boyd, *op. cit.*, 309-10.

FRENCH WOO MOHAWKS: I, 40; Wallace, *op. cit.*, 227.

SARATOGA ATTACK: I, 42-3, 52-3, 201 (this letter misdated); III, 825.

CLINTON—DE LANCEY DONNYBROOK: Livingston, *op. cit.*, 27; Smith, *op. cit.*, 100.

COLDEN DESCRIBED: Hindle, *Colden*.

OSWEGO SUPPLY: I, 49; D, VI, 740; N. Y., (Colony) *Laws*, III, 554.

JUSTICE OF THE PEACE: I, 27.

ASSEMBLY STILL RELUCTANT: D, VI, 620.

J'S BULL FEAST: IX, 4.

CLINTON'S TITLES: I, 151.

INDIANS BOYCOTT CLINTON: D, VI, 739; Colden, *History*, II, 216-7.

POLICY OF NEUTRALITY: Colden, *op cit.*, 219.

J STIRS UP MOHAWKS: I, 54, 199-200; III, 993; IX, 4-5; Colden, *op. cit.*, 218-9.

J ON INDIAN GOVERNMENT: Stone, *J*, II, 484.

JONCAIRES DESCRIBED: Severance, *Frontier*, see index.

MARCHES INTO HISTORY: Colden, *op. cit.*, 220-1; Smith, *op. cit.*, 100-1.

CHAPTER 5

1746 INDIAN CONGRESS: Colden, *History*, II, 226-45; Wallace, *Weiser*, 228, 238; N. Y. (Colony) Assembly, *Journal*, II, 124-5, 130.

WEISER FORESEES J'S MURDER: *Penna. Archives*, 1st Ser., I, 751.

INDIAN RITUAL: III, 483; IV, 468.

WAMPUM NOT MONEY: Stone, *Brant*, II, 354.

J'S COMMISSION: I, 60-1; Assembly, *op. cit.*, 540.

RECRUITING AND CAUGHNAWAGA IMPEDIMENT: I, 40, 63-5, 164; Colden, *op. cit.*, 255-9, 264.

PRISONERS AND PROCESSIONS: Lydius to John Stoddard, 11/20/1746, NYHS; I, 69; D, VI, 314; N. Y. *Gazette,* N. Y. *Journal,* N. Y. *Evening Post,* 11/24/1746.

PETITIONS AND RECOMMENDATIONS: D, VI, 314-5.

LIVINGSTON PURCHASE EXPLAINED: Deed, 2/16/1729-30, photostat, NYHS; undated memo, Alexander Papers, NYHS; I, 432; IV, 166; IX, 148.

HENDRICK'S MISSION: Lydius to Stoddard, *op. cit.*; IX, 15; N. Y. *Gazette,* supp. 12/1-4/1746.

PRISONERS DIVIDED: Lydius to Stoddard, *op. cit.*; IX, 15-6.

DEPUTED TO ONONDAGA: Lydius to Stoddard, 3/26/1747, NYHS; I, 67-8; D, VI, 314.

1747 SPRING PLANS: I, 73-4, 81.

WAR-PARTY RITUAL: Lydius to Stoddard, 5/5/1747, NYHS; Colden, *History,* I, xxv; Stone, *J,* II, 482.

BUTLER'S TRIUMPH: Lydius, *op. cit.*; D, VI, 343-4.

WAR PARTIES FLOURISH: Lydius, *op. cit.*; II, 899.

SENECAS OBJECT: D, VI, 358-61.

INVASION RULED IMPRACTICAL: D, VI, 859.

MILITIA RIOT: Lydius, *op. cit.*

FRENCH REPULSED AT ONONDAGA: D, VI, 361-2.

SUPPLY PROBLEMS: Lydius to Stoddard, 3/26/1747, NYHS; I, 81, 83-4; D, VI, 360-2.

J PLEADS WITH CLINTON: I, 105-9; D, VI, 360-3; Colden, *Papers,* III, 357.

MOUNT JOHNSON FILLS UP: I, 93-6, 109, 898, IX, 8, 15-31; D, VI, 361.

J's FUR MONOPOLY: I, 66; D, VI, 739-40.

LYDIUS DESCRIBED: Horsmanden Papers, appendix, NYHS; Lydius to Stoddard, 11/24/1746; D, VI, 372, 650, 662, Colden, *Papers,* III, 15; *Gentlemen's Mag.,* LXI (1791) 383-5; Hill, *Fort Edward,* 27-49.

MASSACHUSETTS GOODS: Lydius to Stoddard, 6/5 & 7/8/1747; I, 889; D, VI, 385.

J ESCAPES ASSASSINATION: D, VII, 714.

SARATOGA FLIGHT: I, 100-2.

HENDRICK AND CLINTON: Clinton to Hendrick, 6/15/1746, CL; I, 94, 102-4; D, VI, 383-4; Colden, *Papers,* III, 403-8.

MILITIA DISOBEY: I, 108-9; IX, 9-10.

WARRIORS ON THE MARCH: I, 107-8.

CHAPTER 6

LAKE SACRAMENT EXPEDITION: Lydius to Stoddard, 9/10/1747, NYHS; I, 111; IX, 29-30; D, VI, 389; N. Y. *Gazette,* Suppl., 9/10/1747; Stone, *J,* II, 481.

ALBANY PARADE: Lydius, *op. cit.*; IX, 30-1.

IN N.Y.: I, 113, 115, 119, 316-7; D, VI, 619-21; N. Y. *Gazette,* 9/28/1747.

WARREN'S POWER: I, 117; Colden, *Letters,* III, 364, 425-6, 432.

GINGEGO INCIDENT: I, 146-50, 161; D, VI, 422-3.

MILITIA COLONEL: J to Jacob Glen, 9/7/1748, NYHS; I, 148, 150, 166; IX, 11-4; Colden, *Papers,* IV, 64.

RITE ACCOMMODATING MURDER: *Am. Mag.,* I (1747), 14.

MOHAWK PRISONERS: I, 149-50; DH, II, 619.

ONONDAGA TRIP: I, 149-65; DH, II, 619; Bartram, *Observations,* 41-2, 58; *Moravian Journals,* 77.

INDIAN GIRLS: IX, 386; Colden, *History,* I, xxx; Warren J, *Journal,* 10; Bartram, *Observations,* 59.

EUROPEAN PEACE: I, 172.

1747 ALBANY CONFERENCE: I, 177; D, VI, 437-52; DH, II, 620-1.

J RID OF INDIANS: DH, II, 621.

INDIAN CHILDREN ENSLAVED: D, VI, 546.

CHAPTER 7

DISSATISFACTION WITH PEACE: I, 209.

SOVEREIGNTY ISSUE: I, 268; D, VI, 490-1, 506, 515, 517.

IROQUOIS SIGN IN CANADA: D, X, 186-8.

ANGÉLIQUE SENT HOME: I, 189, 253-4; DH, II, 621; NYSL, *Calendar,* 18.

NEGOTIATIONS WITH WARREN & DE LANCEY: I, 238-40; IX, 85; D, VI, 534; Colden, *Papers,* IV, 126-7, 178.

NEW MOUNT JOHNSON: John J, Estimate of his estate, n.d., NYHS; I, 197, 220-3; 230; 260; 264-5; D., X., 479; DH, III, 1039; *Royal Mag.,* I, (1759), 167; Davis, *Memoirs,* I, 281-3; Pouchot, *Memoir,* II, 143-4.

FRIENDS & GAIETIES: I, 210, 242-5, 257, 289, 295-6, 319; Warren J, *Journal,* 6.

J'S CHILDREN: I, 179, 249, 270.

CAROLINE: This story was first published in Reid, *Mohawk,* 122. Gleefully embellishing the error, Buell claimed in his *J,* 52-3, that he was himself a descendant of Caroline. Since then, the mythical Caroline has entrapped many writers. For a refutation, see Hamilton, *Wives.*

BRANT J'S BIRTH DATE: John Butler, Return of loyalists, 12/1/1783, Haldiman's Papers, NAC.

THE LADIES: I, 197-8, 205.

WOLLASTON PORTRAIT: I, 931; original in Albany Inst. of Hist. & Art.

CONTRAST WITH FRENCH EXPENDITURES: I, 288, 343, IX, 57; D, VI, 521.

WANTS ROYAL OFFICE: I, 329; D, VI, 541.

OSWEGATCHIE FOUNDED: I, 199; D, VI, 526, 589; Parkman, *Montcalm*, I, 69-75.

CATAWBA WAR: I, 261; D, VI, 559-60, 742; Wallace, *Weiser*, 308.

MIGRATIONS TO OHIO: I, 303; D, VI, 541, 547.

CÉLERON'S EXPEDITION: IX, 40-1; D, VI, 541, 547-9.

OTTAWA ATTACK SCARE: I, 276-9.

PRISONERS RELEASED: I, 260, 306-7; D, VI, 589-91; Wallace, *Weiser*, 307.

THREATENS RESIGNATION: I, 279-81, 302, 314; IX, 78-9.

ONONDAGA PURCHASE: I, 923-7; D, VI, 590; D, VII, 840.

LEAD PLATE: D, VI, 604, 608-11.

RESIGNS: I, 314, 340; D, VI, 739.

CHAPTER 8

J IS PEEVISH: I, 324, 327, 381; IX, 57-8.

CLINTON'S AND COLDEN'S REACTIONS: Clinton to John Catherwood, 2/18/1752, CL; I, 322, 332; D, VI, 738-47, 750.

APPOINTED TO COUNCIL: I, 273-4, 282, 344.

1751 INDIAN CONGRESS: I, 339-44; D, VI, 715-26; Stone, *J*, I, 393-4; Wallace, *Weiser*, 323-31.

J RECOMMENDS LYDIUS: Colden, *Papers*, IV, 127.

J IN N. Y.: Smith, History, II, 155-79; Stone, *J*, I, 403-4.

J OPPOSED, COMMISSIONERS APPOINTED: I, 383; IX, 103; D, VI, 738-47, 750; Colden, *Papers*, IV, 126-7, 151, 247.

WARREN DEBT CONTROVERSY: Warren Papers, nos. 18-9, 28, 33, 46, NYHS; I, 907-8, 929-30; DH, II, 825, 935-6, 979-80.

CHARLOTTE RIVER PURCHASE: Indian deed, 8/24/1751, NYSL; I, 335, 392, 444, 921-2; D, VI, 748.

ONONDAGA PURCHASE: I, 333-4; D, VI, 840; N. Y. (State), *Land Papers*, 261, 271.

BANYAR DESCRIBED: 3 portraits at NYHS.

KINGSBOROUGH: I, 378-9, 392, 394-5, 565; IX, 98, 109; N. Y., *Land Papers*, 270-3, 276; N. Y. *Wkly. Mercury*, 3/4/1754.

FRENCH OHIO INVASION: D, VI, 778-9, 797; *Penna. Col. Records*, V, 607.

HENDRICK'S PROTEST: D, VI, 781-8; *Penna. Col. Records,* V, 625-6; N. Y., *Laws,* III, 916-7; Wallace, *Weiser,* 350.

1753 ONONDAGA CONFERENCE: D, VI, 808-15.

ENTER CLAUS: Claus, *Narrative,* 3-7; *Penna. Archives,* 1st ser., II, 116-7; Wallace, *Weiser,* 304.

WYOMING CONTROVERSY OPENS: I, 396-401, 405, 454-6; IX, 131, 133-4, 142-5, 150-60; Wallace, *Weiser,* 344, 351-7, 375-7.

1754 ALBANY CONGRESS: D, VI, 853-99; Van Doren, *Franklin,* 209; Wallace, *Weiser,* 346; Alden, *Albany;* Stone, *Hendrick,* 31.

PENNSYLVANIA OHIO PURCHASE: Wallace, *Weiser,* 357-9.

WASHINGTON'S DEFEAT: I, 409-10, 431; *Penna. Col. Records,* VI, 151-2; Wallace, *Weiser,* 373.

DE LANCEY'S OFFER: IX, 123.

SHIRLEY'S OFFER: I, 426-7, 433, 616.

CHAPTER 9

SHIRLEY APPOINTS J: I, 445-51, 455-9.

NIAGARA SUGGESTION: I, 458-60, 462; D, VI, 920-1, 941.

WITH BRADDOCK: D, VII, 573; DH, II, 648-57, 708.

CROGHAN APPOINTED: I, 475-6, 496-7.

CROGHAN DESCRIBED: IV, 399; Volweiler, *Croghan;* Wallace, *Weiser,* 323, 335-6.

SHIRLEY'S APPEARANCE: Portrait after Hudson, in coll. of James G. King.

CABAL AGAINST SHIRLEY: I, 518, 534, 545, 559, 591, 652-3; IX, 655, 676; *Penna. Archives,* II, 326, 331; Livingston, *Review,* 49, 64; Smith, *History,* II, 257.

WRAXALL DESCRIBED: I, 467; Wraxall, *Abridgement.*

TROOP QUOTAS: I, 522, 536, 603.

EYRE: I, 448, 492, 514, 557, 590, 601, 655; II, 393; IX, 207.

RELIGHTS COUNCIL FIRE: I, 505, 514, 524; IX, 171-9.

INDIANS FOR BRADDOCK: I, 475-6, 496-7, 516, 663; IX, 205; D, VII, 203.

REFUSES SHIRLEY: I, 598, 600, 613, 735; IX, 205; DH, II, 695-6.

1755 INDIAN CONGRESS: I, 581, 611-2, 614, 641-4, 706-7, 734, 737-8; IX, 189-90; 203-4; D, VI, 964-89; DH, II, 655, 671-4.

CAUGHNAWAGAS: I, 543, 595-6, 643; D, VI, 973, 980.

FIGHT WITH SHIRLEY: I, 733-6, 740-1, 756-7, 841-2; II, 374; IX, 217-8; D, VII, 184-5, 715; DH, II, 684-8; Livingston, *Review,* 67; Shirley, *Corres.,* II, 233 n.

HEARS OF BRADDOCK'S DEFEAT: I, 759, 794-7.

CHAPTER 10

FRENCH PLANS: D, X, 316.

FIGHT WITH SHIRLEY: See note, previous chapter.

LYMAN APPOINTED: I, 493-5, 518.

BAD WOMEN: I, 783; IX, 210; Kellogg, *Bernardstown*, 44.

J TRAINS TROOPS: I, 747; IX, 206; Boston *Gazette*, 9/1/1755; *Hist. Mag*, 2nd ser., VII (1870), 213.

HOUSEHOLD ROUTINE: IX, 340-1.

JOHN J: Pastel portrait at J Hall; John J, Memorial to Duke of Portland, 4/16/1796, NAC.

JOSEPH JOINS CAMPAIGN: Stone, *Brant*, I, 19.

J MARCHES: I, 730-2, 838-9, 842; DH, II, 678-80; *Mag. N. E. Hist.*, III (1893), 191.

CAUGHNAWAGA NEGOTIATIONS: I, 880, 894; II, 381-2; IX, 200-1.

AT CARRYING PLACE: I, 616, 857, 880, 883, 886: D, VI, 1000-2; DH, II, 668.

MARCH TO LAKE: Trumbull, *Northampton*, II, 266-7.

NAMES LAKE GEORGE: I, 893.

J'S PLAN OF ATTACK: II, 10; DH, II, 689.

HENDRICK'S ACTIONS: I, 893-4; II, 7.

DIESKAU'S ACTIONS: D, IV, 1013-4; D, X, 316-7.

EVE OF BATTLE: II, 16-7; D, VI, 1005; D, X, 317; Claus, *Narrative*, 12.

BLOODY MORNING SCOUT: D, VI, 1013; D, X, 317-8; DH, II, 691-3; Claus, *op. cit.*, 13-5.

HENDRICK'S DEATH: Claus, *op. cit.*, 14. The generally accepted statement that Hendrick was killed, in his conspicuous position at the head of the column, at the first fire, is discredited by the fact that several days passed before anyone in Johnson's camp knew whether he was alive or dead. See: D, VI, 1004, 1007-8; DH, II, 693; N. Y. *Mercury*, 9/15/1755.

CHAPTER 11

BATTLE OF LAKE GEORGE: II, 32, 420; D, VI, 1003-7; D, X, 317-45; DH, II, 691-5; N. Y. *Mercury*, 9/12/1755; Pargellis, *Military*, 138; Warren J, *Journal*, 7; Blodget, *Battle*.

J PROTECTS DIESKAU: D, VI, 1004; D, X, 318, 322-3, 343.

CASUALTIES: IX, 234-7; D, VI, 1006-7; D, X, 356, 360.

CONTROVERSY OVER CREDIT: Boston *Gazette*, 2/23/1756; N. Y. *Gazette*, 10/6 & 10/20/1755; Livingston, *Review*, 85-9; Hutchinson, *History*, III, 27.

J'S INDIANS LEAVE: II, 86, 202, 222; IX, 300; D, VI, 1011-2; DH, II, 699.

ROGER'S RANGERS: II, 187, 263, 269; V, 788; D, VII, 78; DH, IV, 272; Rogers, *Journals.*

WRAXALL'S REPORTS: I, 472-7; DH, II, 380-2; Hutchinson, *op. cit.*

J SICK: II, 153 ff.

REINFORCEMENTS AND PRESSURE TO ADVANCE: II, 58, 74, 107-10, 146, 156, 160, 169, 178, 209, 213-5, 222, 250-4.

FORTS EDWARD AND WILLIAM HENRY: II, 39, 53, 129, 144, 221.

RIOTS AND MILITIA ORGANIZATION: II, 164, 284; *N. Y. Gen. & Biog. Record*, XXXIII (1902), 69-70.

SHIRLEY AS COMMANDER IN CHIEF: II, 271, 283, 299, 309, 338; IX, 299.

J RESTIVE: II, 165, 173; IX, 300.

ARMY DISBANDED: II, 361, 420.

INDIANS ATTACK PENNA.: IX, 328, 333-7, 287-8, 394.

J BLAMES SHIRLEY: D, VI, 1027; DH, II, 708.

SHIRLEY AND J'S INDIAN OFFICE: II, 397; D, VI, 1025-8; Shirley, *Corres.*, II, 362; Wallace, *Weiser*, 435.

N. Y. AND MASS. WELCOMES: N. Y. *Mercury*, 1/5 & 26/1756.

SECRET MEETING AGAINST SHIRLEY: Claus, *Narrative*, 19-20.

J A HERO: II, 206, 343-50, 430; Livingston, *Review*, 95; Walpole, *Letters*, III, 361, 373; Boston *Gazette*, 2/23/1756; Entich, *History*, IV, 141; J, *Relaçao.*

SHIRLEY DISGRACED: II, 430; D, VI, 1022; D, VII, 75; Shirley *op. cit.*, 425, 428-9, 547; Alden, *Gage*, 32-4.

J'S HONORS: II, 434-5; D, VI, 1020; D, VII, 76; Smith, *History*, II, 283.

J'S POWERS: II, 529; Alexander, *Shirley*; Smith, *op. cit.*, 272, 292.

CHAPTER 12

SHOT BY ACCIDENT: N. Y. *Mercury*, 5/10/1756.

TALKS ON BORDER ATTACKS: IX, 558, 574-81; D, VII, 18, 208-15; DH, II, 700-3.

IROQUOIS CONGRESS: II, 388; D, VII, 54-71.

HARDY'S ORDERS: I, 528-30; DH, II, 735-6.

FRANKLIN'S REACTION: Franklin, *Writings*, II, 342.

FORT BULL: IX, 404-15, 449-50; D, VII, 94.

RUMORS OF FRENCH ACTION: IX, 415-6, 424-5, 430.

WAR AND PEACE DECLARED: II, 447, 468-9

TRIP TO ONONDAGA: II, 486-8; D, VII, 82-5, 107, 117-20, 130-53.

TRIP HOME: D, VII, 151-2; D, X, 447-8; N. Y. *Gazette*, 7/19/1756.

TREATY WITH PENNA. INDIANS: D, VII, 119, 152-61; Wallace, *Weiser*, 450.

PATENT AS BARONET: II, 343-50.

TEEDYUSCUNG DESCRIBED: Wallace, *Teedyuscung.*

EASTON CONGRESS: Wallace, *Teedyuscung*, 100-15; Wallace, *Weiser*, 445-51; *Penna. Mag.* XLIV (1920), 109-10.
SCARES AT FORT J: IX, 491-2, 496-7; Claus, *Narrative*, 20-1.
OSWEGO FALLS: II, 506-14; IX, 548-55; DH, II, 733-4.
MOUNT J BECOMES FORT: II, 266-8, 537-8; DH, I, 532.
NICK-NOSED ANTHONY: II, 715; IX, 774.
RESULTS IN CANADA: D, X, 447-8, 451-3, 513.

CHAPTER 13

WILLIAM HENRY MENACED: IX, 666-7.
ACTION TOWARD GERMAN FLATTS: IX, 664-81, 684; D, VII, 245; Parkman, *Montcalm*, II, 80; Gipson, *Empire*, VII, 65.
SYPHILIS: II, 535, V, 760; VI, 30-1; Warren J, *Journal*, 6.
ONONDAGA DECISIONS: IX, 640, 688, 711, 839; D, VII, 254-66.
SCALPS AND BOUNTIES: I, 81; Atkin, *Indians*, xxiv.
SHOCKING SCENE: Parkman, *Montcalm*, I, 355.
NICHUS' RAGE: IX, 796-9.
FRENCH TRIUMPHS AND RUMORS: Lévis, *Coll.*, VII, 301; XI, 110-1.
ATKIN: II, 485; D, VII, 208-15; Atkin, *Indians*; Alden, *Stuart*, 41-2; 68-71.
J URGES PENNA. PURCHASE RETURNED: II, 684-5; D, VII, 222; DH, II, 737.
FALL OF WILLIAM HENRY: II, 730; IX, 809-12, 819-22; Gipson, *Empire*, VII, 149.
GERMAN FLATTS DESTROYED: IX, 852-63; X, 672-4; D, VII, 341.
J SICK: II, 748, 761, 808.
PANIC ON MOHAWK: II, 759-61.
ENGLISH THREATEN IROQUOIS: II, 719-25, 749, 769.
J DEFENDS INDIAN ACTIONS: II, 736-8; IX, 827-8; D, VII, 276-9.
URGES BOUNDARY: II, 737-8.
J GIVES TESTIMONIALS: IX, 815.

CHAPTER 14

MOLLY: Haldimand Papers, B127, p. 388, NAC; Gundy, *Molly*; Jones, *History*, II, 374-5; Stone, *J*, I, 387n; Robertson, *Simcoe*, 274; Tilghman, *Memoir*, 87.
FRENCH STATEMENTS: Lévis, *Colls.*, II, 153; Parkman, *Montcalm*, II, 9.
FRENCH SHORTAGES: II, 778, 791, 858; IV, 888; X, 71.
WHAT J GAVE: III, 171; VIII, 130-1; IX, 21-5; XII, 1000.
1758 ONONDAGA COUNCIL: II, 821-4, 840; IX, 874-5, 879-84.
INDIANS FOR ABERCROMBY: II, 851-4, 871; IX, 901-14, 937-9.

FRANCE'S LACK OF INDIANS: X, 740, 746, 749.

J ON TICONDEROGA CAMPAIGN: IX, 941; D, X, 739-41, 787.

FRONTENAC TAKEN: II, 889-90; IX, 952-3; D, X, 822-3.

STOPS PENNA. CONFERENCE: II, 844, 875; IX, 894; Parkman, *op. cit.*, 154.

CHEROKEE NEGOTIATIONS: II, 742, 797-8, 846-9, 873-5; IX, 847, 898, 946-51; X, 90; D, VII, 208-15.

1758 EASTON CONGRESS: X, 43-8, 55; Wallace, *Weiser*, 532-52; Volweiler, *Croghan*, 210.

DUQUESNE FALLS: Volweiler, *op. cit.*, 139.

CHAPTER 15

COUNCIL AT CANAJOHARIE: D, VII, 378-94.

AMHERST DESCRIBED: II, 44; Long, *Amherst.*

NIAGARA ATTACK PLANNED: III, 19, 27-31, 38-46; Amherst, *Journal,* 105-10; Knox, *Journal,* III, 21; Gipson, *Empire,* VII, 341.

INDIANS KEEP SECRET: III, 271.

NIAGARA BESIEGED: III, 63-77; D, VII, 402; Pouchot, *Memoir,* I, 161ff.

J TAKES COMMAND: III, 62, 77-80, 106, 116; Amherst, *op. cit.*, 147; Lee, *Papers,* I, 21.

INDIAN INTRIGUES: Pouchot, *op. cit.*, 171-86; N. Y. *Wkly. Mercury,* 8/20/1759.

FRENCH PARTISANS APPROACH: III, 107-8; D, VII, 432; Pouchot, *op. cit.*, 186-91.

NIAGARA WON: III, 108-13, 272; D, VII, 399, 402-3; D, X, 990-2; Pouchot, *op. cit.*, 191-201; Knox, *op. cit.*, II, 182-91; *Mercury, op. cit.*

AFTER SURRENDER: III, 110, 174, 272; X, 136; Pouchot, *op. cit.*, 201-5; Pitt, *Corres.*, II, 212; Stone, *J,* II, 395; Mercury, *op. cit.*

MASSY COMPLAINS: Gipson, *op. cit.*, 354.

J PRAISED: III, 128; Walpole, *Letters,* IV, 300.

CHAPTER 16

THE FALL: Stone, *J,* II, 397-8; Lee, *Papers,* I, 22.

AT FORT NIAGARA: III, 114-7, 140; X, 137; D, VIII, 432; Stone, *op. cit.*, 392-9.

AMHERST'S CONGRATULATIONS: Amherst to Gage, 8/16/1759, CL.

AT OSWEGO WITH GAGE: X, 171; Stone, *op. cit.*, 399-429; Alden, *Gage,* 49-52; Amherst, *Journal,* 209; Gipson, *Empire,* VII, 359.

PETER J'S BIRTH DATE: John Ferguson, Petition, 3/4/1793, Draper Papers; Joseph Brant to George Clinton, 1/23/1793, Draper Papers.

PAY AS REGULAR COLONEL: III, 183-5; Amherst, *op. cit.*, 199.

AMHERST AT FORT J: Amherst, *op. cit.*, 213; O'Conor, *Servant,* 147.

GUESSES DIRECTION OF CAMPAIGN: X, 148.

PREPARED INDIANS FOR ENGLISH VICTORY: III, 125-6, 136, 239-41; IV, 308; X, 144, 148-50; Warren J, *Journal*, 10; Pouchot, *Memoir*, II, 6.

AT OSWEGO: X, 175, 246; Amherst, *op. cit.*, 221-5.

OSWEGATCHIE & LA GALLETTE: Jells Fonda, Journal of 1760 campaign, NYHS; X, 176, 180-5; Amherst, *op. cit.*, 231, 239; Warren J, *op. cit.*, 5; Pouchot, *op. cit.*, 30-2.

REST OF CAMPAIGN: III, 272-3; Knox *Journal*, II, 555; Lévis, *Colls.*, I, 301; Warren J, *op. cit.*, 5; Gipson, *op. cit.*, 453-63.

CREDIT FOR VICTORY: X, 878; Knox *Journal*, III, 94.

CHAPTER 17

GOVERNORSHIP: III, 314-5; X, 192.

SETTLEMENTS & GARDENS: III, 296, 355, 566, 574, 591; IV, 90-1; X, 150, 282; DH, IV, 346-50; Stone, *J*, II, 452; Warren J, *Journal*, 10.

IRISH VS. DUTCH: III, 328, 408; X, 275-6; Warren J, *Journal*, 8.

CANAJOHARIE GIFT: III, 296-7; IV, 90; Stone, *Brant*, II, 403; Warren J, *op. cit.*, 5.

CONTROVERSY WITH COUNCIL: III, 288, 305, 319-20, 354, 366-7, 373-4, 397, 607; D, VII, 492.

INCOME REDUCED SINCE ABANDONED TRADE: VI, 94.

LAND FRAUDS: III, 399-400, 409-11, 425-6; DH, II, 847.

CLAUS' ERRANDS: III, 355; X, 248, 348, 355.

CLAUS' COURTSHIP: III, 371-2, 379-84, 393-4, 522-4, 546-9, 564-6, 576-7, 629-30; X, 259-64, 281-3, 323-5, 333-4, 409.

STARTS J HALL: III, 660, 672, 827; IV, 40-1.

JOHN'S EDUCATION: DH, II, 785-6.

GUY DESCRIBED: II, 474, 479, 744-6, 810; III, 186; IV, xi-xiii; V, 403, 629, 724; Stone, *Brant*, II, 167; Recum, *Families*, 5.

CATHERINE'S RETURN: Daniel Campbell, Account Books, 7/28/1756 & 7/28/1759, NYSL; III, 393; DH, II, 785; Hamilton, *Wives*, 22-3; Jones, *History*, II, 641.

GRANDMOTHER: John J to Ann Claus, 12/14/1765 & 8/2/1766, John J to Daniel Claus, 6/4 & 10/12/1766, D. Claus to John J, 5/13/1766, all Claus Papers, NAC; X, 813; XII, 114.

SERVIS CONNECTION: Servis family records; G. Clinton, *Papers*, III, 505, 516; Ontario, *Archives*, II, 957-8; Simms, *Frontiersmen*, I, 204.

BANYAR URGES MARRIAGE: III, 287.

RINGS: Jones, *op. cit.*, II, 641; Stone, *J, II*, 529-30.

SONS-IN-LAW REACT: Claus, *Narrative*, 8; Hamilton, *op. cit.*, 24-5.

J'S MALADY: V, 840-1.

CHAPTER 18

GROSSE ISLE: Warren J, *Journal,* 5.

NEW INDIAN CHARGES: VII, 154; DH, II, 900.

ASKS MORE STAFF: III, 274-5, 277-8.

SAYS INDIANS WON WAR: X, 878.

AMHERST MAKES TROUBLE: III, 269-75, 277, 354, 506; X, 232.

AMHERST'S BITTER FRUIT: III, 506, 513, 515-6; X, 222, 319.

TROUBLES IN PENNA.: X, 212, 215, 317-8.

CHEROKEE WAR: III, 356, 517; Warren J, *Journal,* 10.

J'S REACTIONS: X, 20, 269-70, 291.

TRADE REGULATIONS: III, 331; IV, 444, 473, 531; D, VII, 960-1.

GLADWIN'S ORDERS: X, 294-6.

REPORT OF CONSPIRACY: III, 437-40, 514, 520; Stone, *J,* II, 431-2.

MOLLY'S FAMILY ILL: Stone, *op. cit.,* 448.

TRIP TO DETROIT: XI, 232; Stone, *op. cit.,* 450-7.

AT DETROIT IN GENERAL: III, 468-75; Stone, *op. cit.,* 457-64.

CAMPBELL DESCRIBED: Peckham, *Pontiac,* 67-8.

ANGÉLIQUE: James Sterling to James Duncan, 2/26/1765, CL; D, VII, 963; Stone, *op. cit.,* 459, 463; Bald, *Detroit,* 35.

KYASHUTA: III, 448-53, 456, 484, 488, 493; X, 324; *Mich. Pioneer Hist. Colls.,* XIX (1891), 104; Stone, *op. cit.,* 461-2.

PONTIAC'S SINGLE BELT: D, VII, 862.

J DIVIDES INDIANS: III, 480; IV, 296.

J SUMS UP DETROIT RESULTS: III, 559, 565.

TRIP HOME: Stone, *op. cit.,* 464-77.

END OF ANGÉLIQUE AFFAIR: III, 759; IV, 82.

CHAPTER 19

CRISIS DEEPENS: III, 733; VIII, 1114; X, 381, 385-6, 392, 421, 475.

NEW LAND REGULATIONS: III, 331, 643, 665; IV, 444; X, 340-2, 665.

KLOCK MAKES TROUBLE: Deed, 2/16/1729-30, NYHS; N. Y. Supreme Court, Charge of John Taylor Kempe, 5/1/1762, NYHS; III, 945-6; IV, 50-61, 177; X, 337, 367, 619-20, 717.

QUAKERS ROUTED AT EASTON: III, 759-91, 799-818, 822-3, 826-7, 837-51; IV, 19; X, 211.

EASTON AFTERMATH: III, 844-51, 908-9, 954; X, 556-7; Thayer, *Friendly,* 373-6.

NEW WYOMING ENCROACHMENTS: III, 715-7, 756-7; X, 416-7.

J DESCRIBES INDIAN WAR: X, 460-5.

KANESTIO MURDERS: IV, 288; X, 562-4, 568, 624-5, 629-30, 679, 905, 970; XI, 36.

DREAMS: II, 593; X, 511; Wallace, *Weiser*, 151.

WINTER FEARS: X, 505-6, 534; Peckham, *Pontiac*, 98-9.

ANGÉLIQUE WARNS: Peckham, *op. cit.*, 124-5.

ANGÉLIQUE'S MARRIAGE: James Sterling to James Duncan, 2/26/1765, CL; NYSL, *Calendar*, 265; Paré, *Catholic*, 225.

CHAPTER 20

RAISING THE DEVIL: Parkman, *Pontiac*, I, 266.

J'S FIRST REACTIONS: IV, 178; D, VII, 574.

AMHERST'S FIRST REACTIONS: IV, 149; D, VII, 545; Peckham, *Pontiac*, 173.

BUSHY RUN: D, VII, 962.

MOHAWK VALLEY ALARMS: IV, 232; X, 773; D, VII, 534; Colden, *Letters*, I, 221-2.

CAUGHNAWAGAS THREATEN: X, 852; D, VII, 556.

BICKERS WITH AMHERST: IV, 167, 193; X, 578, 689, 827, 878-80; D, VII, 541, 560; Peckham, *op. cit.*, 226-7.

AND LORDS OF TRADE: D, VII, 559-62, 567, 572-81.

PONTIAC WITHDRAWS: Peckham, *op. cit.*, 236-8.

GAGE REPLACES AMHERST: Amherst to Gage, 11/17/1763, CL; III, 953; IV, 200, 251.

NEW LAND POLICY: X, 973, 976-85.

SENECA NEGOTIATIONS: IV, 361; X, 905, 953, 964-6, 974; XI, 24-7.

WAR PARTIES: IV, 323, 361; XI, 33, 51.

CAPTAIN BULL CAPTURED: IV, 344, 349, 369; XI, 105, 110, 118; Heckewelder, *Account*, 68.

REST OF INDIAN CAMPAIGN: IV, 165, 291, 324, 393.

WHITE ACTION: IV, 289, 291-2; XI, 19, 112, 128.

PAXTON MURDERS: IV, 284-5, 310, 343, 357, 366; XI, 1, 13, 97; *Penna. Mag. Hist. & Biog.*, XXV (1901), 17-8.

PRELIMINARY SENECA PEACE: IV, 57-8, 113, 135-6; IV, 387, 389.

INVITATIONS TO NIAGARA: XI, 176-80; Henry, *Travels*, 158-69; *Mich. Pioneer Hist. Colls.*, XXVII (1897), 665-6.

CHAPTER 21

NIAGARA CONFERENCE: IV, 481, 503, 511-4; XI, 250-328; 336-8; D, VII, 647, 650-3; Henry, *Travels*, 172.

BACK AT J HALL: XI, 336.

MILITARY PLANS: IV, 389-91; D, VII, 632.

BRADSTREETS'S CAMPAIGN: IV, 605; XI, 343, 494, 501, 506-7, 513, 515; D, VII, 629; N. Y. *Gazette*, 11/15/1764.

INDIANS NOT SUBJECTS: XI, 395-6; D, VII, 674.

BOUQUET'S EXPEDITION: IV, 516-7, 585-6, 619-21; XI, 530, 577, 607.

1764 INDIAN PLAN: IV, 558-63; XI, 348; D, VII, 634-41, 661-6, 713-4; Franklin, *Writings*, IV, 467-71; Volweiler, *Croghan*, 173; Washington, *Writings*, II, 468.

STUART: Alden, *Stuart*.

KAYADEROSSERAS: John J, Estimate of his estate, NYHS; I, 432; IV, 609; IX, 148; XI, 376; D, VI, 866; D, VII, 576, 579; N. Y. Assembly, *Journal*, II, 764-5.

ESTIMATE OF INDIAN TRADE: IV, 556-63.

DRAWS TENTATIVE BOUNDARY: D, VII, 711-7, 725-38, 1005.

DELAWARE, SHAWNEE, AND MINGO PEACE: XI, 704-14, 723-34, 748-66, 800; D, VII, 718-41, 750-8.

EXCHANGED CAPTIVES: IV, 783-4; Simms, *Frontiersmen*, I, 263; Parkman, *Pontiac*, II, 254-5.

BRANT J'S WIFE: DP, 13F115; Tryon, *Minute*, 39.

GAUSTARAX: XI, 748.

ILLINOIS: IV, 303-4; XI, 36; D, VII, 688.

CROGHAN'S SMUGGLING: IV, 706, 714; XI, 634-6, 643-5, 664-7, 704, 751, 798.

CROGHAN'S ADVENTURES: XI, 841-2, 906-7; DH, II, 820-1.

PEACE WITH PONTIAC: D, VII, 851-67.

CROGHAN'S SUMMARY: Peckham, *Pontiac*, 219.

CHAPTER 22

INDIANS TO BE PITIED: DH, IV, 305.

SHOULD BRAVES FARM?: XI, 741; DH, IV, 342-3, 345.

EXAMPLE OF DOMESTICATED TRIBES: VII, 597-9; XII, 481.

IMPORTANCE OF MARTIAL SKILLS: V, 530; VII, 597-9.

EVOLUTION TOWARD WHITE WAYS: Kirkland, Journal, 1764-5, 6, Hamilton College; VII, 599; DH, IV, 428, 431-4.

EDWARDS ON J: *Mass. Hist. Soc. Colls.*, Ser. 1, X (1809), 148.

RECEIVES KIRKLAND: Kirkland, *op. cit.*, 1, 3-4, 8, 113, 117.

J ON CONGREGATIONALISTS: IV, 72-3; D, VII, 970.

FEW ANGLICAN MISSIONARIES: V, 415; VII, 602; D, VII, 969.

MOHAWK PRAYER BOOK: III, 363; X, 33; XII, 1172; DH, II, 334-5, 340-1, 384-5; Andrews, *Order*.

MISSIONARIES MISBEHAVE: VI, 17; X, 515, 518; D, VI, 315.

MOHAWKS ON CRUCIFIXION: Lydecker, *Mohawks*, 46.

JOSEPH'S EDUCATION: DH, IV, 330-1; *London Mag.*, XLIV (1776), 339; McCallum, *Letters,* see index; Anon., *Brant;* Wheelock, *Narrative,* 15-7; Stone, *Brant,* I, 182.

MOHAWKS' SITUATION: XII, 747; D, VIII, 303-4; DH, IV, 432; Stone, *Brant,* II, 38; Tilghman, *Memoir,* 82.

ILLINOIS COLONY PROPOSED: IV, 886-8; V, 38, 128-30, 319-30; XII, 555, 561; D, VII, 892-3; *Colls. Ill. State Hist. Library,* XI (1916), 376-7.

FORMAL APPEAL FOR CANAJOHARIE GRANT: IV, 596; D, VII, 659, 839-42.

ROYAL GRANT: V, 8, 10, 417, 476; VI, 735, 769-73; VIII, 1010; D, VII, 896-8.

OTHER PURCHASES: References too numerous for listing.

DAMAGE OF ABSENTEEISM: D, VII, 713, 881.

ADVERTISES FOR ARTISANS: IV, 682-3, 813, 866; XII, 981-2.

JOHNSTOWN BUILT: V, 413; VIII, 328-9; XI, 648-9; XII, 829, 884, 893.

AGRICULTURAL EXPERIMENTS: VII, 645; DH, IV, 346, 348.

ATTITUDE TOWARD RELIGION: V, 29; VIII, 1195; X, 250; XII, 919; DH, IV, 501.

SPG & MINISTER SHORTAGE: V, 414; VIII, 504-5; N. Y. *Gazette,* 3/11/1771.

JOHNSTOWN CHURCHES: VI, 293; VIII, 927; XII, 982; DH, IV, 439, 473; Frothingham, *Fulton,* 238; Jones, *History,* II, 371; Vosburg, *Records,* ii-iii.

SCHENECTADY CHURCH: Hanson, *Schenectady,* I, 39.

CANAJOHARIE CHURCH: VI, 264; VII, 666-8; XII, 655.

SCHOOLS: VII, 290, 693, 892; VIII, 322-3; DH, IV, 416-7; Simms, *Trappers,* 24-7.

RENTALS: V, 502; VIII, 613-4; XII, 1023.

CONNECTICUT EXILES: XII, 1066, 1078; DH, IV, 181n.

SCOTS SETTLE: VIII, 816; XII, 1023, 1041-2, 1111.

EXTENT OF SETTLEMENT: XII, 893-4.

FRONTIER NEEDS LUXURY: DH, IV, 346, 348.

J HALL: J to Saml. Fuller, 1/5/63, NYSL; J, Inventory of his estate, Claus Papers, NAC; John J, Estimate of his estate, NYHS; IV, 788, 845; V, 276, 413; VII, 229; DH, IV, 420; Simms, *Frontiersmen,* I, 249, 251, 278-9: Jones, *op. cit.,* 373-4.

BLIND HARPER: IV, 638, 877; V, 383, 733; VIII, 41, 91.

SHUCKBAUGH: III, 278; D, VII, 433, 694-5; D, VIII, 244; Sonneck, *Report,* 105, 150-4.

COAT OF ARMS: I, 266; III, vi-xii; Pound, *J,* 23-4.

ARISTOCRATIC CRITICISMS: Mereness, *Travels,* 418; Severance, *Niagara,* 340.

ROMANTIC VISION: Johnstone, *Chrysal,* III, 139-55, 163.

SEXUAL JOKING: J to Banyar, 4/12/1762, in Anderson Galleries, N.Y., *Catalogue Theodore Sedgwick Sale,* 11/21/1926.

FETES: Simms, *Frontiersmen,* I, 260-1.

BULLFROG: Simms, *Trappers,* 53.

J'S BENEVOLENCE: III, 643-4; VII, 216-7; VIII, 31, 414, 1027; DH, IV, 490-1; Stone, *J*, II, 386-7.

WANTS A MANOR: XII, 699; DH, II, 937-8.

FEUDAL FIGURE: Turner, *Frontier*, 27; De Tocqueville, *Democracy*, I, 8-9.

CHAPTER 23

REACTIONS TO STAMP ACT: V, 113; XI, 931.

EFFORTS TO ENFORCE TRADE RULES: XII, 16, 23; D, VII, 817, 837, 842-3, 855.

CANNOT PROTECT TRIBES: XI, 890-1; XII, 130; D, VII, 851, 880; DH, II, 885, 975.

ENCROACHMENTS AND MURDERS: IV, 4; V, 492, 548; VII, 154; D, VII, 746, 837, 852, 892-3, 914, 952; DH, II, 866, 886, 888, 892; *Ill. Pioneer Hist. Colls.*, XI (1916), 465.

SEIZURE AND LEBANON SPRINGS: V, 685; VI, 31; D, VII, 946-8, 951; DH, II, 863.

SHELBURNE BESEECHES: V, 374-5.

BASES POLICY ON IROQUOIS: J to Tryon, 10/22/1773, NYHS; XII, 461; D, VII, 958.

POLICY TO DOMESTICATED TRIBES: XI, 910-1; D, VII, 892.

STOCKBRIDGES: IV, 654, 682; V, 503-6; VI, 284, 891; D, VII, 892, 913.

NARRAGANSETTS: IV, 80, 87, 587ff, 659; V, 490ff, 683; XI, 406-35, 483.

MONTAUKS: D, VIII, 476.

MOHICANS: II, 371; IX, 288, 700; XI, 254; XII, 973-4, 1037; D, VII, 94, 152, 253.

WAPPINGERS, DELAWARES, AND NANTICOKES: XII, 242, 802.

DIVIDES INDIAN NATIONS: IV, 296; VII, 151; VIII, 108; DH, II, 950.

CHEROKEE PEACE: V, 449; XI, 863, 942; XII, 34, 56, 99, 468; D, VII, 777-8; DH, II, 849.

PLEASES PRINCIPAL INDIANS: I, 300; II, 827; XII, 468; D, VII, 946-7.

DISTRIBUTES LARGESSE: IV, 370; VII, 130-1.

COUNCILS: IV, 331; X, 721.

LIQUOR: II, 396; IX, 629; XII, 273; D, VII, 665; Chase, *Dartmouth*, 81.

RECORDS LOCKED FROM GUY: VI, 310.

MOLLY'S POSITION: VI, 460-1, 463; VII, 483; Stone, *J*, II, 244.

INTERMARRIAGE: IV, 620; D, V, 88; *Scots Mag.*, XXVIII (1766), 218.

WILLIAM OF CANAJOHARIE: V, 604, 843-5; VI, 66, 170-1; DH, IV, 351, 367-8, 381-3; Stone, *Brant*, I, 23.

PETER'S EDUCATION: VIII, 878, 947, 1019, 1063, 1139, 1179; XII, 961-2, 966, 1010, 1013, 1029; DH, II, 368, 373; *Am. Mag.*, I (1757), 12.

MOLLY'S YOUNGER CHILDREN: John Ferguson, Petition to N. Y. Legislature,

3/4/1793, & J. Bawden to L. C. Draper, 11/19/1877, DP; Stone, *Brant*, II, 341.

LIMITING TRADERS TO POSTS: V, 521-4, 566, 826-30; IX, 95; D, VII, 872, 882, 929, 951, 964-5, 976.

ROGERS CONTROVERSY: Voluminous material in V; VI; VII; D, VII; DH, II.

TRADE RETURNED TO COLONIES: VI, 280; D, VIII, 55-9; DH, II, 896ff.

J TO DRAW BOUNDARY: V, 855; VI, 61, 231; D, VII, 1004-5, D, VIII, 2.

STANWIX TREATY IN GENERAL: VI, 519; D, VIII, 111-37; DH, II, 912-9; Alvord, *Stanwix*; Billington, *Stanwix*.

PREPARATIONS: XII, 665-8.

IROQUOIS CONTROL ALL LAND: VIII, 75-6.

RELIGIOUS FRACAS: VI, 457, 472; DH, IV, 388-394, 397-8; J, *Jacob J*, 115-42; McCallum, *Wheelock*, 123-6; Miner, *Wyoming*, 97-100.

N. Y.'S BOUNDARY: J to Banyar, 11/24/1768, NYHS; XII, 656-7, 945; DH, II, 743.

PRIVATE PURCHASES: VII, 215; XII, 656-7, 767-8; DH, II, 945; *Mass. Hist. Soc. Colls.*, 4th Ser., X (1871), 605-6.

J OBJECTS TO VIRGINIA LINE: VI, 406-8; XII, 746-7; D, VIII, 316; DH, II, 940-4.

COST: VI, 569-70; XII, 745; DH, II, 912.

J SURE CROWN WILL APPLAUD: DH, II, 917, 941.

HILLSBOROUGH OBJECTS, GIVES IN: VI, 652; VII, 16-8; D, VIII, 145; DH, II, 938-9.

CHAPTER 24

J'S POWER: V, 407, 418; XII, 395; D, VII, 485.

IGNORES ENGLISH POLITICS: VI, 773, 779; XII, 512.

AVOIDS OPPOSING PATRIOTS: IV, 843-4; V, 62; XI, 921, 930-1.

SUPPORT FOR ANGLICANS: IV, 309; V, 842; VI, 543; VII, 292, 585; D, VII, 600; DH, II, 489-90; Klingberg, *Anglican*, 87-120.

EARLY POLITICS IN VALLEY: I, 293-4; XII, 692, 789, 796; DH, II, 925.

VS. SCHUYLER: VI, 70, 127, 571, 575-6, 585, 589-90; VII, 587, 627, 634-5, 641; XII, 691-2.

JOHN UNWILLING TO RUN: XII, 692.

TRYON COUNTY ESTABLISHED: VII, 19-21; VIII, 369, 413, 436-7, 478, 492, 678, 823; XII, 932; DH, II, 955.

N. Y. LEADER: VII, 689; Becker, *Nominations*, 262.

GUY IN ASSEMBLY: VIII, 703, 710.

LIVINGSTON GRANT SOLVED: XII, 184, 365, 496, 539-40.

KAYADEROSSERAS SOLVED: Wm. Smith, Jr., to Schuyler, 5/25/1768, NYPL; V, 104, 285, 363, 567, 744-5; VI, 269, 277, 284, 308-10, 342, 399, 404; XI, 821, 864-6, 886-7, 923; D, VII, 78, 92; DH, II, 894, 905.

MILITIA: VIII, 100ff; DH, II, 962-3; N. Y., State Historian *Report,* 880-1, 887-8.

OPPOSES VAN RENSSELAER: VIII, 100-2, 529, 535, etc.

MASON: IV, 434; VIII, 40, 91-2, 357, 534; XII, 792-3.

BOATS NAMED ETC.: III, 749; V, 434; VIII, 368, 534; XII, 792.

SICKNESS: V, 478, 840; VI, 684, 705; VII, 106, 375, 413; VIII, 20, 828; XII, 22, 437.

SARATOGA SPRINGS: VIII, 258, 263.

MONTAUK POINT: VIII, 854, 878-9.

MOUNT JOY: John J, Inventory of his estate, NYHS; VII, 586; VIII, 138; XII, 826, 893; Simms, *Frontiersmen,* I, 258-60; Frothingham, *Fulton,* 490.

FISH HOUSE: Simms, *Trappers,* 27; Frothingham, *op. cit.,* 451-3.

WORMWOOD GIRLS: Simms, *Trappers,* 44-6.

MALE JOKES: Simms, *Trappers,* 42; Frothingham, *op. cit.,* 484-5.

SIGNS STANWIX TREATY: XII, 850; D, VIII, 244-44.

N. Y. CALLS CONFERENCE: D, VIII, 287, 349.

WALPOLE SCHEME: VI, 1125; VIII, 751, 1159; D, VIII, 314; DH, II, 998-1001.

RAMSAY MURDERS: VIII, 541; XII, 999-1000; DH, II, 994-6; *Buffalo Hist. Soc. Pubs.,* VI (1904), 449.

THREATENED SPANISH WAR: VIII, 45; XII, 893.

GAGE'S WAR LETTER: XII, 380.

J REFUSES TO INVOLVE INDIANS: D, VII, 809-10; DH, II, 974.

KIRKLAND'S CHARGES: Kirkland, Journal, 2/3/1771, Hamilton College; VIII, 228-31; XII, 918-9; DH, IV, 460.

TRYON VISITS: D, VIII, 303-4.

CALM IN 1771: VIII, 341; XII, 892.

FORESEES DEATH: VIII, 1198.   n

WILL: VIII, 1189-91; XII, 1062-76.

JOHN IN ENGLAND: V, 120, 371, 603, 605, 705; XII, 252, 316.

CLARISSA: Hanson, *Schenectady,* I, 42, 48; Putnam, *Putnam,* 103, 106-7; Simms, *Frontiersmen,* I, 265.

JOHN AND MARRIAGE: VII, 503, 1114; VIII, 711, 727, 805-6, 836.

GUY'S BLINDNESS: VIII, 706; Stone, *Brant,* I, 84.

J FORESEES TRANQUILLITY: VIII, 640, 837, 1164-5.

CRESAP MURDERS: VII, 640, 837, 1164-5.

DEATH: VIII, 827; D, VIII, 479, 485; Jones, *History,* II, 373; Stone, *Brant,* I, 32; Stone, *J,* II, 374-8.

EPILOGUE

J'S FUNERAL: Simms, *Frontiersmen,* I, 310; Stone, *J,* II, 490-1; N. Y. *Gazette,* 8/1/1774.

INDIANS ACCEPT GUY: D, VIII, 481.

COMMITTEE OF SAFETY: Tryon, *Minute.*

MOLLY'S GREAT INFLUENCE: Claus to Haldimand, 8/30/1779, NAC; Gundy, *Molly,* 100.

WILLIAM'S THREATS: Tryon, *op. cit.,* 95-6.

BRANT J: Brant J, Petition on losses, 1/5/1784, AD, 13bundle80, Public Records Office, London; John Butler, Return of loyalists, 1/1/1783, Haldimand Papers, NAC.

PETER'S FATE: John Ferguson, Petition on losses, 3/4/1793, DP; Loyalist transcripts, XLIV, 106, NYPL; *English Army List* (1770), 80; *Mag. Am. Hist.,* VI (1881), 461.

MOLLY WARNS ON ORISKANY: D, VIII, 721, 725.

DESTRUCTION ON MOHAWK, Tryon, *op. cit.,* xiii.

MOLLY'S CONTINUED ACTIVITY: W. C. Bryant to W. Kirby, 9/9/1899, DP; Simms, *Schoharie,* 513.

CLARISSA'S DAUGHTER CLAIMS PEW: Hanson, *Schenectady,* I, 107.

MOLLY'S LAST YEARS: Haldimand to John J, 5/27/1783, NYHS; Gundy, *Molly,* 103-7; Stone, *Brant,* II, 341; Robertson, *Simcoe,* 166, 247, 274-5.

Index

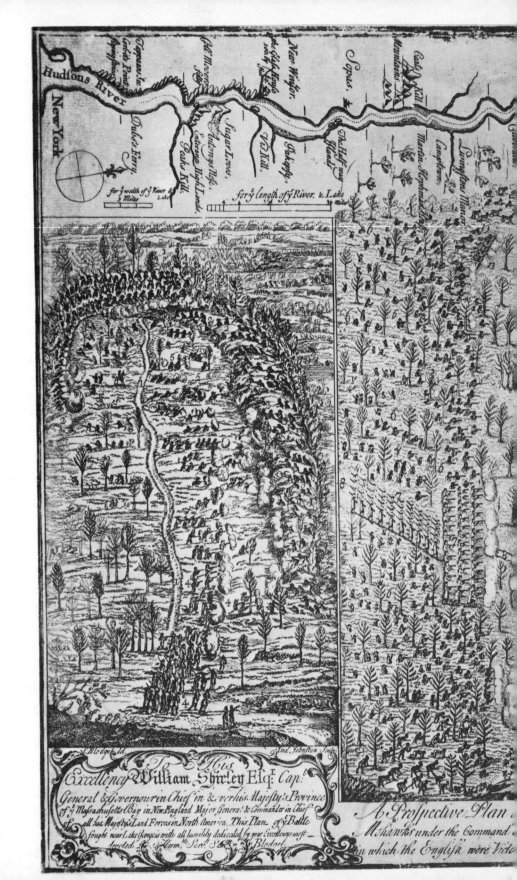

Hudson's River

New York

New Windsor

Sopas.

Caats Kill
Murdurers Kill

Martine Hoofman's Land

Camp Town

Livingston Manor

for ye breadth of ye River &
3 Miles   Lake

for ye length of ye River & Lake
30 Miles

Dubo's Ferry

Anthony's Nose
the enterance High Lands
Peaks Kill.

Sugar Loaves

Pooples Kill
the Clove Hawks
nest by Jett

New Worsser

The Half way Islands

Tappan's Bay
Carits Point
Teaskill.

J. Blodget del.   Ind. Johnston Sculp.

To   His

Excellency William Shirley Esqr Capt.
General & Governour in Chief in & over his Majesty's Province
of ye Massachusetts Bay in New England Major General & Commander in Chief
of all his Majesties Land Forces in North America. This Plan of ye Battle
fought near Lake George is with all humility dedicated by your Excellencys most
devoted Hum.l Ser.t Sa.l Blodget.

A Prospective Plan
Mohawks under the Command
in which the English were Victo